W●RLD WRITERS TODAY

CONTEMPORARY LITERATURE FROM AROUND THE WORLD

FOREWORD BY
JAMAICA KINCAID

ScottForesman

A Division of HarperCollins*Publishers*

EDITORIAL OFFICES: Glenview, Illinois
REGIONAL OFFICES: Sunnyvale, California · Tucker, Georgia
· Glenview, Illinois · Oakland, New Jersey · Dallas, Texas

FOREWORD
Jamaica Kincaid

CONSULTANTS
Bernadette Anand, *English teacher and department chair,* Montclair High School, Montclair, New Jersey. ■ **Jesús Cardona,** *English teacher,* John F. Kennedy High School, San Antonio, Texas. ■ **Kristina Kostopoulos,** *English teacher,* Lincoln Park High School, Chicago, Illinois. ■ **May Lee,** *English and Chinese language teacher,* Baldwin Senior High School, Baldwin, New York. ■ **Emmanuel Sena,** *English and foreign languages teacher,* Wyoming Seminary College Preparatory School, Kingston, Pennsylvania. ■ **Dana Whitaker,** *Ethnic studies, social science, and English teacher,* International Studies Academy, San Francisco, California.

Acknowledgments for quoted matter and illustrations are included in the acknowledgments section on pages 540–544. The acknowledgments section is an extension of the copyright page.

ISBN: 0–673–29431–5

23456789-DQ-04030201009998979695

Contents

UNIT **8** Triumph of the Spirit

The following authors now make their permanent homes in the United States: Isabel Allende, Nina Cassian, Le Ly Hayslip, Jamaica Kincaid, Mark Mathabane, Alicia Partnoy, Ari B. Siletz.

Foreword

BY JAMAICA KINCAID

IN THE WORLD of literature that I grew up in, there was only one literature — that of the people of England. As far as I was allowed to know, a literature belonging to other people did not exist. I grew up in a small patch of what was then the British Empire, an island in the West Indies. To me (and to all the people like me) England and its people and what happened in that place to those people were real and everything else mattered only to the degree that England and its people were affected.

My situation (our situation) was not unique in history, contemporary or ancient: most people at some time or another are "subject people." But, I suppose, being the sort of person I was, and the sort of person I would become, I felt often that the historical weight of colonialism was directed at me solely. I had then, and they remain with me now, feelings about my situation that were violently opposed to each other. I loved the English people and was so very sorry not to be one; I hated the English people and was so very happy that nothing in the world could make me one. Neither of these two emotions, love and hate, could I have ever expressed to anyone I knew.

To the question, Who am I?, I might have answered — A person descended mostly from the captured people of Africa and (through one grandparent) from the vanished Carib Indian people. But beyond that, I had no real cultural identity. We, my people, were alive but dead, cut off from ancestral memory. We no longer had any idea of the people we used to be.

Literature is a powerful tool—the word, a weapon really more powerful than a bullet. A bullet will kill you, and that's the end of that. And the way the words work? By the time I reached adolescence I had never seen a daffodil, I had never seen snow, I had never seen the English countryside, I had never seen the White Cliffs of Dover. And yet, I knew by heart the poem by William Wordsworth, "Daffodils." I knew the feel, the texture of snow through the many characters I had come across in English literature. I had sung a hymn many times in church about seeing the White Cliffs of Dover. Of course, I grew (we all did) to despise the flora of the place I am from, that tiny part of the British Empire. We did not have daffodils, which require a temperate zone. I felt the climate in which I lived to be wanting: it would never snow there; for it is in the tropical zone.

It is surprising, then, that in my own life, this weapon against me, the literature of a people who did not like me and were alien to me, saved me from them and from the other normal forces that from time to time overwhelm an individual life. My mother had taught me to read when I was three-and-a-half years old. She liked to read and wanted to keep me from interrupting her as she did so; she thought that if I knew how to read also, I would leave her alone. That was a success.

MUCH LATER, when I was about eleven or so, in a fit of exasperation, even anger, towards me, my French teacher thrust a copy of a book at me, telling me to read it and perhaps then I would shut up and behave myself. The book was *Jane Eyre*, a novel about a complicated, masochistic nursemaid, though I did not see it that way at the time. I loved that novel then, and I love it now. I reread it almost every two years or so, and I still can find something new in it. I so identified with the strong will and self pity of Jane then that I felt myself to be her, not physically, not racially, only her as I understood her inside herself as she appeared to me in the pages of that book.

If I knew myself better, if I understood myself better, I would perhaps be able to trace my becoming a writer to the day *Jane Eyre* entered my life. It was in that very book too that I came across the word *gloaming*. I did not know what it meant, only that the very sound of it was captivating. I remember looking it up in my *Concise Oxford Dictionary*, a present from my mother on my seventh birthday. And that word, which became so much part of my imagination that I later in my own writing built an entire paragraph around it, describes a part in the cycle of a day — dusk, twilight, which does not really occur in the part of the world that I grew up in. A day there begins and ends far too suddenly, the night becomes day and the day becomes night with an abruptness that startles me even now when I visit this place.

THE GREAT SURPRISE to me is how literature turned out to be my own spiritual rescue. The days I spent as a child in school memorizing vast passages of *Paradise Lost* led to my understanding all too well the position of Lucifer. I wrote a novel and named the heroine after him. It was through this literature that I came to understand the forces of good and the forces of evil. It was through this literature too, that I came to understand the relationship between the powerful and the powerless and how they can exchange places — in my own family, in the small world of the island where I grew up, and in the larger world beyond that. And I know that what freed me from this cycle, apart from making myself physically absent from this environment, was to place some distance between myself and it through my own contribution to Literature, the world of a writer.

What good would it have done me to know of the world, the larger world, the world beyond England and its people, the world of other people both different from me and the same? I can only speculate that such exposure to other people and other cultures might have made me a different person. To have learned that the place where I originated was of some value—human value—would have nourished that delicate thing inside of me, my sense of being.

The world today is as far as I know geographically the same size as it was when I was growing up and yet it is smaller. Many things that were far away are nearer now. Here is this book, *World Writers Today.* Through its stories, poems, nonfiction, and drama it reaches into every corner of the world, making it appear smaller and larger, the same and different, all at once. Anyone living at the other end of the world from China will recognize the fear and conformity in Feng Jicai's "The Mao Button." The quiet awe that comes over the reader at the end of Derek Walcott's "A Lesson for This Sunday" will be familiar and yet new. And Dhu'l Nun Ayyoub's "From Behind the Veil" will strike a responsive chord with anyone who has hidden behind a prop.

The world brought near and made intimate (through these portraits of everyday life from such places as Turkey, China, Russia, Egypt, Nigeria, and Mexico) is not a prescription for anything. It is only a contribution to truth and reality. This is true and real: There are many different kinds of human beings; they are born and sometime, sooner or later, they die. In between, they mostly do regrettable and foolish things. But their lives give meaning to ours—each life in fact gives meaning to another. The writings in this book show us so.

The Need to Succeed

Have you ever wanted to succeed so badly that you made great sacrifices to achieve your goal? Was it worth it? The selections in this unit are about people who *need* to succeed — to be the best, the brightest, or the richest. They all give up something of personal value to get something they see as better. Some are able to say "I made it!" but not everyone ends up better off.

Rules of the Game

I WAS SIX when my mother taught me the art of invisible strength. It was a strategy for winning arguments, respect from others, and eventually, though neither of us knew it at the time, chess games.

"Bite back your tongue," scolded my mother when I cried loudly, yanking her hand toward the store that sold bags of salted plums. At home, she said, "Wise guy, he not go against wind. In Chinese we say, Come from South, blow with wind—poom!—North will follow. Strongest wind cannot be seen."

The next week I bit back my tongue as we entered the store with the forbidden candies. When my mother finished her shopping, she quietly plucked a small bag of plums from the rack and put it on the counter with the rest of the items.

My mother imparted her daily truths so she could help my older brothers and me rise above our circumstances. We lived in San Francisco's Chinatown. Like most of the other Chinese children who played in the back alleys of restaurants and curio shops, I didn't think we were poor. My bowl was always full, three five-course meals every day, beginning with a soup full of mysterious things I didn't want to know the names of.

We lived on Waverly Place, in a warm, clean, two–bedroom flat that sat above a small Chinese bakery specializing in steamed pastries and dim sum. In the early morning, when the alley was still quiet, I could smell fragrant red beans as they were cooked down to a pasty sweetness. By daybreak, our flat was heavy with the odor of fried sesame balls and sweet curried chicken crescents. From my bed, I would listen as my father got ready for work, then locked the door behind him, one-two-three clicks.

At the end of our two-block alley was a small sandlot playground with swings and slides well-shined down the middle with use. The play area was bordered by wood-slat benches where old-country people sat cracking roasted watermelon seeds with their golden teeth and scattering the husks to an impatient gathering of gurgling pigeons. The best playground, however, was the dark alley itself. It was crammed with daily mysteries and adventures. My brothers and I would peer into the medicinal herb shop, watching old Li dole out onto a stiff sheet of white paper the right amount of insect shells, saffron-colored seeds, and pungent leaves for his ailing customers. It was said that he once cured a woman dying of an ancestral curse that had eluded the best of American doctors. Next to the pharmacy was a printer who specialized in gold-embossed wedding invitations and festive red banners.

Culture Note

San Francisco's Chinatown the largest Chinese community outside Asia, a well-established neighborhood area where shops and other businesses provide many of the foods and goods Chinese immigrants depended on in their native country, p. 2

Farther down the street was Ping Yuen Fish Market. The front window displayed a tank crowded with doomed fish and turtles struggling to gain footing on the slimy green-tiled sides. A hand-written sign informed tourists, "Within this store, is all for food, not for pet." Inside, the butchers with their bloodstained white smocks deftly gutted the fish while customers cried out their orders and shouted, "Give me your freshest," to which the butchers always protested, "All are freshest." On less crowded market days, we would inspect the crates of live frogs and crabs which we were warned not to poke, boxes of dried cuttlefish, and row upon row of iced prawns, squid, and slippery fish. The sanddabs made me shiver each time; their eyes lay on one flattened side and reminded me of my mother's story of a careless girl who ran into a crowded street and was crushed by a cab. "Was smash flat," reported my mother.

At the corner of the alley was Hong Sing's, a four-table café with a recessed stairwell in front that led to a door marked "Tradesmen." My brothers and I believed the bad people emerged from this door at night. Tourists never went to Hong Sing's, since the menu was printed only in Chinese. A Caucasian man with a big camera once posed me and my playmates in front of the restaurant. He had us move to the side of the picture window so the photo would capture the roasted duck with its head dangling from a juice-covered rope. After he took the picture, I told him he should go into Hong Sing's and eat dinner. When he smiled and asked me what they served, I shouted, "Guts and duck's feet and octopus gizzards!" Then I ran off with my friends, shrieking with laughter as we scampered across the alley and hid in the entryway grotto of the China Gem Company, my heart pounding with hope that he would chase us.

My mother named me after the street that we lived on: Waverly Place Jong, my official name for important American documents. But my family called me Meimei, "Little Sister." I was the youngest, the only daughter. Each morning before school, my mother would twist and yank on my thick black hair until she had formed two tightly wound pigtails. One day, as she struggled to weave a hard-toothed comb through my disobedient hair, I had a sly thought.

I asked her, "Ma, what is Chinese torture?" My mother shook her head. A bobby pin was wedged between her lips. She wetted her palm and smoothed the hair above my ear, then pushed the pin in so that it nicked sharply against my scalp.

"Who say this word?" she asked without a trace of knowing how wicked I was being. I shrugged my shoulders and said, "Some boy in my class said Chinese people do Chinese torture."

"Chinese people do many things," she said simply. "Chinese people do business, do medicine, do painting. Not lazy like American people. We do torture. Best torture."

M Y OLDER BROTHER Vincent was the one who actually got the chess set. We had gone to the annual Christmas party held at the First Chinese Baptist Church at the end of the alley. The missionary ladies had put together a Santa bag of gifts donated by members of another church. None of the gifts had names on them. There were separate sacks for boys and girls of different ages.

One of the Chinese parishioners had donned a Santa Claus costume and a stiff paper beard with cotton balls glued to it. I think the only children who thought he was the real thing were too young to know that Santa Claus was not Chinese. When my turn came up, the Santa man asked me how old I was. I thought it was a trick question; I was seven according to the American formula and eight by the Chinese calendar. I said I was born on March 17, 1951. That seemed to satisfy him. He then solemnly asked if I had been a very, very good girl this year and did I believe in Jesus Christ and obey my parents. I knew the only answer to that. I nodded back with equal solemnity.

Having watched the other children opening their gifts, I already knew that the big gifts were not necessarily the nicest ones. One girl my age got a large coloring book of biblical characters, while a less greedy girl who selected a smaller box received a glass vial of lavender toilet water. The sound of the box was also important. A ten-year-old boy had chosen a box that jangled when he shook it. It was a tin globe of the world with a slit for inserting money. He must have thought it was full of dimes and nickels, because when he saw that it had just ten pennies, his face fell with such undisguised disappointment that his mother slapped the side of his head and led him out of the church hall, apologizing to the crowd for her son who had such bad manners he couldn't appreciate such a fine gift.

As I peered into the sack, I quickly fingered the remaining presents, testing their weight, imagining what they contained. I chose a heavy, compact one that was wrapped in shiny silver foil and a red satin ribbon. It was a twelve-pack of Life Savers and I spent the rest of the party arranging and rearranging the candy tubes in the order of my favorites. My brother Winston chose wisely as well. His present turned out to be a box of intricate plastic parts; the instructions on the box proclaimed that when they were properly assembled he would have an authentic miniature replica of a World War II submarine.

Vincent got the chess set, which would have been a very decent present to get at a church Christmas party, except it was obviously used and, as we discovered later, it was missing a black pawn and a white knight. My mother graciously thanked the unknown benefactor, saying, "Too good. Cost too much." At which point, an old lady with fine white, wispy hair nodded toward our family and said with a whistling whisper, "Merry, merry Christmas."

When we got home, my mother told Vincent to throw the chess set away. "She not want it. We not want it," she said, tossing her head stiffly to the side with a tight, proud smile. My brothers had deaf ears. They were already lining up the chess pieces and reading from the dog-eared instruction book.

I watched Vincent and Winston play during Christmas week. The chess board seemed to hold elaborate secrets waiting to be untangled. The chessmen were more powerful than Old Li's magic herbs that cured ancestral curses. And my brothers wore such serious faces that I was sure something was at stake that was greater than avoiding the tradesmen's door to Hong Sing's.

"Let me! Let me!" I begged between games when one brother or the other would sit back with a deep sigh of relief and victory, the other annoyed, unable to let go of the outcome. Vincent at first refused to let me play, but when I offered my Life Savers as replacements for the buttons that filled in for the missing pieces, he relented. He chose the flavors: wild cherry for the black pawn and peppermint for the white knight. Winner could eat both.

As our mother sprinkled flour and rolled out small doughy circles for the steamed dumplings that would be our dinner that night, Vincent explained the rules, pointing to each piece. "You have sixteen pieces and so do I. One king and queen, two bishops, two knights, two castles, and eight pawns. The pawns can only move forward one step, except on the first move. Then they can move two. But they can only take men by moving crossways like this, except in the beginning, when you can move ahead and take another pawn."

"Why?" I asked as I moved my pawn. "Why can't they move more steps?"

"Because they're pawns," he said.

"But why do they go crossways to take other men? Why aren't there any women and children?"

"Why is the sky blue? Why must you always ask stupid questions?" asked Vincent. "This is a game. These are the rules. I didn't make them up. See. Here. In the book." He jabbed a page with a pawn in his hand. "Pawn. P-A-W-N. Pawn. Read it yourself."

My mother patted the flour off her hands. "Let me see book," she said quietly. She scanned the pages quickly, not reading the foreign English symbols, seeming to search deliberately for nothing in particular.

"This American rules," she concluded at last. "Every time people come out from foreign country, must know rules. You not know, judge say, Too bad, go back. They not telling you why so you can use their way go forward. They say, Don't know why, you find out yourself. But they knowing all the time. Better you take it, find out why yourself." She tossed her head back with a satisfied smile.

I found out about all the whys later. I read the rules and looked up all the big words in a dictionary. I borrowed books from the Chinatown library. I studied each chess piece, trying to absorb the power each contained.

I learned about opening moves and why it's important to control the center early on; the shortest distance between two points is straight down the middle. I learned about the middle game and why tactics between two adversaries are like clashing ideas; the one who plays better has the clearest plans for both attacking and getting out of traps. I learned why it is essential in the endgame to have foresight, a mathematical understanding of all possible moves, and patience; all weaknesses and advantages become evident to a strong adversary and are obscured to a tiring opponent. I discovered that for the whole game one must gather invisible strengths and see the endgame before the game begins.

I also found out why I should never reveal "why" to others. A little knowledge withheld is a great advantage one should store for future use. That is the power of chess. It is a game of secrets in which one must show and never tell.

I loved the secrets I found within the sixty-four black and white squares. I carefully drew a handmade chessboard and pinned it to the wall next to my bed, where at night I would stare for hours at imaginary battles. Soon I no longer lost any games or Life Savers, but I lost my adversaries. Winston and Vincent decided they were more interested in roaming the streets after school in their Hopalong Cassidy cowboy hats.

O N A COLD SPRING AFTERNOON, while walking home from school, I detoured through the playground at the end of our alley. I saw a group of old men, two seated across a folding table playing a game of chess, others smoking pipes, eating peanuts, and watching. I ran home and grabbed Vincent's chess set, which was bound in a cardboard box with rubber bands. I also carefully selected two prized rolls of Life Savers. I came back to the park and approached a man who was observing the game.

"Want to play?" I asked him. His face widened with surprise and he grinned as he looked at the box under my arm.

"Little sister, been a long time since I play with dolls," he said, smiling benevolently. I quickly put the box down next to him on the bench and displayed my retort.

Lau Po, as he allowed me to call him, turned out to be a much better player than my brothers. I lost many games and many Life Savers. But over the weeks, with each diminishing roll of candies, I added new secrets. Lau Po gave me the names. The Double Attack from the East and West Shores. Throwing Stones on the Drowning Man. The Sudden Meeting of the Clan. The Surprise from the Sleeping Guard. The Humble Servant Who Kills the King. Sand in the Eyes of Advancing Forces. A Double Killing Without Blood.

There were also the fine points of chess etiquette. Keep captured men in neat rows, as well-tended prisoners. Never announce "Check" with vanity, lest someone with an unseen sword slit your throat. Never hurl pieces into the sandbox after you have lost a game, because then you must find them again, by yourself, after apologizing to all around you. By the end of the summer, Lau Po had taught me all he knew, and I had become a better chess player.

A small weekend crowd of Chinese people and tourists would gather as I played and defeated my opponents one by one. My mother would join the crowds during these outdoor exhibition games. She sat proudly on the bench, telling my admirers with proper Chinese humility, "Is luck."

A man who watched me play in the park suggested that my mother allow me to play in local chess tournaments. My mother smiled graciously, an answer that meant nothing. I desperately wanted to go, but I bit back my tongue. I knew she would not let me play among strangers. So as we walked home I said in a small voice that I didn't want to play in the local tournament. They would have American rules. If I lost, I would bring shame on my family.

"Is shame you fall down nobody push you," said my mother.

During my first tournament, my mother sat with me in the front row as I waited for my turn. I frequently bounced my legs to unstick them from the cold metal seat of the folding chair. When my name was called, I leapt up. My mother unwrapped something in her lap. It was her *chang*, a small tablet of red jade which held the sun's fire. "Is luck," she whispered, and tucked it into my dress pocket. I turned to my opponent, a fifteen-year-old boy from Oakland. He looked at me, wrinkling his nose.

As I began to play, the boy disappeared, the color ran out of the room, and I saw only my white pieces and his black ones waiting on the other side. A light wind began blowing past my ears. It whispered secrets only I could hear.

"Blow from the South," it murmured. "The wind leaves no trail." I saw a clear path, the traps to avoid. The crowd rustled. "Shhh! Shhh!" said the corners of the room. The wind blew stronger. "Throw sand from the East to distract him." The knight came forward ready for the sacrifice. The wind hissed, louder and louder. "Blow, blow, blow. He cannot see. He is blind now. Make him lean away from the wind so he is easier to knock down."

"Check," I said, as the wind roared with laughter. The wind died down to little puffs, my own breath.

M̲Y MOTHER placed my first trophy next to a new plastic chess set that the neighborhood Tao society had given to me. As she wiped each piece with a soft cloth, she said, "Next time win more, lose less."

"Ma, it's not how many pieces you lose," I said. "Sometimes you need to lose pieces to get ahead."

"Better to lose less, see if you really need."

At the next tournament, I won again, but it was my mother who wore the triumphant grin.

"Lost eight piece this time. Last time was eleven. What I tell you? Better off lose less!" I was annoyed, but I couldn't say anything.

I attended more tournaments, each one farther away from home. I won all games, in all divisions. The Chinese bakery downstairs from our flat displayed my growing collection of trophies in its window, amidst the dust-covered cakes that were never picked up. The day after I won an important regional tournament, the window encased a fresh sheet cake with whipped-cream frosting and red script saying,

"Congratulations, Waverly Jong, Chinatown Chess Champion." Soon after that, a flower shop, headstone engraver, and funeral parlor offered to sponsor me in national tournaments. That's when my mother decided I no longer had to do the dishes. Winston and Vincent had to do my chores.

"Why does she get to play and we do all the work," complained Vincent.

"Is new American rules," said my mother. "Meimei play, squeeze all her brains out for win chess. You play, worth squeeze towel."

By my ninth birthday, I was a national chess champion. I was still some 429 points away from grand-master status, but I was touted as the Great American Hope, a child prodigy and a girl to boot. They ran a photo of me in *Life* magazine next to a quote in which Bobby Fischer said, "There will never be a woman grand master." "Your move, Bobby," said the caption.

The day they took the magazine picture I wore neatly plaited braids clipped with plastic barrettes trimmed with rhinestones. I was playing in a large high school auditorium that echoed with phlegmy coughs and the squeaky rubber knobs of chair legs sliding across freshly waxed wooden floors. Seated across from me was an American man, about the same age as Lau Po, maybe fifty. I remember that his sweaty brow seemed to weep at my every move. He wore a dark, malodorous suit. One of his pockets was stuffed with a great white kerchief on which he wiped his palm before sweeping his hand over the chosen chess piece with great flourish.

In my crisp pink-and-white dress with scratchy lace at the neck, one of two my mother had sewn for these special occasions, I would clasp my hands under my chin, the delicate points of my elbows poised lightly on the table in the manner my mother had shown me for posing for the press. I would swing my patent leather shoes back and forth like an impatient child riding on a school bus. Then I would pause, suck in my lips, twirl my chosen piece in midair as if undecided, and then firmly plant it in its new threatening place, with a triumphant smile thrown back at my opponent for good measure.

I no longer played in the alley of Waverly Place. I never visited the playground where the pigeons and old men gathered. I went to school, then directly home to learn new chess secrets, cleverly concealed advantages, more escape routes.

But I found it difficult to concentrate at home. My mother had a habit of standing over me while I plotted out my games. I think she thought of herself as my protective ally. Her lips would be sealed tight, and after each move I made, a soft "Hmmmmph" would escape from her nose.

"Ma, I can't practice when you stand there like that," I said one day. She retreated to the kitchen and made loud noises with the pots and pans. When the crashing stopped, I could see out of the corner of my eye that she was standing in the doorway. "Hmmph!" Only this one came out of her tight throat.

My parents made many concessions to allow me to practice. One time I complained that the bedroom I shared was so noisy that I couldn't think. Thereafter, my brothers slept in a bed in the living room facing the street. I said I couldn't finish my rice; my head didn't work right when my stomach was too full. I left the table with half-finished bowls and nobody complained. But there was one duty I couldn't avoid. I had to accompany my mother on Saturday market days when I had no tournament to play. My mother would proudly walk with me, visiting many shops, buying very little. "This my daughter Wave-ly Jong," she said to whoever looked her way.

One day, after we left a shop I said under my breath, "I wish you wouldn't do that, telling everybody I'm your daughter." My mother stopped walking. Crowds of people with heavy bags pushed past us on the sidewalk, bumping into first one shoulder, then another.

"Aiii-ya. So shame be with mother?" She grasped my hand even tighter as she glared at me.

I looked down. "It's not that, it's just so obvious. It's just so embarrassing."

"Embarrass you be my daughter?" Her voice was cracking with anger.

"That's not what I meant. That's not what I said."

"What you say?"

I knew it was a mistake to say anything more, but I heard my voice speaking. "Why do you have to use me to show off? If you want to show off, then why don't you learn to play chess."

My mother's eyes turned into dangerous black slits. She had no words for me, just sharp silence.

I felt the wind rushing around my hot ears. I jerked my hand out of my mother's tight grasp and spun around, knocking into an old woman. Her bag of groceries spilled to the ground.

"Aii-ya! Stupid girl!" my mother and the woman cried. Oranges and tin cans careened down the sidewalk. As my mother stooped to help the old woman pick up the escaping food, I took off.

I raced down the street, dashing between people, not looking back as my mother screamed shrilly, "Meimei! Meimei!" I fled down an alley, past dark curtained shops and merchants washing the grime off their windows. I sped into the sunlight, into a large street crowded with tourists examining trinkets and souvenirs. I ducked into another dark alley, down another street, up another alley. I ran until it hurt and I realized I had nowhere to go, that I was not running from anything. The alleys contained no escape routes.

My breath came out like angry smoke. It was cold. I sat down on an upturned plastic pail next to a stack of empty boxes, cupping my chin with my hands, thinking hard. I imagined my mother, first walking briskly down one street or another looking for me, then giving up and returning home to await my arrival. After two hours, I stood up on creaking legs and slowly walked home.

The alley was quiet and I could see the yellow lights shining from our flat like two tiger's eyes in the night. I climbed the sixteen steps to the door, advancing quietly up each so as not to make any warning sounds. I turned the knob; the door was locked. I heard a chair moving, quick steps, the locks turning — click! click! click! — and then the door opened.

"About time you got home," said Vincent. "Boy, are you in trouble."

He slid back to the dinner table. On a platter were the remains of a large fish, its fleshy head still connected to bones swimming upstream in vain escape. Standing there waiting for my punishment, I heard my mother speak in a dry voice.

"We not concerning this girl. This girl not have concerning for us."

Nobody looked at me. Bone chopsticks clinked against the insides of bowls being emptied into hungry mouths.

I walked into my room, closed the door, and lay down on my bed. The room was dark, the ceiling filled with shadows from the dinnertime lights of neighboring flats.

In my head, I saw a chessboard with sixty-four black and white squares. Opposite me was my opponent, two angry black slits. She wore a triumphant smile. "Strongest wind cannot be seen," she said.

Her black men advanced across the plane, slowly marching to each successive level as a single unit. My white pieces screamed as they scurried and fell off the board one by one. As her men drew closer to my edge, I felt myself growing light. I rose up into the air and flew out the window. Higher and higher, above the alley, over the tops of tiled roofs, where I was gathered up by the wind and pushed up toward the night sky until everything below me disappeared and I was alone.

I closed my eyes and pondered my next move.

ABOUT **AMY TAN**

Amy Tan was born in 1952 in Oakland, California, shortly after her parents emigrated from China. Her father was a minister and electrical engineer, and her mother was a vocational nurse and member of a social club called the Joy Luck Club. Tan's

first novel, named for that club, explores the relationships between Chinese American daughters and their mothers. For a number of years, Tan was a freelance technical writer. She began writing fiction — and studying jazz piano — as a diversion from work.

RESPONDING

1. *Personal Response* Compare your attitude toward competition to Meimei's. Explain whether you feel the same way or differently about winning and losing.

2. *Literary Analysis* The idea that the narrator can get what she wants by using "invisible strengths" is a *motif*, or repeated theme, in this story. Identify two incidents in which this motif is evident.

3. *Multicultural Connection* Examine the relationship between Meimei and her mother. Which aspects do you think are universal, and which are peculiar to the author's culture?

LANGUAGE WORKSHOP

Direct Address When someone is addressed by name or title, commas are used to separate the person's name from the rest of the sentence. Examine these sentences: "Ma, what is Chinese torture?" "You have sixteen pieces, Meimei, and so do I. " Insert commas where needed in the following sentences from the story.
1. "Little sister been a long time since I play with dolls. . . ."
2. "Ma I can't practice when you stand there like that," I said one day.
3. "Your move Bobby" said the caption.

WRITER'S PORTFOLIO

Tan writes, "I also found out why I should never reveal 'why' to others. A little knowledge withheld is a great advantage one should store for future use." Write a brief sketch of a real or imaginary situation in which you use a secret to succeed.

The Mao Button

HE VOWED to get himself a stupendous Mao button tonight after work.

Actually, the one he had worn to the office today was big and novel enough to arouse a good deal of envy.

His brother-in-law had gotten it specially for him from a certain unit in the navy and had brought it to his place just last night. Everyone in his family had wanted it. After squabbling over it for about half an hour, they had agreed to take turns: each would have it for a day until it had circulated once, then each would keep it for a week at a time. He had gotten it first, not because he was head of the house, but because he had wanted so desperately to show it off at work. He had insisted, and he had won.

He was delighted with himself all morning at the office. He created a real sensation. "You've outdone us all today, Mr. Kong!" said everyone who saw him, as they bent down to pore over the button as if it were some kind of jewel.

Their envious looks went straight to his head. He was certain that his Mao button was the best at the office today. At lunch he paraded around the cafeteria to make sure everyone noticed him. But then Mr. Chen, from the production department, approached him sporting an even bigger, newer, more eye-catching button on his neatly pressed jacket. An embossed portrait of the Leader was centered in a great red enamel sun, below which a giant golden steamship forged through the waves. The Leader was depicted from the front instead of the usual profile. He was wearing an army cap, and his cap and collar bore insignia. The gilding was superb: the flash of gold against red dazzled the eye. The button was a collector's item. Kong felt his own button darken like a light that had gone out. And it was so small by comparison—his whole button was no bigger than the portrait on Mr. Chen's, whose entire button must have been more than three inches across: about as big as a sesame cake.

Mr. Chen was extremely coolheaded and always kept a straight face. As they walked by each other, Mr. Chen just eyed Kong's chest and passed him like some champion athlete meeting a young amateur. Hurt, jealous, and angry, Kong made up his mind to go right out and get an enormous Mao button, even if it cost him his life's savings. He just had to bring Mr. Chen down a peg or two.

When he got home in the evening he told his family about his failure. After a quick dinner he found all the Mao buttons in the house, wrapped them in a handkerchief, and stuffed them into his pocket. He even snatched up the buttons his wife and son were wearing. Then he dashed out to The East Is Red Avenue, the busiest shopping street in town. He had heard that the open space beyond the parking lot of the big department store was the place to go to trade Mao buttons. People said you could get all the latest styles there. He had never been before.

Bʏ THE TIME he got there the sky was dark and all the lights were on, but shoppers still crowded the street. Practically everyone was wearing Mao buttons; they seemed to have become another part of the human

body. Some people wore four or five across their chests, the way European generals used to wear their medals a hundred years ago. It seemed to Kong that people with unusual Mao buttons held their heads higher than the rest, while those with ordinary little outmoded buttons moved drearily through the crowd. No matter how much status, income, or power you had, the quality of your Mao button was all-determining at this particular moment. Had the Mao button become the acid test of the wearer's political stance and loyalty to the Leader? A touchstone? A monitor of the heart?

As he walked he paid no attention to the people coming toward him; he had eyes only for their Mao buttons. Colorful, glittering buttons of all sizes were rushing at him like stars shooting by a rocket ship in outer space. Then he spotted a button exactly like Mr. Chen's. He reached out and grabbed its wearer by the arm.

"Just what do you think you're doing?" the man demanded, obviously startled.

Kong took a closer look at him: a short, fat, paunchy old soldier. Perhaps he was an officer.

"Excuse me, uh—" Kong asked with an ingratiating laugh, "could you spare your Mao button? I have all kinds—you could have your pick. Do you think we could make a deal?"

The soldier sneered as if to say that his button was a priceless family heirloom. He looked annoyed at Kong's effrontery. Kong was still clutching his sleeve. "No way," he snapped, shoving Kong aside, and waddled away.

KONG WAS ANGRY, but he comforted himself with the thought that even if he had gotten the button, it would merely have put him on an equal footing with Mr. Chen. What he wanted was to outdo him. Then he caught sight of the swarm of button traders beyond the parking lot. His heart began to pound like that of a fisherman who spots a shimmering school of fish, and he broke into a run.

Once in the crowd, Kong felt hot and flushed, but the sight was mind-boggling: an endless variety of Mao buttons and an assortment of hawkers to match.

Some wore the buttons they hoped to trade and called out what kinds they were looking for:

"Who has a Wuhan Steelworks 'two-and-a-half'?"—a button two-and-a-half inches in diameter—"I'll swap you for it!"

Some displayed their buttons on hand towels; others, who mistook flashy colors for beauty, had their wares in flat glass cases lined with colored paper on the sides and green satin on the bottom. Still others pinned their buttons to their caps so that people had to crane their necks to see them. The crowd thronged the south and east edges of the parking lot. Some people had even spilled over into the lot and squeezed their way in between the cars. With their haggling, shouts, and laughter, the place was noisier than an open-air market at the busiest hour of the morning.

Someone tapped him on the shoulder. "What kind are you looking for?"

The speaker was a big, tall middle-aged man with the unctuous manner of a practiced salesman. But he was wearing a baggy blue jacket with only a single bottlecap-sized Mao button on the chest. He did not look as though he had any special goods.

"I want a big one. At least a 'three-and-a-half.' Do you have any?"

"Oh-ho—no little trinkets for you, eh! Do you mind if the workmanship is a bit rough?" the man asked. He seemed to have what Kong wanted.

"Let me see it."

"First tell me what you have," the man replied without batting an eyelid. He was as haughty as a Mao-button millionaire.

"I've got dozens of different kinds," said Kong, reaching for his pocket.

The man touched Kong's wrist. "Don't take them out in this mob. Somebody'll swipe them. Come with me!"

They elbowed their way out of the crowd, crossed the street, and entered the dark alley beside the Revolution Hat and Shoe Store. The man led him to the second lamppost.

"Let me see your goods," he ordered.

Kong handed the man his handkerchief of Mao buttons. The man inspected them, shaking his head and clucking in disapproval, and gave them back.

"You got any better ones?" he asked after a moment's thought.

"No, these are all I have."

THE MAN PAUSED AGAIN. "You're going to have a hard time trading that bunch of buttons for a 'three-and-a-half,'" he said, pointing at Kong's handkerchief of buttons. "Don't forget—the big ones are hot items now."

"Well, I should have a look at yours, whether you're going to trade or not. Then we'll see what's what," Kong retorted scornfully. After all, he had not even seen the man's wares.

Instead of answering, the man unfastened his outer jacket and whisked it open. Kong's eyes nearly popped out of his head: at least a hundred different Mao buttons were pinned to the man's inner jacket. He was a walking Mao-button treasure house. Kong had never seen any of the styles before.

"You haven't seen anything yet," the man said before Kong could look his fill. "Take a peek inside—that's where the big ones are." And he opened the button-covered jacket to reveal yet another garment laden with row upon row of shiny buttons. They were huge: all were at least as big as a fist, and one, the size of the lid of a mug, caught the eye like a crane among chickens.

"That's the one I want!" cried Kong in delight, his heart thumping.

"What? This one?" the man asked with a chuckle. "Do you know how big it is? It's a 'four.' You see where it says 'Loyalty' three times in gold along here? This is a 'Triple Loyalty' button from Xinjiang. Nobody around here has seen these yet. I guess you don't know the market: even four times the buttons you've got here wouldn't buy you one of these. All your buttons put together are worth at most a 'three-and-a-half.' And that's only if you trade with me—nobody else would give you such a good deal. Your buttons are too little and too ordinary."

"Why don't you just let me have this 'four'? I've got forty or fifty buttons here, and—" Kong pleaded. He was madly in love with the button. If only he could just wear it tomorrow, Mr. Chen and everyone else at the office would be green with envy.

Just then a swarthy little man appeared on the left and approached to look at the Mao buttons on the tall man's chest.

The tall man glanced at the newcomer and yanked his outer jacket shut. "No deal!" he announced rudely, and stalked away, jingling like a horse in bell harness.

Kong thought, "I can't let him get away—at least I've got to trade him for a 'three-and-a-half.'" He was about to run after the tall man when the swarthy little man put out an arm to stop him. With his chin of bristly black stubble and his dark clothes, he looked as if he were carved in jet. His round gleaming eyes seemed to cast a black luster over his entire person.

"Don't trade with him—gypping beginners is his racket," he said in a rasping voice. "Those 'Triple Loyalty' buttons from Xinjiang are a dime a dozen; they're considered passé. Now tell me what you've got—I'll make you a deal. *I've* got a Mao button like nothing you've ever seen before."

"Is it big?"

"Big! Well, it's bigger than that 'Triple Loyalty' button of his. But it's not just big—it's a real novelty. But let me see yours first."

KONG PRODUCED HIS PACKAGE of buttons again and let the man examine them like a customs inspector. Then the man led him deeper into the alley. The streetlights were burned out, and it was pitch-dark. Kong was afraid that the stranger was going to mug him. The farther they went, the darker it got, until the man's murky silhouette almost blended into the gloomy black shadows.

"Couldn't I take a look at it here?" he asked, making a supreme effort to be brave.

"All right," agreed the swarthy little man, and like the tall man before him he unfastened his jacket, but his chest was a dark blur without a single Mao button. Before Kong could ask any questions he heard a click, and a round, glowing, moonlike object magically appeared on the man's left breast. It seemed to Kong that a luminous hole had opened up in the man's chest or that his heart had lit up. And inside was a picture: a color portrait of Chairman Mao waving from the Tian Anmen Rostrum!

When he recovered from his momentary stupefaction, Kong understood: the man was wearing a round glass case lit by a flashlight bulb. In the case a color photo of the Leader waving a giant hand was mounted behind a red cardboard railing. The light bulb was probably between the photo and the cardboard. The battery was concealed on the man's person; the wiring hung down from the back of the case; and the switch was in his hand. A flip of the switch and presto! The Mao button would light up like a color television. A truly great invention!

The man clicked the light off. "Well, how do you like it?" came his smug, wheedling voice in the dark. "Isn't it incredible? What'll you give me for it? But don't forget that the batteries and switch alone are worth a lot of money!"

Kong had to agree that the button was a real novelty. But his interest quickly faded. This was some homemade contraption, not a proper button. And you had to carry around a complete set of electrical equipment — wiring, batteries, a switch — as if you were an electric fan. Besides, it might be eye-catching at night, but it would be totally lackluster by day.

"It's very nice," he said politely after a moment's thought, "but I think I won't take it, since it's not a proper button. What I'd like is a regular button, at least a 'three-and-a-half,' if you have any."

The man launched into a sales pitch, but Kong would not change his mind. Then the man grabbed him eagerly by the wrist. Kong, who had been afraid to start with, thought the man was going to rob him of his Mao buttons. Jerking his arm free, he ran for the brightly lit entrance to the alley.

"Stop him!" he heard the man shout behind him.

It occurred to Kong that some of the man's cronies might be lurking nearby. He shot out of the alley and into the street, where he almost collided with an approaching bicycle. Skittish as a hare, he jumped over the front wheel and darted back into the crowd of button traders by the parking lot. For fear that the swarthy little man might spot him, he stooped over, hiding his face, and stole through the crowd. Luckily he escaped without further mishap and ran all the way home.

WHEN HIS WIFE saw how pale and breathless he was, she thought he was ill. She scolded him, once she found out what had happened, and poured him a hot cup of tea to calm him down.

"You've got Mao buttons on the brain!" she said. "You never do what you're supposed to when you get home from work — and tonight, of all things, you run out onto the streets to swap buttons. Don't you know what kind of riffraff you could have run into out there? And you took the kid's and my buttons too! If they'd been stolen, what would we have worn tomorrow? People would say I'd gone without my button because I didn't love Chairman Mao. They'd arrest me as a counterrevolutionary, and there wouldn't be anybody here to cook for you when you got home from work every day. It takes finesse to get good Mao buttons. Look at Mr. Wang — now there's a real operator. He may be unassuming, but he's got more buttons than anybody."

"Which Mr. Wang?"

"The one who lives on the third floor of the front building. You still don't know who I mean? Of course you do — Mrs. Wang's husband. What's the matter with you? Did they scare you silly out there?"

"Oh—yes—I see. So where does he get so many buttons?"

"He's on the staff of a badge factory where they make nothing but Mao buttons. His boss gives him hundreds of them to take along on every business trip. You have to grease palms with them nowadays to get a hotel room, buy train tickets, or ask anyone a favor. They're worth more than cash. A little while ago Mrs. Wang told me that her husband paid for a new truck for his factory with nothing but Mao buttons."

"How many buttons did that cost?"

"The man's clever—he may not have parted with all that many. My guess is that a shrewd fellow like him lines his own pocket on the sly whenever he has the chance. Why else would Mrs. Wang have a new Mao button every time I see her? When I ask her about them she just laughs it off instead of answering, but I'm sure she gets them all from her husband. Just now I went over there to collect their water bill and found them gloating over their buttons. I burst in without knocking and really got an eyeful."

"Did you get a good look at them? What kinds did they have?"

"I couldn't begin to tell you. There were at least a thousand—the bed and table were both covered with them."

"Were there any big ones?"

"Big ones? I swear one of them was as big as a saucepan lid."

So THE OBJECT of his far-flung search had been right next door all along. Leaving his tea untouched on the table, he ran to the front building as fast as his legs could carry him. "Mr. Wang!" he began to shout, even before he got to the third floor. Like some invisible hand, joy clutched at his vocal cords and made his voice tremble.

Once inside Mr. Wang's apartment, he begged him to show his treasures. Mr. Wang grudgingly obliged, since Kong was an old neighbor. Now here was a great Mao-button collection! Mr. Wang was a Mao-button millionaire if there ever was one. Kong was developing an inferiority complex.

Then he spotted the enormous button that his wife had mentioned. Mr. Wang said that it was a "five-and-a-half." Kong weighed it in his palm. It was surprisingly heavy: at least half a pound. But the picture was commonplace: a big red sun with a profile of the Leader in the middle and a chain of nine sunflowers across the bottom. The flowers looked more like coarse sieves. The buffing, painting, and gilding were shoddy. However, it was definitely the biggest in the world — Mr. Chen's would look tiny by comparison. Kong wanted a big one: they were the best — they stood out and really made a statement. He begged Mr. Wang for it and showed his buttons one more time. Luckily he had one with a picture of the globe and the caption: "The People of the World Yearn for the Red Sun." Mr. Wang happened to need this one to complete a set of four, so Kong gave it to him, along with two others, in exchange for the biggest button in history. He arrived home cradling his treasure in trembling hands.

"Wow!" his wife and son exclaimed when they saw it.

THE NEXT MORNING he rose early, shaved, washed his face and neck, and put on clean clothes, as carefully as if he were going to be awarded a medal. Next, ignoring his wife's protests, he used one of her soft new handkerchiefs to polish the huge button with petroleum jelly. He had some trouble pinning it on. It covered half of his narrow chest when he wore it on the side, but placed in the middle it looked frivolous, like the breastplate of an ancient general. And his jacket sagged under its tremendous weight. Worst of all, since the pin was right in the center of the back, the button tilted outward like a picture frame instead of lying flat. Kong was at a loss until his wife suggested that he change into his denim jacket; although the weather was still too warm for denim, the stiff material allowed the button to lie flat the way it was supposed to.

With the button on, he struck a few poses and admired himself in the mirror.

"Hooray!" his son cheered, clapping his hands. "My dad is tops! My dad is number one!"

The child was adorable—his compliments were the icing on the cake.

Yes, he really was the sensation of the day! People ogled him as he rode his bicycle down the street. Some pointed him out to their companions, but he sped past them before they could get a good look at him. He was on cloud nine. To prolong the gratification, he took the long way to work. People on a passing bus pressed their noses flat against the windows to stare. As he approached the gate of his office building he tensed up like an actor about to take his first plunge through a brightly lit stage door. He was headed for the limelight.

He entered the gate and locked his bicycle in the yard.

"Hey, everybody," someone shouted, "come see Mr. Kong's Mao button!" In no time flat he was surrounded by a crowd. People were jostling each other and craning their necks to see. They were looking at his button with amazement and envy, and at him with a new respect. Everyone was yelling, which attracted more people.

"Now that's a big button. Where did you get it?"

"Mr. Kong, you're a real go-getter!"

"Of course! I'm loyal to Chairman Mao," he said with a smug laugh, keeping one hand on the button in case anyone tried to snatch it.

Some people tried to move his fingers out of the way so that they could get a better look at the button; others tried to peek at the back to find out where it was made.

"It doesn't say anything on the back," he cried, clutching the button. "It was produced by a classified military factory. Please quit yanking on it, the pin is too small—" He

Culture Note

After Mao's death, new leaders reversed many of his policies and looked to the United States and Europe to help modernize China. This story was written in 1980, four years after Mao's death and almost a decade before the massacre of anti-Communist demonstrators in Tiananmen (Tian Anmen) Square.

seemed anxious, but in fact he was jubilant. The excitement he was causing was a sign that his button was without compare not only at the office, but probably in the whole city. Unless someone made a button as big as a crock lid, which only a giant could wear. Then he remembered Mr. Chen: where was yesterday's victor now?

The crowd had swelled to thirty or forty people. Everyone was babbling at once. He could not hear anything. His heavy denim jacket had brought the sweat out on his forehead. Unable to stand it any longer, he began to wriggle his way out of the unbearable crush, away from the hands that were pulling on him.

"Let me out, you're squashing me!"

He was tickled pink.

Finally he squeezed his way out like a noodle out of a noodle machine. He was exhilarated. But just then he heard a clank, as though a heavy metal platter had fallen to the ground. Then he heard it rolling around. He did not realize what the sound was until he reached up and found that his Mao button was gone.

"Oh, oh! My button fell off!" he cried. Everyone froze and he began a frantic search. It was not on the ground in front of him, so he stepped back to turn around and look behind him. He felt something hard and slippery underfoot.

"Oh, no! You're standing on a button with a portrait of Chairman Mao!" he heard a woman say, before he could grasp what had happened.

In terror he looked down and saw the Mao button under his heel. He should have been able to lift his foot quickly, but it was as unresponsive as a piece of wood. His body went limp and his weight sank into the offending leg. With all eyes riveted upon him, he stood rooted to the spot.

THIS BLUNDER was a heinous crime that brought him to the brink of destruction. There is no need to recount the details here. Suffice it to say that he recovered from his Mao-button mania and came to look upon these former objects of his affection with fear and trembling. These events are all behind him now. But there is one question that puzzles him to this day. Perhaps the only clue to its answer lies in the following "natural phenomenon": you can travel the entire three million seven hundred and seven thousand square miles of our country today and see hardly a single Mao button. . . .

ABOUT **FENG JICAI**

Feng Jicai (**fəh′ tsə′chi**) is both a writer and a painter. (Note that his family name *Feng* appears first, according to Chinese custom.) He lives in Tianjin, where he has been Vice Chairman of a branch of the Chinese Writers' Association. "The Mao Button" is from his collection of nine stories of China, called *Chrysanthemums and Other Stories,* which offers a gently satirical portrait of the country during and after Mao's Cultural Revolution.

RESPONDING

1. *Personal Response* What parallels can you draw between Mr. Kong, who is obsessed with outdoing his associates, and competitive people you know today?

2. *Literary Analysis* Satire is a literary form in which human actions are held up for ridicule. Describe the author's use of satire, especially at the end of the story when Mr. Kong's button falls off. What is the author trying to say in this satiric story?

3. *Multicultural Connection* Mao was once considered a hero by many Chinese communists. Name current heroes in two or three cultures and explain why you think people admire them.

LANGUAGE WORKSHOP

Simile A *simile* is a kind of figurative language that makes a comparison using the words *like* or *as.* Similes can help convey physical images as well as mental or emotional states. Find three similes in "The Mao Button" that convey physical qualities such as size, shape, speed, and smell, and three that convey emotional qualities such as fear, excitement, and joy.

WRITER'S PORTFOLIO

How do people compete by their appearance in your school or neighborhood? Outline the plot for a story in which someone who is obsessed with this kind of competition learns something about how it feels to "win" or "lose."

The Censors

Poor Juan! One day they caught him
with his guard down before he could even realize that what
he had taken as a stroke of luck was really one of fate's dirty
tricks. These things happen the minute you're careless and
you let down your guard, as one often does. Juancito let
happiness — a feeling you can't trust — get the better of him
when he received from a confidential source Mariana's new
address in Paris and he knew that she hadn't forgotten him.
Without thinking twice, he sat down at his table and wrote
her a letter. *The* letter that keeps his mind off his job during
the day and won't let him sleep at night (what had he
scrawled, what had he put on that sheet of paper he sent
to Mariana?).

Juan knows there won't be a problem with the letter's
contents, that it's irreproachable, harmless. But what about
the rest? He knows that they examine, sniff, feel, and read
between the lines of each and every letter, and check its tiniest comma and most accidental stain. He knows that all letters pass from hand to hand and go through all sorts of tests
in the huge censorship offices and that, in the end, very few
continue on their way. Usually it takes months, even years,
if there aren't any snags; all this time the freedom, maybe
even the life, of both sender and receiver is in jeopardy. And
that's why Juan's so down in the dumps; thinking that
something might happen to Mariana because of his letters.
Of all people, Mariana, who must finally feel safe there

where she always dreamed she'd live. But he knows that the *Censor's Secret Command* operates all over the world and cashes in on the discount in air rates; there's nothing to stop them from going as far as that hidden Paris neighborhood, kidnapping Mariana, and returning to their cozy homes, certain of having fulfilled their noble mission.

Well, you've got to beat them to the punch, do what everyone tries to do: sabotage the machinery, throw sand in its gears, get to the bottom of the problem so as to stop it.

This was Juan's sound plan when he, like many others, applied for a censor's job—not because he had a calling or needed a job: no, he applied simply to intercept his own letter, a consoling but unoriginal idea. He was hired immediately, for each day more and more censors are needed and no one would bother to check on his references.

Ulterior motives couldn't be overlooked by the *Censorship Division*, but they needn't be too strict with those who applied. They knew how hard it would be for those poor guys to find the letter they wanted and even if they did, what's a letter or two when the new censor would snap up so many others? That's how Juan managed to join the *Post Office's Censorship Division*, with a certain goal in mind.

The building had a festive air on the outside which contrasted with its inner staidness. Little by little, Juan was absorbed by his job and he felt at peace since he was doing everything he could to get his letter for Mariana. He didn't even worry when, in his first month, he was sent to *Section K* where envelopes are very carefully screened for explosives.

It's true that on the third day, a fellow worker had his right hand blown off by a letter, but the division chief claimed it was sheer negligence on the victim's part. Juan and the other employees were allowed to go back to their work, albeit feeling less secure. After work, one of them tried to organize a strike to demand higher wages for unhealthy work, but Juan didn't join in; after thinking it over, he reported him to his superiors and thus got promoted.

You don't form a habit by doing something once, he told himself as he left his boss's office. And when he was transferred to *Section J*, where letters are carefully checked for poison dust, he felt he had climbed a rung in the ladder.

By working hard, he quickly reached *Section E* where the work was more interesting, for he could now read and analyze the letters' contents. Here he could even hope to get hold of his letter which, judging by the time that had elapsed, had gone through the other sections and was probably floating around in this one.

Soon his work became so absorbing that his noble mission blurred in his mind. Day after day he crossed out whole paragraphs in red ink, pitilessly chucking many letters into the censored basket. These were horrible days when he was shocked by the subtle and conniving ways employed by people to pass on subversive messages; his instincts were so sharp that he found behind a simple 'the weather's unsettled' or 'prices continue to soar' the wavering hand of someone secretly scheming to overthrow the Government.

His zeal brought him swift promotion. We don't know if this made him happy. Very few letters reached him in *Section B* — only a handful passed the other hurdles — so he read them over and over again, passed them under a magnifying glass, searched for microprint with an electronic microscope, and tuned his sense of smell so that he was beat by the time he made it home. He'd barely manage to warm up his soup, eat some fruit, and fall into bed, satisfied with having done his duty. Only his darling mother worried, but she couldn't get him back on the right road. She'd say, though it wasn't always true: Lola called, she's at the bar with the girls, they miss you, they're waiting for you. Or else she'd leave a bottle of red wine on the table. But Juan wouldn't overdo it: any distraction could make him lose his edge and the perfect censor had to be alert, keen, attentive, and sharp to nab cheats. He had a truly patriotic task, both self-denying and uplifting.

His basket for censored letters became the best fed as well as the most cunning basket in the whole *Censorship Division*. He was about to congratulate himself for having finally discovered his true mission, when his letter to Mariana reached his hands. Naturally, he censored it without regret. And just as naturally, he couldn't stop them from executing him the following morning, another victim of his devotion to his work.

ABOUT **LUISA VALENZUELA**

One of Argentina's most famous authors, Luisa Valenzuela (lü ē′sə val′ənz wā′lə) was born in Buenos Aires in 1938, the daughter of a physician and a well-respected writer. She wrote and published her first story when she was eighteen years old. Many of her works deal with the repressive world of Argentinian national politics after the brief return of Juan Perón to the presidency in 1973.  Valenzuela became a writer-in-residence at New York University in 1979. She currently divides her time between Buenos Aires and New York City, where she teaches creative writing.

RESPONDING

1. *Personal Response* Describe a time when what began as a clever idea ended up as a disaster. Did you become obsessed with the idea as Juan does in this story, or did something else cause the unfortunate outcome? Explain.

2. *Literary Analysis* Irony is a literary technique in which things turn out different from what is expected. Reread the story to find clues that might have alerted a careful reader to the ending.

3. *Multicultural Connection* Do you think a government has the right to enforce censorship on its people? Why or why not? Can you think of any forms of censorship that are practiced in your own country?

LANGUAGE WORKSHOP

Dash As a means of punctuation, a *dash* can signal an explanation or set off an interruption. Explain what purpose the dash serves in the following passage from the selection: "Very few letters reached him in *Section B* — only a handful passed the other hurdles — so he read them over and over again. . . ." Find two other passages in which Valenzuela uses a dash. Try substituting a colon, comma, or parentheses, and see if you like the results as well.

WRITER'S PORTFOLIO

Draft the letter Juan wrote to Mariana that eventually got him executed. Be imaginative!

RALPH ELLISON

From The Little Man
at Chehaw Station

It WAS AT TUSKEGEE INSTITUTE dur-
ing the mid-1930s that I was made aware of the little man
behind the stove. At the time I was a trumpeter majoring in
music and had aspirations of becoming a classical composer. As such, shortly before the little man came to my
attention, I had outraged the faculty members who judged
my monthly student's recital by substituting a certain skill
of lips and fingers for the intelligent and artistic structuring
of emotion that was demanded in performing the music
assigned to me. Afterward, still
dressed in my hired tuxedo, my ears
burning from the harsh negatives of
their criticism, I had sought solace in
the basement studio of Hazel
Harrison, a highly respected concert
pianist and teacher. Miss Harrison
had been one of Ferruccio Busoni's
prize pupils, had lived (until the rise
of Hitler had driven her back to a
U.S.A. that was not yet ready to recognize her talents) in Busoni's home in
Berlin, and was a friend of such masters as Egon Petri, Percy Grainger, and
Sergei Prokofiev. It was not the first
time that I had appealed to Miss
Harrison's generosity of spirit, but

About Music

Ferruccio Busoni
(1866–1924), Italian
composer and pianist,
p. 35

Egon Petri (1881–
1962), distinguished
pianist and student of
Busoni, p. 35

Percy Grainger
(1882–1961), Australian
composer, p. 35

Sergei Prokofiev
(1891–1953), Russian
composer, p. 35

today her reaction to my rather adolescent complaint was less than sympathetic.

"But, baby," she said, "in this country you must always prepare yourself to play your very best wherever you are, and on all occasions."

"But everybody tells you that," I said.

"Yes," she said, "but there's more to it than you're usually told. Of course you've always been taught to *do* your best, *look* your best, *be* your best. You've been told such things all your life. But now you're becoming a musician, an artist, and when it comes to performing the classics in this country, there's something more involved."

Watching me closely, she paused. "Are you ready to listen?"

"Yes, ma'am."

"All right," she said, "you must *always* play your best, even if it's only in the waiting room at Chehaw Station, because in this country there'll always be a little man hidden behind the stove."

"A *what*?"

She nodded. "That's right," she said. "There'll always be the little man whom you don't expect, and he'll know the *music*, and the *tradition*, and the standards of *musicianship* required for whatever you set out to perform!"

Speechless, I stared at her. After the working-over I'd just received from the faculty, I was in no mood for joking. But no, Miss Harrison's face was quite serious. So what did she mean? Chehaw Station was a lonely whistle-stop where swift north- or southbound trains paused with haughty impatience to drop off or take on passengers; the point where, on homecoming weekends, special coaches crowded with festive visitors were cut loose, coupled to a waiting switch engine, and hauled to Tuskegee's railroad siding. I knew it well, and as I stood beside Miss Harrison's piano, visualizing the station, I told myself, *She has GOT to be kidding!*

For, in my view, the atmosphere of Chehaw's claustrophobic little waiting room was enough to discourage even a blind street musician from picking out blues on his guitar, no matter how tedious his wait for a train. Biased toward disaster by bruised feelings, my imagination pictured the vibrations set in motion by the winding of a trumpet within that drab, utilitarian structure: first shattering, then bringing its walls "a-tumbling down"—like Jericho's at the sounding of Joshua's priest-blown ram horns.

Culture Note

like Jericho's . . . horns
Jericho, a stronghold commanding the valley of the lower Jordan River, was captured and destroyed by Joshua and his troops, according to the Old Testament. p. 37

True, Tuskegee possessed a rich musical tradition, both classical and folk, and many music lovers and musicians lived or moved through its environs, but—and my regard for Miss Harrison notwithstanding—Chehaw Station was the last place in the area where I would expect to encounter a connoisseur lying in wait to pounce upon some rash, unsuspecting musician. Sure, a connoisseur might hear the haunting, blues-echoing, train-whistle rhapsodies blared by fast express trains as they thundered past—but the classics? Not a chance!

So as Miss Harrison watched to see the effect of her words, I said with a shrug, "Yes, ma'am."

She smiled, her prominent eyes a-twinkle. "I hope so," she said. "But if you don't just now, you will by the time you become an artist. So remember the little man behind the stove."

With that, seating herself at the piano, she began thumbing through a sheaf of scores—a signal that our discussion was ended.

So, I thought, *you ask for sympathy and you get a riddle.* I would have felt better if she had said, "Sorry, baby, I know how you feel, but after all, I was *there,* I *heard* you; and you treated your audience as though you were some kind of confidence man with a horn. So forget it, because I will not violate my own standards by condoning sterile musicianship." Some such reply, by reaffirming the "sacred principles" of art to which we were both committed, would have done much to supply the emotional catharsis for which I was appealing. By refusing, she forced me to accept full responsibility and thus learn from my offense. The condition of artistic communication is, as the saying goes, hard but fair.

But although disappointed and puzzled by Miss Harrison's sibylline response, I respected her artistry and experience too highly to dismiss it. Besides, something about her warning of a cultivated taste that asserted its authority out of obscurity sounded faintly familiar. Hadn't I once worked for an eccentric millionaire who prowled the halls and ballrooms of his fine hotel looking like a derelict who had wandered in off the street? Yes! And woe unto the busboy or waiter, hallman or maid — or anyone else — caught debasing the standards of that old man's house. For then, lashing out with the abruptness of reality shattering the contrived façade of a practical joke, the apparent beggar revealed himself as an extremely irate, and exacting, host of taste.

Thus, as I leaned into the curve of Miss Harrison's Steinway and listened to an interpretation of a Liszt rhapsody (during which she carried on an enthusiastic, stylistic analysis of passages that Busoni himself had marked for expressional subtlety), the little man of Chehaw Station fixed himself in my memory. And so vividly that today he not only continues to engage my mind, but often materializes when I least expect him.

ABOUT **RALPH ELLISON**

Ralph Ellison was born in Oklahoma City in 1914 and entered Tuskegee Institute in Alabama in 1933. He intended to study classical music, but was also inspired by the improvisations of jazz musicians. Ellison's literary career was launched by his novel, *Invisible Man*, published in

1952. He has also published a great deal of nonfiction, most of which emphasizes the potential of America's diverse cultures. At the time of his death in 1994, Ellison was still working on his second novel, begun in the 1960s.

RESPONDING

1. *Personal Response* Who or what plays the role of the little man in your life? Who introduced you to the little man, and when are you most aware of his presence?

2. *Literary Analysis* How would you describe the *tone* of Ellison's writing? Is it humorous, philosophical, ironic, or chiding? Explain.

3. *Multicultural Connection* Artistic communities often develop a culture of their own, with standards community members must meet. Describe at least three standards this excerpt suggests were held by the musical community at Tuskegee.

LANGUAGE WORKSHOP

Greek and Latin Words The following words from *The Little Man at Chehaw Station* have their roots in classical Greek or Latin. Use a dictionary to look up their meanings and etymologies, or origins: *catharsis, sibylline, connoisseur, tedious.*

WRITER'S PORTFOLIO

Imagine you are playing an instrument in the waiting room at Chehaw Station—or a public waiting area near you. Use images appealing to sight and sound to write a paragraph describing the instrument, how it would sound, and how others might react.

The Shoe Breaker

WHERE IS PINCELOUP?"

"I don't know, sir," replied the clerk.

"Baron," the owner said, as he turned to speak to the client who had just come in, "my staff and I saw him leave early this morning on your behalf."

"What I see," retorted the other, "is that I was counting on my shoes being ready at four o'clock. You assured me they would be. It is now six o'clock and the dinner is at eight. I don't intend to stand here cooling my heels."

"But, sir. . . ."

"Don't tell me you're sorry. It is I, my dear man, who am sorry. You can't depend on anyone nowadays."

The baron looked down at his feet and wiggled his toes under the worn calfskin. He'd have to go to the dinner party in his old shoes, bulging from his bunions and bubbled by his corns. Obviously he was comfortable in them, but aren't we always anxious to try out our latest purchase? The pair of dress shoes that he had bought the day before that tortured him so when he first put them on were still walking the streets of Paris, being broken in by a fellow named Pinceloup.

"May I make a suggestion?" ventured the owner. "I know the man well. I have used him for more than thirty years, Sir. He has broken in over twelve thousand pairs of shoes for me, following the customers' directives. He figures a morning per pair for normal feet, but an entire after-noon should there be any deformity. Our exceptional patrons. . . ."

The baron didn't readily count himself among the latter.

". . . I mean those whom it was nature's whim to deform, and God knows I pity them, will sometimes cost Pinceloup an entire day."

With the tip of his cane, the baron maliciously applied pressure to the corn crowning the big toe of his right foot, swollen by gout.

"Pinceloup is, moreover, a great judge of physiognomy and I shall miss him. He knows at a glance whether to walk pigeon-toed or duck-footed, or to stuff a wad of cotton in the shoe at just the right place, that is to say at the place that . . . Baron, sir?"

"Yes?"

"People like Pinceloup will be hard to come by in the future. Love for one's work is a thing of the past. Love for art is disappearing. But please sit down, he should be here any time now."

"Art?" cried out the baron. "Indeed I shall sit down."

"Pinceloup," the owner continued, "belonged to my father before I took over the business."

This sort of talk the baron savored, and time wore on. The salesmen, mean-while, were coming and going, carry-ing piles of boxes, kneeling, wielding their shoehorns, here lacing up an Oxford, there vaunting the quality of the alligator and, over in the women's section, assuming feminine poses as they side-saddled their fitting stools, clamping their knees together like women in bathing suits, not hesitating to look away should gaping thighs offer them the forbidden view. The owner kept a watchful eye on his people without diverting his

About Feet

bunions inflamed swellings near the first joint of the big toe, p. 40

corn a hardening and thickening of the skin, usually on the toes, p. 40

gout a disease that results in painful irritation of the joints, especially of the big toe, p. 41

attention from the baron who, though not a particularly good customer, was a man of great renown. The Petit-Chablis clan, lest one forget, still owned half of the country's railroads, and that is indeed what drew a good part of the clientele.

"Honestly, I can't understand what's keeping him."

"And it's getting dark," the baron sighed.

They were about to give up when the door opened and Pinceloup appeared, green around the gills and dragging at the heels.

"Ah! There you are."

THE BARON LOOKED at his dress shoes now gracing the shoe breaker's feet. They no longer bore a resemblance to the ones the Baron had purchased, but rather to the good old pair he now wore. His eyes wandered from the one to the other.

"My dear fellow," he exclaimed, putting his hand on Pinceloup's shoulder, "did everything go well?"

"Everything, Baron, sir. There might still be a hint of stiffness in the reinforcement of the outer left heel. I apologize for that."

Am I getting old, Pinceloup wondered. Is the leather less supple due to the new fangled methods of tanning and splicing? Or might the stitching or the lining be too heavy?

"Unshoe him," the owner told a clerk.

"I'd appreciate it," Pinceloup uttered feebly.

"Are you otherwise satisfied?" Baron Petit-Chablis inquired.

With the tip of his cane, he pointed to the already bloated shoes, now emptied of Pinceloup's feet, as well as of the scraps of cardboard, cotton balls, strips of cork, rubber disks and the like.

"They've put in eighteen kilometers," Pinceloup declared. "I advise you to put them on right away while they're still warm. We'll obtain a more generous contact. Talcum powder. . . ."

"The talc," shouted the owner.

The talcum powder will save the day, mused Pinceloup.

The baron had himself shod, laced up and helped to his feet. He shook hands with the owner. At the same time, he extended his left hand which held his cane, trying discreetly to offer Pinceloup a coin. He nearly blinded the poor devil in the process.

The breaker watched the baron as he left with short and hesitant steps.

Seeing him stop in the middle of the street for relief, Pinceloup felt the pain and even a twinge of shame.

"Monsieur," he said to the owner. "I just can't do it any more."

"What's that?"

"I've lost my touch. Look!" They could see the baron limping off.

"I did what I could," Pinceloup muttered as he examined his lacerated feet. His socks were embedded in his flesh and darkened in spots with blood stains.

"Come on now, don't give up for heaven's sake. You're the best breaker in all of Paris, Pinceloup. The main thing in life is to be tops at something. Remember. . . ."

"And tomorrow?" interrupted Pinceloup, his sense of honor reviving.

"You'll do two pairs for me. They'll be a snap."

"But I didn't see them on the customers' feet." The owner went to his file and pulled two sheets of vellum.

"Here." He knows that Pinceloup can't read and Pinceloup knows that he knows. If the boss is being mean again, it's because he esteems him, needs him, and can boast that no one else in all of Paris can break in shoes as well as Pinceloup.

"See you tomorrow," Pinceloup murmured.

Since his feet hurt him so, he put on his espadrilles, which he saved for the bad evenings. The boss, despite the fact that it was closing time, asked him to leave through the back service door.

ABOUT **DANIEL BOULANGER**

Daniel Boulanger (**bü läN zhā⁄**) was born in Compiègne, France, in 1922. He has written novels, short stories, children's stories, and film scripts. In addition, he acted in movies in the 1960s, most notably in the classics *Shoot the Piano Player, King of Hearts,* and *Breathless.*

RESPONDING

1. *Personal Response* Shoes were once a symbol of status, especially for people who could pay someone else to make them comfortable. Do you choose *your* shoes for status, for comfort, or for other reasons? Explain.

2. *Literary Analysis* Explain what the following *dialogue* reveals about each character who speaks these words.
• "Pinceloup," the owner continued, "belonged to my father before I took over the business."
• ". . . Baron, sir. There might still be a hint of stiffness in the reinforcement of the outer left heel. I apologize for that."
• "Don't tell me you're sorry. It is I, my dear man, who am sorry. You can't depend on anyone nowadays."

3. *Multicultural Connection* "The Shoe Breaker" illustrates class distinctions in French society. Find at least three indications that Pinceloup occupies a low social position.

LANGUAGE WORKSHOP

Idiom An *idiom* is an expression whose meaning cannot be understood from the ordinary meanings of the words that make it up. For example, "fed up," which has nothing to do with eating, means "bored or disgusted." Give the meanings of the following idioms from "The Shoe Breaker."
1. cooling my heels
2. green around the gills

3. dragging at the heels
4. save the day
Give a current idiom for each of the following meanings:
the best, tired, anxious, full of food.

WRITER'S PORTFOLIO

List what you would have to do to break in a pair of
shoes for a person sitting near you right now. Include
any physical, mental, and emotional preparations and
efforts you would make.

A Man

Nina Cassian

While fighting for his country, he lost an arm
and was suddenly afraid:
"From now on, I shall only be able to do things by
        halves.

I shall reap half a harvest.
I shall be able to play either the tune
or the accompaniment on the piano,
but never both parts together.
I shall be able to bang with only one fist
on doors, and worst of all
I shall only be able to half hold
my love close to me.
There will be things I cannot do at all,
applaud for example,
at shows where everyone applauds."

From that moment on, he set himself to do
everything with twice as much enthusiasm.
And where the arm had been torn away
a wing grew.

Black Hair

Gary Soto

At eight I was brilliant with my body.
In July, that ring of heat
We all jumped through, I sat in the bleachers
Of Romain Playground, in the lengthening
Shade that rose from our dirty feet.
The game before us was more than baseball.
It was a figure—Hector Moreno
Quick and hard with turned muscles,
His crouch the one I assumed before an altar
Of worn baseball cards, in my room.

I came here because I was Mexican, a stick
Of brown light in love with those
Who could do it—the triple and hard slide,
The gloves eating balls into double plays.
What could I do with 50 pounds, my shyness,
My black torch of hair, about to go out?
Father was dead, his face no longer
Hanging over the table or our sleep,
And mother was the terror of mouths
Twisting hurt by butter knives.

In the bleachers I was brilliant with my body,
Waving players in and stomping my feet,
Growing sweaty in the presence of white shirts.
I chewed sunflower seeds. I drank water
And bit my arm through the late innings.
When Hector lined balls into deep
Center, in my mind I rounded the bases
With him, my face flared, my hair lifting
Beautifully, because we were coming home
To the arms of brown people.

ABOUT **NINA CASSIAN**

Born in Galati, Romania, in 1924, Nina Cassian (ka╱ sē ən) studied drama and painting in Bucharest and eventually became a film critic and composer as well as a writer. She enjoyed success in her native country until, while visiting New York in 1985, her satirical writings about the Romanian government were discovered in a friend's diary. Cassian's work was immediately banned and her friend was tortured to death. Now living in the United States, Cassian teaches creative writing at New York University.

ABOUT **GARY SOTO**

Gary Soto grew up in Fresno, California, where he was born in 1952. As a child he worked as a migrant laborer, and much of his early poetry draws on childhood memories of the conditions of farm laborers and urban factory workers and his dreams of a better life. A prose writer as well as a poet, Soto reflects on his experiences as a Chicano in works such as *The Elements of San Joaquin, Black Hair,* and *Baseball in April.*

RESPONDING

1. *Personal Response* When in your life have you overcome a fear of failure? Compare the way you felt to the way the characters in these poems probably felt.

2. *Literary Analysis* How does each poem reflect the unit *theme,* The Need to Succeed?

3. *Multicultural Connection* Compare the treatment of wounded war veterans with that of sports heroes in our culture. Then decide what this comparison suggests about our society.

LANGUAGE WORKSHOP

Stanzas Poets arrange groups of lines in *stanzas* rather than in paragraphs. Stanzas may have similar patterns of rhythm and rhyme. They may also separate units of thought in a poem. After examining Cassian's poem, explain why you think it is organized into three stanzas.

WRITER'S PORTFOLIO

Draft a three-stanza poem or song about an event, real or imagined, in which someone succeeds against the odds. You might want to include a refrain that is repeated after each stanza.

Paper

H E WANTED IT, he dreamed of it, he hankered after it, as an addict after his opiate. Once the notion of a big beautiful house had lodged itself in his imagination, Tay Soon nurtured it until it became the consuming passion of his life. A house. A dream house such as he had seen on his drives with his wife and children along the roads bordering the prestigious housing estates on the island, and in the glossy pages of *Homes* and *Modern Living*. Or rather, it was a house which was an amalgam of the best, the most beautiful aspects of the houses he had seen. He knew every detail of his dream house already, from the aluminium sliding doors to the actual shade of the dining room carpet to the shape of the swimming pool. Kidney. He rather liked the shape. He was not ashamed of the enthusiasm with which he spoke of the dream house, an enthusiasm that belonged to women only, he was told. Indeed, his enthusiasm was so great that it had infected his wife and even his children, small though they were. Soon his wife Yee Lian was describing to her sister Yee Yeng, the dream house in all its perfection of shape and decor, and the children were telling their cousins and friends. "My daddy says that when our house is ready. . ."

They talked of the dream house endlessly. It had become a reality stronger than the reality of the small terrace house which they were sharing with Tay Soon's mother, to whom it belonged. Tay Soon's mother, whose little business of selling bottled curries and vegetable preserves which she made herself, left her little time for dreams, clucked her tongue and shook her head and made sarcastic remarks about the ambitiousness of young people nowadays.

"What's wrong with this house we're staying in?" she asked petulantly. "Aren't we all comfortable in it?"

Not as long as you have your horrid ancestral altars all over the place, and your grotesque sense of colour—imagine painting the kitchen wall bright pink. But Yee Lian was tactful enough to keep the remarks to herself, or to make them only to her sister Yee Yeng, otherwise they were sure to reach the old lady, and there would be no end to her sharp tongue.

The house—the dream house—it would be a far cry from the little terrace house in which they were all staying now, and Tay Soon and Yee Lian talked endlessly about it, and it grew magnificently in their imaginations, this dream house of theirs with its timbered ceiling and panelled walls and sunken circular sitting room which was to be carpeted in rich amber. It was no empty dream, for there was much money in the bank already. Forty thousand dollars had been saved. The house would cost many times that, but Tay Soon and Yee Lian with their good salaries would be able to manage very well. Once they took care of the down payment, they would be able to pay back monthly over a period of ten years—fifteen, twenty—what did it matter how long it took as long as the dream house was theirs? It had become the symbol of the peak of earthly achievement, and all of Tay Soon's energies and devotion were directed towards its realisation. His mother said, "You're a show-off, what's so grand about marble flooring and a swimming pool? Why don't you put your money to better use?" But the forty thousand grew steadily, and after Tay Soon and Yee Lian had put in every cent of their annual bonuses, it grew to forty-eight thousand, and husband and wife smiled at the smooth way their plans were going.

It was a time of growing interest in the stock market. The quotations for stocks and shares were climbing the charts, and the crowds in the rooms of the broking houses were growing perceptibly. Might we not do something about this, Yee Lian said to her husband. Do you know that Dr. Soo bought Rustan Banking for four dollars and today the shares are worth seven dollars each? The temptation was great. The rewards were almost immediate. Thirty thousand dollars' worth of NBE became fifty-five thousand almost overnight. Tay Soon and Yee Lian whooped. They put their remaining eighteen thousand in Far East Mart. Three days later the shares were worth twice that much. It was not to be imagined that things could stop here. Tay Soon secured a loan from his bank and put twenty thousand in OHTE. This was a particularly lucky share; it shot up to four times its value in three days.

"Oh, this is too much, too much," cried Yee Lian in her ecstasy, and she sat down with pencil and paper, and found after a few minutes' calculation that they had made a cool one hundred thousand in a matter of days.

AND NOW THERE WAS to be no stopping. The newspapers were full of it, everybody was talking about it, it was in the very air. There was plenty of money to be made in the stock exchange by those who had guts—money to be made by the hour, by the minute, for the prices of stocks and shares were rising faster than anyone could keep track of them! Dr. Soo was said—he laughingly dismissed it as a silly rumour—Dr. Soo was said to have made two million dollars already. If he sold all his shares now, he would be a millionaire twice over. And Yee Yeng, Yee Lian's sister, who had been urged with sisterly goodwill to come join the others make money, laughed happily to find that the shares she had bought for four twenty on Tuesday had risen to seven ninety-five on Friday—she laughed and thanked Yee Lian who advised her not to sell yet, it was going further, it would hit the ten dollar mark by next week. And Tay Soon both laughed and cursed—cursed that he had failed to buy a share at nine dollars which a few days later had hit seventeen dollars! Yee Lian said reproachfully, "I thought I told you to buy it, darling," and Tay Soon had beaten his forehead in despair and said, "I know, I know, why didn't I! Big fool that I am!" And he had another reason to curse himself—he sold five thousand West Parkes at sixteen twenty-three per share, and saw, to his horror, West Parkes climb to eighteen ninety the very next day!

"I'll never sell now," he vowed. "I'll hold on. I won't be so foolish." And the frenzy continued. Husband and wife couldn't talk or think of anything else. They thought fondly of their shares—going to be worth a million altogether soon. A million! In the peak of good humour, Yee Lian went to her mother-in-law, forgetting the past insults, and advised her to join the others by buying some shares, she would get her broker to buy them immediately for her, there was sure money in it. The old lady refused curtly, and to her son later, she showed great annoyance, scolding him for being so foolish as to put all his money in those worthless shares. "Worthless!" exploded Tay Soon. "Do you know, Mother, if I sold all my shares today, I would have the money to buy fifty terrace houses like the one you have?"

His wife said, "Oh, we'll just leave her alone. I was kind enough to offer to help her make money, but since she's so nasty and ungrateful, we'll leave her alone." The comforting, triumphant thought was that soon, very soon, they would be able to purchase their dream house; it would be even more magnificent than the one they had dreamt of, since they had made almost a — Yee Lian preferred not say the sum. There was the old superstitious fear of losing something when it is too often or too directly referred to, and Yee Lian had cautioned her husband not to make mention of their gains.

"Not to worry, not to worry," he said jovially, not superstitious like his wife, "After all, it's just paper gains so far."

The downward slide, or the bursting of the bubble as the newspapers dramatically called it, did not initially cause much alarm, for the speculators all expected the shares to bounce back to their original strength and thence continue the phenomenal growth. But that did not happen. The slide continued.

Tay Soon said nervously, "Shall we sell? Do you think we should sell?" but Yee Lian said stoutly, "There is talk that this decline is a technical thing only—it will be over soon, and then the rise will continue. After all, see what is happening in Hong Kong and London and New York. Things are as good as ever."

"We're still making, so not to worry," said Yee Lian after a few days. Their gains were pared by half. A few days later, their gains were pared to marginal.

There is talk of a recovery, insisted Yee Lian. Do you know, Tay Soon, Dr. Soo's wife is buying up some OHTE and West Parkes now? She says these two are sure to rise. She has some inside information that these two are going to climb past the forty dollar mark—

Tay Soon sold all his shares and put the money in OHTE and West Parkes. OHTE and West Parkes crashed shortly afterwards. Some began to say the shares were not worth the paper of the certificates.

"Oh, I can't believe, I can't believe it," gasped Yee Lian, pale and sick. Tay Soon looked in mute horror at her.

"All our money was in OHTE and West Parkes," he said, his lips dry.

"That stupid Soo woman!" shrieked Yee Lian. "I think she deliberately led me astray with her advice! She's always been jealous of me—ever since she knew we were going to build a house grander than hers!"

"How are we going to get our house now?" asked Tay Soon in deep distress, and for the first time he wept. He wept like a child, for the loss of all his money, for the loss of the dream house that he had never stopped loving and worshipping.

The pain bit into his very mind and soul, so that he was like a madman, unable to go to his office to work, unable to do anything but haunt the broking houses, watching with frenzied anxiety for OHTE and West Parkes to show him hope. But there was no hope. The decline continued with gleeful rapidity. His broker advised him to sell, before it was too late, but he shrieked angrily, "What! Sell at a fraction at which I bought them! How can this be tolerated?"

And he went on hoping against hope.

He began to have wild dreams in which he sometimes laughed and sometimes screamed. His wife Yee Lian was afraid and she ran sobbing to her sister who never failed to remind her curtly that all her savings were gone, simply because when she had wanted to sell, Yee Lian had advised her not to.

"But what is your sorrow compared to mine," wept Yee Lian, "see what's happening to my husband. He's cracking up! He talks to himself, he doesn't eat, he has nightmares, he beats the children. Oh, he's finished!"

Her MOTHER-IN-LAW TOOK CHARGE of the situation, while Yee Lian, wide-eyed in mute horror at the terrible change that had come over her husband, shrank away and looked to her two small children for comfort. Tight-lipped and grim, the elderly woman made herbal medicines for Tay Soon, brewing and straining for hours, and got a Chinese medicine man to come to have a look at him.

"There is a devil in him," said the medicine man, and he proceeded to make him a drink which he mixed with the ashes of a piece of prayer paper. But Tay Soon grew worse. He lay in bed, white, haggard and delirious, seeming to be beyond the touch of healing. In the end, Yee Lian, on the advice of her sister and friends, put him in hospital.

"I have money left for the funeral," whimpered the frightened Yee Lian only a week later, but her mother-in-law sharply retorted, "You leave everything to me! I have the money for his funeral, and I shall give him the best! He wanted a beautiful house all his life; I shall give him a beautiful house now!"

She went to the man who was well-known on the island for his beautiful houses, and she ordered the best. It would come to nearly a thousand dollars, said the man, a thin, wizened fellow whose funereal gauntness and pallor seemed to be a concession to his calling.

That doesn't matter, she said, I want the best. The house is to be made of superior paper, she instructed, and he was to make it to her specifications. She recollected that he, Tay Soon, had often spoken of marble flooring, a timbered ceiling and a kidney-shaped swimming pool. Could he simulate all these in paper?

The thin, wizened man said, "I've never done anything like that before. All my paper houses for the dead have been the usual kind—I can put in paper furniture and paper cars, paper utensils for the kitchen and paper servants, all that the dead will need in the other world. But I shall try to put in what you've asked for. Only it will cost more."

The house, when it was ready, was most beautiful to see. It stood seven feet tall, a delicate framework of wire and thin bamboo strips covered with finely worked paper of a myriad colours. Little silver flowers scattered liberally throughout the entire structure, gave a carnival atmosphere. There was a paper swimming pool (round, as the man had not understood "kidney") which had to be fitted inside the house itself, as there was no provision for a garden or surrounding grounds. Inside the house were paper figures; there were at least four servants to attend to the needs of the master who was posed beside two cars, one distinctly a Chevrolet and the other a Mercedes.

At the appointed time, the paper house was brought to Tay Soon's grave and set on fire there. It burned brilliantly, and in three minutes was a heap of ashes on the grave.

ABOUT **CATHERINE LIM**

Catherine Lim was born in a small Malaysian town in 1942. After careers as a schoolteacher and a lecturer in linguistics, she turned to writing full time. She has published one novel, as well as several collections of short stories, including ghost stories, love stories, and satirical fantasies. She is noted for her ironic perspective on life in Singapore.

RESPONDING

1. *Personal Response* What would your dream house be like, inside and out? How would you go about attaining this dream house?

2. *Literary Analysis* What does paper *symbolize* in this story? Use examples from the story to support your answer.

3. *Multicultural Connection* Singapore is an island of about 221 square miles with a population of over 2.5 million people. This works out to an average of nearly 12,000 people per each square mile. In a culture with this sort of population density, what do you think Tay Soon's dream house would represent?

LANGUAGE WORKSHOP

Analogies Verbal *analogies* are words that are related in some way. For example, *paper* and *money* are related because one can be made of the other. Decide what the relationship is between the first pair of words in each analogy below. Then complete the analogy for the second pair by providing a word that shows the same relationship.

1. nurture: care for:: neglect:
   a. worry   b. guard   c. treasure   d. overlook
2. tactful: rude:: wise:
   a. scholarly   b. foolish   c. obvious   d. bold
3. simulate: imitate:: dismiss:
   a. send away   b. welcome   c. maintain   d. ponder
4. addict: opiate:: athlete:
   a. fatigue   b. grace   c. exercise   d. Olympics

WRITER'S PORTFOLIO

Using an incident from your personal experience or something you have seen or read about, write a description of a funeral that related to the deceased person's goals and successes or failures in life.

Projects

MODEL OF SUCCESS

Work with a small group to build a model of what "success" could look like. Use common objects from around school and home. The model can be realistic or imaginative, of any size and medium—for instance, a collage of good report cards and papers for academic success; objects such as medals that suggest fulfilled goals; photographs of successful people in a career; clothes logos and advertisements that indicate material success; a tape by a successful performer; and so on. Present your model to the class.

THE ROAD TO SUCCESS

Make up a board game called "The Road to Success" to be played with 4 player markers, 32 cards, and a board. Squares on the board lead from a starting point to a goal of your choosing. Make up cards based on information from selections in the unit. ("You have become a national chess champion. Advance 3 squares." "You have lost money on the stock market. Go back 2 squares." "If you can explain who Mao is, advance 2 squares. If not, go back 2 squares.") Board squares may have traps and bonuses as well. Players in turn draw a card from the pile to determine their moves.

COMPOSITION ON COMPETITION

Write an essay about competition, examining at least one character from the selections in this unit, a person you know, and a world figure. Tell about both the advantages and the disadvantages of competing, using these people to illustrate.

Further Reading

The following books, many by authors represented in this unit, offer insights into the varied roads that can lead to success.

Cassian, Nina. *Life Sentences: Selected Poems.* Norton, 1990. The poems in this volume show the range of Cassian's perceptions of love, loss, and country.

Ellison, Ralph. *Going to the Territory.* Random House, 1986. The collection that opens with *The Little Man at Chehaw Station* includes lectures, memoirs, and provocative essays written from the 1960s into the 1980s.

Feng, Jicai. *Chrysanthemums and Other Stories.* Harcourt Brace Jovanovich, 1985. Nine stories inspired by China's Cultural Revolution show people surviving by their wits during turbulent years.

Hurston, Zora Neale. *Their Eyes Were Watching God.* Harper & Row, Perennial Library, 1990 (first published in 1937). This is the story of Janie Crawford's evolving selfhood through three marriages, the final one with Tea Cake, a man who engages her heart and spirit.

Lim, Catherine. *Little Ironies: Stories of Singapore.* Heinemann, 1978. The author's first collection offers views of the universal human condition as well as portraits of Singapore's customs and institutions.

Tan, Amy. *The Joy Luck Club.* Putnam, 1989. Mothers and daughters struggle to overcome generational barriers as they balance aspects of two cultures.

It's Not
Fair!

Life isn't always fair, and its injustices may range from small personal ones to large-scale social ones. Think of a time when you said—aloud or silently—"It's not fair!" Were you misjudged or deceived? Did you have a chance to make the situation better? Each selection in this unit relates someone's complicated feelings when geography, family, culture, or even the writer's own personality creates a situation perceived as unfair.

Another Evening
at the Club

IN A STATE OF TENSION, she awaited the return of her husband. At a loss to predict what would happen between them, she moved herself back and forth in the rocking chair on the wide wooden verandah that ran along the bank and occupied part of the river itself, its supports being fixed in the river bed, while around it grew grasses and reeds. As though to banish her apprehension, she passed her fingers across her hair. The spectres of the eucalyptus trees ranged along the garden fence rocked before her gaze, with white egrets slumbering on their high branches like huge white flowers among the thin leaves.

The crescent moon rose from behind the eastern mountains and the peaks of the gently stirring waves glistened in its feeble rays, intermingled with threads of light leaking from the houses of Manfalout scattered along the opposite bank. The coloured bulbs fixed to the trees in the garden of the club at the far end of the town stood out against the surrounding darkness. Somewhere over there her husband now sat, most likely engrossed in a game of chess.

It was only a few years ago that she had first laid eyes on him at her father's house, meeting his gaze that weighed up her beauty and priced it before offering the dowry. She had noted his eyes ranging over her as she presented him with the coffee in the Japanese cups that were kept safely locked away in the cupboard for important guests. Her mother had herself laid them out on the silver-plated tray with its elaborately embroidered spread. When the two men had taken their coffee, her father had looked up at her with a smile and had told her to sit down, and she had seated herself on the sofa facing them, drawing the end of her dress over her knees and looking through lowered lids at the man who might choose her as his wife. She had been glad to see that he was tall, well-built and clean-shaven except for a thin greying moustache. In particular she noticed the well-cut coat of English tweed and the silk shirt with gold links. She had felt herself blushing as she saw him returning her gaze. Then the man turned to her father and took out a gold case and offered him a cigarette.

"You really shouldn't, my dear sir," said her father, patting his chest with his left hand and extracting a cigarette with trembling fingers. Before he could bring out his box of matches Abboud Bey had produced his lighter.

"No, after you, my dear sir," said her father in embarrassment. Mingled with her sense of excitement at this man who gave out such an air of worldly self-confidence was a guilty shame at her father's inadequacy.

After lighting her father's cigarette Abboud Bey sat back, crossing his legs, and took out a cigarette for himself. He tapped it against the case before putting it in the corner of his mouth and lighting it, then blew out circles of smoke that followed each other across the room.

"It's a great honour for us, my son," said her father, smiling first at Abboud Bey, then at his daughter, at which Abboud Bey looked across at her and asked:

"And the beautiful little girl's still at secondary school?"

She lowered her head modestly and her father had answered:

"As from today she'll be staying at home in readiness for your happy life together, Allah permitting," and at a glance from her father she had hurried off to join her mother in the kitchen.

"You're a lucky girl," her mother had told her. "He's a real find. Any girl would be happy to have him. He's an Inspector of Irrigation though he's not yet forty. He earns a big salary and gets a fully furnished government house wherever he's posted, which will save us the expense of setting up a house—and I don't have to tell you what our situation is—and that's besides the house he owns in Alexandria where you'll be spending your holidays."

Samia had wondered to herself how such a splendid suitor had found his way to her door. Who had told him that Mr. Mahmoud Barakat, a mere clerk at the Court of Appeal, had a beautiful daughter of good reputation?

The days were then taken up with going the rounds of Cairo's shops and choosing clothes for the new grand life she would be living. This was made possible by her father borrowing on the security of his government pension. Abboud Bey, on his part, never visited her without bringing a present. For her birthday, just before they were married, he bought her an emerald ring that came in a plush box bearing the name of a well-known jeweller in Kasr el-Nil Street. On her wedding night, as he put a diamond bracelet round her wrist, he had reminded her that she was marrying someone with a brilliant career in front of him and that one of the most important things in life was the opinion of others, particularly one's equals and seniors. Though she was still only a young girl she must try to act with suitable dignity.

"Tell people you're from the well-known Barakat family and that your father was a judge," and he went up to her and gently patted her cheeks in a fatherly, reassuring gesture that he was often to repeat during their times together.

THEN, YESTERDAY EVENING, she had returned from the club somewhat light-headed from the bottle of beer she had been required to drink on the occasion of someone's birthday. Her husband, noting the state she was in, hurriedly took her back home. She had undressed and put on her nightgown, leaving her jewellery on the dressing-table, and was fast asleep seconds after getting into bed. The following morning, fully recovered, she slept late, then rang the bell as usual and had breakfast brought to her. It was only as she was putting her jewellery away in the wooden and mother-of-pearl box that she realized that her emerald ring was missing.

Could it have dropped from her finger at the club? In the car on the way back? No, she distinctly remembered it last thing at night, remembered the usual difficulty she had in getting it off her finger. She stripped the bed of its sheets, turned over the mattress, looked inside the pillow cases, crawled on hands and knees under the bed. The tray of breakfast lying on the small bedside table caught her eye and she remembered the young servant coming in that morning with it, remembered the noise of the tray being put down, the curtains being drawn, the tray then being lifted up again and placed on the bedside table. No one but the servant had entered the room. Should she call her and question her?

Eventually, having taken two aspirins, she decided to do nothing and await the return of her husband from work.

Directly he arrived she told him what had happened and he took her by the arm and seated her down beside him:

"Let's just calm down and go over what happened."

She repeated, this time with further details, the whole story.

"And you've looked for it?"

"Everywhere. Every possible and impossible place in the bedroom and the bathroom. You see, I remember distinctly taking it off last night."

He grimaced at the thought of last night, then said:

"Anybody been in the room since Gazia when she brought in the breakfast?"

"Not a soul. I've even told Gazia not to do the room today."

"And you've not mentioned anything to her?"

"I thought I'd better leave it to you."

"Fine, go and tell her I want to speak to her. There's no point in your saying anything but I think it would be as well if you were present when I talk to her."

Five minutes later Gazia, the young servant girl they had recently employed, entered behind her mistress. Samia took herself to a far corner of the room while Gazia stood in front of Abboud Bey, her hands folded across her chest, her eyes lowered.

"Yes, sir?"

"Where's the ring?"

"What ring are you talking about, sir?"

"Now don't make out you don't know. The one with the green stone. It would be better for you if you hand it over and then nothing more need be said."

"May Allah blind me if I've ever set eyes on it."

He stood up and gave her a sudden slap on the face. The girl reeled back, put one hand to her cheek, then lowered it again to her chest and made no answer to any of Abboud's questions. Finally he said to her:

"You've got just fifteen seconds to say where you've hidden the ring or else, I swear to you, you're not going to have a good time of it."

As he lifted up his arm to look at his watch the girl flinched slightly but continued in her silence. When he went to the telephone Samia raised her head and saw that the girl's cheeks were wet with tears. Abboud Bey got through to the Superintendent of Police and told him briefly what had occurred.

"Of course I haven't got any actual proof but seeing that no one else entered the room, it's obvious she's pinched it. Anyway I'll leave the matter in your capable hands — I know your people have their ways and means."

He gave a short laugh, then listened for a while and said: "I'm really most grateful to you."

He put down the receiver and turned round to Samia:

"That's it, my dear. There's nothing more to worry about. The Superintendent has promised me we'll get it back. The patrol car's on the way."

The following day, in the late afternoon, she'd been sitting in front of her dressing-table rearranging her jewellery in its box when an earring slipped from her grasp and fell to the floor. As she bent to pick it up she saw the emerald ring stuck between the leg of the table and the wall. Since that moment she had sat in a state of panic awaiting her husband's return from the club. She even felt tempted to walk down to the water's edge and throw it into the river so as to be rid of the unpleasantness that lay ahead.

At the sound of the screech of tyres rounding the house to the garage, she slipped the ring on to her finger. As he entered she stood up and raised her hand to show him the ring. Quickly, trying to choose her words but knowing that she was expressing herself clumsily, she explained what an extraordinary thing it was that it should have lodged itself between the dressing-table and the wall, what an extraordinary coincidence she should have dropped the earring and so seen it, how she'd thought of ringing him at the club to tell him the good news but. . .

She stopped in mid-sentence when she saw his frown and added weakly: "I'm sorry. I can't think how it could have happened. What do we do now?"

He shrugged his shoulders as though in surprise.

"Are you asking me, my dear lady? Nothing, of course."

"But they've been beating up the girl — you yourself said they'd not let her be till she confessed."

UNHURRIEDLY, he sat himself down as though to consider this new aspect of the matter. Taking out his case, he tapped a cigarette against it in his accustomed manner, then moistened his lips, put the cigarette in place and lit it. The smoke rings hovered in the still air as he looked at his watch and said:

"In any case she's not got all that long before they let her go. They can't keep her for more than forty-eight hours without getting any evidence or a confession. It won't kill her to put up with things for a while longer. By now the whole town knows the servant stole the ring — or would you like me to tell everyone: 'Look, folks, the fact is that the wife got a bit tiddly on a couple of sips of beer and the ring took off on its own and hid itself behind the dressing-table.'? What do you think?"

"I know the situation's a bit awkward. . ."

"Awkward? It's downright ludicrous. Listen, there's nothing to be done but to give it to me and next time I go down to Cairo I'll sell it and get something else in its place. We'd be the laughing-stock of the town."

He stretched out his hand and she found herself taking off the ring and placing it in the outstretched palm. She was careful that their eyes should not meet. For a moment she was on the point of protesting and in fact uttered a few words:

"I'd just like to say we could. . ."

Putting the ring away in his pocket, he bent over her and with both hands gently patted her on the cheeks. It was a gesture she had long become used to, a gesture that promised her continued security, that told her that this man who was her husband and the father of her child had also taken the place of her father who, as though assured that he had found her a suitable substitute, had followed up her marriage with his own funeral. The gesture told her more eloquently than any words that he was the man, she the woman, he the one who carried the responsibilities, made the decisions, she the one whose role it was to be beautiful, happy, carefree. Now, though, for the first time in their life together the gesture came like a slap in the face.

Directly he removed his hands her whole body was seized with an uncontrollable trembling. Frightened he would notice, she rose to her feet and walked with deliberate steps towards the large window. She leaned her forehead against the comforting cold surface and closed her eyes tightly for several seconds. When she opened them she noticed that the café lights strung between the trees on the opposite shore had been turned on and that there were men seated under them and a waiter moving among the tables. The dark shape of a boat momentarily blocked out the café scene; in the light from the hurricane lamp hanging from its bow she saw it cutting through several of those floating islands of Nile waterlilies that, rootless, are swept along with the current.

Suddenly she became aware of his presence alongside her.

"Why don't you go and change quickly while I take the car out? It's hot and it would be nice to have supper at the club."

"As you like. Why not?"

By the time she had turned round from the window she was smiling.

ABOUT **ALIFA RIFAAT**

Alifa Rifaat (ə lē′fə ri fät′) lives in Cairo, the city near the Nile Delta where she was born in 1930. Rifaat's father insisted that she marry rather than get a university education, and her husband disapproved of her writing. She published under a pseudonym from 1955 to 1960, then stopped writing for almost fifteen years. During that time she read world literature, studied religion and the sciences, and raised three children. Rifaat is faithful to her Moslem roots and writes primarily about women, particularly about the problems women encounter in marriage.

RESPONDING

1. *Personal Response* If you were Abboud Bey, would you have covered up Samia's discovery of the ring or not? Explain.

2. *Literary Analysis* What details about Abboud Bey and Samia's relationship are provided in the *flashback* on page 62 that begins "It was only a few years ago. . ."?

3. *Multicultural Connection* What does the story tell you about the social position of women in traditional Egyptian marriages?

LANGUAGE WORKSHOP

Cause and Effect *Cause-and-effect* relationships can advance the plot. What effect does each of the following incidents cause in "Another Evening at the Club"?
1. Samia reports the loss of her ring to Abboud Bey.
2. Abboud Bey reports Gazia to the Police.
3. Samia searches for a dropped earring.
4. Samia reports she has found the ring.

WRITER'S PORTFOLIO

Use evidence from the story to explain in a paragraph why you think Samia is smiling at the end of the story.

Forbidden Fruit

Neither children nor grown-ups in our family ever ate pork. Though another of Mohammed's commandments—the one on alcoholic drinks—was broken (and without constraint, as I know now), no latitude was allowed with respect to pork.

The ban provoked hot dreams and icy abstinence. I dreamt interminably of eating pork. The smell of fried pork made me faint. I would loiter for hours in front of food-store showcases and contemplate sausages beaded with fat and dappled with pork. I imagined myself skinning these sausages and letting my teeth sink into the juicy, luxuriant meat. I imagined the taste of sausage so accurately that, when I tasted it later, I was surprised at how truly my imagination had anticipated reality.

Of course, in childhood there were occasions when I could have tasted pork in kindergarten or at the home of a friend, but I never broke the commandment.

When we had rice and pork in kindergarten, I fished out all the pieces of pork and gave them to my friends. I conquered the agony of yearning by the sweetness of self-denial. I enjoyed my ideological superiority. It was pleasant to be an enigma, to behave in a way baffling to everyone around. And yet, all the more intensely did I dream of a transgression.

One of our neighbors was a nurse called Auntie Sonya. For some reason or other, we believed Auntie Sonya was a doctor. In general, I notice that as one grows older, the status of people seems to drop.

Auntie Sonya was an elderly woman with bobbed hair and a sorrowing expression never absent from her face. She always spoke in a low voice as though she had long ago realized that there was nothing in life worth speaking up about.

When she quarreled with her neighbors, she rarely raised her voice. That created problems for her adversaries because they could not grasp her last words, lost the thread, and the quarrel flagged disastrously.

Auntie Sonya and our family were friends, and Mother used to say that Auntie Sonya had saved me. I had been very sick, and she and my mother had taken turns looking after me for a whole month. To tell the truth, I did not feel properly grateful for my saved life, but, out of politeness, whenever the incident came up, I wore the expression of a person happy to have been saved.

Auntie Sonya spent evenings with our family and often told us the story of her life, and the principal hero was her first husband, who had been killed in the Civil War. I had heard the story many times, but my heart always dropped when she reached the point where she found her husband among the corpses. Here she would begin to cry, and my mother and older sister would weep too. Then they would comfort her, beg her to have some tea, or bring her a glass of water. I was always astonished at how quickly the

Culture Note

Civil War This is a reference to the conflict waged in Russia following the November Revolution in 1917 between those who supported Lenin and the revolution and those who resisted the revolution, favoring less radical change or no change at all. p. 71

women composed themselves and chattered with fresh, and even cheery, animation about all sorts of trifles. Then Auntie Sonya would leave because it was time for her husband, Uncle Shura, to come home.

I liked Uncle Shura. I liked his black hair and that unruly lock over his forehead, his neatly rolled-up sleeves and strong arms. I even liked his stoop. His was not a clerk's stoop but a pleasant old worker's stoop, though Uncle Shura was neither an old man nor a worker.

After hours he would always tinker with something: a desk lamp, or an electric iron, or a radio set, or even a watch which his neighbors brought and which he repaired, charging them nothing.

Auntie Sonya sat across the table, smoked prodigiously, and poked fun at him, telling him that he was a jack of all trades, that he would never fix what he was trying to fix, and so on and so forth.

"We'll see if I won't fix it," Uncle Shura muttered through his teeth because he had a cigarette in his mouth. He would handle the thing a neighbor had brought with graceful confidence, dust it off, and then suddenly look at it from some unexpected angle.

"I can see them laughing at you," Auntie Sonya would counter with an arrogant puff of smoke, wrapping her robe tighter around her.

Finally, he would wind the watch, or the radio set would crackle snatches of music.

"I like to see them laughing at me. I don't mind a bit," he would say with a wink at me.

I wanted my smile to show that I had nothing to do with his triumph but that I appreciated his trust.

"You brag too much," Auntie Sonya would say. "Lay the table for tea."

In her voice I detected hidden pride, and I wondered if Uncle Shura was of a less heroic mold than that hero of the Civil War whom Auntie Sonya could not forget.

ONCE, WHEN I WAS SPENDING an evening with them, my sister dropped in, and they invited her to tea. Auntie Sonya sliced some pork fat of an unbelievably delicate pink and put a cruet of mustard on the table. They had often eaten pork before and asked me to have some, but I invariably and firmly refused, which always moved Uncle Shura to mirth for some reason or other. This time they also asked me to have some, but they did not insist. Uncle Shura put several slices of pork fat on a chunk of bread and gave it to my sister. After the few no's required by decency, she accepted the horrible sandwich and began to eat it. Indignation stiffened my throat, and I had difficulty getting my tea down.

"That's what it is," said Uncle Shura. "You're a monk, that's what you are!"

I could say nothing. She ate the sandwich with shameless neatness, a vacant look in her eyes. That vacancy was meant to show that she was eating officially, purely out of respect for her hosts. It was meant to suggest that the sacrilege was not to be taken seriously and did not count at all.

"It does count!" I thought maliciously, watching the sandwich becoming smaller at an agonizingly slow rate.

I felt she was enjoying it. It was evident from the way she licked at the crumbs, from the way she swallowed each bite — slowed her chewing in the silliest way as though listening to the sound the food made going down her gullet. The slices of fat were thinner at the edge she nibbled, the surest sign that she was enjoying it because all normal children leave the tidbit for last. In other words, all the evidence was there.

Now she was coming to the edge of the sandwich where the piece of pork was thickest. She kept her enjoyment in crescendo. Meanwhile, she was serenely (woman's infinite ability to pretend) telling how my brother jumped out of a window when the teacher called on our parents. The story had a dual purpose: first, to divert attention from what she was doing, and second, to flatter me in a very subtle way since everyone knew that the teacher had no reason to complain of me, and still less had I any reason to flee from her through a window.

As she was telling all this, she would look at me from time to time to see whether I was still watching her or, carried away by her story, was forgetting about her sin. But my expression was not to be doubted: my vigilance never flagged. In self-defense she goggled her eyes like one surprised that so much attention was being paid to a trifling matter. I only smirked, a hint of the retribution to come.

For a moment I thought that it had come already because she began to cough. I watched transfixed. Uncle

Shura slapped her on the back, and she stopped coughing to indicate that his cure had helped and that her discomfort was insignificant. But I felt that the piece was still stuck in her throat. She pretended she was all right now and took another bite.

"Chew away!" I thought. "Let's see you swallow it."

But evidently, somewhere on high the retribution was rescheduled. My sister swallowed this bite without difficulty, and perhaps it even helped her swallow down its predecessor because she gave a sigh of relief and looked around cheerfully. Now she chewed and licked her lips after each bite with special care, or maybe she was simply sticking out her tongue at me.

She was at the edge of the sandwich with the thickest piece of fat. Before committing it to her mouth, she bit off the last edge of the bread uncovered by fat. That climaxed the last tidbit even more. Then she swallowed it down, too, and licked her lips as though trying to prolong the pleasure and show that there were no traces of the sin left.

All this did not take much time, of course, and was almost imperceptible to an outsider. At any rate, Uncle Shura and Auntie Sonya did not seem to notice anything. Her sandwich finished, my sister proceeded to her tea, still pretending that nothing had happened. As soon as she touched her cup, I gulped mine down. I did not want to share anything with her. A few minutes before, I had refused to eat some cookies so I could run the whole gamut of suffering and have no earthly joys in her presence. Besides, I resented Uncle Shura, who had not urged me nearly as much as he had my sister. I would not have accepted the cookies anyway, but his urging would have made my refusal a better lesson in principles for my sister.

In short, I was terribly let down and went home as soon as I finished my tea. They begged me to stay, but I was adamant.

"I have to do my lessons!" I said piously.

My sister asked me to stay with special insistence. She was sure that I would tell on her at home, and, besides, she was afraid to cross the yard alone.

At home, I slipped out of my clothes and into my bed to luxuriate in the contemplation of my sister's apostasy. All kinds of visions rushed through my mind. Here I was, a Red partisan captured by the Whites, who are forcing me to eat pork. They torture me, but I will not touch it. Surprised, the officers shake their heads: What sort of boy is this? As a matter of fact, I'm surprised myself. I just won't eat pork. Kill me, but eat pork I will not.

Culture Note

Red partisan . . . Whites
In the Civil War, the Communists (or Bolsheviks) were known as "Reds." The anti-Communist forces were called "Whites." p. 75

The door creaked and my sister came in. She immediately asked about me.

"He's gone to bed," I heard my mother reply. "He came home in the dumps. Anything happen?"

"Why, nothing," my sister answered and went over to my bed. I was afraid she would begin coaxing me and all that. Pardon was out of the question, anyway, and besides I did not want her to change the state of mind I was in. I, therefore, pretended to be asleep. She stood for a while and stroked my hair, but I turned over to show that I knew her treacherous hand even in my sleep. She stood there for a while longer and then went away. I thought she was feeling guilty and did not know how to redeem herself.

I was sorry for her, but, as it turned out, she was not worth it. A minute later she was saying something to mother in a loud whisper; they began to giggle and then stopped, afraid to wake me up. Gradually they settled to a mood fit for going to bed.

Next day we sat at the table waiting dinner for father. He was late and angry at being waited for. Something was wrong on the job, and he was often gloomy and absent-minded.

I WAS ALL PREPARED to divulge my sister's crime, but I realized that this was not a proper time for my exposure. Nevertheless, I looked at my sister from time to time and pretended I was going to tell. I even opened my mouth but said something else instead. As soon as I opened my mouth, she dropped her eyes and bent her head as though expecting a blow. I discovered that keeping her on the verge of exposure was even more fun than exposing her right away could possibly be.

She would turn pale and then blush. From time to time she would toss her head contemptuously, and then her eyes would beg me to forgive her this gesture of wild defiance. She barely touched her soup, but mother insisted that she eat it.

"Of course," I said, "yesterday she ate so much at Uncle Shura's that—"

"What did you eat there?" my brother asked—as always, he understood nothing.

Mother looked at me anxiously and shook her head imperceptibly for father. My sister pulled up the plate and continued eating. I was getting a full taste of it. I fished a boiled onion out of my soup and spooned it into hers; we all hated boiled onions. Mother looked at me severely.

"She likes onions," I said. "You like onions, don't you?" I asked my sister with velvety softness.

She said nothing but her head went down still lower.

"If you like onions, take mine too!" my brother said, and started to transfer his. However, my father looked at him in a way to make his spoon freeze in midair and beat a hasty retreat.

Between the first and second course I invented another diversion. I put some slices of cucumber from the salad on a slice of bread and began to eat it, pausing from time to time as though the sandwich was too delicious to proceed. That was a witty little skit recreating her fall. She looked at me in pretended puzzlement, refusing to recognize the picture or to admit that it was so shameful. That was the limit to which her protest rose.

In short, the dinner was magnificent. Virtue black-mailed, and vice lowered its head in disgrace. Dinner was followed by tea. Father cheered up, and we shared his mood, especially my sister. Her cheeks reddened and her eyes shone. She started telling some school story, calling on me to testify as though nothing had happened. Her familiarity shocked me. It seemed to me that a person with such a record ought to be more diffident, more self-effacing, ought to wait for worthier people to tell the story. I was on the point of calling her to order, but father produced a package and unwrapped it. It turned out to be a batch of brand-new notebooks.

In those years before the war, it was difficult to get notebooks, just as it was some other things. The notebooks father had brought were of the best kind, made of wonderful paper, cool, heavy, bluish white like skimmed milk, with clear red lines for the margins.

There were nine notebooks in all, and father divided them, three notebooks apiece. My elation went. This egalitarian approach seemed to me simply unjust.

The fact was that I did well in school and sometimes even got high marks. The family would tell relatives and friends that all my marks were very high, but probably that was done to balance my brother's academic notoriety.

At school he was considered one of the laziest and most unruly boys. As his teacher put it, his ability to evaluate his behavior lagged far behind his temperament. I imagined my brother's temperament as a little ruffian running helter-skelter far ahead of him, my brother unable to catch up. It was perhaps to overtake him that my brother had wanted to become a car driver ever since the fourth grade. On every scrap of paper he would write the same text:

"To: Transport Office
     Chief Manager
"I hereby request that you employ me at your agency since I am a third-class driver."

Later he realized his childhood dream, but it turned out that he had to exceed speed limits to overtake his temperament and finally had to change his trade.

And here I, with my almost invariably high marks, was equalized with my brother, who would, of course, use those beautiful notebooks to pen his idiotic car-driving applications. And my sister, who gobbled up pork fat yesterday, would receive an undeserved gift today.

I put my notebooks aside. I felt hard and humiliating tears scalding my eyes and a big lump in my throat. Father coaxed and soothed me and promised to take me to a mountain river for fishing. But the more he consoled me, the more acutely I felt the injustice of it all.

"I have two blotters!" my sister suddenly yelled as she opened one of her notebooks. That was the last straw. Everything might have been different if it hadn't been for those two blotters.

I stood up and said in a trembling voice, addressing myself to father, "She ate pork yesterday."

There was a horrible silence. I realized that something was wrong. Perhaps I hadn't expressed myself properly, or maybe Mohammed's great tenets and a little urge to capture someone else's notebooks didn't go together.

Father looked at me, his glance growing heavy with wrath. I made the last pathetic attempt to redeem the situation and direct his wrath into the proper channel.

"She ate pork at Uncle Shura's," I said in despair, and felt that everything was lost.

Father grabbed me by my ears, shook my head as though to make sure that it would not come off, and then flung me to the floor. For a fleeting instant I felt a flash of pain and the crunch of pulled ears.

"You little louse!" he yelled. "All I need now is a stool pigeon at home!"

Grabbing his leather coat, he left the room, slamming the door so hard that plaster crumbled off the wall. I was not crushed by the pain or his words but by that expression of hatred and disgust on his face, as though I were a dangerous snake.

I lay on the floor. Mother tried to pick me up while my brother pranced around me in frantic ecstasy.

"He always gets high marks!" he screamed, pointing to my ears.

I liked my father, and this was the first time he had treated me so.

Many years have passed since. I have long been eating pork like everyone else, though perhaps this does not make me any happier. Still, at that time I realized that no principle justifies treachery, and besides, that treachery is always a hairy caterpillar bred of a small butterfly called envy, no matter how lofty the principles involved.

ABOUT **FAZIL ISKANDER**

Fazil Iskander (fä zil′ is kan′der) was born in 1929 in southern Russia between the Black and Caspian Seas in a small republic where Islam was once the predominant religion. Known for poking fun at officialdom, Iskander's works have been censored. Many of his short stories are based on recollections of his childhood. "Forbidden Fruit" appears in his collection, *The Thirteenth Exploit of Hercules.*

RESPONDING

1. *Personal Response* Do you think that the father is justified in reacting so harshly to his son at the end of the story? Explain.

2. *Literary Analysis* In the final paragraph, Iskander writes, ". . . treachery is always a hairy caterpillar bred of a small butterfly called envy." What does he mean by this *metaphor*?

3. *Multicultural Connection* Why is the eating of pork not allowed among certain cultural or religious groups?

LANGUAGE WORKSHOP

Images *Images* are vivid word pictures that appeal to the senses. Find the paragraphs in "Forbidden Fruit" that begin with the sentences indicated below, and explain to what senses the images appeal.
1. "The ban provoked hot dreams. . . ." (page 70)
2. "I felt she was enjoying it." (page 73)
3. "She was at the edge of the sandwich. . . ." (page 74)

WRITER'S PORTFOLIO

Imagine that you are Miss Manners. Someone has written a letter to you asking what is appropriate table etiquette when you have been served something you cannot eat. Now write a reply.

From The Woman Warrior

Normal Chinese women's voices are strong and bossy. We American-Chinese girls had to whisper to make ourselves American-feminine. Apparently we whispered even more softly than the Americans. Once a year the teachers referred my sister and me to speech therapy, but our voices would straighten out, unpredictably normal, for the therapists. Some of us gave up, shook our heads, and said nothing, not one word. Some of us could not even shake our heads. At times shaking my head no is more self-assertion than I can manage. Most of us eventually found some voice, however faltering. We invented an American-feminine speaking personality, except for that one girl who could not speak up even in Chinese school.

She was a year older than I and was in my class for twelve years. During all those years she read aloud but would not talk. Her older sister was usually beside her; their parents kept the older daughter back to protect the younger one. They were six and seven years old when they began school. Although I had flunked kindergarten, I was the same age as most other students in our class; my parents had probably lied about my age, so I had had a head start and came out even. My younger sister was in the class below me; we were normal ages and normally separated. The parents of the quiet girl, on the other hand, protected both daughters. When it sprinkled, they kept them home from school. The girls did not work for a living the way we did. But in other ways we were the same.

We were similar in sports. We held the bat on our shoulders until we walked to first base. (You got a strike only when you actually struck at the ball.) Sometimes the pitcher wouldn't bother to throw to us. "Automatic walk," the other children would call, sending us on our way. By fourth or fifth grade, though, some of us would try to hit the ball. "Easy out," the other kids would say. I hit the ball a couple of times. Baseball was nice in that there was a definite spot to run to after hitting the ball. Basketball confused me because when I caught the ball I didn't know whom to throw it to. "Me. Me," the kids would be yelling. "Over here." Suddenly it would occur to me I hadn't memorized which ghosts were on my team and which were on the other. When the kids said, "Automatic walk," the girl who was quieter than I kneeled with one end of the bat in each hand and placed it carefully on the plate. Then she dusted her hands as she walked to first base, where she rubbed her hands softly, fingers spread. She always got tagged out before second base. She would whisper-read but not talk. Her whisper was as soft as if she had no muscles. She seemed to be breathing from a distance. I heard no anger or tension.

Culture Note

ghosts in this story, white Americans; in others, dead ancestors and relatives, p. 81

I joined in at lunchtime when the other students, the Chinese too, talked about whether or not she was mute, although obviously she was not if she could read aloud. People told me how *they* had tried *their* best to be friendly. *They* said hello, but if she refused to answer, well, they didn't see why they had to say hello anymore. She had no friends of her own but followed her sister everywhere, although people and she herself probably thought I was her friend. I also followed her sister about, who was fairly normal. She was almost two years older and read more than anyone else.

I hated the younger sister, the quiet one. I hated her when she was the last chosen for her team and I, the last chosen for my team. I hated her for her China doll hair cut. I hated her at music time for the wheezes that came out of her plastic flute.

One afternoon in the sixth grade (that year I was arrogant with talk, not knowing there were going to be high school dances and college seminars to set me back), I and my little sister and the quiet girl and her big sister stayed late after school for some reason. The cement was cooling, and the tetherball poles made shadows across the gravel. The hooks at the rope ends were clinking against the poles. We shouldn't have been so late; there was laundry work to do and Chinese school to get to by 5:00. The last time we had stayed late, my mother had phoned the police and told them we had been kidnapped by bandits. The radio stations broadcast our descriptions. I had to get home before she did that again. But sometimes if you loitered long enough in the schoolyard, the other children would have gone home and you could play with the equipment before the office took it away. We were chasing one another through the playground and in and out of the basement, where the playroom and the lavatory were. During air raid drills (it was during the Korean War, which you knew about because every day the front page of the newspaper printed a map of Korea with the top part red and going up and down like a window shade), we curled up in this basement. Now everyone was gone. The playroom was army green and had nothing in it but a long trough with drinking spigots in rows. Pipes across the ceiling led to the drinking fountains and to the toilets in the next room. When someone flushed you could hear the water and other matter, which the children named, running inside the big pipe above the drinking spigots. There was one playroom for girls next to the girls' lavatory and one playroom for boys next to the boys' lavatory. The stalls were open and the toilets had no lids, by which we knew that ghosts have no sense of shame or privacy.

Inside the playroom the lightbulbs in cages had already been turned off. Daylight came in x̌-patterns through the caging at the windows. I looked out and, seeing no one in the schoolyard, ran outside to climb the fire escape upside down, hanging on to the metal stairs with fingers and toes.

I did a flip off the fire escape and ran across the school-yard. The day was a great eye, and it was not paying much attention to me now. I could disappear with the sun; I could turn quickly sideways and slip into a different world. It seemed I could run faster at this time, and by evening I would be able to fly. As the afternoon wore on we could run into the forbidden places—the boys' big yard, the boys' playroom. We could go into the boys' lavatory and look at the urinals. The only time during school hours I had crossed the boys' yard was when a flatbed truck with a giant thing covered with canvas and tied down with ropes had parked across the street. The children had told one another that it was a gorilla in captivity; we couldn't decide whether the sign said "Trail of the Gorilla" or "Trial of the Gorilla." The thing was as big as a house. The teachers couldn't stop us from hysterically rushing to the fence and clinging to the wire mesh. Now I ran across the boys' yard clear to the Cyclone fence and thought about the hair that I had seen sticking out of the canvas. It was going to be summer soon, so you could feel that freedom coming on too.

I RAN BACK into the girls' yard, and there was the quiet sister all by herself. I ran past her, and she followed me into the girls' lavatory. My footsteps rang hard against the cement and tile because of the taps I had nailed into my shoes. Her footsteps were soft, padding after me. There was no one in the lavatory but the two of us. I ran all around the rows of twenty-five open stalls to make sure of that. No sisters. I think we must have been playing hide-and-go-seek. She was not good at hiding by herself and usually followed her sister; they'd hide in the same place. They must have gotten separated. In this growing twilight, a child could hide and never be found.

I stopped abruptly in front of the sinks, and she came running toward me before she could stop herself, so that she almost collided with me. I walked closer. She backed away, puzzlement, then alarm in her eyes.

"You're going to talk," I said, my voice steady and normal, as it is when I'm talking to the familiar, the weak, and the small. "I am going to make you talk, you sissy-girl." She stopped backing away and stood fixed.

I looked into her face so I could hate it close up. She wore black bangs, and her cheeks were pink and white. She was baby soft. I thought I could put my thumb on her nose and push it bonelessly in, indent her face. I could poke dimples into her cheeks. I could work her face around like dough. She stood still, and I did not want to look at her face anymore; I hated fragility. I walked around her, looked her up and down the way the Mexican and Negro girls did when they fought, so tough. I hated her weak neck, the way it did not support her head but let it droop; her head would fall backward. I stared at the curve of her nape. I wished I was able to see what my own neck looked like from the back and sides. I hoped it did not look like hers; I wanted a stout neck. I grew my hair long to hide it in case it was a flower-stem neck. I walked around to the front of her to hate her face some more.

I REACHED UP and took the fatty part of her cheek, not dough, but meat, between my thumb and finger. This close, and I saw no pores. "Talk," I said. "Are you going to talk?" Her skin was fleshy, like squid out of which the glassy blades of bones had been pulled. I wanted tough skin, hard brown skin. I had callused my hands; I had scratched dirt to blacken the nails, which I had cut straight across to make stubby fingers. I gave her face a squeeze. "Talk." When I let go, the pink rushed back into my white thumbprint on her skin. I walked around to her side. "Talk!" I shouted into the side of her head. Her straight hair hung, the same all these years, no ringlets or braids or permanents. I squeezed her other cheek. "Are you? Huh? Are you going to talk?" She tried to shake her head, but I had hold of her face. She had no muscles to jerk away. Her skin seemed to stretch. I let go in horror. What if it came away in my hand? "No, huh?" I said, rubbing the touch of her off my fingers. "Say, 'No' then," I said. I gave her another pinch and a twist. "Say, 'No.' " She shook her head, her straight hair turning with her head, not swinging side to side like the pretty girls'. She was so neat. Her neatness bothered me. I hated the way she folded the wax paper from her lunch; she did not wad her brown paper bag and her school papers. I hated her clothes—the blue pastel cardigan, the white blouse with the collar that lay flat over the cardigan, the homemade flat, cotton skirt she wore when everybody else was wearing flared skirts. I hated pastels; I would wear black always. I squeezed again, harder, even though her cheek had a weak rubbery feeling I did not like. I squeezed one cheek, then the other, back and forth until the tears ran out of her eyes as if I had pulled them out. "Stop crying," I said, but although she habitually followed me around, she did not obey. Her eyes dripped; her nose dripped. She wiped her eyes with her papery fingers. The skin on her hands and arms seemed powdery-dry, like tracing paper, onion skin. I hated her fingers. I could snap them like bread-sticks. I pushed her hands down. "Say, 'Hi,' " I said.

" 'Hi.' Like that. Say your name. Go ahead. Say it. Or are you stupid? You're so stupid, you don't know your own name, is that it? When I say, 'What's your name?' you just blurt it out, okay? What's your name?" Last year the whole class had laughed at a boy who couldn't fill out a form because he didn't know his father's name. The teacher sighed, exasperated, and was very sarcastic. "Don't you notice things? What does your mother call him?" she said. The class laughed at how dumb he was not to notice things. "She calls him father of me," he said. Even we laughed, although we knew that his mother did not call his father by name, and a son does not know his father's name. We laughed and were relieved that our parents had had the foresight to tell us some names we could give the teachers. "If you're not stupid," I said to the quiet girl, "what's your name?" She shook her head, and some hair caught in the tears; wet black hair stuck to the side of the pink and white face. I reached up (she was taller than I) and took a strand of hair. I pulled it. "Well, then, let's honk your hair," I said. "Honk. Honk." Then I pulled the other side—"ho-o-n-nk" —a long pull; "ho-o-n-n-nk"—a longer pull. I could see her little white ears, like white cutworms curled underneath the hair. "Talk!" I yelled into each cutworm.

I looked right at her. "I know you talk," I said. "I've heard you." Her eyebrows flew up. Something in those black eyes was startled, and I pursued it. "I was walking past your house when you didn't know I was there. I heard you yell in English and Chinese. You weren't just talking. You were shouting. I heard you shout. You were saying, 'Where are you?' Say that again. Go ahead, just the way you did at home." I yanked harder on the hair, but steadily, not jerking. I did not want to pull it out. "Go ahead. Say, 'Where are you?' Say it loud enough for your sister to come. Call her. Make her come help you. Call her name. I'll stop if she comes. So call. Go ahead."

She shook her head, her mouth curved down, crying. I could see her tiny white teeth, baby teeth. I wanted to grow big strong yellow teeth. "You do have a tongue," I said. "So use it." I pulled the hair at her temples, pulled the tears out of her eyes. "Say, 'Ow,' " I said. "Just 'Ow.' Say, 'Let go.' Go ahead. Say it. I'll honk you again if you don't say, 'Let me alone.' Say, 'Leave me alone,' and I'll let you go. I will. I'll let you go if you say it. You can stop this anytime you want to, you know. All you have to do is tell me to stop. Just say, 'Stop.' You're asking for it, aren't you? You're just asking for another honk. Well then, I'll have to give you another honk. Say 'Stop.' " But she didn't. I had to pull again and again.

Sounds did come out of her mouth, sobs, chokes, noises that were almost words. Snot ran out of her nose. She tried to wipe it on her hands, but there was too much of it. She used her sleeve. "You're disgusting," I told her. "Look at you, snot streaming down your nose, and you won't say a word to stop it. You're such a nothing." I moved behind her and pulled the hair growing out of her weak neck. I let go. I stood silent for a long time. Then I screamed, "Talk!" I would scare the words out of her. If she had had little bound feet, the toes twisted under the balls, I would have jumped up and landed on them—crunch!—stomped on them with my iron shoes. She cried hard, sobbing

Culture Note

bound feet In the past, young upper-class Chinese girls' feet were bound tightly so they were tiny and deformed, making walking almost impossible. p. 86

aloud. "Cry, 'Mama,' " I said. "Come on. Cry, 'Mama.' Say, 'Stop it.' "

I put my finger on her pointed chin. "I don't like you. I don't like the weak little toots you make on your flute. Wheeze. Wheeze. I don't like the way you don't swing at the ball. I don't like the way you are the last one chosen. I don't like the way you can't make a fist for tetherball. Why don't you make a fist? Come on. Get tough. Come on. Throw fists." I pushed at her long hands; they swung limply at her sides. Her fingers were so long, I thought maybe they had an extra joint. They couldn't possibly make fists like other people's. "Make a fist," I said. "Come on. Just fold those fingers up; fingers on the inside, thumbs on the outside. Say something. Honk me back. You're so tall, and you let me pick on you.

"Would you like a hanky? I can't get you one with embroidery on it or crocheting along the edges, but I'll get you some toilet paper if you tell me to. Go ahead. Ask me. I'll get it for you if you ask." She did not stop crying. "Why don't you scream, 'Help'?" I suggested. "Say, 'Help.' Go ahead." She cried on. "Okay. Okay. Don't talk. Just scream, and I'll let you go. Won't that feel good? Go ahead. Like this." I screamed, not too loudly. My voice hit the tile and rang it as if I had thrown a rock at it. The stalls opened wider and the toilets wider and darker. Shadows leaned at angles I had not seen before. It was very late. Maybe a janitor had locked me in with this girl for the night. Her black eyes blinked and stared, blinked and stared. I felt dizzy from hunger. We had been in this lavatory together forever. My mother would call the police again if I didn't bring my sister home soon. "I'll let you go if you say just one word," I said. "You can even say 'a' or 'the,' and I'll let you go. Come on. Please." She didn't shake her head anymore, only cried steadily, so much water coming out of her. I could see the two duct holes where the tears welled out. Quarts of tears but no words. I grabbed her by the shoulder. I could feel bones. The light was coming in queerly through the frosted glass with the chicken wire embedded in it. Her crying was like an animal's—a seal's—and it echoed around the basement. "Do you want to stay here all night?" I asked.

"Your mother is wondering what happened to her baby. You wouldn't want to have her mad at you. You'd better say something." I shook her shoulder. I pulled her hair again. I squeezed her face. "Come on! Talk! Talk! Talk!" She didn't seem to feel it anymore when I pulled her hair. "There's nobody here but you and me. This isn't a classroom or a playground or a crowd. I'm just one person. You can talk in front of one person. Don't make me pull harder and harder until you talk." But her hair seemed to stretch; she did not say a word. "I'm going to pull harder. Don't make me pull anymore, or your hair will come out and you're going to be bald. Do you want to be bald? You don't want to be bald, do you?"

Far away, coming from the edge of town, I heard whistles blow. The cannery was changing shifts, letting out the afternoon people, and still we were here at school. It was a sad sound — work done. The air was lonelier after the sound died.

"Why won't you talk?" I started to cry. What if I couldn't stop, and everyone would want to know what happened? "Now look what you've done," I scolded. "You're going to pay for this. I want to know why. And you're going to tell me why. You don't see I'm trying to help you out, do you? Do you want to be like this, dumb (do you know what dumb means?), your whole life? Don't you ever want to be a cheerleader? Or a pompon girl? What are you going to do for a living? Yeah, you're going to have to work because you can't be a housewife. Somebody has to marry you before you can be a housewife. And you, you are a plant. Do you know that? That's all you are if you don't talk. If you don't talk, you can't have a personality. You'll have no personality and no hair. You've got to let people know you have a personality and a brain. You think somebody is going to take care of you all your stupid life? You think you'll always have your big sister? You think somebody's going to marry you, is that it? Well, you're not the type that gets dates, let alone gets married. Nobody's going to notice you. And you have to talk for interviews, speak right up in front of the boss. Don't you know that? You're so dumb. Why do I waste my time on you?" Sniffling and snorting, I couldn't stop crying and talking at the same time. I kept wiping my nose on my arm, my sweater lost somewhere (probably not worn because my mother said to wear a sweater). It seemed as if I had spent my life in that basement, doing the worst thing I had yet done to another person. "I'm doing this for your own good," I said. "Don't you dare tell anyone I've been bad to you. Talk. Please talk."

I was getting dizzy from the air I was gulping. Her sobs and my sobs were bouncing wildly off the tile, sometimes together, sometimes alternating. "I don't understand why you won't say just one word," I cried, clenching my teeth. My knees were shaking, and I hung on to her hair to stand up. Another time I'd stayed too late, I had had to walk around two Negro kids who were bonking each other's head on the concrete. I went back later to see if the concrete had cracks in it. "Look, I'll give you something if you talk. I'll give you my pencil box. I'll buy you some candy. Okay? What do you want? Tell me. Just say it, and I'll give it to you. Just say, 'Yes,' or 'Okay,' or 'Baby Ruth.' " But she didn't want anything.

I had stopped pinching her cheek because I did not like the feel of her skin. I would go crazy if it came away in my hands. "I skinned her," I would have to confess.

Suddenly I heard footsteps hurrying through the basement, and her sister ran into the lavatory calling her name. "Oh, there you are," I said. "We've been waiting for you. I was only trying to teach her to talk. She wouldn't cooperate, though." Her sister went into one of the stalls and got handfuls of toilet paper and wiped her off. Then we found my sister, and we walked home together. "Your family really ought to force her to speak," I advised all the way home. "You mustn't pamper her."

The world is sometimes just, and I spent the next eighteen months sick in bed with a mysterious illness. There was no pain and no symptoms, though the middle line in my left palm broke in two. Instead of starting junior high school, I lived like the Victorian recluses I read about. I had a rented hospital bed in the living room, where I watched soap operas on TV, and my family cranked me up and down. I saw no one but my family, who took good care of me. I could have no visitors, no other relatives, no villagers. My bed was against the west window, and I watched the seasons change the peach tree. I had a bell to ring for help. I used a bedpan. It was the best year and a half of my life. Nothing happened.

But one day my mother, the doctor, said, "You're ready to get up today. It's time to get up and go to school." I walked about outside to get my legs working, leaning on a staff I cut from the peach tree. The sky and trees, the sun were immense — no longer framed by a window, no longer grayed with a fly screen. I sat down on the sidewalk in amazement — the night, the stars. But at school I had to figure out again how to talk. I met again the poor girl I had tormented. She had not changed. She wore the same clothes, hair cut, and manner as when we were in elementary school, no make-up on the pink and white face, while the other Asian girls were starting to tape their eyelids. She continued to be able to read aloud. But there was hardly any reading aloud anymore, less and less as we got into high school.

I was wrong about nobody taking care of her. Her sister became a clerk-typist and stayed unmarried. They lived with their mother and father. She did not have to leave the house except to go to the movies. She was supported. She was protected by her family, as they would normally have done in China if they could have afforded it, not sent off to school with strangers, ghosts, boys.

ABOUT **MAXINE HONG KINGSTON**

Maxine Hong Kingston was born in the Chinatown area of Stockton, California. She worked in her family's laundry and attended Chinese school at the close of the regular school day. After graduating from college, she became a college English teacher and started to explore the rich mine of "talk-story," tales of Chinese heroes and history that her mother had told her when she was young. Some of them she incorporated into her book, *The Woman Warrior: Memoirs of a Girlhood Among Ghosts*.

RESPONDING

1. *Personal Response* If you learned that your younger sister had bullied a quiet girl as the narrator did, how would you react? Before taking action or giving advice, try to figure out why she might have acted this way.

2. *Literary Analysis* Use evidence from the story to make some *inferences* about why the narrator becomes so angry with the quiet girl and about why she becomes ill afterwards.

3. *Multicultural Connection* In the first and last few paragraphs of this selection, Kingston refers to what is "normal" for Chinese people. Do you consider these qualities normal or stereotypical? Explain the difference.

LANGUAGE WORKSHOP

Personal Pronouns Personal *pronouns* can serve as subjects (I, we, he, she, they) or objects (me, us, him, her, them) in a sentence. People sometimes have problems determining which form of pronoun to use with a compound subject or object. Use the correct form of the pronoun in the following sentences from the story.
1. "Once a year the teachers referred my sister and (I, me) to speech therapy. . . ."
2. "(We, Us) American-Chinese girls had to whisper. . . ."
3. ". . . (I, Me) and my little sister and the quiet girl and her big sister stayed late after school for some reason."

WRITER'S PORTFOLIO

Public places, like Kingston's school, that are familiar and friendly during regular working hours can be lonely, hostile, or frightening after hours. Write a thumbnail sketch of your school (job site, place of worship, or meeting place) after hours.

Getting Nowhere

James Berry

Next week I'll leave school.
Next week, nil, fulltime —
me — for good!

Yonks now
nobody bothered.
No teacher scrawled, "work harder."
Or, "Use your potential."

They'd twigged on.
Their words were whispers
to a rock. So
They gave up on me.

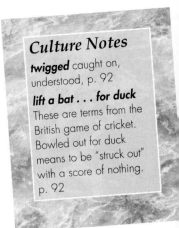

Culture Notes

twigged caught on,
understood, p. 92

lift a bat . . . for duck
These are terms from the
British game of cricket.
Bowled out for duck
means to be "struck out"
with a score of nothing.
p. 92

They had no grasp —
none to give.
Had no power to kick
my motor into clatter.

Not to lift a bat, next week
I'm bowled out for duck.
Year in year out
terrible need took
nothing teachers served.

I couldn't win them.
They couldn't win me.
Their mouthings reached me jammed.
So routines to me will end next week.

Lamp of workshop drawing got built
only as far as the base
and abandoned. Made scrap.

And a relief will grab them.
Relieved, the teachers will sigh —
"Clearly, a non-achiever."

Next week, I'll leave school
but stay held on poverty street.
Held hostage by myself, they'll say.

Clouds on the Sea

Ruth Dallas

I walk among men with tall bones,
With shoes of leather, and pink faces;
I meet no man holding a begging bowl;
All have their dwelling places.

In my country
Every child is taught to read and write,
Every child has shoes and a warm coat,
Every child must eat his dinner,
No one must grow any thinner;
It is considered remarkable and not nice
To meet bed-bugs or lice.
Oh we live like the rich
With music at the touch of a switch,
Light in the middle of the night,
Water in the house as from a spring,
Hot, if you wish, or cold, anything
For the comfort of the flesh,
In my country. Fragment
Of new skin at the edge of the world's ulcer.

For the question
That troubled you as you watched the reapers
And a poor woman following,

Gleaning the ears on the ground,
Why should I have grain and this woman none?
No satisfactory answer has been found.

ABOUT **JAMES BERRY**

James Berry lived in Jamaica from his birth in 1924 until he immigrated to England in 1948. He currently resides in London and makes a living as a writer, editor, and educator. His collection of stories set in the Caribbean, *A Thief in the Village and Other Stories,* was named a Coretta Scott King Award honor book in 1989. Berry has also published *Ajeemah and His Son,* winner of the *Boston Globe Horn Book* Award in 1993, as well as a poetry collection, *When I Dance,* from which "Getting Nowhere" is taken. In his stories and poems Berry often uses the Creole language spoken in Jamaica to capture the character of the island's people.

ABOUT **RUTH DALLAS**

Ruth Dallas was born in 1919 in Invercargill, New Zealand, and now lives in nearby Dunedin. She grew up near the southern tip

of the South Island of New Zealand, almost as far south as the Falkland Islands off the coast of Argentina. Her great-grandparents and grandparents were early settlers to the area, and her work has strong historical and regional themes. She has published a number of children's novels about pioneering, as well as many poetry collections. Dallas was awarded a CBE (Cross of the British Empire) in 1989 in recognition of her work.

RESPONDING

1. *Personal Response* Imagine that you could do one thing for the student in Berry's poem or the reaper in Dallas's

poem to make their life better. What would you do and why?

2. *Literary Analysis* Which of these poems would be easier to memorize? Why? Do *rhyme* or *rhythm* have anything to do with your choice? Explain.

3. *Multicultural Connection* Do you think that the student and the hungry gleaner described in these poems are victims of society and culture, or could they take control of their own fates? Explain.

LANGUAGE WORKSHOP

Contractions In *contractions,* apostrophes show where letters are missing. Identify the missing letters in the following contractions from Berry's poem: *I'll, they'd, I'm, couldn't, they'll.* Now make a contraction for each of the following phrases, placing the apostrophe properly: *we would, she will, I have, you have.*

WRITER'S PORTFOLIO

Write lyrics for a three-verse song about a question to which you think there is "no satisfactory answer."

Amnesty

W<small>HEN WE HEARD</small> he was released I ran all over the farm and through the fence to our people on the next farm to tell everybody. I only saw afterwards I'd torn my dress on the barbed wire, and there was a scratch, with blood, on my shoulder.

He went away from this place eight years ago, signed up to work in town with what they call a construction company—building glass walls up to the sky. For the first two years he came home for the weekend once a month and two weeks at Christmas; that was when he asked my father for me. And he began to pay. He and I thought that in three years he would have paid enough for us to get married. But then he started wearing that T-shirt, he told us he'd joined the union, he told us about the strike, how he was one of the men who went to talk to the bosses because some others had been laid off after the strike. He's always been good at talking, even in English—he was the best at the farm school, he used to read the newspapers the Indian wraps soap and sugar in when you buy at the store.

There was trouble at the hostel where he had a bed, and riots over paying rent in the townships and he told me— just me, not the old ones—that wherever people were fighting against the way we are treated they were doing it for all of us, on the farms as well as the towns, and the unions were with them, he was with them, making speeches, marching. The third year, we heard he was in prison. Instead of getting married. We didn't know where to find him, until he went on trial. The case was heard in a town far away. I couldn't go often to the court because by that time I had passed my Standard 8 and I was working in the farm school. Also my parents were short of money. Two of my brothers who had gone away to work in town didn't send home; I suppose they lived with girlfriends and had to buy things for them. My father and other brother work here for the Boer and the pay is very small, we have two goats, a few cows we're allowed to graze, and a patch of land where my mother can grow vegetables. No cash from that.

When I saw him in the court he looked beautiful in a blue suit with a striped shirt and brown tie. All the accused—his comrades, he said— were well dressed. The union bought the clothes so that the judge and the prosecutor would know they weren't dealing with stupid yes-baas black men who didn't know their rights. These things and everything else about the court and trial he explained to me when I was allowed to visit him in jail. Our little girl was born while the trial went on and when I brought the baby to court the first time to show him, his comrades hugged him and then hugged me across the barrier of the prisoners' dock and they had clubbed together to give me some money as a present for the baby. He chose the name for her, Inkululeko.

Then the trial was over and he got six years. He was sent to the Island. We all knew about the Island. Our leaders had been there so long. But I have never seen the sea except to colour it in blue at school, and I couldn't imagine a piece of earth surrounded by it. I could only think of a cake of dung, dropped by the cattle, floating in a pool of rainwater they'd crossed, the water showing the sky like a looking-glass, blue. I was ashamed only to think that. He had told me how the glass walls showed the pavement, trees and the other buildings in the street and the colours of

Culture Notes

townships areas of South Africa set aside for black citizens, where they are often forced to live, p. 96

Boer a white South African of Dutch or Huguenot descent, p. 97

baas term of address used by a black laborer to a white landowner, p. 97

Inkululeko (in´kü lü la´kō), p. 97

the cars and the clouds as the crane lifted him on a platform higher and higher through the sky to work at the top of a building.

He was allowed one letter a month. It was my letter because his parents didn't know how to write. I used to go to them where they worked on another farm to ask what message they wanted to send. The mother always cried and put her hands on her head and said nothing, and the old man, who preached to us in the veld every Sunday, said tell my son we are praying, God will make everything all right for him. Once he wrote back, That's the trouble — our people on the farms, they're told God will decide what's good for them so that they won't find the force to do anything to change their lives.

AFTER TWO YEARS HAD PASSED, we — his parents and I — had saved up enough money to go to Cape Town to visit him. We went by train and slept on the floor at the station and asked the way, next day, to the ferry. People were kind; they all knew that if you wanted the ferry it was because you had somebody of yours on the Island.

And there it was — there was the sea. It was green *and* blue, climbing and falling, bursting white, all the way to the sky. A terrible wind was slapping it this way and that; it hid the Island, but people like us, also waiting for the ferry, pointed where the Island must be, far out in the sea that I never thought would be like it really was.

There were other boats, and ships as big as buildings that go to other places, all over the world, but the ferry is only for the Island, it doesn't go anywhere else in the world, only to the Island. So everybody waiting there was waiting for the Island, there could be no mistake we were not in the right place. We had sweets and biscuits, trousers and a warm coat for him (a woman standing with us said we wouldn't be allowed to give him the clothes) and I wasn't wearing, any more, the old beret pulled down over my head that farm girls wear, I had bought relaxer cream from the man who comes round the farms selling things out of a box on his bicycle, and my hair was combed up thick under a flowered scarf that didn't cover the gold-coloured rings in my ears. His mother had her blanket tied round her waist over her dress, a farm woman, but I looked just as good as any of the other girls there. When the ferry was ready to take us, we stood all pressed together and quiet like the cattle waiting to be let through a gate. One man kept looking round with his chin moving up and down, he was counting, he must have been afraid there were too many to get on and he didn't want to be left behind. We all moved up to the policeman in charge and everyone ahead of us went on to the boat. But when our turn came and he put out his hand for something, I didn't know what.

We didn't have a permit. We didn't know that before you come to Cape Town, before you come to the ferry for the Island, you have to have a police permit to visit a prisoner on the Island. I tried to ask him nicely. The wind blew the voice out of my mouth.

We were turned away. We saw the ferry rock, bumping the landing where we stood, moving, lifted and dropped by all that water, getting smaller and smaller until we didn't know if we were really seeing it or one of the birds that looked black dipping up and down, out there.

The only good thing was one of the other people took the sweets and biscuits for him. He wrote and said he got them. But it wasn't a good letter. Of course not. He was cross with me; I should have found out, I should have known about the permit. He was right — I bought the train tickets, I asked where to go for the ferry, I should have known about the permit. I have passed Standard 8. There was an advice office to go to in town, the churches ran it, he wrote. But the farm is so far from town, we on the farms don't know about these things. It was as he said; our ignorance is the way we are kept down, this ignorance must go.

We took the train back and we never went to the Island — never saw him in the three more years he was there. Not once. We couldn't find the money for the train. His father died and I had to help his mother from my pay. For our people the worry is always money, I wrote. When will we ever have money? Then he sent such a good letter. That's what I'm on the Island for, far away from you, I'm here so that one day our people will have the things they need, land, food, the end of ignorance. There was something else—I could just read the word "power" the prison had blacked out. All his letters were not just for me; the prison officer read them before I could.

He was coming home after only five years!
That's what it seemed to me, when I heard—the five years was suddenly disappeared—nothing!—there was no whole year still to wait. I showed my—our—little girl his photo again. That's your daddy, he's coming, you're going to see him. She told the other children at school, I've got a daddy, just as she showed off about the kid goat she had at home.
We wanted him to come at once, and at the same time we wanted time to prepare. His mother lived with one of his uncles; now that his father was dead there was no house of his father for him to take me to as soon as we married. If there had been time, my father would have cut poles, my mother and I would have baked bricks, cut thatch, and built a house for him and me and the child.

W̲E WERE NOT SURE what day he would arrive. We only heard on my radio his name and the names of some others who were released. Then at the Indian's store I noticed the newspaper, *The Nation*, written by black people, and on the front a picture of a lot of people dancing and waving—I saw at once it was at that ferry. Some men were being carried on other men's shoulders. I couldn't see which one was him. We were waiting. The ferry had brought him from the Island but we remembered Cape Town is a long way from us. Then he did come. On a Saturday, no school, so I was working with my mother, hoeing and weeding round the pumpkins and mealies, my hair, that I meant to keep nice, tied in an old *doek*. A combi came over the veld and his comrades had brought him. I wanted to run away and wash but he stood there stretching his legs, calling, hey! hey! with his comrades making a noise around him, and my mother started shrieking in the old style aie!

aie! and my father was clapping and stamping towards him. He held his arms open to us, this big man in town clothes, polished shoes, and all the time while he hugged me I was holding my dirty hands, full of mud, away from him behind his back. His teeth hit me hard through his lips, he grabbed at my mother and she struggled to hold the child up to him. I thought we would all fall down! Then everyone was quiet. The child hid behind my mother. He picked her up but she turned her

Culture Notes

doek a cloth, especially a head cloth, p.100

combi a motorcycle with a side-car, p.100

head away to her shoulder. He spoke to her gently but she wouldn't speak to him. She's nearly six years old! I told her not to be a baby. She said, That's not him.

The comrades all laughed, we laughed, she ran off and he said, She has to have time to get used to me.

He has put on weight, yes; a lot. You couldn't believe it. He used to be so thin his feet looked too big for him. I used to feel his bones but now — that night — when he lay on me he was so heavy, I didn't remember it was like that. Such a long time. It's strange to get stronger in prison; I thought he wouldn't have enough to eat and would come out weak. Everyone said, Look at him! — he's a man, now. He laughed and banged his fist on his chest, told them how the comrades exercised in their cells, he would run three miles a day, stepping up and down on one place on the floor of that small cell where he was kept. After we were together at night we used to whisper a long time but now I can feel he's thinking of some things I don't know and I can't worry him with talk. Also I don't know what to say. To ask him what it was like, five years shut away there; or to tell him something about school or about the child. What else has happened, here? Nothing. Just waiting. Sometimes in the daytime I do try to tell him what it was like for me, here at home on the farm, five years. He listens, he's interested, just like he's interested when people from the other farms come to visit and talk to him about little things that happened to them while he was away all that time on the Island. He smiles and nods, asks a couple of questions and then stands up and stretches. I see it's to show them it's enough, his mind is going back to something he was busy with before they came. And we farm people are very slow; we tell things slowly, he used to, too.

He hasn't signed on for another job. But he can't stay at home with us; we thought, after five years over there in the middle of that green and blue sea, so far, he would rest with us a little while. The combi or some car comes to fetch him and he says don't worry, I don't know what day I'll be back. At first I asked, what week, next week? He tried to explain to me: in the Movement it's not like it was in the union, where you do your work every day and after that you are busy with meetings; in the Movement you never know where you will have to go and what is going to come up next. And the same with money. In the Movement, it's not like a job, with regular pay—I know that, he doesn't have to tell me—it's like it was going to the Island, you do it for all our people who suffer because we haven't got money, we haven't got land—look, he said, speaking of my parents', my home, the home that has been waiting for him, with his child: look at this place where the white man owns the ground and lets you squat in mud and tin huts here only as long as you work for him—*Baba* and your brother planting his crops and looking after his cattle, Mama cleaning his house and you in the school without even having the chance to train properly as a teacher. The farmer owns us, he says. I've been thinking we haven't got a home because there wasn't time to build a house before he came from the Island; but we haven't got a home at all. Now I've understood that.

I'm not stupid. When the comrades come to this place in the combi to talk to him here I don't go away with my mother after we've brought them tea or (if she's made it for the weekend) beer. They like her beer, they talk about our culture and there's one of them who makes a point of putting his arm around my mother, calling her the mama of all of them, the mama of Africa. Sometimes they please her very much by telling her how they used to sing on the Island and getting her to sing an old song we all know from our grandmothers. Then they join in with their strong voices. My father doesn't like this noise travelling across the veld; he's afraid that if the Boer finds out my man is a political, from the Island, and he's holding meetings on the Boer's land, he'll tell my father to go, and take his family with him. But my brother says if the Boer asks anything just tell him it's a prayer meeting. Then the singing is over; my mother knows she must go away into the house.

I STAY, AND LISTEN. He forgets I'm there when he's talking and arguing about something I can see is important, more important than anything we could ever have to say to each other when we're alone. But now and then, when one of the other comrades is speaking I see him look at me for a moment the way I will look up at one of my favourite children in school to encourage the child to understand. The men don't speak to me and I don't speak. One of the things they talk about is organising the people on the farms — the workers, like my father and brother, and like his parents used to be. I learn what all these things are: minimum wage, limitation of working hours, the right to strike, annual leave, accident compensation, pensions, sick and even maternity leave. I am pregnant, at last I have another child inside me, but that's women's business. When they talk about the Big Man, the Old Men, I know who these are: our leaders are also back from prison. I told him about the child coming; he said, And this one belongs to a new country, he'll build the freedom we've fought for! I know he wants to get married but there's no time for that at present. There was hardly time for him to make the child. He comes to me just like he comes here to eat a meal or put on clean clothes. He picks up the little girl and swings her round and there! — it's done, he's getting into the combi, he's already turning to his comrade that face of his that knows only what's inside his head, those eyes that move quickly as if he's chasing something you can't see. The little girl hasn't had time to get used to this man. But I know she'll be proud of him, one day!

How can you tell that to a child six years old? But I tell her about the Big Man and the Old Men, our leaders, so she'll know that her father was with them on the Island, this man is a great man, too.

On Saturday, no school and I plant and weed with my mother, she sings but I don't; I think. On Sunday there's no work, only prayer meetings out of the farmer's way under the trees, and beer drinks at the mud and tin huts where the farmers allow us to squat on their land. I go off on my own as I used to do when I was a child, making up games and talking to myself where no one would hear me or look for me. I sit on a warm stone in the late afternoon, high up, and the whole valley is a path between the hills, leading away from my feet. It's the Boer's farm but that's not true, it belongs to nobody. The cattle don't know that anyone says he owns it, the sheep—they are grey stones, and then they become a thick grey snake moving—don't know. Our huts and the old mulberry tree and the little brown mat of earth that my mother dug over yesterday, way down there, and way over there the clump of trees round the chimneys and the shiny thing that is the TV mast of the farmhouse—they are nothing, on the back of this earth. It could twitch them away like a dog does a fly.

I am up with the clouds. The sun behind me is changing the colours of the sky and the clouds are changing themselves, slowly, slowly. Some are white, blowing themselves up like bubbles. Underneath is a bar of grey, not enough to make rain. It gets longer and darker while the other clouds are all pink, it grows a thin snout and long body and then the end of it is a tail. There's a huge grey rat moving across the sky, eating the sky.

The child remembered the photo; she said, That's not him. I'm sitting here where I came often when he was on the Island. I came to get away from the others, to wait by myself.

I'm watching the rat, it's losing itself, its shape, eating the sky, and I'm waiting. Waiting for him to come back.

Waiting. I'm waiting to come back home.

ABOUT **NADINE GORDIMER**

Recipient of the 1991 Nobel Prize for Literature, Nadine Gordimer is one of South Africa's most widely respected authors. She was born in 1923 in Springs, South Africa, and now makes her home in Johannesburg. Since 1953 she has published novels, short stories, and nonfiction collections, most of them about issues of race and oppression in her native country.

RESPONDING

1. *Personal Response* Who do you think has faced greater challenges, the narrator or the man she is to marry? Why?

2. *Literary Analysis* How would you describe the *narrator*? Do you think she appears to be a good match for her husband-to-be? Why or why not?

3. *Multicultural Connection* The speaker is surprised that her future husband gained weight in prison. Is that typical of prisons in most cultures? How does the Island compare to the prisons in your own culture?

LANGUAGE WORKSHOP

Fragments and Run-ons A *sentence fragment* is a group of words punctuated like a sentence but not expressing a complete thought. *Run-ons* are sentences run together without proper punctuation in between. Authors may use sentence fragments or run-ons in formal writing to establish a conversational tone or convey a choppy, spontaneous thought process. Find two fragments and two run-ons in "Amnesty" and generalize about Gordimer's reason for using them.

WRITER'S PORTFOLIO

Review the speaker's descriptions of the Island and the homes of her parents and future in-laws. Then compose a short essay that compares the ways people are treated on the Boer farm and on the Island.

Lot's Wife

Anna Akhmatova

The just man followed then his angel guide
Where he strode on the black highway, hulking and
    bright;
But a wild grief in his wife's bosom cried,
Look back, it is not too late for a last sight

Of the red towers of your native Sodom, the square
Where once you sang, the gardens you shall mourn,
And the tall house with empty windows where
You loved your husband and your babes were born.

She turned, and looking on the bitter view
Her eyes were welded shut by mortal pain;
Into transparent salt her body grew,
And her quick feet were rooted in the plain.

Who would waste tears upon her? Is she not
The least of our losses, this unhappy wife?
Yet in my heart she will not be forgot
Who, for a single glance, gave up her life.

Fable

János Pilinszky

Once upon a time
there was a lonely wolf
lonelier than the angels.

He happened to come to a village.
He fell in love with the first house he saw.

Already he loved its walls

the caresses of its bricklayers.
But the windows stopped him.

In the room sat people.
Apart from God nobody ever
found them so beautiful
as this child-like beast.

So at night he went into the house.
He stopped in the middle of the room
and never moved from there any more.

He stood all through the night, with wide eyes
and on into the morning when he was beaten to
death.

ABOUT **ANNA AKHMATOVA**

Anna Akhmatova (uk mät′ə və, äk′mə tō′və; 1889–1966)
was born near Odessa, Ukraine. She began her writing
career in St. Petersburg, publishing seven
books of poetry between 1912 and
1921. From 1922 to 1940 she was not
allowed to publish officially. During World
War II, she published four books of poems,
then was silenced again until Stalin's death
in 1953. Like Lot's wife in Genesis,
Akhmatova at times felt alienated from the homeland she loved,
particularly under Soviet rule. Akhmatova was a candidate for the
Nobel Prize in 1946 and 1965 (in each case, a male Soviet
writer won).

ABOUT **JÁNOS PILINSZKY**

János Pilinszky (yah′nôsh pi lin′skē) was
born in Budapest, Hungary, in 1921 and
died there in 1981. As a soldier at the
end of World War II, Pilinszky was deeply
affected by witnessing experiences of

victims of the Holocaust. Critics also note that his Catholicism profoundly influenced his poetry. Although simple, direct, and traditional in form, his poems are unusually musical and intense.

RESPONDING

1. *Personal Response* Have you ever felt as strongly about a place where you lived as Lot's wife does? What things can make a home or a place so desirable?

2. *Literary Analysis* *Tone* is an author's attitude toward a subject. For example, an author may feel pity, admiration, or ridicule toward a subject. Choose a word or words to describe the tone of each of these poems and explain your choice.

3. *Multicultural Connection* Describe one or two current situations in which love of a country has led to pain for its people.

LANGUAGE WORKSHOP

Fable A *fable* is a story with a moral, or lesson, often using animals as characters. What moral would you assign to "Fable"? Do you think that "Lot's Wife" teaches a moral? Why or why not?

WRITER'S PORTFOLIO

In a poem or a prose fable of no more than one page, tell the story of a person or animal that gives up its life for love.

ALICIA PARTNOY

Bread

. . . Give us this day our daily bread,
the one that, yesterday, you took away from us.

A Latin American's Lord's Prayer
Mario Benedetti

I N THIS CLIMATE of overall uncertainty, bread is the only reliable thing. I mean, it is the only reliable thing besides the belief that we have always been right, that betting our blood in the fight against these killers was the only intelligent option. We don't know when it is time for screams, time for torture, or time for death, but we do know when it is time for bread. At noon we wait to hear the sound of the bread bag sweeping the floor, that smell purifying everything; we wait to touch that bread: crunchy outside, soothingly soft inside. We wait for it so we can either devour it with greed or treasure it with love. One day I was given two extra pieces of bread and an apple. I kept them under my pillow. That day I felt rich, very rich. Every now and then I lifted the edge of the pillow to breathe that vivifying mixture of

Culture Note

This account takes place in The Little School (*La Escuelita*), a detention center in Argentina, where the narrator was detained for what were considered subversive student activities.

scents. By the time that happened I'd already been at the Little School some three months.

In the beginning, when I was a new arrival I almost didn't eat. I passed my portion of bread to other prisoners. I did that until the fellow in the bunk on top of mine told me to stop. He told me to eat so I wouldn't lose strength. But once, when I still wasn't desperately hungry, and lying on that mattress made me unbearably impatient, I cut twenty-five little pieces of bread and made twenty-five tiny balls out of them; I played with the balls, rolling them around in my palm. Vaca passed by, and noticing such an unusual activity, he asked:

"What's that?"

"Little bread balls."

"What for?"

"To play with."

He kept silent for two minutes while he meticulously calculated the danger level of that toy.

"It's okay," he said solemnly, and left, probably convinced that I was one step closer to madness. You were wrong, Mr. Vaca.

BREAD IS ALSO A MEANS of communicating, a way of telling the person next to me: "I'm here. I care for you. I want to share the only possession I have." Sometimes it is easy to convey the message: When bread distribution is over, we ask, "Sir, is there any more?" When the guard answers that there isn't any, another prisoner will say, "Sir, I have some bread left, can I pass it to her?" If we are lucky enough, a deal can finally be made. Sometimes it is more difficult; but when hunger hits, the brain becomes sharper. The blanket on the top bed is made into a kind of stage curtain that covers the wall, and behind the curtain, pieces of bread go up and down at the will of stomachs and hearts.

When tedium mixes with hunger, and four claws of anxiety pierce the pits of our stomachs, eating a piece of bread, very slowly, fiber by fiber, is our great relief. When we feel our isolation growing, the world we seek vanishing in the shadows, to give a brother some bread is a reminder that true values are still alive. To be given some bread is to receive a comforting hug.

One day I peeked under the blindfold and saw little María Elena. I made up a silly poem for her: *María Elena/sweet and small/sitting on her bed/eating some bread/Two little tears/slide down her face/People will never learn/of María Elena/sitting on her bed/eating some bread. . .*

Once Pato was blind drunk and I wanted to pass some bread to Hugo, who was on the bed in front of mine. Pato refused to answer my calls. I decided to do it myself. I called Vasca.

"What?" she whispered.

"Look at me!" I got out of bed and tiptoed the four steps that separated me from Hugo's bed. I left the piece of bread by his face and went back. It was the first, and last, time I got up that way, illegally. I felt as if I was returning from an adventure, and my heart beat crazily. The operation had taken two seconds.

"But . . . what are you doing?" asked Vasca, half amused and half shocked.

"If he's seen me," I replied, "he'll think it's all part of his *delirium tremens.*" We laughed, feeling like accomplices.

There are also stories about bread crumbs. When we blindly look for them on the mattress, to devour them, the tiny crumbs hide and, several days later, they are the occasion for a rare event, an event that—provided it isn't accompanied by blows with the rubber stick—can even be labeled entertainment: the "shaking" of the beds. First, we remove the crumbs from the mattress; after that we shake the blanket and, while the dust and crumbs are flying around, we wave our arms as if—with blanket and all— we can take off from the ground. After that we lay the blanket on the bed, smooth any folds and put back the pillows. Under the pillow is the lunch bread. It is then time to wait until our hands are bound again, and afterwards to lie down and slowly eat that piece of bread that reminds us that our present is a result of our fight—so that bread, our daily bread, the very same bread that has been taken away from our people, will be given back because it is our right, no pleas to God needed, forever and ever. Amen.

ABOUT **ALICIA PARTNOY**

In 1986 Alicia Partnoy published a book, *The Little School: Tales of Disappearance and Survival in Argentina,* that chronicles her six years as a political prisoner. In 1976 Partnoy and her husband were "disappeared" with thousands of other Argentinians by members of the military who had taken over the government. "Disappearances" are kidnappings, usually followed by torture and secret jailing. Unlike many of "the disappeared," Partnoy and her husband

survived, and her testimony helped convict four generals who had helped overthrow the government. "Bread" is an excerpt from her book about life in the secret prison. Partnoy and her husband now live in the United States.

RESPONDING

1. *Personal Response* What one food or drink would you want to have every day if you were imprisoned or suffering in another way? Why?

2. *Literary Analysis* How would you describe the *mood* established in the first three sentences of the story? How does Partnoy create this mood?

3. *Multicultural Connection* What does Partnoy mean when she says "to give a brother some bread is a reminder that true values are still alive"?

LANGUAGE WORKSHOP

Prefixes and Suffixes *Prefixes* and *suffixes* are combining forms that come at the beginnings and ends of words, respectively. They can alter the meaning of a word and change its role in a sentence. For example, *disregard* means the opposite of *regard; vacation* is a noun form of the verb *vacate*. Locate the prefix or suffix in the following words from "Bread." Then write another word that contains the same combining form.

1. entertainment
2. solemnly
3. illegal
4. isolation
5. impatient

WRITER'S PORTFOLIO

Create a one-page dialogue between two people in which food plays an important role. Before you write, decide what sort of food they will use—for example, breakfast food? a health snack? a banquet? berries off a vine?

Tell Them
Not to Kill Me!

"TELL THEM NOT TO KILL ME, Justino! Go on and tell them that. For God's sake! Tell them. Tell them please for God's sake."

"I can't. There's a sergeant there who doesn't want to hear anything about you."

"Make him listen to you. Use your wits and tell him that scaring me has been enough. Tell him please for God's sake."

"But it's not just to scare you. It seems they really mean to kill you. And I don't want to go back there."

"Go on once more. Just once, to see what you can do."

"No. I don't feel like going. Because if I do they'll know I'm your son. If I keep bothering them they'll end up knowing who I am and will decide to shoot me too. Better leave things the way they are now."

"Go on, Justino. Tell them to take a little pity on me. Just tell them that."

Justino clenched his teeth and shook his head saying no.

And he kept on shaking his head for some time.

"Tell the sergeant to let you see the colonel. And tell him how old I am—How little I'm worth. What will he get out of killing me? Nothing. After all he must have a soul. Tell him to do it for the blessed salvation of his soul."

Justino got up from the pile of stones which he was sitting on and walked to the gate of the corral. Then he turned around to say, "All right, I'll go. But if they decide to shoot me too, who'll take care of my wife and kids?"

"Providence will take care of them, Justino. You go there now and see what you can do for me. That's what matters."

They'd brought him in at dawn. The morning was well along now and he was still there, tied to a post, waiting. He couldn't keep still. He'd tried to sleep for a while to calm down, but he couldn't. He wasn't hungry either. All he wanted was to live. Now that he knew they were really going to kill him, all he could feel was his great desire to stay alive, like a recently resuscitated man.

Who would've thought that old business that happened so long ago and that was buried the way he thought it was would turn up? That business when he had to kill Don Lupe. Not for nothing either, as the Alimas tried to make out, but because he had his reasons. He remembered: Don Lupe Terreros, the owner of the Puerta de Piedra—and besides that, his compadre—was the one he, Juvencio Nava, had to kill, because he'd refused to let him pasture his animals, when he was the owner of the Puerta de Piedra and his compadre too.

At first he didn't do anything because he felt compromised. But later, when the drouth came, when he saw how his animals were dying off one by one, plagued by hunger, and how his compadre Lupe continued to refuse to let him use his pastures, then was when he began breaking through the fence and driving his herd of skinny animals to the pasture where they could get their fill of grass. And Don Lupe didn't like it and ordered the fence mended, so that he, Juvencio Nava, had to cut open the hole again. So, during the day the hole was stopped up and at night it was opened again, while the stock stayed right next to the fence, always waiting—his stock that before had lived just smelling the grass without being able to taste it.

And he and Don Lupe argued again and again without coming to any agreement.

Until one day Don Lupe said to him, "Look here, Juvencio, if you let another animal in my pasture, I'll kill it."

And he answered him, "Look here, Don Lupe, it's not my fault that the animals look out for themselves. They're innocent. You'll have to pay for it, if you kill them."

And he killed one of my yearlings.

This happened thirty-five years ago in March, because in April I was already up in the mountains, running away from the summons. The ten cows I gave the judge didn't do me any good, or the lien on my house either, to pay for getting me out of jail. Still later they used up what was left to pay so they wouldn't keep after me, but they kept after me just the same. That's why I came to live with my son on this other piece of land of mine which is called Palo de Venado. And my son grew up and got married to my daughter-in-law Ignacia and has had eight children now. So it happened a long time ago and ought to be forgotten by now. But I guess it's not.

I FIGURED THEN that with about a hundred pesos everything could be fixed up. The dead Don Lupe left just his wife and two little kids still crawling. And his widow died soon afterward too—they say from grief. They took the kids far off to some relatives. So there was nothing to fear from them.

But the rest of the people took the position that I was still summoned to be tried just to scare me so they could keep on robbing me. Every time someone came to the village they told me, "There are some strangers in town, Juvencio."

And I would take off to the mountains, hiding among the madrone thickets and passing the days with nothing to eat but herbs. Sometimes I had to go out at midnight, as though the dogs were after me. It's been that way my whole life. Not just a year or two. My whole life.

And now they've come for him when he no longer expected anyone, confident that people had forgotten all about it, believing that he'd spend at least his last days peacefully. "At least," he thought, "I'll have some peace in my old age. They'll leave me alone."

He'd clung to this hope with all his heart. That's why it was hard for him to imagine that he'd die like this, suddenly, at this time of life, after having fought so much to ward off death, after having spent his best years running from one place to another because of the alarms, now when his body had become all dried up and leathery from the bad days when he had to be in hiding from everybody.

Hadn't he even let his wife go off and leave him? The day when he learned his wife had left him, the idea of going out in search of her didn't even cross his mind. He let her go without trying to find out at all who she went with or where, so he wouldn't have to go down to the village. He let her go as he'd let everything else go, without putting up a fight. All he had left to take care of was his life, and he'd do that, if nothing else. He couldn't let them kill him. He couldn't. Much less now.

But that's why they brought him from there, from Palo de Venado. They didn't need to tie him so he'd follow them. He walked alone, tied by his fear. They realized he couldn't run with his old body, with those skinny legs of his like dry bark, cramped up with the fear of dying. Because that's where he was headed. For death. They told him so.

That's when he knew. He began to feel that stinging in his stomach that always came on suddenly when he saw death nearby, making his eyes big with fear and his mouth swell up with those mouthfuls of sour water he had to swallow unwillingly. And that thing that made his feet heavy while his head felt soft and his heart pounded with all its force against his ribs. No, he couldn't get used to the idea that they were going to kill him.

There must be some hope. Somewhere there must still be some hope left. Maybe they'd made a mistake. Perhaps they were looking for another Juvencio Nava and not him.

He walked along in silence between those men, with his arms fallen at his sides. The early morning hour was dark, starless. The wind blew slowly, whipping the dry earth back and forth, which was filled with that odor like urine that dusty roads have.

His eyes, that had become squinty with the years, were looking down at the ground, here under his feet, in spite of the darkness. There in the earth was his whole life. Sixty years of living on it, of holding it tight in his hands, of tasting it like one tastes the flavor of meat. For a long time he'd been crumbling it with his eyes, savoring each piece as if it were the last one, almost knowing it would be the last.

Then, as if wanting to say something, he looked at the men who were marching along next to him. He was going to tell them to let him loose, to let him go; "I haven't hurt anybody, boys," he was going to say to them, but he kept silent. "A little further on I'll tell them," he thought. And he just looked at them. He could even imagine they were his friends, but he didn't want to. They weren't. He didn't know who they were. He watched them moving at his side and bending down from time to time to see where the road continued.

H E'D SEEN THEM FOR THE FIRST TIME at nightfall, that dusky hour when everything seems scorched. They'd crossed the furrows trodding on the tender corn. And he'd gone down on account of that—to tell them that the corn was beginning to grow there. But that didn't stop them.

He'd seen them in time. He'd always had the luck to see everything in time. He could've hidden, gone up in the mountains for a few hours until they left and then come down again. Already it was time for the rains to have come, but the rains didn't come and the corn was beginning to wither. Soon it'd be all dried up.

So it hadn't even been worthwhile, his coming down and placing himself among those men like in a hole, never to get out again.

And now he continued beside them, holding back how he wanted to tell them to let him go. He didn't see their faces, he only saw their bodies, which swung toward him and then away from him. So when he started talking he didn't know if they'd heard him. He said, "I've never hurt anybody." That's what he said. But nothing changed. Not one of the bodies seemed to pay attention. The faces didn't turn to look at him. They kept right on, as if they were walking in their sleep.

Then he thought that there was nothing else he could say, that he would have to look for hope somewhere else. He let his arms fall again to his sides and went by the first houses of the village, among those four men, darkened by the black color of the night.

"Colonel, here is the man."

They'd stopped in front of the narrow doorway. He stood with his hat in his hand, respectfully, waiting to see someone come out. But only the voice came out, "Which man?"

"From Palo de Venado, colonel. The one you ordered us to bring in."

"Ask him if he ever lived in Alima," came the voice from inside again.

"Hey, you. Ever lived in Alima?" the sergeant facing him repeated the question.

"Yes. Tell the colonel that's where I'm from. And that I lived there till not long ago."

"Ask him if he knew Guadalupe Terreros."

"He says did you know Guadalupe Terreros?"

"Don Lupe? Yes. Tell him that I knew him. He's dead."

Then the voice inside changed tone: "I know he died," it said. And the voice continued talking, as if it was conversing with someone there on the other side of the reed wall.

"Guadalupe Terreros was my father. When I grew up and looked for him they told me he was dead. It's hard to grow up knowing that the thing we have to hang on to, to take roots from is dead. That's what happened to us.

"Later on I learned that he was killed by being hacked first with a machete and then an ox goad stuck in his belly. They told me he lasted more than two days and that when they found him, lying in an arroyo, he was still in agony and begging that his family be taken care of.

"As time goes by you seem to forget this. You try to forget it. What you can't forget is finding out that the one who did it is still alive, feeding his rotten soul with the illusion of eternal life. I couldn't forgive that man, even though I don't know him; but the fact that I know where he is makes me want to finish him off. I can't forgive his still living. He should never have been born."

From here, from outside, all he said was clearly heard. Then he ordered, "Take him and tie him up awhile, so he'll suffer, and then shoot him!"

"Look at me, colonel!" he begged. "I'm not worth anything now. It won't be long before I die all by myself, crippled by old age. Don't kill me!"

"Take him away!" repeated the voice from inside.

"I've already paid, colonel. I've paid many times over. They took everything away from me. They punished me in many ways. I've spent about forty years hiding like a leper, always with the fear they'd kill me at any moment. I don't deserve to die like this, colonel. Let the Lord pardon me, at least. Don't kill me! Tell them not to kill me!"

There he was, as if they'd beaten him, waving his hat against the ground. Shouting.

Immediately the voice from inside said, "Tie him up and give him something to drink until he gets drunk so the shots won't hurt him."

Finally, now, he'd been quieted. There he was, slumped down at the foot of the post. His son Justino had come and his son Justino had gone and had returned and now was coming again.

He slung him on top of the burro. He cinched him up tight against the saddle so he wouldn't fall off on the road. He put his head in a sack so it wouldn't give such a bad impression. And then he made the burro giddap, and away they went in a hurry to reach Palo de Venado in time to arrange the wake for the dead man.

"Your daughter-in-law and grandchildren will miss you," he was saying to him. "They'll look at your face and won't believe it's you. They'll think the coyote has been eating on you when they see your face full of holes from all those bullets they shot at you."

ABOUT **JUAN RULFO**

One of Mexico's most respected writers of the mid-1900s, Juan Rulfo (hwän rül⁄fō) was born in 1918 in the town of Sayula. He began publishing short stories in the 1940s, when he also worked impounding German warships. "Tell Them Not to Kill Me!," from the collection *El llano en llamas y otros cuentos*, was translated into English in 1967 as *The Burning Plain and Other Stories*. Rulfo is best known for his novel *Pedro Páramo*, which paints a bleak picture of the life of

the rural poor. Rulfo lived in Mexico City from the age of fifteen, when he left an orphanage, until he died in 1986.

RESPONDING

1. *Personal Response* Do you think that after thirty-five years Juvencio Nava should have been allowed to live? Why or why not?

2. *Literary Analysis* What argument does Nava make for his life in the opening *dialogue* with his son?

3. *Multicultural Connection* Why does Juvencio Nava believe he had a right to kill Don Lupe Terreros? On what tradition might his belief be based?

LANGUAGE WORKSHOP

Point of View The vantage point from which a story is told is called *point of view*. This vantage point is established through an author's choice of narrator. The story may be related by a character (first-person point of view) or by a narrator who is outside of the story (third-person point of view). "Tell Them Not to Kill Me!" is told alternately in the first person (Nava is referred to as *I* and tells his own story) and the third person (Nava is referred to as *he*). What different effects are achieved by hearing details of Nava's crime from him, from an outside narrator, and later from the victim's son?

WRITER'S PORTFOLIO

Weigh the evidence and deliver a verdict for Nava — guilty or innocent. Explain in a paragraph how you arrived at your decision.

Projects

CLASSROOM POSTER

Create a poster for classroom display about an unfair situation in the world today. Choose a single incident—political, personal, geographical, religious, or familial—and illustrate its effects on all the people involved in words and/or pictures. You might use newsclippings, magazine pictures, or your own art, poetry, or headlines.

DRAMATIC READING

With several classmates, prepare a dramatic reading of "Forbidden Fruit," the excerpt from *The Woman Warrior,* or "Tell Them Not to Kill Me!" Rather than presenting the entire story, you might select scenes that you think have the best dramatic possibilities, creating narrative links that tie the readings together. Assign the speaking parts and the role of narrator, practice your parts, and present your reading to the class.

ADD ANOTHER ENDING

Add a paragraph or a stanza to the end of one of the selections in which you restore justice or right a wrong that exists. Try to make your addition in keeping with the tone and style of the original work. When you have finished, ask a classmate to read the entire work with your addition, and decide whether or not you have improved on the original.

Further Reading

The following books, many by authors represented in this unit, explore personal, social, and political situations and tensions that echo the theme, "It's not fair."

Akhmatova, Anna. *Complete Poems of Anna Akhmatova,* trans. Judith Hemschemeyer. Zephyr Press, 1992. These poems, spanning nearly six decades, address themes of love, suffering, and politics.

Berry, James. *When I Dance,* ed. Bonnie V. Ingber. Harcourt Brace, 1991. Poems for today's young people, many written in a Caribbean voice, examine the tension between Jamaican and British cultures.

Ellison, Ralph. *Invisible Man.* Random House, 1952. A young African American man from the South confronts a hostile society in New York City's Harlem.

Partnoy, Alicia. *The Little School: Tales of Disappearance and Survival in Argentina,* trans. Lois Athey *et al.* Cleis Press, 1991. Partnoy describes her detention as a political prisoner, along with thirty thousand other Argentinians, after the military coup in 1976.

Rifaat, Alifa. *Distant View of a Minaret,* trans. Denys Johnson-Davies. Interlink Publishers, 1993. These stories, translated from Arabic, describe the experiences of contemporary Egyptian women.

Rulfo, Juan. *The Burning Plain and Other Stories,* trans. George D. Schade, University of Texas Press, 1967. These short stories brilliantly portray Mexico's disenfranchised rural poor and their fading culture.

Standing Apart

What is the difference between being extraordinary and being odd, being one-of-a-kind and being weird? Sometimes there's a fine line between what's unique and what's bizarre. The characters in this unit illustrate that standing apart can be painful or enviable, valued or ridiculed, depending on the culture and the situation.

The Handsomest Drowned Man in the World

THE FIRST CHILDREN who saw the dark and slinky bulge approaching through the sea let themselves think it was an enemy ship. Then they saw it had no flags or masts and they thought it was a whale. But when it washed up on the beach, they removed the clumps of seaweed, the jellyfish tentacles, and the remains of fish and flotsam, and only then did they see that it was a drowned man.

They had been playing with him all afternoon, burying him in the sand and digging him up again, when someone chanced to see them and spread the alarm in the village. The men who carried him to the nearest house noticed that he weighed more than any dead man they had ever known, almost as much as a horse, and they said to each other that maybe he'd been floating too long and the water had got into his bones. When they laid him on the floor they said he'd been taller than all other men because there was barely enough room for him in the house, but they thought that maybe the ability to keep on growing after death was part of the nature of certain drowned men. He had the smell of the sea about him and only his shape gave one to suppose that it was the corpse of a human being, because the skin was covered with a crust of mud and scales.

They did not even have to clean off his face to know that the dead man was a stranger. The village was made up of only twenty-odd wooden houses that had stone courtyards with no flowers and which were spread about on the end of a desertlike cape. There was so little land that mothers always went about with the fear that the wind would carry off their children and the few dead that the years had caused among them had to be thrown off the cliffs. But the sea was calm and bountiful and all the men fit into seven boats. So when they found the drowned man they simply had to look at one another to see that they were all there.

That night they did not go out to work at sea. While the men went to find out if anyone was missing in neighboring villages, the women stayed behind to care for the drowned man. They took the mud off with grass swabs, they removed the underwater stones entangled in his hair, and they scraped the crust off with tools used for scaling fish. As they were doing that they noticed that the vegetation on him came from faraway oceans and deep water and that his clothes were in tatters, as if he had sailed through labyrinths of coral. They noticed too that he bore his death with pride, for he did not have the lonely look of other drowned men who came out of the sea or that haggard, needy look of men who drowned in rivers. But only when they finished cleaning him off did they become aware of the kind of man he was and it left them breathless. Not only was he the tallest, strongest, most virile, and best built man they had ever seen, but even though they were looking at him there was no room for him in their imagination.

Culture Note

Brabant linen especially fine cloth from the Brabant region, a former province of Belgium, p.128

They could not find a bed in the village large enough to lay him on nor was there a table solid enough to use for his wake. The tallest men's holiday pants would not fit him, nor the fattest ones' Sunday shirts, nor the shoes of the one with the biggest feet. Fascinated by his huge size and his beauty, the women then decided to make him some pants from a large piece of sail and a shirt from some bridal Brabant linen so that he could continue through his death with dignity. As they sewed, sitting in a circle and gazing at the corpse between stitches, it seemed to them that the wind had never been so steady nor the sea so restless as on that night and they supposed that the change had something to do with the dead man. They thought that if that magnificent man had lived in the village, his house would have had the widest doors, the highest ceiling, and the strongest floor, his bedstead would have been made from a midship frame held together by iron bolts, and his wife would have been the happiest woman. They thought that he would have had so much authority that he could have drawn fish out of the sea simply by calling their names and that he would have put so much work into his land that springs would have burst forth from among the rocks so that he would have been able to plant flowers on the cliffs. They secretly compared him to their own men, thinking that for all their lives theirs were incapable of doing what he could do in one night, and they ended up dismissing them deep in their hearts as the weakest, meanest, and most useless creatures on earth. They were wandering through that maze of fantasy when the oldest woman, who as the oldest had looked upon the drowned man with more compassion than passion, sighed:

"He has the face of someone called Esteban."

It WAS TRUE. Most of them had only to take another look at him to see that he could not have any other name. The more stubborn among them, who were the youngest, still lived for a few hours with the illusion that when they put his clothes on and he lay among the flowers in patent leather shoes his name might be Lautaro. But it was a vain illusion. There had not been enough canvas, the poorly cut and worse sewn pants were too tight, and the hidden strength of his heart popped the buttons on his shirt. After midnight the whistling of the wind died down and the sea fell into its Wednesday drowsiness. The silence put an end to any last doubts: he was Esteban. The women who had dressed him, who had combed his hair, had cut his nails and shaved him were unable to hold back a shudder of pity when they had to resign themselves to his being dragged along the ground. It was then that they understood how unhappy he must have been with that huge body since it bothered him even after death. They could see him in life, condemned to going through doors sideways, cracking his head on crossbeams, remaining on his feet during visits, not knowing what to do with his soft, pink, sea lion hands while the lady of the house looked for her most resistant chair and begged him, frightened to death, sit here, Esteban, please, and he, leaning against the wall, smiling, don't bother, ma'am, I'm fine where I am, his heels raw and his back roasted from having done the same thing so many times whenever he paid a visit, don't bother, ma'am, I'm fine where I am, just to avoid the embarrassment of breaking up the chair, and never knowing perhaps that the ones who said don't go, Esteban, at least wait till the coffee's ready, were the ones who later on would whisper the big boob finally left, how nice, the handsome fool has gone. That was what the women were thinking beside the body a little before dawn. Later, when they covered his face with a handkerchief so that the light would not bother him, he looked so forever dead, so defenseless, so much like their men that the first furrows of tears opened in their hearts. It was one of the younger ones who began the weeping. The others, coming to, went from sighs to wails, and the more they sobbed the more they felt like weeping, because the drowned man was becoming all the more Esteban for them, and so they wept so much, for he was the most destitute, most peaceful, and most obliging man on earth, poor Esteban. So when the men returned with the news that the drowned man was not from the neighboring villages either, the women felt an opening of jubilation in the midst of their tears.

"Praise the Lord," they sighed, "he's ours!"

The men thought the fuss was only womanish frivolity. Fatigued because of the difficult nighttime inquiries, all they wanted was to get rid of the bother of the newcomer once and for all before the sun grew strong on that arid, windless

day. They improvised a litter with the remains of foremasts and gaffs, tying it together with rigging so that it would bear the weight of the body until they reached the cliffs. They wanted to tie the anchor from a cargo ship to him so that he would sink easily into the deepest waves, where fish are blind and divers die of nostalgia, and bad currents would not bring him back to shore, as had happened with other bodies. But the more they hurried, the more the women thought of ways to waste time. They walked about like startled hens, pecking with the sea charms on their breasts, some interfering on one side to put a scapular of the good wind on the drowned man, some on the other side to put a wrist compass on him, and after a great deal of *get away from there, woman, stay out of the way, look, you almost made me fall on top of the dead man,* the men began to feel mistrust in their livers and started grumbling about why so many main-altar decorations for a stranger, because no matter how many nails and holy-water jars he had on him, the sharks would chew him all the same, but the women kept piling on their junk relics, running back and forth, stumbling, while they released in sighs what they did not in tears, so that the men finally exploded with *since when has there ever been such a fuss over a drifting corpse, a drowned nobody, a piece of cold Wednesday meat.* One of the women, mortified by so much lack of care, then removed the handkerchief from the dead man's face and the men were left breathless too.

He was Esteban. It was not necessary to repeat it for them to recognize him. If they had been told Sir Walter Raleigh, even they might have been impressed with his gringo accent, the macaw on his shoulder, his cannibal-killing blunderbuss, but there could be only one Esteban in the world and there he was, stretched out like a sperm whale, shoeless, wearing the pants of an undersized child, and with those stony nails that had to be cut with a knife.

They only had to take the handkerchief off his face to see that he was ashamed, that it was not his fault that he was so big or so heavy or so handsome, and if he had known that this was going to happen, he would have looked for a more discreet place to drown in, seriously, I even would have tied the anchor off a galleon around my neck and staggered off a cliff like someone who doesn't like things in order not to be upsetting people now with this Wednesday dead body, as you people say, in order not to be bothering anyone with this filthy piece of cold meat that doesn't have anything to do with me. There was so much truth in his manner that even the most mistrustful men, the ones who felt the bitterness of endless nights at sea fearing that their women would tire of dreaming about them and begin to dream of drowned men, even they and others who were harder still shuddered in the marrow of their bones at Esteban's sincerity.

That was how they came to hold the most splendid funeral they could conceive of for an abandoned drowned man. Some women who had gone to get flowers in the neighboring villages returned with other women who could not believe what they had been told, and those women went back for more flowers when they saw the dead man, and they brought more and more until there were so many flowers and so many people that it was hard to walk about. At the final moment it pained them to return him to the waters as an orphan and they chose a father and mother from among the best people, and aunts and uncles and cousins, so that through him all the inhabitants of the village became kinsmen. Some sailors who heard the weeping from a distance went off course and people heard of one who had himself tied to the mainmast, remembering ancient fables about sirens. While they fought for the privilege of carrying him on

the steep escarpment by the cliffs, men and women became aware for the first time of the desolation of their streets, the dryness of their courtyards, the narrowness of their dreams as they faced the splendor and beauty of their drowned man. They let him go without an anchor so that he could come back if he wished and whenever he wished, and they all held their breath for the fraction of centuries the body took to fall into the abyss. They did not need to look at one another to realize that they were no longer all present, that they would never be. But they also knew that everything would be different from then on, that their houses would have wider doors, higher ceilings, and stronger floors so that Esteban's memory could go everywhere without bumping into beams and so that no one in the future would dare whisper the big boob finally died, too bad, the handsome fool has finally died, because they were going to paint their house fronts gay colors to make Esteban's memory eternal and they were going to break their backs digging for springs among the stones and planting flowers on the cliffs so that in future years at dawn the passengers on great liners would awaken, suffocated by the smell of gardens on the high seas, and the captain would have to come down from the bridge in his dress uniform, with his astrolabe, his pole star, and his row of war medals and, pointing to the promontory of roses on the horizon, he would say in fourteen languages, look there, where the wind is so peaceful now that it's gone to sleep beneath the beds, over there, where the sun's so bright that the sunflowers don't know which way to turn, yes, over there, that's Esteban's village.

ABOUT **GABRIEL GARCÍA MÁRQUEZ**

Gabriel García Márquez (gäv´rē el´ gär sē´ə mär´kez) was born in 1928 in Aracataca, Colombia, a coastal town like the ones in which he later set much of his fiction. His best-known novel, *One Hundred Years of Solitude*, has sold over ten million copies and been translated into more than thirty languages. Winner of the Nobel Prize for Literature in 1982, García

Márquez is recognized as a major practitioner of magical realism, a style in which incredible and marvelous events are mixed with realistic details and told with complete seriousness.

RESPONDING

1. *Personal Response* If this drowned man were found in your community, how would you react? What would *you* name him? Why?

2. *Literary Analysis* This story contains elements of *magical realism,* the mixing of real and fantastic, or unbelievable, qualities. Identify things about the drowned man that are realistic, as well as those that are fantastic.

3. *Multicultural Connection* Describe this culture's rituals surrounding death and burial based on evidence in the story. How do these rituals regarding death compare with those you know about?

LANGUAGE WORKSHOP

Comparative and Superlative Adjectives The drowned man in this story is described as the handsomest, tallest, and strongest man in the world. Most adjectives and adverbs of one syllable (and some of two syllables such as *happy*) form their *comparative* and *superlative* degrees by adding *-er* and *-est.* Adjectives of more than two syllables (and some of two syllables such as *eager*) form their comparative and superlative degrees by means of *more* and *most,* or *less* and *least.* Form the comparative or superlative of the following adjectives, as indicated.

Comparative: *virile, old, useless, helpless*
Superlative: *young, destitute, near, mistrustful*

WRITER'S PORTFOLIO

A *eulogy* is a speech or piece of writing in praise of a person or thing. Write a one- or two-paragraph eulogy to deliver at the drowned man's funeral. Review the story for ideas about the dead man's good qualities before you begin.

Wanted: a Town
Without a Crazy

O N THE TABLE crouched someone my age with a messy beard and untidy hair. Using the broom in his hand sometimes as a guitar, sometimes as a microphone, his singing and dancing had the people in the coffeehouse dying with laughter. My brother-in-law explained, "That's our town crazy."

He did a little act between verses. Moving the broom handle forward and back and making a series of sounds, then holding the handle in his mouth, undulating his hips and dancing, the loony shouted, "Dem dérula, dem dérula!" The crowd picked up the tempo, became exuberant and from time to time shouted, "Hurrah for Crazy Hilmi!"

For a moment, the name Hilmi stuck in my mind. Could this Hilmi be that *same* Hilmi? Even behind a tangled beard, the face resembled his. The squinty eyes, the forehead protruding like a fist, ears like the back of a shovel, even the arms, long like a bear's, were his.

"Look here!" I told my brother-in-law, "I probably know this crazy guy."

"You wouldn't know him," he replied. "This is your first visit to this town, so where could you have met him?"

"Is he from around here?"

"By God, I really don't know. I've lived here for three years and he was here when I came."

At this point the loony finished his concert, walked among the tables and after collecting fifty piastres from this one, a lira from that and a "Get outa here!" from others, he left, crestfallen. I had to find out, so I arose quickly. I not only knew this man, but knew him well, having worked with him seven years previously in the same district office. After handing in my resignation and leaving, I had heard no news of Hilmi Bey again. But the Hilmi Bey I knew was a very serious-minded, sober man. I fell in behind him and just as he "lifted" a handful of chestnuts from a bag at the grocery store, saying, "Hilmi Bey!" I caught him.

He threw me a guilty glance then turned to the grocer. After the grocer pressed eight or ten more chestnuts into his hand, he said to me, "He brings good luck. Whatever store he takes something from does very good business that day."

Hilmi Bey moved off from there in a hurry; he was almost running. I started running too. I intended to learn whether this was my Hilmi or some other Hilmi. He was running toward the gardens. They say that a lunatic's strength is superior but I managed to keep close behind him. When he speeded up, I ran even faster to try and catch up with him. Finally, however, I lost him in a wooded area and started calling, "Hilmi Bey! Hilmi Bey!"

No answer. Who knew which tree he was hiding behind! After calling a few times, I heard his crazy laugh close by. There he was. He appeared from behind a bush and grinned.

"Hilmi Bey," I repeated.

"Huh!"

Right, it was him . . . Yet inside I still had doubts. Approaching closer, I said, "See here, Hilmi Bey, what's the matter with you?"

"Hey," he replied, "I'm the town lunatic."

"Are you really crazy?"

He laughed again. "When you heard my laugh, you really thought at first that I was loony." He bounded over the bush to my side and placed before me things he took out of his pockets: candy, chestnuts, expensive cigarettes, nylon ribbons, a big chocolate bar, four large oranges, some first class glasses, then he unwound from around his waist, three meters of greatcoat cloth . . . Hilmi's pockets could completely stock a sundries shop.

"Tell me," I insisted, "when did you lose your mind?"

"Come on, lose what mind! Thank God there's nothing wrong with my head."

"Are you really all right?"

"Of course I'm all right. I understood when you resigned from the civil service, it was because there was nothing in it. If we paid the rent we couldn't eat or if we ate we couldn't pay the rent so I took a month's leave, rolled up my sleeves, and started searching for a town without a lunatic. Wearing a heavy overcoat, dark glasses and carrying a large suitcase, I went from town to town. Every place I went, my first task was to find out if the place had a crazy. If they told me there was, I immediately moved on. In twenty-five days I went through nearly a hundred towns, but each one had a loony. Though I struggled and economized, I was down to my last piastre when finally I came to this town. I sat down in a coffeehouse and, after drinking a tea, called the waiter: 'Brother, I wonder if this town happens to have a lunatic.' "

WHERE, SIR? Here? Eight years ago, we had a cuckoo but ever since he got run over by a truck, the whole town has missed him greatly. What a great guy he was, our cuckoo. He sang songs in the coffeehouses, wandered through the neighborhoods tying cloth on this door and that and played music when there was a wedding, using his nose for a pipe and his chest for a drum. It happened one Friday, Sefer the truckdriver ran him over. Believe me, we gave Crazy Davut a funeral that the town won't even give Mayor Riza Bey when he dies."

The waiter heaved a great sigh, "Ah, ah, after Davut left there was no joy in town. Where could you find another loony like him?"

"Well, after this conversation I left for home and my family. After packing a few things, I said to my wife, 'Well, tell me good-bye.'

"Surprised, she asked, 'Where are you going?'

" 'I'm going crazy. I found a town without a lunatic.'

" 'Sounds like you're already loony!'

" 'Would you listen to her! Of course I've gone mad!'

" 'Very well. So what will *we* do?'

" 'You'll be the wife and children of a loony.'

"So to enter the town with the honor and glory befitting a loony, I had to start with my clothes. First, I went and had an extra long, bright red topcoat made. I smeared it with mud to make it look old and ripped holes in it left and right. Then I went to the flea market and bought piles of worthless old money and bizarre medals. These I pinned here and there on the coat. Around my waist I bound a thick belt and hung a frying pan to one end on a cord. The frying pan was to be my guitar. I hung things all around my belt: a ladle, wooden spoons, a potty, an old electric clock, a women's umbrella, a cast-iron stove-lid. Clanging and rattling all over, I boarded the bus. The people on the minibus broke into laughter, so I stood up, and using my frying pan as a guitar, sang all the songs I knew. Laughing and clapping, they were so light-hearted it was indescribable. Some threw oranges for me to eat, others gave me candy, and some money. Not only that, the bus driver not only failed to ask me for the fare but invited me to his home: 'Where have you been all this time? Come every day, the food and drinks are on me.'

I GOT OFF THE BUS in town to the same laughter. As soon as I landed, eight or ten kids followed me. Their numbers grew to fifty, one hundred. You know kids! Everyone heard about me from them; that's how my fame spread through the town from the first day.

" 'Did you hear, huh? A cuckoo came to town.'

" 'Man, is he loony. Davut couldn't hold a candle to him!'

"God bless them! From that first day, I drank tea free, coffee too. I ate the best food in the restaurants free, and in addition, they gave me pocket money. It kills me to think that while these poor people were suffering all those years from the lack of a loony, I was putting numbers on documents, kowtowing when I entered the director's office, and wasting all that time for a mere thousand lira a month. If I'd known, wouldn't I have come to this town long before?

"The people are so happy at finding a loony that they don't even ask who or what he is or even where he comes from. Now when I enter the mayor's office, I don't say *selam* or hello and don't even bother to knock. I walk right in, lean against the mayor's arm then settle myself into an easy chair. After thrusting an expensive cigarette into my hand, he lights it with his own lighter and orders me a coffee. While I drink my coffee, he asks, 'You have any problems or anything, Hilmi?'

"I grin. So that means I have no difficulties. As I'm leaving the mayor puts his hand into his pocket and slips me a fiver. From there I go to the director of finance and from there to the doctor, then to the commissar. God bless them, they stick fives and tens into my pockets. Then I go out among tradesmen. Grinning, I enter the shops and tug at the owners' sleeves; they quickly open the drawer, saying, 'May your fortune be bountiful, God willing, Hilmi.' They take out a ten or a five and hand it to me. If my hand happens to brush a bolt of cloth, they immediately tell an apprentice to cut off a couple of meters for me. I wind the two meters around my waist and enter a second store. Then the health services. It's as if they're at my beck and call. Recently, I developed a pain, so I lay down in the middle of the road. In an instant, God, what a commotion broke loose!

PEOPLE RUSHED THERE crying, 'Our loony's fallen ill!' You won't believe it; not only the doctor but also the mayor came. People flocked around saying, 'Please, doctor, if you haven't made a diagnosis, let's get a taxi and take him to town. We have a pretty good loony and in return for our respect, God blesses our pocketbooks.'

"For a week I was treated like a king in the hospital. The mayor came to visit me three times, and the townspeople every day. What a departure I had from the hospital! It was as if one of the country's greats had had an important operation and was returning from the brink of death."

"Very well," I said, "what about your wife and children? How are they getting along?"

He grinned again: "I disappear for two or three days a month; the town is used to this. They say the poor fellow is having another fit of nervous agitation so he takes off in order not to bring any harm on the townspeople. As a matter of fact, I send some of the money and things I've collected by mail and others I forward to a place agreed upon with my wife. Thus my family gets along very well. One of my sons is attending the university and a daughter has finished high school. We bought a flat in an apartment building and my wife has had it furnished to suit her heart's desire."

"OK," I continued, "but when are you going to put an end to this lunacy?"

He grinned: "Are you nuts? There are lots of professional lunatics in this country. One of them would snatch my spot, so I can't leave town. What's more, I'm sort of used to this insanity."

As he leaped up and skipped away, he said, "Don't tell anyone. Even if you did, they wouldn't believe you!"

ABOUT **MUZAFFER IZGÜ**

Muzaffer Izgü (mə zä′fer iz gü′) was born in 1933 in Adana, Turkey. He works as a teacher and writes stories for adults and children, as well as stage and radio plays. Anthologized in several countries, his work is gaining international recognition.

RESPONDING

1. *Personal Response* What kind of treatment would Hilmi receive if he visited your community? Why?

2. *Literary Analysis* *Irony* occurs when events lead to an unexpected result. What is ironic in this story? Explain your answer.

3. *Multicultural Connection* Why do you think that in some cultures, prophets and other people who behave in an unconventional manner are revered or respected?

LANGUAGE WORKSHOP

Simile *Similes* are comparisons between things that are essentially unlike, using the words *like* or *as*. We read, for instance, that Hilmi's forehead protrudes "like a fist" and his ears are "like the back of a shovel." Make up a simile that describes each of the following by comparing it to something else using *like* or *as*: an old hat, two kittens, angry words, a brand new car.

WRITER'S PORTFOLIO

Imagine that another town had lost its crazy and had to advertise for a new one. Write a job description stating the necessary qualifications, as well as the benefits connected with the job.

A Vision Beyond
Time and Place

Wʜᴇɴ ᴍʏ ғᴀᴛʜᴇʀ ᴡᴀs ᴀ ʙᴏʏ, an old man used to come to (my grandfather) Mammedaty's house and pay his respects. He was a lean old man in braids and was impressive in his age and bearing. His name was Cheney, and he was an arrowmaker. Each morning, my father tells me, Cheney would paint his wrinkled face, go out, and pray aloud to the rising sun. In my mind I can see that man as if he were there now. I like to watch him as he makes his prayer. I know where he stands and where his voice goes on the rolling grasses and where the sun comes up on the land. There, at dawn, you can feel the silence. It is cold and clear and deep like water. It takes hold of you and will not let you go. (From *The Way to Rainy Mountain*. The University of New Mexico Press.)

I ᴏғᴛᴇɴ ᴛʜɪɴᴋ ᴏғ ᴏʟᴅ ᴍᴀɴ Cʜᴇɴᴇʏ, and of his daily devotion to the sun. He died before I was born, and I never knew where he came from or what of good and bad entered into his life. But I think I know who he was, essentially, and what his view of the world meant to him and to me. He was a man who saw very deeply into the distance, I believe, one whose vision extended far beyond the physical boundaries of his time and place. He perceived the wonder and meaning of Creation itself. In his mind's eye he could integrate all the realities and illusions of the earth and sky; they became for him profoundly intelligible and whole.

Once, in the first light, I stood where Cheney has stood, next to the house which my grandfather Mammedaty had built on a rise of land near Rainy Mountain Creek, and watched the sun come out of the black horizon of the world. It was an irresistible and awesome emergence, as waters gather to the flood, of weather and of light. I could not have been more sensitive to the cold nor than to the heat which came upon it. And I could not have *foreseen* the break of day. The shadows on the rolling plains became large and luminous in a moment, impalpable, then faceted, dark and distinct again as they were run through with splinters of light. And the sun itself, when it appeared, was pale and immense, original in the deepest sense of the word. It is no wonder, I thought, that an old man should pray to it. It is no wonder . . . and yet, of course, wonder is the principal part of such a vision. Cheney's prayer was an affirmation of his wonder and regard, a testament to the realization of a quest for vision.

This native vision, this gift of seeing truly, with wonder and delight, into the natural world, is informed by a certain attitude of reverence and self-respect. It is a matter of extrasensory as well as sensory perception, I believe. In addition to the eye, it involves the intelligence, the instinct, and the imagination. It is the perception not only of objects and forms but also of essences and ideals, as in this Chippewa song:

> *as my eyes*
> *search*
> *the prairie*
> *I feel the summer*
> *in the spring*

Even as the singer sees into the immediate landscape, he perceives a now and future dimension that is altogether remote, yet nonetheless real and inherent within it, a quality of evanescence and evolution, a state at once of being and of becoming. He beholds what is there; nothing of the scene is lost upon him. In the integrity of his vision he is wholly in possession of himself and of the world around him; he is quintessentially alive.

Most Indian people are able to see in these terms. Their view of the world is peculiarly native and distinct, and it determines who and what they are to a great extent. It is indeed the basis upon which they identify themselves as individuals and as a race. There is something of genetic significance in such a thing, perhaps, an element of being which resides in the blood and which is, after all, the very nucleus of the self. When old man Cheney looked into the sunrise, he saw as far into himself, I suspect, as he saw into the distance. He knew certainly of his existence and of his place in the scheme of things.

In contrast, most of us in this society are afflicted with a kind of cultural nearsightedness. Our eyes, it may be, have been trained too long upon the superficial, and *artificial*, aspects of our environment; we do not see beyond the buildings and billboards that seem at times to be the monuments of our civilization, and consequently we fail to see into the nature and meaning of our own humanity. Now, more than ever, we might do well to enter upon a vision quest of our own, that is, a quest after vision itself. And in this the Indian stands to lead by his example. For with respect to such things as a sense of heritage, of a vital continuity in terms of origin and of destiny, a profound investment of the mind and spirit in the oral traditions of literature, philosophy, and religion — those things, in short, which constitute his vision of the world — the Indian is perhaps the most culturally secure of all Americans.

As I see him, that old man, he walks very slowly to the place where he will make his prayer, and it is always the same place, a small mound where the grass is sparse and the hard red earth shows through. He limps a little, with age, but when he plants his feet he is tall and straight and hard. The bones are fine and prominent in his face and hands. And his face is painted. There are red and yellow bars under his eyes, neither bright nor sharply defined on the dark, furrowed skin, but soft and organic, the colors of sandstone and of pollen. His long braids are wrapped with blood-red cloth. His eyes are deep and open to the wide world. At sunrise, precisely, they catch fire and close, having seen. The low light descends upon him. And when he lifts his voice, it enters upon the silence and carries there, like the call of a bird.

ABOUT N. SCOTT MOMADAY

N(avarre) Scott Momaday (mä mä′dä) was born in Lawton, Oklahoma, in 1934. His father was Kiowa, his mother part Anglo and part Cherokee. In 1969 Momaday received a Pulitzer Prize for the novel *House Made of Dawn*. He has also published poetry collections and a set of reminiscences called *The Way to Rainy Mountain*, which is illustrated by his father. A central theme in all of his writing is the dilemma Native Americans face living within two opposing cultures — the traditional and the modern.

RESPONDING

1. *Personal Response* Do you agree with Momaday about today's "cultural nearsightedness"? For instance, do you think people are so concerned with superficial appearances that they fail to see the deep meaning in life? Explain.

2. *Literary Analysis* What *images,* or word pictures that appeal to the senses, does Momaday use to communicate the Native American vision?

3. *Multicultural Connection* Momaday says that "the Indian is perhaps the most culturally secure of all Americans." What do you think he means?

LANGUAGE WORKSHOP

Prefixes and Roots Knowing word parts can help you figure out meanings of words. For example, in "A Vision

Beyond Time and Place," Momaday says that the native vision is "a matter of extrasensory as well as sensory perception." If you know that *extra-* is a *prefix* meaning "beyond" and you associate *sensory* with *sense*, a *root* that refers to sight, touch, hearing, taste, and smell, you can probably figure out that *extrasensory* means "beyond the normal range of the senses."

Figure out the meanings of the italicized words below, which have the same prefix or root as *extrasensory*.

1. Cheney had *extraordinary* insight into the natural world.
2. When the narrator stands where Cheney stood, he feels very *sensitive* to heat and cold.
3. Momaday says that silence can give one a *sensation* of being cold.
4. The existence of *extraterrestrial* life is not discussed in this essay.

WRITER'S PORTFOLIO

Spend several minutes watching, imagining, or studying a picture of the sun rising or setting. Under the headings Physical Description and Personal Feelings, write your reactions to this scene. Include images that appeal to several of the senses.

Ashamanja Babu's Dog

On a visit to a friend in Hashimara, Ashamanja Babu had one of his long cherished wishes fulfilled. Ashamanja Babu lives in a room and a half, in a flat on Mohini Mohan Road in Bhowanipore. As a clerk in the registry department of Lajpat Rai Post Office, Ashamanja Babu is able to avoid the hassle of riding in trams and buses, because it takes him only seven minutes to walk to work. Not being one to sit and brood about what he might have been or done had Fate been kinder to him, Ashamanja Babu is quite content with his lot. Two Hindi films, a dozen packets of cigarettes a month, and fish twice a week—these are enough to keep him happy. But being a bachelor and lacking friends, he has often wished to possess a pet dog. Not a large dog like the Talukdar's Alsatian, two houses away to the east, but a medium-sized dog which would keep him company, wag its tail when he came home from work and show love and devotion by obeying his orders. One of Ashamanja Babu's pet conceits was that he would speak to his dog in English. "Stand up," "Sit down," "Shake hands"—how nice it would be if his dog obeyed such commands! Ashamanja Babu liked to believe that

Culture Notes

Bhowanipore (bu vä′nē pôr) suburb of Calcutta, in southeast West Bengal, India, p. 146

Bhutanese (büt′ən ēz′) resident of Bhutan, an Asian country on the northeast border of India, p. 147

dogs belonged to the English race. Yes, an English dog, and he would be its master. That would make him really happy.

On a cloudy day marked by a steady drizzle, Ashamanja Babu had gone to the market in Hashimara to buy some oranges. At one end of the market sat a Bhutanese by a stunted *kul* tree holding a cigarette between his thumb and forefinger. As their eyes met, the man smiled. Was he a beggar? His clothes made him seem like one, for there were five patches on his jacket and trousers. But the man didn't have a begging bowl. Instead, by his side was a shoe-box with a little pup sticking its head out from it.

"Good morning!" said the Bhutanese in English, his eyes reduced to slits in a smile. Ashamanja Babu was obliged to return the greeting.

"Buy dog? Dog buy? Very good dog." The man had taken the pup out of the box and put it down on the ground. "Very cheap. Very good. Happy dog."

The pup shook itself free of the raindrops, looked at Ashamanja Babu and wagged its two-inch tail. Nice pup.

Ashamanja Babu moved closer to the pup, crouched on the ground and put his hand towards it. The pup gave his ring finger a lick with his pink tongue. Nice, friendly pup.

"How much? What price?"

"Ten rupees."

A little haggling, and the price came down to seven-fifty. Ashamanja Babu paid the money, put the pup back in the shoe-box, closed the lid to save it from the drizzle, and turned homewards, forgetting all about the oranges.

Biren Babu, who worked in the Hashimara State Bank, didn't know of his friend's wish to own a dog. He was naturally surprised and a bit alarmed to see what the shoe-box contained. But when he heard the price, he heaved a sigh of relief. He said in a tone of mild reprimand, "Why come all the way to Hashimara to buy a mongrel? You could easily have bought one in Bhowanipore."

That was not true. Ashamanja Babu knew it. He had often seen mongrel pups in the streets in his neighbour-hood. None of them had ever wagged their tail at him or licked his fingers. Whatever Biren might say, this dog was something special. But the fact that the pup was a mongrel was something of a disappointment to Ashamanja Babu, and he said so. But Biren Babu's retort came sharp and quick. "But do you know what it means to keep a pedigree dog as a pet? The vet's fees alone would cost you half a month's salary. With this dog you have no worries. You don't even need a special diet for him. He'll eat what you eat. But don't give him fish. Fish is for cats; dogs have trouble with the bones."

Back in Calcutta, it occurred to Ashamanja Babu that he had to think of a name for the pup. He wanted to give it an English name, but the only one he could think of was Tom. Then, looking at the pup one day, it struck him that since it was brown in colour, Brownie would be a good name for it. A cousin of his had a camera of an English make called Brownie, so the name must be an English one. The moment he decided on the name and tried it on the pup, it jumped off a wicker stool and padded up to him wagging its tail. Ashamanja Babu said, "Sit down." Right away the pup sat on its haunches and opened its mouth in a tiny yawn. Ashamanja Babu had a fleeting vision of Brownie winning the first prize for cleverness in a dog show.

IT WAS LUCKY that his servant Bipin had also taken a fancy to the dog. While Ashamanja Babu was away at work, Bipin gladly took it upon himself to look after Brownie. Ashamanja Babu had warned Bipin against feeding the dog rubbish. "And see that he doesn't go out into the street. The car drivers these days seem to wear blinkers." But however much he might instruct his servant, his worry would linger until, after returning from work, he would be greeted by Brownie with his wagging tail.

The incident took place three months after returning from Hashimara. It was a Saturday, and the date was November the twenty-third. Ashamanja Babu had just got back from work and sat down on the old wooden chair — the only piece of furniture in the room apart from the bed and the wicker stool—when it suddenly gave under him and sent him sprawling on the floor. He was naturally hurt and, in fact, was led to wonder if, like the rickety leg of the chair, his right elbow was also out of commission, when an unexpected sound made him forget all about his pain.

The sound had come from the bed. It was the sound of laughter or, more accurately, a giggle, the source of which was undoubtedly Brownie, who sat on the bed and whose lips were still curled up.

If Ashamanja Babu's general knowledge had been wider, he would surely have known that dogs never laughed. And if he had a modicum of imagination, the incident would have robbed him of his sleep. In the absence of either, what Ashamanja Babu did was to sit down with the book *All About Dogs* which he had bought for two rupees from a second-hand book shop in Free School Street. He searched for an hour but found no mention in the book about laughing dogs.

And yet there wasn't the slightest doubt that Brownie had laughed. Not only that, he had laughed because there had been cause for laughter. Ashamanja Babu could clearly recall an incident from his own childhood. A doctor had come on a visit to their house in Chandernagore and had sat on a chair which had collapsed under him. Ashamanja Babu had burst out laughing, and had his ears twisted by his father for doing so.

Ashamanja Babu shut the book and looked at Brownie. As their eyes met, Brownie put his front paws on the pillow and wagged his tail, which had grown an inch and a half longer in three months. There was no trace of a smile on his face now. Why should there be? To laugh without reason was a sign of madness. Ashamanja Babu felt relieved that Brownie was not a mad dog.

On two more occasions within a week of this incident, Brownie had occasion to laugh. The first took place at night, at nine-thirty. Ashamanja Babu had just spread a white sheet on the floor for Brownie to sleep on when a cockroach came fluttering into the room and settled on the wall. Ashamanja Babu picked up a slipper and flung it at the insect. But it missed its target, landed on a hanging mirror, and sent it crashing to the floor. This time Brownie's laughter more than compensated for the loss of his mirror.

The second time it was not laughter, but a brief snicker. Ashamanja Babu was puzzled, because nothing had really happened. So why the snicker? The servant Bipin provided the answer. He came into the room, glanced at his master and said, smiling, "There's shaving-soap right by your ears, sir." With his mirror broken, Ashamanja Babu had to use one of the window panes for shaving. He now felt with his fingers and found that Bipin was right.

That Brownie should laugh even when the reason was so trifling surprised Ashamanja Babu a great deal. Sitting at his desk in the post office he found his thoughts turning again and again to the smile on Brownie's face and the sound of the snicker. *All About Dogs* may say nothing about a dog's laughter, but if he could get hold of something like an encyclopaedia of dogs, there was sure to be a mention of laughter in it.

When four book shops in Bhowanipore—and all the ones in the New Market—failed to produce such an encyclopaedia, Ashamanja Babu wondered whether he should call on Mr. Rajani Chatterji. The retired professor lived not far from his house on the same street. Ashamanja Babu didn't know what subject Rajani Chatterji had taught, but he had seen through the window of his house many fat books in a book-case in what appeared to be the professor's study.

On a Sunday morning, Ashamanja Babu invoked the name of the goddess Durga for good luck and turned up at Professor Chatterji's. He had seen him several times from a distance, and had no idea he had such thick eyebrows and a voice so grating. But since the professor hadn't turned him away, Ashamanja Babu took courage in occupying a seat on a sofa across the room from him. Then he gave a short cough and waited. Professor Chatterji

Culture Notes

Durga goddess and renowned slayer of demons, p.150

ganja, charas, hashish potent preparations of cannabis with narcotic effects, p.151

King of Bombardia well-known Bengali nonsense verse, p.152

put aside the newspaper and turned his attention to the visitor.

"Your face seems familiar."

"I live close by."

"I see. Well?"

"I have seen a dog in your house; that is why. . ."

"So what? We have two dogs, not one."

"I see, I have one too."

"Are you employed to count the number of dogs in the city?"

Being a simple man, Ashamanja Babu missed the sarcasm in the question. He said, "I have come to ask if you have something I've been looking for."

"What is it?"

"I wonder if you have a dog encyclopaedia."

"No, I don't. Why do you need one?"

"You see, my dog laughs. So I wanted to find out if it was natural for dogs to laugh. Do your dogs laugh?"

Throughout the time it took the wall clock in the room to strike eight, Professor Chatterji kept looking at Ashamanja Babu. Then he asked: "Does your dog laugh at night?"

"Well, yes—even at night."

"And what are your preferences in drugs? Only *ganja* can't produce such symptoms. Perhaps you take charas and hashish as well?"

Ashamanja Babu meekly answered that his only vice was smoking—and even that he had had to reduce from four packets a week to three ever since the arrival of his dog.

"And yet you say your dog laughs?"

"I have seen and heard him laugh, with my own eyes and ears."

"Listen." Professor Chatterji took off his spectacles, cleaned them with his handkerchief, put them on again and fixed Ashamanja Babu with a hard stare. Then he declaimed in the tones of a classroom lecture. "I am amazed at your ignorance concerning a fundamental fact of nature. Of all the creatures created by God, only the human species is capable of laughter. This is one of the prime differences between *homo sapiens* and other creatures. Don't ask me why it should be so, because I do not know. I have heard that a marine species called the dolphin has a sense of humour. Dolphins may be the single exception. Apart from them there are none. It is not clearly understood why human beings should laugh. Great philosophers have racked their brains to find out why; but have not succeeded. Do you understand?"

Ashamanja Babu understood, and he also understood that it was time for him to take his leave because the professor had once again taken up his newspaper.

DOCTOR SUKHOMOY BHOWMICK — some called him Doctor Bhow-wowmick — was a well-known vet. In the belief that if ordinary people didn't listen to him a vet might, Ashamanja Babu made an appointment with him on the phone and turned up at his residence on Gokhale Road. Brownie had laughed seventeen times during the last four months. One thing Ashamanja Babu had noticed is that Brownie didn't laugh at funny remarks; only at funny incidents. Ashamanja Babu had recited the *King of Bombardia* to Brownie, and it had produced no effect on him. And yet when a potato from a curry slipped from Ashamanja Babu's fingers and landed on a plate of curd, Brownie had almost choked with laughter. Professor Chatterji had said that none of God's creatures laughed except human beings, and yet here was proof that the learned gentleman was wrong.

So Ashamanja Babu went to the vet in spite of knowing that the latter charged twenty rupees per visit.

Even before he had heard of the dog's unique trait, its very appearance had the vet's eyebrows shooting up. "I've seen mongrels, but never one like this."

The vet lifted the dog and placed him on the table. Brownie sniffed at the brass paperweight at his feet.

"What do you feed him?"

"He eats what I eat, sir. He has no pedigree, you see. . ."

Doctor Bhowmick frowned. He was observing the dog with great interest. "We can tell a pedigree dog when we see one. But sometimes we are not so sure. This one, for instance. I should hesitate to call him a mongrel. I suggest that you stop feeding him rice and *dal*. I'll make a diet chart for him."

Ashamanja Babu now made an attempt to come out with the real reason for his visit. "I—er, my dog has a speciality—which is why I have brought him to you."

"Speciality?"

"The dog laughs."

"Laughs—?"

"Yes. Laughs, like you and me."

"You don't say! Well, can you make him laugh now so I can see?"

And now Ashamanja Babu was in a quandary. As it is he was a very shy person, so he was quite unable to make faces at Brownie to make him laugh, nor was it likely that something funny should happen here at this very moment. So Ashamanja Babu had to tell the doctor that Brownie didn't laugh when asked to, but only when he saw something funny happening.

After this Doctor Bhowmick didn't have much time left for Ashamanja Babu. He said, "Your dog looks distinctive enough; don't try to make him more so by claiming that he laughs. I can tell you from my twenty-two years' experience that dogs cry, dogs feel afraid, dogs show anger, hatred, distrust and jealousy. Dogs even dream, but dogs don't laugh."

After this encounter, Ashamanja Babu decided that he would never tell anyone about Brownie's laughter. When immediate proof was not forthcoming, to talk about it was to court embarrassment. What did it matter if others never knew? He himself knew, Brownie was his own dog, his own property. Why drag outsiders into their own private world?

But man proposes, God disposes. Even Brownie's laughter was one day revealed to an outsider.

For some time now, Ashamanja Babu had developed the habit of taking Brownie for a walk in the afternoon near the Victoria Memorial. One April day, in the middle of their walk, a big storm came up suddenly. Ashamanja Babu glanced at the sky and decided that it wasn't safe to try to get back home as it might start raining any moment. So he ran with Brownie and took shelter below the marble arch with the black equestrian statue on it.

Meanwhile, huge drops of rain had started to fall and people were running this way and that for shelter. A stout man in white bush shirt and trousers, twenty paces away from the arch, opened his umbrella and held it over his head when a sudden strong gust of wind turned the umbrella inside out with a loud snap.

To tell the truth, Ashamanja Babu was himself about to burst out laughing, but Brownie beat him by a neck with a canine guffaw which rose above the sound of the storm and reached the ear of the hapless gentleman. He stopped trying to bring the umbrella back to its original shape and stared at Brownie in utter amazement. Brownie was now quite helpless with laughter, Ashamanja Babu had given up trying to suppress it by clapping his hand over the dog's mouth.

Culture Notes

Bengali (ben gô′lē) resident of the Bengal region, now West Bengal and Bangladesh, p.154

Gujarati (gŭj ə rät′ē) resident of a state in western India, p.154

Parsi (pär′sē) a Zoroastrian descended from Persian refugees, p. 154

The dumbfounded gentleman now walked over to Ashamanja Babu as if he had seen a ghost. Brownie's paroxysm was now subsiding, but it was still enough to make the gentleman's eyes pop out of his head.

"A laughing dog!"

"Yes, a laughing dog," said Ashamanja Babu.

"But how extraordinary!"

Ashamanja Babu could make out that the man was not a Bengali. Perhaps he was a Gujarati or a Parsi. Ashamanja Babu braced himself to answer in English the questions he knew he would soon be bombarded with.

The rain had turned into a heavy shower. The gentleman took shelter alongside Ashamanja Babu, and in ten minutes had found out all there was to know about Brownie. He also took Ashamanja Babu's address. He said his name was Piloo Pochkanwalla, that he knew a lot about dogs and wrote about them occasionally, and that his experience today had surpassed everything that had ever happened to him, or was likely to happen in the future. He felt something had to be done about it, since Ashamanja Babu himself was obviously unaware of what a priceless treasure he owned.

IT WOULDN'T BE WRONG to say that Brownie was responsible for Mr. Pochkanwalla being knocked down by a minibus while crossing Chowringhee Road soon after the rain had stopped — it was the thought of the laughing dog running through his head which made him a little unmindful of the traffic. After spending two and a half months in hospital, Pochkanwalla had gone off to Naini Tal for a change. He had come back to Calcutta after a month in the hills, and the same evening had described the incident of the laughing dog to his friends Mr. Balaporia and Mr. Biswas at the Bengal Club. Within half an hour, the story had reached the ears of twenty-seven other members and three bearers of the Club. By next morning, the incident was known to a least a thousand citizens of Calcutta.

Brownie hadn't laughed once during these three and a half months. One good reason was that he had seen no funny incidents. Ashamanja Babu didn't see it as cause for alarm; it had never crossed his mind to cash in on Brownie's unique gift. He was happy with the way Brownie had filled a yawning gap in his life, and felt more drawn to him than he had to any human being.

Among those who got the news of the laughing dog was an executive in the office of the *Statesman*. He sent for the reporter Rajat Chowdhury and suggested that he should interview Ashamanja Babu.

Ashamanja Babu was greatly surprised that a reporter should think of calling on him. It was when Rajat Chowdhury mentioned Pochkanwalla that the reason for the visit became clear. Ashamanja Babu asked the reporter into his bedroom. The wooden chair had been fitted with a new leg, and Ashamanja Babu offered it to the reporter while he himself sat on the bed. Brownie had been observing a line of ants crawling up the wall; he now jumped up on the bed and sat beside Ashamanja Babu.

Rajat Chowdhury was about to press the switch on his recorder when it suddenly occurred to Ashamanja Babu that a word of warning was needed. "By the way, sir, my dog used to laugh quite frequently, but in the last few months he hasn't laughed at all. So you may be disappointed if you are expecting to see him laugh."

Like many a young, energetic reporter, Rajat Chowdhury exuded a cheerful confidence in the presence of a good story. Although he was slightly disappointed he was careful not to show it. He said, "That's all right. I just want to get some details from you. To start with, his name. What do you call your dog?"

Ashamanja Babu bent down to reach closer to the mike. "Brownie."

"Brownie..." The watchful eye of the reporter had noted that the dog had wagged his tail at the mention of his name. "How old is he?"

"A year and a month."

"Where did you f-f-find the dog?"

This had happened before. The impediment Rajat Chowdhury suffered often showed itself in the middle of interviews, causing him no end of embarrassment. Here too the same thing might have happened but for the fact that the stammer was unexpectedly helpful in drawing out Brownie's unique trait. Thus Rajat Chowdhury was the second outsider after Pochkanwalla to see with his own eyes a dog laughing like a human being.

THE MORNING OF THE FOLLOWING Sunday, sitting in his air-conditioned room in the Grand Hotel, Mr. William P. Moody of Cincinnati, USA, read in the papers about the laughing dog and at once asked the hotel operator to put him through to Mr. Nandy of the Indian Tourist Bureau. That Mr. Nandy knew his way about the city had been made abundantly clear in the last couple of days when Mr. Moody had occasion to use his services. The *Statesman* had printed the name and address of the owner of the laughing dog. Mr. Moody was very anxious to meet this character.

Ashamanja Babu didn't read the *Statesman*. Besides, Rajat Chowdhury hadn't told him when the interview would come out, or he might have bought a copy. It was in the fish market that his neighbor Kalikrishna Dutt told him about it.

"You're a fine man," said Mr. Dutt. "You've been guarding such a treasure in your house for over a year, and you haven't breathed a word to anybody about it? I must drop in at your place some time this evening and say hello to your dog."

Ashamanja Babu's heart sank. He could see there was trouble ahead. There were many more like Mr. Dutt in and around his neighbourhood who read the *Statesman* and who would want "to drop in and say hello" to his dog. A most unnerving prospect.

Ashamanja Babu made up his mind. He decided to spend the day away from home. Taking Brownie with him, he took a taxi for the first time, went straight to the Ballygunge station and boarded a train to Port Canning. Half-way through, the train pulled up at a station called Palsit. Ashamanja Babu liked the look of the place and got off. He spent the whole day in quiet bamboo groves and mango orchards and felt greatly refreshed. Brownie, too, seemed to enjoy himself. The gentle smile that played around his lips was something Ashamanja Babu had never noticed before. This was a benign smile, a smile of peace and contentment, a smile of inner happiness. Ashamanja Babu had read somewhere that a year in the life of a dog equalled seven years in the life of a human being. And yet he could scarcely imagine such tranquil behaviour in such sylvan surroundings from a seven-year-old human child.

It was past seven in the evening when Ashamanja Babu got back home. He asked Bipin if anyone had called. Bipin said he had to open the door to callers at least forty times. Ashamanja Babu couldn't help congratulating himself on his foresight. He had just taken off his shoes and asked Bipin for a cup of tea when there was a knock on the front door. "Oh, hell!" swore Ashamanja Babu. He went to the door and opened it, and found himself facing a foreigner. "Wrong number" he was at the point of saying, when he caught sight of a young Bengali standing behind the foreigner. "Whom do you want?"

"You," said Shyamol Nandy of the Indian Tourist Bureau, "in case the dog standing behind you belongs to you. He certainly looks like the one described in the papers today. May we come in?"

Ashamanja Babu was obliged to ask them into his bedroom. The foreigner sat in the chair, Mr. Nandy on the wicker stool, and Ashamanja Babu on his bed. Brownie, who seemed a bit ill at ease, chose to stay outside the threshold; probably because he had never seen two strangers in the room before.

"Brownie! Brownie! Brownie!" The foreigner had leaned forward towards the dog and called him repeatedly by name to entice him into the room. Brownie, who didn't move, had his eyes fixed on the stranger.

Who were these people? The question had naturally occurred to Ashamanja Babu when Mr. Nandy provided the answer. The foreigner was a wealthy and distinguished citizen of the United States whose main purpose in coming to India was to look for old Rolls-Royce cars.

The American had now got off the chair and, sitting on his haunches, was making faces at the dog.

After three minutes of abortive clowning, the man gave up, turned to Ashamanja Babu and said, "Is he sick?"

Ashamanja Babu shook his head.

"Does he really laugh?" asked the American.

In case Ashamanja Babu was unable to follow the American's speech, Mr. Nandy translated it for him.

"Brownie laughs," said Ashamanja Babu, "but only when he feels amused."

A TINGE OF RED spread over the American's face when Nandy translated Ashamanja Babu's answer to him. Next, he let it be known that he wasn't willing to squander any money on the dog unless he had proof that the dog really laughed. He refused to be saddled with something which might later cause embarrassment. He further let it be known that in his house he had precious objects from China to Peru, and that he had a parrot which spoke only Latin. "I have brought my chequebook with me to pay for the laughing dog, but only if it laughed."

The American now pulled out a blue chequebook from his pocket to prove his statement. Ashamanja Babu glanced at it out of the corner of his eyes. CitiBank of New York, it said on the cover.

"You would be walking on air," said Mr. Nandy temptingly. "If you know a way to make the dog laugh, then out with it. This gentleman is ready to pay up to 20,000 dollars. That's two lakhs of rupees."

The Bible says that God created the universe in six days. A human being, using his imagination, can do the same thing in six seconds. The image that Mr. Nandy's words conjured up in Ashamanja Babu's mind was of himself in a spacious air-conditioned office, sitting in a swivel chair with his legs up on the table, with the heady smell of *hasu-no-hana* wafting in through the window. But the image vanished like a pricked balloon at a sudden sound.

Brownie was laughing.

This was like no laugh he had ever laughed before.

"But he *is* laughing!"

Mr. Moody had gone down on his knees, tense with excitement, watching the extraordinary spectacle. The chequebook came out again and, along with that, his gold Parker pen.

Brownie was still laughing. Ashamanja Babu was puzzled because he couldn't make out the reason for the laughter. Nobody had stammered, nobody had stumbled, nobody's umbrella had turned inside out, and no mirror on the wall had been hit with a slipper. Why then was Brownie laughing?

"You're very lucky," commented Mr. Nandy. "I think I ought to get a percentage on the sale—wouldn't you say so?"

Mr. Moody had now risen from the floor and sat down on the chair. He said, "Ask him how he spells his name."

Although Mr. Nandy had relayed the question in Bengali, Ashamanja Babu didn't answer, because he had just seen the light, and the light filled his heart with a great sense of wonder. Instead of spelling his name, he said, "Please tell the foreign gentleman that if he only knew why the dog was laughing, he wouldn't have opened his chequebook."

"Why don't you tell me?" Mr. Nandy snapped in a dry voice. He certainly didn't like the way events were shaping. If the mission failed, he knew the American's wrath would fall on him.

Brownie had at last stopped laughing. Ashamanja Babu lifted him up on his lap, wiped his tears and said, "My dog's laughing because the gentleman thinks money can buy everything."

"I see," said Mr. Nandy. "So your dog's a philosopher, is he?"

"Yes, sir."

"That means you won't sell him?"

"No, sir."

To Mr. Moody, Shyamol Nandy only said that the owner had no intention of selling the dog. Mr. Moody put the chequebook back in his pocket, slapped the dust off his knees and, on his way out of the room, said with a shake of his head, "The guy must be crazy."

When the sound of the American car had faded away, Ashamanja Babu looked into Brownie's eyes and said, "I was right about why you laughed, wasn't I?"

Brownie chuckled in assent.

ABOUT SATYAJIT RAY

Satyajit Ray (sôt yäj/ət rā; 1921–1992), India's most acclaimed filmmaker, was noted for his emphasis on emotion over action. A lifelong resident of Calcutta, he produced or directed over thirty films, and in 1992 received an honorary Academy Award as well as India's highest civilian honor. In 1961, he began writing and illustrating stories for a revival of the monthly children's magazine *Sandesh*, which his grandfather had launched in 1914.

RESPONDING

1. *Personal Response* Would you like to have a pet that behaves as Brownie does? Why or why not?

2. *Literary Analysis* How does the fact that a *character* like Ashamanja Babu owns a dog as unusual as Brownie contribute to the humor in this story?

3. *Multicultural Connection* Speculate on why Ray might have portrayed Mr. Moody as an American rather than an Indian. Given Moody's personality and mission, do you consider him a cultural stereotype? Why or why not?

LANGUAGE WORKSHOP

Possessives and Plurals *Possessive nouns* are usually formed by adding an apostrophe and an *s* to the end of a word. *Plural nouns* are usually formed by adding only an *s*. *Possessive pronouns* such as *his, hers, theirs, ours,* and *its* have no apostrophe. Under the two heads, Possessives and Plurals, write the appropriate words from the following sentences.
1. "One of Ashamanja Babu's pet conceits was that he would speak to his dog in English."
2. "Even before he had heard of the dog's unique trait, its very appearance had the vet's eyebrows shooting up."
3. "Brownie's paroxysm was now subsiding, but it was still enough to make the gentleman's eyes pop out of his head."

WRITER'S PORTFOLIO

Imagine what Brownie is thinking as Mr. Moody negotiates with Ashamanja Babu for his purchase. Draw a cartoon of the scene and write Brownie's thoughts in a bubble over his head.

Telephone Conversation

Wole Soyinka

The price seemed reasonable, location
Indifferent. The landlady swore she lived
Off premises. Nothing remained
But self-confession. "Madam," I warned,
"I hate a wasted journey — I am African."
Silence. Silenced transmission of
Pressurised good-breeding. Voice, when it came,
Lipstick-coated, long gold-rolled
Cigarette-holder pipped. Caught I was, foully.

"HOW DARK?" . . . I had not misheard. . . ."ARE YOU
    LIGHT
"OR VERY DARK?" Button B. Button A. Stench
Of rancid breath of public hide-and-speak.
Red booth. Red pillar-box. Red double-tiered
Omnibus squelching tar. It *was* real! Shamed
By ill-mannered silence, surrender
Pushed dumbfoundment to beg simplification.
Considerate she was, varying the emphasis —

"ARE YOU DARK? OR VERY LIGHT?" Revelation came.
"You mean — like plain or milk chocolate?"

Words to Know

pillar-box mailbox, p.162

Omnibus a double-decker bus, p.162

sepia dark brown, p.163

spectroscopic . . . fancy The poet compares the landlady's imagination, which runs wild trying to visualize the speaker's color, to a spectroscope, an instrument that measures a variety, or spectrum, of colors. p.163

Her assent was clinical, crushing in its light
Impersonality. Rapidly, wave-length adjusted,
I chose, "West African sepia"—and as an after-
    thought,
"Down in my passport." Silence for spectroscopic
Flight of fancy, till truthfulness clanged her accent
Hard on the mouthpiece "WHAT'S THAT?" conceding,
"DON'T KNOW WHAT THAT IS." "Like brunette."

"THAT'S DARK, ISN'T IT?" "Not altogether.
Facially, I am brunette, but madam, you should see
The rest of me. Palm of my hand, soles of my feet
Are a peroxide blonde. Friction, caused—
Foolishly, madam—by sitting down, has turned
My bottom raven black—One moment
    madam!"—sensing
Her receiver rearing on the thunder clap
About my ears—"Madam," I pleaded, "wouldn't
    you rather
See for yourself?"

La Migra

Pat Mora

1
Let's play *La Migra*
I'll be the Border Patrol.
You be the Mexican maid.
I get the badge and sunglasses.
You can hide and run,
but you can't get away
because I have a jeep.
I can take you wherever
I want, but don't ask
questions because
I don't speak Spanish.

Culture Notes

La Migra term used along
the Mexican American
border for border patrol
agents, p.163

**Agua dulce brota aquí,
aquí, aquí** Sweet water
gushes here, here, here.
p.164

I can touch you wherever
I want but don't complain
too much because I've got
boots and kick—if I have to,
and I have handcuffs.
Oh, and a gun.
Get ready, get set, run.

2
Let's play *La Migra*
You be the Border Patrol.
I'll be the Mexican woman.
Your jeep has a flat,
and you have been spotted
by the sun.
All you have is heavy: hat,
glasses, badge, shoes, gun.
I know this desert,
where to rest,
where to drink.
Oh, I am not alone.
You hear us singing
and laughing with the wind,
Agua dulce brota aquí,
aquí, aquí, but since you
can't speak Spanish
you do not understand.
Get ready.

ABOUT **WOLE SOYINKA**

Wole Soyinka (wō′lā swoi ing′kə) was born in Isara, Nigeria, in 1934. He has been a playwright, poet, novelist, professor, and director of his own theater group. Soyinka was imprisoned from 1967 to 1969, but never charged with a crime, during Nigeria's civil war. The notes and poems he was able to smuggle out let his friends and supporters know he was still alive.

He received Amnesty International's Prisoner of Conscience Prize, as well as the 1986 Nobel Prize for Literature.

ABOUT **PAT MORA**

Pat(ricia) Mora, born in 1942, lived in El Paso, Texas, for most of her life before moving to Ohio in 1989. In her work as a university administrator and part-time teacher, she has been active in efforts to conserve Mexican American culture. Mora has published children's books and a collection of essays as well as several poetry collections.

RESPONDING

1. *Personal Response* Which poem affected you more? Why?

2. *Literary Analysis* What words would you use to describe the *speaker* of each poem? Explain your choices.

3. *Multicultural Connection* What two cultures are clashing in each of these poems, and how are the clashes resolved, if at all?

LANGUAGE WORKSHOP

Proper Nouns and Adjectives *Proper nouns* name a particular person (Pat Mora), place (Mexico), or thing (Border Patrol). Proper adjectives are based on proper nouns (Mexican maid). Find six more proper nouns or adjectives in Mora's and Soyinka's poems or biographies.

WRITER'S PORTFOLIO

Both poets write about dealing with stereotypes. More than likely you yourself have been "pegged" as a type— an athlete, a brain, a comic, a loner, or a "typical teenager." Write a brief phone conversation in which you confront such a stereotype and set someone straight about what and who you really are.

Nobel Lecture — 1993

ONCE UPON A TIME there was an old woman. Blind but wise." Or was it an old man? A guru, perhaps. Or a griot soothing restless children. I have heard this story, or one exactly like it, in the lore of several cultures.

"Once upon a time there was an old woman. Blind. Wise."

In the version I know the woman is the daughter of slaves, black, American, and lives alone in a small house outside of town. Her reputation for wisdom is without peer and without question. Among her people she is both the law and its transgression. The honor she is paid and the awe in which she is held reach beyond her neighborhood to places far away; to the city where the intelligence of rural prophets is the source of much amusement.

One day the woman is visited by some young people who seem to be bent on disproving her clairvoyance and showing her up for the fraud they believe she is. Their plan is simple: they enter her house and ask the one question the answer to which rides solely on her difference from them, a difference they regard as a profound disability: her blindness. They stand before her, and one of them says, "Old woman, I hold in my hand a bird. Tell me whether it is living or dead."

She does not answer, and the question is repeated. "Is the bird I am holding living or dead?"

Still she doesn't answer. She is blind and cannot see her visitors, let alone what is in their hands. She does not know their color, gender or homeland. She only knows their motive.

The old woman's silence is so long, the young people have trouble holding their laughter.

Finally she speaks and her voice is soft but stern. "I don't know," she says. "I don't know whether the bird you are holding is dead or alive, but what I do know is that it is in your hands. It is in your hands."

Her answer can be taken to mean: if it is dead, you have either found it that way or you have killed it. If it is alive, you can still kill it. Whether it is to stay alive, it is your decision. Whatever the case, it is your responsibility.

For parading their power and her helplessness, the young visitors are reprimanded, told they are responsible not only for the act of mockery but also for the small bundle of life sacrificed to achieve its aims. The blind woman shifts attention away from assertions of power to the instrument through which that power is exercised.

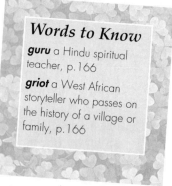

Words to Know

guru a Hindu spiritual teacher, p. 166

griot a West African storyteller who passes on the history of a village or family, p. 166

Speculation on what (other than its own frail body) that bird-in-the-hand might signify has always been attractive to me, but especially so now, thinking as I have been, about the work I do that has brought me to this company. So I choose to read the bird as language and the woman as a practiced writer. She is worried about how the language she dreams in, given to her at birth, is handled, put into service, even withheld from her for certain nefarious purposes. Being a writer she thinks of language partly as a system, partly as a living thing over which one has control, but mostly as agency—as an act with consequences. So the question the children put to her: "Is it living or dead?" is not unreal because she thinks of language as susceptible to death, erasure; certainly imperiled and salvageable only by an effort of the will. She believes that if the bird in the hands of her visitors is dead the custodians are responsible for the corpse. For her a dead language is not only one no longer spoken or written, it is unyielding language content to admire its own paralysis. Like statist language, censored and censoring. Ruthless in its policing duties, it has no desire or purpose other than maintaining the free range of its own narcotic narcissism, its own exclusivity and dominance. However, moribund, it is not without effect for it actively thwarts the intellect, stalls conscience, suppresses human potential. Unreceptive to interrogation, it cannot form or tolerate new ideas, shape other thoughts, tell another story, fill baffling silences. Official language smitheried to sanction ignorance and preserve privilege is a suit of armor, polished to shocking glitter, a husk from which the knight departed long ago. Yet there it is: dumb, predatory, sentimental. Exciting reverence in schoolchildren, providing shelter for despots, summoning false memories of stability, harmony among the public.

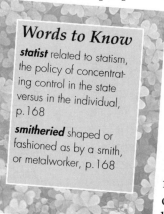

Words to Know

statist related to statism, the policy of concentrating control in the state versus in the individual, p. 168

smitheried shaped or fashioned as by a smith, or metalworker, p. 168

She is convinced that when language dies, out of carelessness, disuse, and absence of esteem, indifference or killed by fiat, not only she herself, but all users and makers are accountable for its demise. In her country children have bitten their tongues off and use bullets instead to iterate the voice of speechlessness, of disabled and disabling language, of language adults have abandoned altogether as a device for grappling with meaning, providing guidance, or expressing love. But she knows tongue-suicide is not only the choice of children. It is common among the infantile heads of state and power merchants whose evacuated language leaves them with no access to what is left of their human instincts for they speak only to those who obey, or in order to force obedience.

The systematic looting of language can be recognized by the tendency of its users to forgo its nuanced, complex, midwifery properties for menace and subjugation. Oppressive language does more than represent violence; it is violence; does more than represent the limits of knowledge; it limits knowledge. Whether it is obscuring state language or the faux-language of mindless media; whether it is the proud but calcified language of the academy or the commodity driven language of science; whether it is the malign language of law-without-ethics, or language designed for the estrangement of minorities, hiding its racist plunder in its literary cheek—it must be rejected, altered and exposed. It is the language that drinks blood, laps vulnerabilities, tucks its fascist boots under crinolines of respectability and patriotism as it moves relentlessly toward the bottom line and the bottomed-out mind. Sexist language, racist language, theistic language—all are typical of the policing languages of mastery, and cannot, do not permit new knowledge or encourage the mutual exchange of ideas.

The old woman is keenly aware that no intellectual mercenary, nor insatiable dictator, no paid-for politician or demagogue, no counterfeit journalist would be persuaded by her thoughts. There is and will be rousing language to keep citizens armed and arming; slaughtered and slaughtering in the malls, courthouses, post offices, playgrounds, bedrooms and boulevards; stirring, memorializing language to mask the pity and waste of needless death. There will be more diplomatic language to countenance rape, torture, assassination. There is and will be more seductive, mutant language designed to throttle women, to pack their throats like pâté-producing geese with their own unsayable, transgressive words; there will be more of the language of surveillance disguised as research; of politics and history calculated to render the suffering of millions mute; language glamorized to thrill the dissatisfied and bereft into assaulting their neighbors; arrogant pseudo-empirical language crafted to lock creative people into cages of inferiority and hopelessness.

Culture Notes

fascist of the governmental system led by a dictator, enforcing oppression and regimenting the economy, p.169

bottom line business lingo for profit, p.169

theistic concerning belief in God, p.169

pack their throats like pâté-producing geese Geese are force-fed so that their livers reach enormous size, to be used in pâté de foie gras, a rich spread savored by gourmets. p.169

Underneath the eloquence, the glamour, the scholarly associations, however, stirring or seductive, the heart of such language is languishing, or perhaps not beating at all — if the bird is already dead.

She has thought about what could have been the intellectual history of any discipline if it had not insisted upon, or been forced into, the waste of time and life that rationalizations for and representations of dominance required — lethal discourses of exclusion blocking access to cognition for both the excluder and the excluded.

The conventional wisdom of the Tower of Babel story is that the collapse was a misfortune. That it was the distraction, or weight of many languages that precipitated the tower's failed architecture. That one monolithic language would have expedited the building and heaven would have been reached. Whose heaven, she wonders? And what kind? Perhaps the achievement of Paradise was premature, a little hasty if no one could take the time to understand other languages, other views, other narratives. Had they, the heaven they imagined might have been found at their feet. Complicated, demanding yes, but a view of heaven as life; not heaven as post-life.

She would not want to leave her young visitors with the impression that language should be forced to stay alive merely to be. The vitality of language lies in its ability to limn the actual, imagined and possible lives of its speakers, readers, writers. Although its poise is sometimes in displacing experience it is not a substitute for it. It arcs toward the place where meaning may lie. When a President of the United States thought about the graveyard his country had become, and said "The world will little note nor long remember what we say here. But it will never forget what they did here." His simple words are exhilarating in their life-sustaining properties because they refused to encapsulate the reality of 600,000 dead men in a cata-

Culture Notes

Tower of Babel a biblical reference (Genesis 11:4-9) to the place where an original language became separated into several "tongues" or languages, p. 170

When a President . . . did here a reference to Lincoln's Gettysburg Address, p. 170

clysmic race war. Refusing to monumentalize, disdaining the "final word," the precise "summing up," acknowledging their "poor power to add or detract," his words signal deference to the uncapturability of the life it mourns. It is the deference that moves her, that recognition that language can never live up to life once and for all. Nor should it. Language can never "pin down" slavery, genocide, war. Nor should it yearn for the arrogance to be able to do so. Its force, its felicity is in its reach toward the ineffable.

Be it grand or slender, burrowing, blasting, or refusing to sanctify; whether it laughs out loud or is a cry without an alphabet, the choice word, the chosen silence, unmolested language surges toward knowledge, not its destruction. But who does not know of literature banned because it is interrogative; discredited because it is critical; erased because alternate? And how many are outraged by the thought of a self-ravaged tongue?

Word-work is sublime, she thinks, because it is generative; it makes meaning that secures our difference, our human difference—the way in which we are like no other life.

We die. That may be the meaning of life. But we do language. That may be the measure of our lives.

"Once upon a time, . . ." visitors ask an old woman a question. Who are they, these children? What did they make of that encounter? What did they hear in those final words: "The bird is in your hands"? A sentence that gestures toward possibility or one that drops a latch? Perhaps what the children heard was "It's not my problem. I am old, female, black, blind. What wisdom I have now is in knowing I can not help you. The future of language is yours."

They stand there. Suppose nothing was in their hands? Suppose the visit was only a ruse, a trick to get to be spoken to, taken seriously as they have not been before? A chance to interrupt, to violate the adult world, its miasma of discourse about them, for them, but never to them? Urgent questions are at stake, including the one they have asked: "Is the bird we hold living or dead?" Perhaps the question meant: "Could some one tell us what is life? What is death?" No trick at all; no silliness. A straightforward question worthy of the attention of a wise one. An old one. And if the old and wise who have lived life and faced death cannot describe either, who can?

But she does not; she keeps her secret; her good opinion of herself; her gnomic pronouncements; her art without commitment. She keeps her distance, enforces it and retreats into the singularity of isolation, in sophisticated, privileged space.

N OTHING, no word follows her declarations of transfer. That silence is deep, deeper than the meaning available in the words she has spoken. It shivers, this silence, and the children, annoyed, fill it with language invented on the spot.

"Is there no speech," they ask her, "no words you can give us that helps us break through your dossier of failures? Through the education you have just given us that is no education at all because we are paying close attention to what you have done as well as to what you have said? To the barrier you have erected between generosity and wisdom?

"We have no bird in our hands, living or dead. We have only you and our important question. Is the nothing in our hands something you could not bear to contemplate, to even guess? Don't you remember being young when language was magic without meaning? When what you could say, could not mean? When the invisible was what imagination strove to see? When questions and demands for answers burned so brightly you trembled with fury at not knowing?

"Do we have to begin consciousness with a battle heroines and heroes like you have already fought and lost leaving us with nothing in our hands except what you have imagined is there? Your answer is artful, but its artiness embarrasses us and ought to embarrass you. Your answer is indecent in its self-congratulation. A made-for-television script that makes no sense if there is nothing in our hands.

"Why didn't you reach out, touch us with your soft fingers, delay the sound bite, the lesson, until you knew who we were? Did you so despise our trick, our modus operandi you could not see that we were baffled about how to get your attention? We are young. Unripe. We have heard all our short lives that we have to be responsible. What could that possibly mean in the catastrophe this word has become; where, as a poet said, "nothing needs to be exposed since it is already barefaced." Our inheritance is an affront. You want us to have your old, blank eyes and see only cruelty and mediocrity. Do you think we are stupid enough to perjure ourselves again and again with the fiction of nationhood? How dare you talk to us of duty when we stand waist deep in the toxin of your past?

"You trivialize us and trivialize the bird that is not in our hands. Is there no context for our lives? No song, no literature, no poem full of vitamins, no history connected to experience that you can pass along to help us start strong? You are an adult. The old one, the wise one. Stop thinking about saving your face. Think of our lives and tell us your particularized world. Make up a story. Narrative is radical, creating us at the very moment it is being created. We will not blame you if your reach exceeds your grasp; if love so ignites your words they go down in flames and nothing is left but their scald. Or if, with the reticence of a surgeon's hands, your words suture only the places where blood might flow. We know you can never do it properly—once and for all. Passion is never enough; neither is skill. But try. For our sake and yours forget your name in the street; tell us what the world has been to you in the dark places and in the light. Don't tell us what to believe, what to fear. Show us belief's wide skirt and the stitch that unravels fear's caul. You, old woman, blessed with blindness, can speak the language that tells us what only language can: how to see without pictures. Language alone protects us from the scariness of things with no names. Language alone is meditation.

"Tell us what it is to be a woman so that we may know what it is to be a man. What moves at the margin. What it is to have no home on this place. To be set adrift from the one you knew. What it is to live at the edge of towns that cannot bear your company.

"Tell us about ships turned away from shorelines at Easter, placenta in a field. Tell us about a wagonload of slaves, how they sang so softly their breath was indistinguishable from the falling snow. How they knew from the hunch of the nearest shoulder that the next stop would be their last. How, with hands prayered in their sex they thought of heat, then suns. Lifting their faces, as though it was there for the taking. Turning as though there for the taking. They stop at an inn. The driver and his mate go in with the lamp leaving them humming in the dark. The horse's void steams into the snow beneath its hooves and its hiss and melt is the envy of the freezing slaves.

"The inn door opens: a girl and a boy step away from its light. They climb into the wagon bed. The boy will have a gun in three years, but now he carries a lamp and a jug of warm cider. They pass it from mouth to mouth. The girl offers bread, pieces of meat and something more: a glance into the eye of the one she serves. One helping for each man, two for each woman. And a look. They look back. The next stop will be their last. But not this one. This one is warmed."

It's quiet again when the children finish speaking, until the woman breaks into the silence.

"Finally," she says, " I trust you now. I trust you with the bird that is now in your hands because you have truly caught it. Look. How lovely it is, this thing we have done—together."

ABOUT **TONI MORRISON**

Recipient of the 1993 Nobel Prize for Literature, Toni Morrison has produced novels that follow her own prescription for writing—to provide a means of discovery, to open doors and point the way. Her first novel, *The Bluest Eye*, published in 1970, was followed by *Sula, Song of Solomon, Tar Baby, Beloved*—which won a Pulitzer Prize in 1988—and *Jazz*. Morrison's works, which draw on myth and legend, portray in lyrical language the suffering and richness of the African American experience.

RESPONDING

1. *Personal Response* What single question would you ask the old woman today? Why?

2. *Literary Analysis* How would you describe Morrison's *diction*—or choice of words? For example, put the following sentence into simple, literal language and explain how this differs from Morrison's original: "The systematic looting of language can be recognized by the tendency of its users to forgo its nuanced, complex, mid-wifery properties for menace and subjugation." (page 168)

3. *Multicultural Connection* What do you think makes this woman so highly regarded in her culture? Would she be as highly regarded in your culture? Why or why not?

LANGUAGE WORKSHOP

Figurative Language *Figurative language* is the use of words outside their literal, or usual, meanings. Often, figurative language suggests comparisons and associations between things not normally linked, as Morrison makes when she compares language to a bird and the death (or misuse) of language to its corpse. Working with a small group, explain what Morrison means by the figurative language in the following items.
1. "Being a writer she thinks of language . . . as an act with consequences." (page 167)
2. "Official language . . . is a suit of armor, polished to shocking glitter, a husk from which the knight departed long ago." (page 168)
3. "The bird is in your hands." (page 171)

WRITER'S PORTFOLIO

Morrison writes "Language protects us from the scariness of things with no names." In your journal, explain what you think she means. Use examples to illustrate.

Snapshots of
a Wedding

W EDDING DAYS ALWAYS STARTED at the haunting, magical hour of early dawn when there was only a pale crack of light on the horizon. For those who were awake, it took the earth hours to adjust to daylight. The cool and damp of the night slowly arose in shimmering waves like water and even the forms of the people who bestirred themselves at this unearthly hour were distorted in the haze; they appeared to be dancers in slow motion, with fluid, watery forms. In the dim light, four men, the relatives of the bridegroom, Kegoletile, slowly herded an ox before them towards the yard of MmaKhudu, where the bride, Neo, lived. People were already astir in MmaKhudu's yard, yet for a while they all came and peered closely at the distorted fluid forms that approached, to ascertain if it were indeed the relatives of the bridegroom. Then the ox, who was a rather stupid fellow and unaware of his sudden and impending end as meat for the wedding feast, bellowed casually his early morning yawn. At this the beautiful ululating of the women rose and swelled over the air like water bubbling rapidly and melo-

Culture Notes

Kegoletile (kə gō′lə tēl′), p.176

MmaKhudu (mä kü′dü), p.176

Neo (nā′ō), p.176

ululating wailing on an emotional occasion; in this story, crying for joy at a wedding, p.176

diously over the stones of a clear, sparkling stream. In between ululating all the while, the women began to weave about the yard in the wedding dance; now and then they bent over and shook their buttocks in the air. As they handed over the ox, one of the bridegroom's relatives joked:

"This is going to be a modern wedding." He meant that a lot of the traditional courtesies had been left out of the planning for the wedding day; no one had been awake all night preparing diphiri or the traditional wedding breakfast of pounded meat and samp; the bridegroom said he had no church and did not care about such things; the bride was six months pregnant and showing it, so there was just going to be a quick marriage ceremony at the police camp.

Culture Notes

diphiri (də pē′rē), a soft cereal, p. 177

samp a coarse hominy boiled into a cereal, p. 177

"O" levels an examination for college entrance, p. 177

Mathata (mä tä′tə), p. 178

R10.00 ten rands (the monetary unit in South Africa), worth about $10, p. 178

"Oh, we all have our own ways," one of the bride's relatives joked back. "If the times are changing, we keep up with them." And she weaved away ululating joyously.

Whenever there was a wedding the talk and gossip that preceded it were appalling, except that this time the relatives of the bride, Neo, kept their talk a strict secret among themselves. They were anxious to be rid of her; she was an impossible girl with haughty, arrogant ways. Of all her family and relatives, she was the only one who had completed her "O" levels and she never failed to rub in this fact. She walked around with her nose in the air; illiterate relatives were beneath her greeting — it was done in a clever way, she just turned her head to one side and smiled to herself or when she greeted it was like an insult; she stretched her hand out, palm outspread, swung it down laughing with a gesture that plainly said: "Oh, that's you!" Only her mother seemed bemused by her education. At her own home Neo was waited on hand and foot. Outside her home nasty remarks were passed. People bitterly disliked conceit and pride.

"That girl has no manners!" the relatives would remark. "What's the good of education if it goes to someone's head so badly they have no respect for the people? Oh, she is not a person."

Then they would nod their heads in that fatal way, with predictions that one day life would bring her down. Actually, life had treated Neo rather nicely. Two months after completing her "O" levels she became pregnant by Kegoletile with their first child. It soon became known that another girl, Mathata, was also pregnant by Kegoletile. The difference between the two girls was that Mathata was completely uneducated; the only work she would ever do was that of a housemaid, while Neo had endless opportunities before her—typist, bookkeeper, or secretary. So Neo merely smiled; Mathata was no rival. It was as though the decision had been worked out by circumstance because when the families converged on Kegoletile at the birth of the children—he was rich in cattle and they wanted to see what they could get—he of course immediately proposed marriage to Neo; and for Mathata, he agreed to a court order to pay a maintenance of R10.00 a month until the child was twenty years old. Mathata merely smiled too. Girls like her offered no resistance to the approaches of men; when they lost them, they just let things ride.

"He is of course just running after the education and not the manners," Neo's relatives commented, to show they were not fooled by human nature. "He thinks that since she is as educated as he is they will both get good jobs and be rich in no time. . ."

Educated as he was, Kegoletile seemed to go through a secret conflict during the year he prepared a yard for his future married life with Neo. He spent most of his free time in the yard of Mathata. His behaviour there wasn't too alarming but he showered Mathata with gifts of all kinds—food, fancy dresses, shoes and underwear. Each time he came, he brought a gift and each time Mathata would burst out laughing and comment: "Ow, Kegoletile, how can I wear all these dresses? It's just a waste of money! Besides, I manage quite well with the R10.00 you give every month for the child. . ."

She was a very pretty girl with black eyes like stars; she was always smiling and happy; immediately and always her own natural self. He knew what he was marrying—something quite the opposite, a new kind of girl with false postures and acquired, grand-madame ways. And yet, it didn't pay a man these days to look too closely into his heart. They all wanted as wives, women who were big money-earners and they were so ruthless about it! And yet it was as though the society itself stamped each of its individuals with its own particular brand of wealth and Kegoletile had not yet escaped it; he had about him an engaging humility and eagerness to help and please that made him loved and respected by all who knew him. During those times he sat in Mathata's yard, he communicated nothing of the conflict he felt but he would sit on a chair with his arms spread out across its back, turn his head sideways and stare at what seemed to be an empty space beside him. Then he would smile, stand up and walk away. Nothing dramatic. During the year he prepared the huts in his new yard, he frequently slept at the home of Neo.

RELATIVES ON BOTH SIDES watched this division of interest between the two yards and one day when Neo walked patronisingly into the yard of an aunt, the aunt decided to frighten her a little.

"Well aunt," she said, with the familiar careless disrespect which went with her so-called, educated, status. "Will you make me some tea? And how's things?"

The aunt spoke very quietly.

"You may not know it, my girl, but you are hated by everyone around here. The debate we have going is whether a nice young man like Kegoletile should marry bad-mannered rubbish like you. He would be far better off if he married a girl like Mathata, who though uneducated, still treats people with respect."

The shock the silly girl received made her stare for a terrified moment at her aunt. Then she stood up and ran out of the house. It wiped the superior smile off her face and brought her down a little. She developed an anxiety to greet people and also an anxiety about securing Kegoletile as a husband — that was why she became pregnant six months before the marriage could take place. In spite of this, her own relatives still disliked her and right up to the day of the wedding they were still debating whether Neo was a suitable wife for any man. No one would have guessed it though with all the dancing, ululating and happiness expressed in the yard and streams of guests gaily ululated themselves along the pathways with wedding gifts precariously balanced on their heads. Neo's maternal aunts, all sedately decked up in shawls, sat in a select group by themselves in a corner of the yard. They sat on the bare ground with their legs stretched out before them but they were served like queens the whole day long. Trays of tea, dry white bread, plates of meat, rice, and salad were constantly placed before them. Their important task was to formally hand over the bride to Kegoletile's maternal aunts when they approached the yard at sunset. So they sat the whole day with still, expressionless faces, waiting to fulfil this ancient rite.

EQUALLY STILL AND EXPRESSIONLESS were the faces of the long column of women, Kegoletile's maternal aunts, who appeared outside the yard just as the sun sank low. They walked slowly into the yard indifferent to the ululating that greeted them and seated themselves in a group opposite Neo's maternal aunts. The yard became very silent while each group made its report. Kegoletile had provided all the food for the wedding feast and a maternal aunt from his side first asked:

"Is there any complaint? Has all gone well?"

"We have no complaint," the opposite party replied.

"We have come to ask for water," Kegoletile's side said, meaning that from times past the bride was supposed to carry water in her in-laws' home.

"It is agreed to," the opposite party replied.

Neo's maternal aunts then turned to the bridegroom and counselled him: "Son, you must plough and supply us with corn each year."

Then Kegoletile's maternal aunts turned to the bride and counselled her: "Daughter, you must carry water for your husband. Beware, that at all times, he is the owner of the house and must be obeyed. Do not mind if he stops now and then and talks to other ladies. Let him feel free to come and go as he likes. . ."

THE FORMALITIES OVER, it was now time for Kegoletile's maternal aunts to get up, ululate and weave and dance about the yard. Then, still dancing and ululating, accompanied by the bride and groom they slowly wound their way to the yard of Kegoletile where another feast had been prepared. As they approached his yard, an old woman suddenly dashed out and chopped at the ground with a hoe. It was all only a formality. Neo would never be the kind of wife who went to the lands to plough. She already had a well-paid job in an office as a secretary. Following on this another old woman took the bride by the hand and led her to a smeared and decorated courtyard wherein had been placed a traditional animal-skin Tswana mat. She was made to sit on the mat and a shawl and kerchief were placed before her. The shawl was ceremonially wrapped around her shoulders; the kerchief tied around her head—the symbols that she was now a married woman.

Guests quietly moved forward to greet the bride. Then two girls started to ululate and dance in front of the bride. As they both turned and bent over to shake their buttocks in the air, they bumped into each other and toppled over.

The wedding guests roared with laughter. Neo, who had all this time been stiff, immobile, and rigid, bent forward and her shoulders shook with laughter.

The hoe, the mat, the shawl, the kerchief, the beautiful flute-like ululating of the women seemed in itself a blessing on the marriage but all the guests were deeply moved when out of the crowd, a woman of majestic, regal bearing slowly approached the bride. It was the aunt who had scolded Neo for her bad manners and modern ways. She dropped to her knees before the bride, clenched her fists together and pounded the ground hard with each clenched fist on either side of the bride's legs. As she pounded her fists she said loudly:

"Be a good wife! Be a good wife!"

ABOUT BESSIE HEAD

Bessie Head (1937–1986), born of racially mixed parentage, was raised by foster parents in South Africa until she was thirteen. When she was twenty-six, she left South Africa for Botswana, where she lived in a refugee city for another fifteen years before being granted citizenship. Issues of caste, personal identity, and exile deeply influenced her novels and short stories, as did tensions between old and new ways.

RESPONDING

1. *Personal Response* How would you treat a proud or conceited person such as Neo? How would your classmates treat such a person?

2. *Literary Analysis* Explain how Head uses the *setting* to evoke a sense of tradition in the story. For example, what traditions are associated with the time of day, the landscape, and the places in which people live?

3. *Multicultural Connection* Kegoletile fathers children by one woman who is "immediately and always her own natural self" and by another who is "a new kind of girl

with false postures and acquired, grand-madame ways."
Which woman seems more valued by Kegoletile's culture? Explain.

LANGUAGE WORKSHOP

Comparing and Contrasting This story paints pictures
of two very different women by *comparing* their similarities and *contrasting* their differences. Compare and contrast Neo and Mathata in terms of each of the following:
education, attitude toward relatives, attitude toward
Kegoletile.

WRITER'S PORTFOLIO

List seven elements you would include in an important
ceremony such as your own wedding that would reflect
your culture, tradition, and personality in an arrangement "all your own."

A Refuge of Nocturnal Birds

Salvatore Quasimodo

High on a cliff there's a twisted pine;
intently it listens into the abyss
with its trunk curved down like a crossbow.

A refuge of nocturnal birds,
in the deepest hours of night it resounds
with the swift fluttering of wings.

Even my heart has a nest
suspended into the darkness, and a voice;
it, too, lies awake listening at night.

A perpetual stranger. . .

Bei Dao

a perpetual stranger
am I to the world
I don't understand its language
my silence it can't comprehend
all we have to exchange
is a touch of contempt
as if we meet in a mirror

a perpetual stranger
am I to myself
I fear the dark
but block with my body
the only lamp
my shadow is my beloved
heart the enemy

The Street

Octavio Paz

The street is very long and filled with silence.
I walk in shadow and I trip and fall,
And then get up and walk with unseeing feet
Over the silent stones and the dry leaves,
And someone close behind, tramples them, too.
If I slow down and stop, he also stops.
If I run, so does he. I look. No one!
The whole street seems so dark, with no way out,
And though I turn and turn, I can't escape.
I always find myself on the same street
Where no one waits for me and none pursues.
Where I pursue, a man who trips and falls
Gets up and seeing me, keeps saying: "No one!"

ABOUT **SALVATORE QUASIMODO**

Salvatore Quasimodo (säl′və tō′rä kwä′zē mä′dō; 1901–1968) was born in Modica, Sicily, and lived much of his life in Milan, Italy. He worked as an engineer before becoming an editor and professor of literature. In addition to his poems, which range from the highly symbolic and political to those having simple, concrete images, he pub-lished many translations of classical and  modern poetry and plays. Quasimodo received the Nobel Prize for Literature in 1959.

ABOUT **BEI DAO**

Bei Dao (bā′ dou′; pen name of Zhao Zhenkai) was born in Beijing, China, in 1949, shortly before the establishment of the

People's Republic of China. After attending the country's most elite secondary schools, he joined the Red Guard Movement, but later rejected orthodox politics and became an underground poet. The simple words of his poems — even those that seem quite personal — mask views that were long considered subversive by the Chinese government. Bei Dao was in involuntary exile during and after the Tiananmen Massacre of 1989.

ABOUT **OCTAVIO PAZ**

Winner of the 1990 Nobel Prize for Literature, Octavio Paz (ôk tä´vyō päs; päz) was born in Mexico City in 1914. He served as a diplomat for over twenty years, including seven years as Mexico's ambassador to India. Paz often writes in two or more languages and examines tensions among ideas and actions. Many of Paz's works deal with alienation and human attempts to transcend it.

RESPONDING

1. *Personal Response* How do these poems make you feel? What words or images contribute to this feeling?

2. *Literary Analysis* Look at the first line of each poem. What word or words would you use to describe the *mood*?

3. *Multicultural Connection* Do you think that these poems, written by an Italian, a Chinese, and a Mexican author, express universal feelings? Explain. Can you describe a poem or a song written by someone from your country that expresses similar feelings?

LANGUAGE WORKSHOP

Personification Personification is a figure of speech in

which human characteristics are attributed to animals, objects, or ideas. When we speak of a lonely tree, an angry wind, or humble flowers, we are using personification. In his poem, Quasimodo says that his heart has a voice and "lies awake listening at night." What do you think he means?

Make up a sentence for each of the following items that includes personification: beans cooking in a pot, a pair of dancing shoes, a large doll, an old car.

WRITER'S PORTFOLIO

Where do you go when you want to be alone? If you could go anywhere you liked in order to be alone, what would that place look like? How would it sound, smell, and feel? Use these details to write a paragraph describing your special place.

Projects

A *SINGULAR* PERSON

Write a song that celebrates a person who is one of a kind (perhaps you yourself). Think of images, figurative comparisons, and/or a refrain after each stanza that reinforces the theme of uniqueness. You might want to perform your song for the class.

CLASS IMAGE

As a class or in small groups, decide what characteristics make your English or language arts class stand apart from all the other classes this year. Is it the room? the teacher? the mix of students? the reading? the tests? the projects? the class discussions? a combination of all these? Decorate your door with a poster, a marquee, or an archway that will tell everyone who passes by exactly what kind of class is inside.

TRACING A SPECIAL TRADITION

Investigate traditions of your grandparents' or great-grandparents' generation connected to a holiday, birthday, graduation, death, wedding, or other occasion. Then track how the traditions have been altered or maintained in recent years for your family members. Determine if factors such as the passage of time, economic conditions, or changes in the culture have had an effect on these traditions. Then write an essay that presents your findings. You may want to make some predictions about how this occasion or celebration could change for your grandchildren.

Further Reading

The following books, some by authors represented in this unit, reveal qualities that make both people and their cultures unique.

Angelou, Maya. *Wouldn't Take Nothing for My Journey Now.* Random House, 1993. Brief essays provide distilled wisdom about being true to oneself and living according to one's own standards.

Head, Bessie. *A Woman Alone.* Heinemann, 1990. Published after Head's death, these autobiographical writings reveal an independent person who overcame tremendous odds to achieve her goals.

Momaday, N. Scott. *House Made of Dawn.* Harper & Row, Publishers, 1968. Abel, the protagonist of this novel, is a young Native American back from war who cannot find a place in white society nor in his ancestral surroundings.

————. *In the Presence of the Sun: Stories and Poems, 1961–1991.* St. Martin's, 1992. Over seventy poems, plus sixteen stories behind traditional Native American shields, offer glimpses into tradition and its contemporary translations.

Ray, Satyajit. *The Unicorn Expedition and Other Fantastic Tales of India.* E. P. Dutton, 1987. Eleven stories, first published in a children's magazine, chronicle odd things that happen to remarkable people.

Soyinka, Wole. *Aké: The Years of Childhood.* Random House, 1991. This autobiographical account of the author's first ten years grows serious and offers insight into his artistic vision.

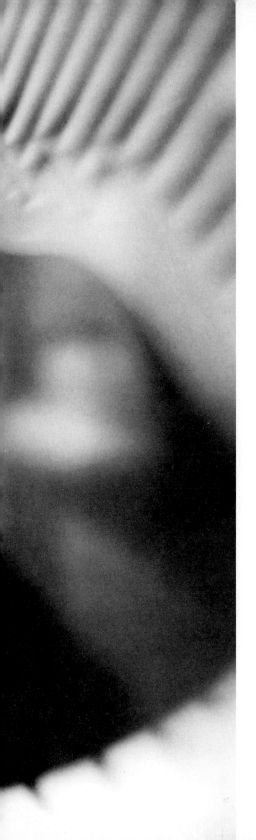

Secrets and Deceptions

There's something fascinating about secrets and deceptions. Think of the fairy tales, myths, movies, and TV shows whose plots revolve around undisclosed truths or cover-ups. Think of how exciting it is to know something that most other people don't know, how frustrating it is to keep a secret, or how much fun it is to share a secret. This unit is about secrets kept, secrets shared, and secrets discovered — and about political secrets and deceptions revealed by writers who recognize their mission to tell the truth.

The Voter

Rufus Okeke — Roof, for short — was
a very popular man in his village. Although the villagers
did not explain it in so many words Roof's popularity was
a measure of their gratitude to an energetic young man
who, unlike most of his fellows nowadays, had not abandoned the village in order to seek work — any work — in
the towns. And Roof was not a village lout either. Everyone
knew how he had spent two years as a bicycle repairer's
apprentice in Port Harcourt and had given up of his own
free will a bright future to return to his people and guide
them in these political times. Not that Umuofia needed a lot
of guidance. The village already belonged *en masse* to the
People's Alliance Party, and its most illustrious son — Chief
the Honourable Marcus Ibe — was Minister of Culture in
the out-going government (which was pretty certain to be
the in-coming one as well). Nobody doubted that the
Honourable Minister would be re-elected in his constituency. Opposition to him was like the proverbial fly trying to move a dunghill. It would have been ridiculous
enough without coming, as it did now, from a complete
nonentity.

As was to be expected Roof was in the service of the
Honourable Minister for the coming elections. He had
become a real expert in election campaigning at all levels —
village, local government or national. He could tell the

mood and temper of the electorate at any given time. For instance he had warned the Minister months ago about the radical change that had come into the thinking of Umuofia since the last national election.

The villagers had had five years in which to see how quickly and plentifully politics brought wealth, chieftaincy titles, doctorate degrees and other honours, some of which like the last had still to be explained satisfactorily to them; for they expected a doctor to heal the sick. Anyhow, these honours had come so readily to the man they had given their votes to free of charge five years ago that they were now ready to think again.

Their point was that only the other day Marcus Ibe was a not too successful Mission-school teacher. Then politics had come to their village and he had wisely joined up, some say just in time to avoid imminent dismissal arising from a female teacher's pregnancy. Today he was Chief the Honourable; he had two long cars and had just built himself the biggest house anyone had seen in those parts. But let it be said that none of these successes had gone to Marcus's head — as they well might. He remained a man of the people. Whenever he could he left the good things of the capital and returned to his village which had neither running water nor electricity. He knew the source of his good fortune, unlike the little bird who ate and drank and went out to challenge his personal spirit. Marcus had christened his new house "Umuofia Mansions" in honour of his village and slaughtered five bulls and countless goats to entertain the people on the day it was opened by the Archbishop.

Everyone was full of praise for him. One old man said: "Our son is a good man; he is not like the mortar which as soon as food comes its way turns its back on the ground." But when the feasting was over the villagers told themselves that they had underrated the power of the ballot-paper before and should not do so again. Chief the Honourable Marcus Ibe was not unprepared. He had drawn five months' salary in advance, changed a few hundred pounds into shining shillings and armed his campaign boys with eloquent little jute bags. In the day he made his speeches; at night his stalwarts conducted their whispering campaign. Roof was the most trusted of these campaigners.

"We have a Minister from our village, one of our own sons," he said to a group of elders in the house of Ogbuefi Ezenwa, a man of high traditional title. "What greater honour can a village have? Do you ever stop to ask yourselves why we should be singled out for this honour? I will tell you: it is because we are favoured by the leaders of PAP. Whether we cast our paper for Marcus or not PAP will continue to rule. Think of the pipe-borne water they have promised us. . ."

Besides Roof and his assistant there were five elders in the room. An old hurricane lamp with a cracked, sooty, glass chimney gave out yellowish light in their midst. The elders sat on very low stools. On the floor, directly in front of each of them, lay two shilling pieces. Outside the moon kept a straight face.

"We believe every word you say to be true," said Ezenwa. "We shall every one of us drop his paper for Marcus. Who would leave an *ozo* feast and go to a poor ritual meal? Tell Marcus he has our papers, and our wives' papers too. But what we do say is that two shillings is shameful." He brought the lamp close and tilted it at the money before him as if to make sure he had not mistaken its value. "Yes, two shillings; it is too shameful. If Marcus were a poor man — which our ancestors forbid — I should be the first to give him my paper free, as I did before. But today Marcus is a great man and does his things like a great man. We did not ask him for money yesterday; we shall not ask him tomorrow. But today is our day; we have climbed the *iroko* tree today and would be foolish not to take down all the fire-wood we need."

Roof had to agree. He had lately been taking down a lot of fire-wood himself. Only yesterday he had asked Marcus for one of his many rich robes — and had got it. Last Sunday Marcus's wife (the teacher that nearly got him in trouble) had objected (like the woman she was) when Roof pulled out his fifth bottle of beer from the kerosene refrigerator, and was roundly and publicly rebuked by her husband. To cap it all Roof had won a land case recently because, among other things, he had been chauffeur-driven to the disputed site. So he understood the elders about the fire-wood.

"Alright," he said in English and then reverted to Ibo. "Let us not quarrel about small things." He stood up and adjusted his robes. Then he bent down like a priest distributing the host and gave one shilling more to every man: only he did not put it into their palms but on the floor in front of them. The men, who had so far not deigned to touch the things, looked at the floor and shook their heads. Roof got up again and gave each man another shilling.

"I am through," he said with a defiance that was no less effective for being transparently faked. The elders too knew how far to go without losing decorum. So when Roof added: "Go cast your paper for the enemy if you like!" they quickly calmed him down with a suitable speech from each of them. By the time the last man had spoken it was possible — without great loss of dignity — to pick up the things from the floor.

THE ENEMY Roof had referred to was the Progressive Organisation Party (POP) which had been formed by the tribes down the coast to save themselves — as the founders of the party proclaimed — from "total political, cultural, social and religious annihilation." Although it was clear the party had no chance here it had plunged — with typical foolishness — into a straight fight with PAP, providing cars and loudspeakers to a few local rascals and thugs to go around and make a lot of noise. No one knew for certain how much money POP had let loose in Umuofia but it was said to be very considerable. Their local campaigners would end up very rich, no doubt.

Up to last night everything had been "moving according to plan"—as Roof would have put it. Then he had received a strange visit from the leader of the POP campaign team. Although he and Roof were well known to each other and might even be called friends his visit was cold and business-like. No words were wasted. He placed five pounds on the floor before Roof and said, "We want your vote." Roof got up from his chair, went to the outside door, closed it carefully and returned to his chair. The brief exercise gave him enough time to weigh the proposition. As he spoke his eyes never left the red notes on the floor.

"You know I work for Marcus," he said feebly. "It will be very bad. . ."

"Marcus will not be there when you put in your paper. We have plenty of work to do tonight; are you taking this or not?"

"It will not be heard outside this room?" asked Roof.

"We are after votes not gossip."

"Alright," said Roof in English.

The man nudged his companion and he brought forward an object covered with red cloth and proceeded to remove the cover. It was a fearsome little affair contained in a clay pot with feathers stuck into it.

"This *iyi* comes from Mbanta. You know what that means. Swear that you will vote for Maduka. If you fail to do so, this *iyi* is to note."

ROOF'S HEART had nearly flown out of his mouth when he saw the *iyi;* and indeed he knew the fame of Mbanta in these things. But he was a man of quick decision. What could a single vote cast in secret for Maduka take away from Marcus's certain victory? Nothing.

"I will cast my paper for Maduka; if not, this *iyi* take note."

"Das all," said the man as he rose with his companion, who had covered up the object again and was taking it back to their car.

"You know he has no chance against Marcus," said Roof at the door.

"It is enough that he gets a few votes now; next time he will get more. People will hear that he gives out pounds, not shillings, and they will listen."

Election morning. The great day every five years when the people exercised power — or thought they did. Weather-beaten posters on walls of houses, tree trunks and telegraph poles. The few that were still whole called out their message to those who could read. Vote for the People's Alliance Party! Vote for the Progressive Organisation Party! Vote for PAP! Vote for POP! The posters that were torn called out as much of the message as they could.

As usual Chief the Honourable Marcus Ibe was doing things in grand style. He had hired a highlife band from Umuru and stationed it at such a distance from the voting booths as just managed to be lawful. Many villagers danced to the music, their ballot papers held aloft, before proceeding to the booths. Chief the Honourable Marcus Ibe sat in the "owner's corner" of his enormous green car and smiled and nodded. One enlightened villager came up to the car, shook hands with the great man and said in advance: "Congrats!" This immediately set the pattern. Hundreds of admirers shook Marcus's hand and said "Corngrass!"

Roof and the other organisers were prancing up and down, giving last minute advice to the voters and pouring with sweat.

"Do not forget," he said again to a group of illiterate women who seemed ready to burst with enthusiasm and good humour, "our sign is the motor-car. . ."

"Like the one Marcus is sitting inside."

"Thank you, mother," said Roof. "It is the same car. The box with the car shown on its body is the box for you. Don't look at the other with the man's head: it is for those whose heads are not correct."

> **Culture Note**
>
> **owner's corner** In this hierarchical society, the seat diagonally behind the driver's seat is specifically reserved for the owner of the car as a mark of his wealth and the respect due him. p. 197

This was greeted with loud laughter. Roof cast a quick and busy-like glance towards the Minister and received a smile of appreciation.

"Vote for the car," he shouted, all the veins in his neck standing out. "Vote for the car and you will ride in it!"

"Or if we don't our children will," piped the same sharp old girl.

The band struck up a new number: "Why walk when you can ride?"

In spite of his apparent calm and confidence Chief the Honourable Marcus was a relentless stickler for detail. He knew he would win what the newspapers called "a land-slide victory" but he did not wish even so to throw away a single vote. So as soon as the first rush of voters was over he promptly asked his campaign boys to go one at a time and put in their ballot-papers.

"Roof, you had better go first," he said.

Roof's spirits fell; but he let no one see it. All morning he had masked his deep worry with a surface exertion which was unusual even for him. Now he dashed off in his springy fashion towards the booths. A policeman at the entrance searched him for illegal ballot papers and passed him. Then the electoral officer explained to him about the two boxes. By this time the spring had gone clean out of his walk. He sidled in and was confronted by the car and the head. He brought out his ballot paper from his pocket and looked at it. How could he betray Marcus even in secret? He resolved to go back to the other man and return his five pounds ... FIVE POUNDS! He knew at once it was impossible. He had sworn on that *iyi*.

At this point he heard the muffled voice of the policeman asking the electoral officer what the man was doing inside. "Abi na pickin im de born?"

Quick as lightning a thought leapt into Roof's mind. He folded the paper,

Culture Note

Abi na pickin im de born? a question in pidgin English that is commonly asked in Nigeria and means literally, "Is he giving birth to a child in there?" (Why is he taking so long?) p. 198

tore it in two along the crease and put one half in each box. He took the precaution of putting the first half into Maduka's box and confirming the action verbally: "I vote for Maduka."

They marked his thumb with indelible purple ink to prevent his return, and he went out of the booth as jauntily as he had gone in.

ABOUT **CHINUA ACHEBE**

Chinua Achebe (chin/wä/ ä chä/bä) was born in 1930 in Ogidi, a village of the Ibo people in eastern Nigeria. During his professional career, he has been a writer, teacher, editor, and lecturer. Many of his works concern the way Africans have dealt with the imposition of Western cultures and values. In addition to his best-known novel, *Things Fall Apart*, he has written other novels, poetry, a children's book, and collections of essays and short stories.

RESPONDING

1. *Personal Response* If you had made Roof's commitments, would you have voted as he did, differently, or not at all? Why?

2. *Literary Analysis* This story is narrated from a third-person *point of view*. How might the paragraph beginning "Roof's spirits fell. . ." (page 198) change if Roof were telling his own story in the first person?

3. *Multicultural Connection* In what countries might a candidate buy votes? Could it happen in your country? Explain.

LANGUAGE WORKSHOP

Proverbs Proverbs, brief traditional sayings containing popular wisdom, are an important component of the West African culture. For example, Achebe says of

Marcus Ibe: "He knew the source of his good fortune, unlike the little bird who ate and drank and went out to challenge his personal spirit." Nigerians believe that all creatures have a personal guiding spirit. The bird here symbolizes someone who has been fortunate in life but does not show gratitude to those who helped him along the way to success. Explain the following proverbs from the story.

1. "Opposition to him was like the proverbial fly trying to move a dunghill."
2. "But today is our day; we have climbed the *iroko* tree today and would be foolish not to take down all the fire-wood we need."

WRITER'S PORTFOLIO

Pretend you are running for election in Umuofia. Make up a campaign poster you think would convince the villagers to vote for you.

The Elephant

THE DIRECTOR of the Zoological Gardens has shown himself to be an upstart. He regarded his animals simply as stepping stones on the road of his own career. He was indifferent to the educational importance of his establishment. In his Zoo the giraffe had a short neck, the badger had no burrow and the whistlers, having lost all interest, whistled rarely and with some reluctance. These shortcomings should not have been allowed, especially as the Zoo was often visited by parties of school-children.

The Zoo was in a provincial town, and it was short of some of the most important animals, among them the elephant. Three thousand rabbits were a poor substitute for the noble giant. However, as our country developed, the gaps were being filled in a well-planned manner. On the occasion of the anniversary of the liberation, on 22nd July, the Zoo was notified that it had at long last been allocated an elephant. All the staff, who were devoted to their work, rejoiced at this news. All the greater was their surprise when they learnt that the director had sent a letter to Warsaw, renouncing the allocation and putting forward a plan for obtaining an elephant by more economic means.

"I, and all the staff," he had written, "are fully aware how heavy a burden falls upon the shoulders of Polish miners and foundry men because of the elephant. Desirous of reducing our costs, I suggest that the elephant mentioned in your communication should be replaced by one of our own procurement. We can make an elephant out of rubber, of the correct size, fill it with air and place it behind railings. It will be carefully painted the correct colour and even on close inspection will be indistinguishable from the real animal. It is well known that the elephant is a sluggish animal and it does not run and jump about. In the notice on the railings we can state that this particular elephant is exceptionally sluggish. The money saved in this way can be turned to the purchase of a jet plane or the conservation of some church monument.

"Kindly note that both the idea and its execution are my modest contribution to the common task and struggle.

"I am, etc."

THIS COMMUNICATION must have reached a soulless official, who regarded his duties in a purely bureaucratic manner and did not examine the heart of the matter but, following only the directive about reduction of expenditure, accepted the director's plan. On hearing the Ministry's approval, the director issued instructions for the making of the rubber elephant.

The carcase was to have been filled with air by two keepers blowing into it from opposite ends. To keep the operation secret the work was to be completed during the night because the people of the town, having heard that an elephant was joining the Zoo, were anxious to see it. The director insisted on haste also because he expected a bonus, should his idea turn out to be a success.

The two keepers locked themselves in a shed normally housing a workshop, and began to blow. After two hours of hard blowing they discovered that the rubber skin had risen only a few inches above the floor and

Culture Notes

liberation After World War II, July 22 was proclaimed Polish National Day by the communist regime. Since the fall of communism, November 11 is celebrated instead. p. 201

carcase British variant of carcass, p. 202

its bulge in no way resembled an elephant. The night progressed. Outside, human voices were stilled and only the cry of the jackass interrupted the silence. Exhausted, the keepers stopped blowing and made sure that the air already inside the elephant should not escape. They were not young and were unaccustomed to this kind of work.

"If we go on at this rate," said one of them, "we shan't finish before the morning. And what am I to tell my Missus? She'll never believe me if I say that I spent the night blowing up an elephant."

"Quite right," agreed the second keeper. "Blowing up an elephant is not an everyday job. And it's all because our director is a leftist."

They resumed their blowing, but after another half-an-hour they felt too tired to continue. The bulge on the floor was larger but still nothing like the shape of an elephant.

"It's getting harder all the time," said the first keeper.

"It's an uphill job, all right," agreed the second. "Let's have a little rest."

While they were resting, one of them noticed a gas pipe ending in a valve. Could they not fill the elephant with gas? He suggested it to his mate.

THEY DECIDED TO TRY. They connected the elephant to the gas pipe, turned the valve, and to their joy in a few minutes there was a full-sized beast standing in the shed. It looked real: the enormous body, legs like columns, huge ears and the inevitable trunk. Driven by ambition the director had made sure of having in his Zoo a very large elephant indeed.

"First class," declared the keeper who had the idea of using gas. "Now we can go home."

In the morning the elephant was moved to a special run in a central position, next to the monkey cage. Placed in front of a large real rock it looked fierce and magnificent. A big notice proclaimed: "Particularly sluggish. Hardly moves."

Among the first visitors that morning was a party of children from the local school. The teacher in charge of them was planning to give them an object-lesson about the elephant. He halted the group in front of the animal and began:

"The elephant is a herbivorous mammal. By means of its trunk it pulls out young trees and eats their leaves."

The children were looking at the elephant with enraptured admiration. They were waiting for it to pull out a young tree, but the beast stood still behind its railings.

". . . The elephant is a direct descendant of the now extinct mammoth. It's not surprising, therefore, that it's the largest living land animal."

The more conscientious pupils were making notes.

". . . Only the whale is heavier than the elephant, but then the whale lives in the sea. We can safely say that on land the elephant reigns supreme."

A slight breeze moved the branches of the trees in the Zoo.

". . . The weight of a fully grown elephant is between nine and thirteen thousand pounds."

At THAT MOMENT the elephant shuddered and rose in the air. For a few seconds it swayed just above the ground but a gust of wind blew it upwards until its mighty silhouette was against the sky. For a short while people on the ground could still see the four circles of its feet, its bulging belly and the trunk, but soon, propelled by the wind, the elephant sailed above the fence and disappeared above the tree-tops. Astonished monkeys in the cage continued staring into the sky.

They found the elephant in the neighbouring botanical gardens. It had landed on a cactus and punctured its rubber hide.

The schoolchildren who had witnessed the scene in the Zoo soon started neglecting their studies and turned into hooligans. It is reported that they drink liquor and break windows. And they no longer believe in elephants.

ABOUT **SLAWOMIR MROŻEK**

First published in English in 1962, "The Elephant" is typical of the satirical stories by Slawomir Mrożek (swäf/mēr mrō/zhək) that led to the banning of his work in Poland in 1968. This story drama- tizes the absurdity of life under the commu- nist bureaucracy when Soviet control extended even to zoo animals. With the fall of communism in 1989, Mrożek's writing was again published in his native country.

RESPONDING

1. *Personal Response* What is your opinion of this story? Would you share it with a friend? Why or why not?

2. *Literary Analysis* Where is the *humor* in this story most obvious to you? Cite a line or two.

3. *Multicultural Connection* Based on this story, what do you think it was like living in a country under commu- nist control? What were the educational and cultural programs like?

LANGUAGE WORKSHOP

Fable A *fable* is a brief tale, in which the characters are often animals, told to point out a moral. What are some fables, such as those by Aesop, that you know? According to this definition, is "The Elephant" a fable? Why or why not?

WRITER'S PORTFOLIO

As a zoo director, you must construct an animal that will look real enough to fool visitors, at least for a day. Which animal would you build, and what would you be sure to include so people would think it is real? Give a detailed plan in paragraph or list form. Illustrate it if you wish.

An Incident in the Ghobashi Household

Z EINAT WOKE TO THE STRIDENT CALL of the red cockerel from the rooftop above where she was sleeping. The Ghobashi house stood on the outskirts of the village and in front of it the fields stretched out to the river and the railway track.

The call of the red cockerel released answering calls from neighbouring rooftops. Then they were silenced by the voice of the muezzin from the lofty minaret among the mulberry trees calling: "Prayer is better than sleep."

She stretched out her arm to the pile of children sleeping alongside her and tucked the end of the old rag-woven kilim round their bodies, then shook her eldest daughter's shoulder.

"It's morning, another of the Lord's mornings. Get up, Ni'ma — today's market day."

Ni'ma rolled onto her back and lazily stretched herself. Like someone alerted by the sudden slap of a gust of wind, Zeinat stared down at the body spread out before her. Ni'ma sat up and pulled her djellaba over her thighs, rubbing at her sleep-heavy eyes in the rounded face with the prominent cheekbones.

"Are you going to be able to carry the grain to the market, daughter, or will it be too heavy for you?"

Culture Notes

muezzin (myü ez′n) in Islamic communities, a crier who summons the faithful to prayer from a minaret or other part of a mosque, p. 206

kilim (kē lēm′) a hand-woven floor covering, often used as a prayer rug but also made into bags, p. 206

"Of course, mother. After all, who else is there to go?"

Zeinat rose to her feet and went out with sluggish steps to the courtyard, where she made her ablutions. Having finished the ritual prayer, she remained in the seated position as she counted off on her fingers her glorifications of Allah. Sensing that Ni'ma was standing behind her, she turned round to her:

"What are you standing there for? Why don't you go off and get the tea ready?"

Zeinat walked towards the corner where Ghobashi had stored the maize crop in sacks; he had left them as a provision for them after he had taken his air ticket from the office that had found him work in Libya and which would be bringing him back in a year's time.

"May the Lord keep you safe while you're away, Ghobashi," she muttered.

Squatting in front of a sack, the grain measure between her thighs, she scooped up the grain with both hands till the measure was full, then poured it into a basket. Coughing, she waved away the dust that rose up into her face, then returned to her work.

The girl went to the large clay jar, removed the wooden covering and dipped the mug into it and sprinkled water on her face; she wetted the tips of her fingers and parted her plaits, then tied her handkerchief over her head. She turned to her mother:

"Isn't that enough, mother? What do we want the money for?"

Zeinat struck her knees with the palms of her hands and tossed her head back.

"Don't we have to pay off Hamdan's wage?—or was he cultivating the beans for us for nothing, just for the fun of hard work?"

Ni'ma turned away and brought the stove from the window shelf, arranging the dried corn-cobs in a pyramid and lighting them. She put it alongside her mother, then filled the teapot with water from the jar and thrust it into the embers. She squatted down and the two sat in silence. Suddenly Zeinat said:

"Since when has the buffalo been with young?"

"From after my father went away."

"That's to say, right after the Great Feast, daughter?"

Ni'ma nodded her head in assent, then lowered it and began drawing lines in the dust.

"Why don't you go off and see how many eggs have been laid while the tea's getting ready."

Zeinat gazed into the glow of the embers. She had a sense of peace as she stared into the dancing flames. Ghobashi had gone and left the whole load on her shoulders: the children, the two kirats of land and the buffalo. "Take care of Ni'ma," he had said the night before he left. "The girl's body has ripened." He had then spread out his palms and said: "O Lord, for the sake of the Prophet's honour, let me bring back with me a marriage dress for her of pure silk." She had said to him: "May your words go straight from your lips to Heaven's gate, Ghobashi." He wouldn't be returning before the following Great Feast.

Culture Note

the Prophet Mohammed, the founder of Islam, p. 208

What would happen when he returned and found out the state of affairs? She put her head between the palms of her hands and leaned over the fire, blowing away the ashes. "How strange," she thought, "are the girls of today! The cunning little thing was hanging out her towels at the time of her period every month just as though nothing had happened, and here she is in her fourth month and there's nothing showing."

Ni'ma returned and untied the cloth from round the eggs, put two of them in the fire and the rest in a dish. She then brought two glasses and the tin of sugar and sat down next to her mother, who was still immersed in her thoughts.

"Didn't you try to find some way out?"

Ni'ma hunched her shoulders in a gesture of helplessness.

"Your father's been gone four months. Isn't there still time?"

"What's the use? If only the Lord were to spare you the trouble of me. Wouldn't it be for the best, mother, if my foot were to slip as I was filling the water jar from the canal and we'd be done with it?"

Zeinat struck herself on the breast and drew her daughter to her.

"Don't say such a wicked thing. Don't listen to such promptings of the Devil. Calm down and let's find some solution before your father returns."

Zeinat poured out the tea. In silence she took quick sips at it, then put the glass in front of her and shelled the egg and bit into it. Ni'ma sat watching her, her fingers held round the hot glass. From outside came the raised voices of women discussing the prospects at the day's market, while men exchanged greetings as they made their way to the fields. Amidst the voices could be heard Hamdan's laughter as he led the buffalo to the two kirats of land surrounding the house.

"His account is with Allah," muttered Zeinat. "He's fine and doesn't have a worry in the world."

Ni'ma got up and began winding round the end of her headcloth so as to form a pad on her head. Zeinat turned round and saw her preparing herself to go off to the market. She pulled her by her djellaba and the young girl sat down again. At this moment they heard a knocking at the door and the voice of their neighbour, Umm al-Khair, calling:

"Good health to you, folk. Isn't Ni'ma coming with me to market as usual, Auntie Zeinat? Or isn't she up yet?"

"Sister, she's just going off to stay with our relatives."

"May Allah bring her back safely."

Ni'ma looked at her mother enquiringly, while Zeinat placed her finger to her mouth. When the sound of Umm al-Khair's footsteps died away, Ni'ma whispered:

"What are you intending to do, mother? What relatives are you talking about?"

Zeinat got up and rummaged in her clothes box and took out a handkerchief tied round some money, also old clothes. She placed the handkerchief in Ni'ma's palm and closed her fingers over it.

"Take it—they're my life savings."

Ni'ma remained silent as her mother went on:

"Get together your clothes and go straight away to the station and take a ticket to Cairo. Cairo's a big place, daughter, where you'll find protection and a way to make a living till Allah brings you safely to your time. Then bring it back with you at dead of night without anyone seeing you or hearing you."

Zeinat raised the end of her djellaba and put it between her teeth. Taking hold of the old cloths, she began winding them round her waist. Then she let fall the djellaba. Ni'ma regarded her in astonishment:

"And what will we say to my father?"

"It's not time for talking. Before you go off to the station, help me with the basket so that I can go to the market for people to see me like this. Isn't it better, when he returns, for your father to find himself with a legitimate son than an illegitimate grandson?"

ABOUT **ALIFA RIFAAT**

Alifa Rifaat (ə lē′fə ri fot′) is the pen name of Fatma Abdallah Rifaat, who lives in Cairo, Egypt. Rifaat is known for her stories about Moslem traditions and the role of women in family life. She also wrote "Another Evening at the Club," page 62.

RESPONDING

1. *Personal Response* Why do you think Zeinat chooses to deceive her neighbors and her husband? Is she doing it for Ni'ma's benefit alone, or for other reasons?

2. *Literary Analysis* What does the *dialogue* between Zeinat and Ni'ma reveal about the relationship between mother and daughter?

3. *Multicultural Connection* What responsibilities or powers would you say women have in the culture portrayed in this story? What responsibilities and powers do men have? How do these compare with male/female roles in your culture?

LANGUAGE WORKSHOP

Sequence You can often gain insight into a story by examining the *sequence* of events, especially when they are reported out of order. Number the following events from "An Incident in the Ghobashi Household" in their chronological order.

a. Zeinat asks if the grain is too heavy for Ni'ma to carry.
b. Father goes away.
c. Zeinat reveals her plan to deceive her husband.
d. Zeinat gives Ni'ma money to go to Cairo.
e. Father says, "Take care of Ni'ma."

WRITER'S PORTFOLIO

Are you a good keeper of secrets? Do you know someone else who is? Have you ever told someone else's secret? Have you ever made someone pledge secrecy? In your journal, write down your feelings about secrets.

The Mother of the Child in Question

HIGH ON A WALKWAY connecting
two tower blocks Stephen Bentley, social worker, stopped to
survey the view. Cement, everywhere he looked. Stained
grey piles went up into the sky, and down below lay grey
acres where only one person moved among puddles, soft
drink cans and bits of damp paper. This was an old man
with a stick and a shopping bag. In front of Stephen, hori-
zontally dividing the heavy building from pavement to low
cloud, were rows of many-coloured curtains where people
kept out of sight. They were probably watching him, but he
had his credentials, the file under his arm. The end of this
walkway was on the fourth floor. The lift smelled bad:
someone had been sick in it. He walked up grey urine-
smelling stairs to the eighth floor, Number 15. The very
moment he rang, the door was opened by a smiling brown
boy. This must be Hassan, the twelve-year-old. His white
teeth, his bright blue jersey, the white collar of his shirt, all
dazzled, and behind him the small room crammed with
furniture was too tidy for a family room, everything just so,
polished, shining. Thorough preparations had been made
for this visit. In front of a red plush sofa was the oblong of a
low table, and on it waited cups, saucers and a sugar bowl
full to the brim. A glinting spoon stood upright in it.
Hassan sat down on the sofa, smiling hard. Apart from the
sofa, there were three chairs, full of shiny cushions. In one
of them sat Mrs. Khan, a plump pretty lady wearing the

outfit Stephen thought of as "pyjamas"—trousers and tunic in flowered pink silk. They looked like best clothes, and the ten-year-old girl in the other chair wore a blue tunic and trousers, with earrings, bangles and rings. Mother wore a pink gauzy scarf, the child a blue one. These, in Pakistan, would be there ready to be pulled modestly up at the sight of a man, but here they added to the festive atmosphere. Stephen sat down in the empty chair at Mrs. Khan's (Stephen particularly noted) peremptory gesture. But she smiled. Hassan smiled and smiled. The little girl had not, it seemed, noticed the visitor, but she smiled too. She was pretty, like a kitten.

"Where is Mr. Khan?" asked Stephen of Mrs. Khan, who nodded commandingly at her son. Hassan at once said, "No, he cannot come, he is at work."

"But he told me he would be here. I spoke to him on the telephone yesterday."

Again the mother gave Hassan an order with her eyes, and he said, smiling with all his white teeth, "No, he is not here."

In the file that had the name Shireen Khan on the front, the last note, dated nine months before, said, "Father did not keep appointment. His presence essential."

Mrs. Khan said something in a low voice to her son, who allowed the smile to have a rest just as long as it took to fetch a tray with a pot of tea on it, and biscuits, from the sideboard. They must have been watching from the windows and made the tea when they saw him down there, file under his arm. Hassan put the smile back on his face when he sat down again. Mrs. Khan poured strong tea. The boy handed Stephen a cup, and the plate of biscuits. Mrs. Khan set a cup before her daughter, and counted five biscuits on to a separate plate and put this near the cup. The little girl was smiling at—it seemed—attractive private fancies. Mrs. Khan clicked her tongue with annoyance and said something to her in Urdu. But Shireen took no notice. She was bursting with internal merriment, and the result of her mother's prompting was that she tried to share this with her brother, reaching out to poke him mischievously, and laughing. Hassan could not prevent a real smile at her, tender, warm, charmed. He instantly removed this smile and put back the polite false one.

"Five," said Mrs. Khan in English. "She can count. Say five, Shireen." It was poor English, and she repeated the command in Urdu.

The little girl smiled delightfully and began breaking up the biscuits and eating them.

"If your husband would agree to it, Shireen could go to the school we discussed — my colleague William Smith discussed with you — when he came last year. It is a good school. It would cost a little but not much. It is Government funded but there is a small charge this year. Unfortunately."

Mrs. Khan said something sharp and the boy translated. His English was fluent. "It is not money. My father has the money."

"Then I am sorry but I don't understand. The school would be good for Shireen."

Well, within limits. In the file was a medical report, part of which read, "The child in question would possibly benefit to a limited extent from special tuition."

Mrs. Khan said something loud and angry. Her amiable face was twisted with anger. Anxiety and anger had become the air in this small overfilled overclean room, and now the little girl's face was woeful and her lips quivered. Hassan at once put out his hand to her and made soothing noises. Mrs. Khan tried simultaneously to smile at the child and show a formal cold face to the intrusive visitor.

Hassan said, "My mother says Shireen must go to the big school, Beavertree School."

"Is that where you go, Hassan?"

"Yes, sir."

"My name is Stephen, Stephen Bentley."

"Yes, sir."

"Your father should be here," said Stephen, trying not to sound peevish. There was something going on, but he could not make out what. If it wasn't that two daughters were doing well at school Stephen would have thought perhaps Mr. Khan was old-fashioned and didn't want Shireen educated. (The two girls were both older than Hassan, but being girls did not count. It was the oldest son who had to be here representing the father.) Not that there was any question of "educating" Shireen. So what was it? Certainly he had sounded perfunctory yesterday on the telephone, agreeing to be here today.

Mrs. Khan now took out a child's picture book she had put down the side of the armchair for this very moment, and held it in front of Shireen. It was a brightly coloured book, for a three-year-old, perhaps. Shireen smiled at it in a vacant willing way. Mrs. Khan turned the big pages, frowning and nodding encouragingly at Shireen. Then she made herself smile. The boy was smiling away like anything. Shireen was happy and smiling.

"Look," said Stephen, smiling but desperate, "I'm not saying that Shireen will learn to read well, or anything like that, but. . ."

At this Mrs. Khan slammed the book shut and faced him. No smiles. A proud, cold, stubborn woman, eyes flashing, she demolished him in Urdu.

Hassan translated the long tirade thus. "My mother says Shireen must go to the big school with the rest of us."

"But, Mrs. Khan, she can't go to the big school. How can she?" As Mrs. Khan did not seem to have taken this in, he addressed the question again to Hassan. "How can she go to the big school? It's not possible!"

Hassan's smile was wan, and Stephen could swear there were tears in his eyes. But he turned his face away.

ANOTHER ANGRY FLOOD from Mrs. Khan, but Hassan did not interpret. He sat silent and looked sombrely at the chuckling and delighted little girl who was stirring biscuit crumbs around her plate with her finger. Mrs. Khan got up, full of imperious anger, pulled Shireen up from her chair, and went stormily out of the room, tugging the child after her by the hand. Stephen could hear her exclaiming and sighing and moving around the next room, and addressing alternately admonishing and tender remarks to the child. Then she wept loudly.

Hassan said, "Excuse me, sir, but I must go to my school. I asked permission to be here, and my teacher said yes, but I must go back quickly."

"Did your father tell you to be here?"

Hassan hesitated. "No, sir. My mother said I must be here."

For the first time Hassan was really looking at him. It even seemed that he might say something, explain. . . His eyes were full of a plea. For understanding? There was pride there, hurt.

"Thank you for staying to interpret, Hassan," said the social worker. "I wish I could talk to your father. . ."

"Excuse me, excuse me," said Hassan, and went running out. Stephen called, "Goodbye, Mrs. Khan," got no reply, and followed the boy. Along the dismal, stained and smelly corridors. Down the grey cement stairs. On to the walkway. A wind was blowing, fresh and strong. He looked down and saw Hassan four storeys below, a small urgent figure racing across the cement, leaping puddles, kicking bits of paper. He reached the street and vanished. He was running from a situation he hated: his whole body shouted it. What on earth. . . Just *what* was all that about?

And then Stephen understood. Suddenly. Just like that. But he couldn't believe it. But yes, he had to believe it. No, it wasn't possible. . .

Not impossible. It was true.

Mrs. Khan did not know that Shireen was "subnormal" as the medical record put it. She was not going to admit it. Although she had two normal sons and two normal daughters, all doing well at school, and she knew what normal bright children were like, she was not going to make the comparison. For her, Shireen was normal. No good saying this was impossible. For Stephen was muttering, "No, it simply isn't *on*, it's crazy." Anyway, he found these "impossibilities" in his work every day. A rich and various lunacy inspired the human race and you could almost say the greater part of his work was dealing with this lunacy.

Stephen stood clutching the balustrade and gripping the file, because the wind was swirling noisily around the high walkway. His eyes were shut because he was examining in his mind's eye the picture of Mrs. Khan's face, that proud, cold, refusing look. So would a woman look while her husband shouted at her, "You stupid woman, she can't go to the big school with the others, why are you so stubborn? Do I have to explain it to you again?" She must have confronted her husband with this look and her silence a hundred times! And so he had not turned up for the appointment, or for the other appointment, because he knew it was no good. He didn't want to have to say to some social worker, "My wife's a fine woman, but she has this little peculiarity!" And Hassan wasn't going to say, "You see, sir, there's a little problem with my mother."

S TEPHEN, EYES STILL SHUT, went on replaying what he had seen in that room: the tenderness on Mrs. Khan's face for her afflicted child, the smile on the boy's face, the real, warm, affectionate smile, at his sister. The little girl was swaddled in their tenderness, the family adored her, what was she going to learn at the special school better than she was getting from her family?

Stephen found he was filling with emotions that threatened to lift him off the walkway with the wind and float him off into the sky like a balloon. He wanted to laugh, or clap his hands, or sing with exhilaration. That woman, that *mother*, would not admit her little girl was simple. She just wouldn't agree to it! Why, it was a wonderful thing, a miracle! Good for you, Mrs. Khan, said Stephen Bentley opening his eyes, looking at the curtained windows four floors above him where he had no doubt Mrs. Khan was watching him, proud she had won yet another victory against those busybodies who would class her Shireen as stupid.

"Bloody marvellous," shouted the social worker into the wind. He opened his file against his knee then and there and wrote, "Father did not turn up as arranged. His presence essential." The date. His own name.

ABOUT **DORIS LESSING**

Doris Lessing was born in 1919 in Iran, and her family moved to Rhodesia in 1924. She has made her home in England since 1949. Known for her frank treatment of social and political change, she has written complex novels such as *The Golden Notebook,* a science fiction series entitled *Canopus in Argos: Archives,* essays, and several collections of short stories.

RESPONDING

1. *Personal Response* Do you think Stephen Bentley is a conscientious social worker? Why or why not?

2. *Literary Analysis* Do you think Mrs. Khan actually realizes that her daughter is "subnormal"? What insights into her *character* does her reaction to the social worker provide?

3. *Multicultural Connection* Do you think that Mrs. Khan's behavior is influenced by her culture, or do you feel that she behaves the way any mother would? Explain.

LANGUAGE WORKSHOP

Ellipsis An *ellipsis* (. . .) indicates an omission or unfinished element in writing. In this story, ellipses are used to express that information is being withheld or is incomplete: "It even seemed that he might say something, explain. . ." Find two other examples of ellipses in the story and explain what information has been left out.

WRITER'S PORTFOLIO

Write a report in which you revise Stephen Bentley's files to accurately describe Shireen Khan's case. Make suggestions about how to proceed with her case in the future.

The Thief

IT WAS YEARS AGO, at the school where I was preparing for Tokyo Imperial University.

My dormitory roommates and I used to spend a lot of time at what we called "candlelight study" (there was very little studying to it), and one night, long after lights-out, the four of us were doing just that, huddled around a candle talking on and on.

I recall that we were having one of our confused, heated arguments about love — a problem of great concern to us in those days. Then, by a natural course of development, the conversation turned to the subject of crime: we found ourselves talking about such things as swindling, theft, and murder.

"Of all crimes, the one we're most likely to commit is murder." It was Higuchi, the son of a well-known professor, who declared this. "But I don't believe I'd ever steal — I just couldn't do it. I think I could be friends with any other kind of person, but a thief seems to belong to a different species." A shadow of distaste darkened his handsome features. Somehow that frown emphasized his good looks.

"I hear there's been a rash of stealing in the dormitory lately." This time it was Hirata who spoke. "Isn't that so?" he asked, turning to Nakamura, our other roommate.

"Yes, and they say it's one of the students."

"How do they know?" I asked.

"Well, I haven't heard all the details—" Nakamura dropped his voice to a confidential whisper. "But it's happened so often it must be an inside job."

"Not only that," Higuchi put in, "one of the fellows in the north wing was just going into his room the other day when somebody pushed the door open from the inside, caught him with a hard slap in the face, and ran away down the hall. He chased after him, but by the time he got to the bottom of the stairs the other one was out of sight. Back in his room, he found his trunk and bookshelves in a mess, which proves it was the thief."

"Did he see his face?"

"No, it all happened too fast, but he says he looked like one of us, the way he was dressed. Apparently he ran down the hall with his coat pulled up over his head—the one thing sure is that his coat had a wisteria crest."

"A wisteria crest?" said Hirata. "You can't prove anything by that." Maybe it was only my imagination, but I thought he flashed a suspicious look at me. At the same moment I felt that I instinctively made a wry face, since my own family crest is a wisteria design. It was only by chance that I wasn't wearing my crested coat that night.

"If he's one of us it won't be easy to catch him. Nobody wants to believe there's a thief among us." I was trying to get over my embarrassment because of that moment of weakness.

"No, they'll get him in a couple of days," Higuchi said emphatically. His eyes were sparkling. "This is a secret, but they say he usually steals things in the dressing room of the bathhouse, and for two or three days now the proctors have been keeping watch. They hide overhead and look down through a little hole."

"Oh? Who told you that?" Nakamura asked.

"One of the proctors. But don't go around talking about it."

"If *you* know so much, the thief probably knows it too!" said Hirata, looking disgusted.

Here I must explain that Hirata and I were not on very good terms. In fact, by that time we barely tolerated each other. I say "we," but it was Hirata who had taken a strong dislike to me. According to a friend of mine, he once remarked scornfully that I wasn't what everyone seemed to think I was, that he'd had a chance to see through me. And again: "I'm sick of him. He'll never be a friend of mine. It's only out of pity that I have anything to do with him."

He only said such things behind my back; I never heard them from him directly, though it was obvious that he loathed me. But it wasn't in my nature to demand an explanation. "If there's something wrong with me he ought to say so," I told myself. "If he doesn't have the kindness to tell me what it is, or if he thinks I'm not worth bothering with, then I won't think of *him* as a friend either." I felt a little lonely when I thought of his contempt for me, but I didn't really worry about it.

Hirata had an admirable physique and was the very type of masculinity that our school prides itself on, while I was skinny and pale and high-strung. There was something basically incompatible about us: I had to resign myself to the fact that we lived in separate worlds. Furthermore, Hirata was a judo expert of high rank, and displayed his muscles as if to say: "Watch out, or I'll give you a thrashing!" Perhaps it seemed cowardly of me to take such a meek attitude toward him, and no doubt I *was* afraid of his physical strength; but fortunately I was quite indifferent to matters of trivial pride or prestige. "I don't care how contemptuous the other fellow is; as long as I can go on believing in myself I don't need to feel bitter toward him." That was how I made up my mind, and so I was able to match Hirata's arrogance with my own cool magnanimity. I even told one of the other boys: "I can't help it if Hirata doesn't understand me, but I appreciate his good points anyway." And I actually believed it. I never considered myself a coward. I was even rather conceited, thinking I must be a person of noble character to be able to praise Hirata from the bottom of my heart.

"A wisteria crest?" That night, when Hirata cast his sudden glance at me, the malicious look in his eyes set my nerves on edge. What could that look possibly mean? Did he know that my family crest was Wisteria? Or did I take it that way simply because of my own private feelings? If Hirata suspected *me*, how was I to handle the situation? Perhaps I should laugh good-naturedly and say: "Then I'm under suspicion too, because I have the same crest." If the others laughed along with me, I'd be all right. But suppose one of them, say Hirata, only began looking grimmer and grimmer—what then? When I visualized that scene I couldn't very well speak out impulsively.

It sounds foolish to worry about such a thing, but during that brief silence all sorts of thoughts raced through my mind. "In this kind of situation what difference is there, really, between an innocent man and an actual criminal?" By then I felt that I was experiencing a criminal's anxiety and isolation. Until a moment ago I had been one of their friends, one of the elite of our famous school. But now, if only in my own mind, I was an outcast. It was absurd, but I suffered from my inability to confide in them. I was uneasy about Hirata's slightest mood—Hirata who was supposed to be my equal.

"A thief seems to belong to a different species." Higuchi had probably said this casually enough, but now his words echoed ominously in my mind.

"A thief belongs to a different species. . . ." A thief! What a detestable name to be called! I suppose what makes a thief different from other men is not so much his criminal act itself as his effort to hide it at all costs, the strain of trying to put it out of his mind, the dark fears that he can never confess. And now I was becoming enshrouded by that darkness. I was trying not to believe that I was under suspicion; I was worrying about fears that I could not admit to my closest friend. Of course it must have been because Higuchi trusted me that he told us what he'd heard from the proctor. "Don't go around talking about it," he had said, and I was glad. But why should I feel glad? I thought. After all, Higuchi has never suspected me. Somehow I began to wonder about his motive for telling us.

It also struck me that if even the most virtuous person has criminal tendencies, maybe I wasn't the only one who imagined the possibility of being a thief. Maybe the others were experiencing a little of the same discomfort, the same elation. If so, then Higuchi, who had been singled out by the proctor to share his secret, must have felt very proud. Among the four of us it was he who was most trusted, he who was thought least likely to belong to that "other species." And if he won that trust because he came from a wealthy family and was the son of a famous professor, then I could hardly avoid envying him. Just as his social status improved his moral character, so my own background—I was acutely conscious of being a scholarship student, the son of a poor farmer—debased mine. For me to feel a kind of awe in his presence had nothing to do with whether or not I was a thief. We *did* belong to different species. I felt that the more he trusted me, with his frank, open attitude, the more the gulf between us deepened. The more friendly we tried to be, joking with each other in apparent intimacy, gossiping and laughing together, the more the distance between us increased. There was nothing I could do about it.

For a long time afterward I worried about whether or not I ought to wear that coat of mine with the "wisteria crest." Perhaps if I wore it around nonchalantly no one would pay any attention. But suppose they looked at me as much as to say: "Ah, he's wearing it!" Some would suspect me, or try to suppress their doubts of me, or feel sorry for me because I was under suspicion. If I became embarrassed and uneasy not only with Hirata and Higuchi but with all the students, and if I then felt obliged to put my coat away, that would seem even more sinister. What I dreaded was not the bare fact of being suspect, but all the unpleasant emotions that would be stirred up in others. If I were to cause doubt in other people's minds I would create a barrier between myself and those who had always been my friends. Even theft itself was not as ugly as the suspicions that would be aroused by it. No one would want to think of me as a thief: as long as it hadn't been proved, they'd want to go on associating with me as freely as ever, forcing themselves to trust me. Otherwise, what would friendship mean? Thief or not, I might be guilty of a worse sin than stealing from a friend: the sin of spoiling a friendship. Sowing seeds of doubt about myself was criminal. It *was* worse than stealing. If I were a prudent, clever thief — no, I mustn't put it that way — if I were a thief with the least bit of conscience and consideration for other people, I'd try to keep my friendships untarnished, try to be open with my friends, treat them with a sincerity and warmth that I need never be ashamed of, while carrying out my thefts in secrecy. Perhaps I'd be what people call "a brazen thief," but if you look at it from the thief's point of view, it's the most honest attitude to take. "It's true that I steal, but it's equally true that I value my friends," such a man would say. "That is typical of a thief, that's why he belongs to a different species." Anyhow, when I started thinking that way, I couldn't help becoming more and more aware of the distance between me and my friends. Before I knew it I felt like a full-fledged thief.

ONE DAY I mustered up my courage and wore the crested coat out on the school grounds. I happened to meet Nakamura, and we began walking along together.

"By the way," I remarked, "I hear they haven't caught the thief yet."

"That's right," Nakamura answered, looking away.

"Why not? Couldn't they trap him at the bathhouse?"

"He didn't show up there again, but you still hear about lots of things being stolen in other places. They say the proctors called Higuchi in the other day and gave him the devil for letting their plan leak out."

"Higuchi?" I felt the color drain from my face.

"Yes. . . ." He sighed painfully, and a tear rolled down his cheek. "You've got to forgive me! I've kept it from you till now, but I think you ought to know the truth. You won't like this, but you're the one the proctors suspect. I hate to talk about it — I've never suspected you for a minute. I believe in you. And because I believe in you, I just had to tell you. I hope you won't hold it against me."

"Thanks for telling me. I'm grateful to you." I was almost in tears myself, but at the same time I thought: "It's come at last!" As much as I dreaded it, I'd been expecting this day to arrive.

"Let's drop the subject," said Nakamura, to comfort me. "I feel better now that I've told you."

"But we can't put it out of our minds just because we hate to talk about it. I appreciate your kindness, but I'm not the only one who's been humiliated—I've brought shame on you too, as my friend. The mere fact that I'm under suspicion makes me unworthy of friendship. Any way you look at it, my reputation is ruined. Isn't that so? I imagine you'll turn your back on me too."

"I swear I never will—and I don't think you've brought any shame on me." Nakamura seemed alarmed by my reproachful tone. "Neither does Higuchi. They say he did his best to defend you in front of the proctors. He told them he'd doubt himself before he doubted you."

"But they still suspect me, don't they? There's no use trying to spare my feelings. Tell me everything you know. I'd rather have it that way."

Then Nakamura hesitantly explained: "Well, it seems the proctors get all kinds of tips. Ever since Higuchi talked too much that night there haven't been any more thefts at the bathhouse, and that's why they suspect you."

"But I wasn't the only one who heard him!"—I didn't say this, but the thought occurred to me immediately. It made me feel even more lonely and wretched.

"But how did they know Higuchi told us? There were only the four of us that night, so if nobody else knew it, and if you and Higuchi trust me—"

"You'll have to draw your own conclusions," Nakamura said, with an imploring look. "You know who it is. He's misjudged you, but I don't want to criticize him."

A sudden chill came over me. I felt as if Hirata's eyes were glaring into mine.

"Did you talk to him about me?"

"Yes.... But I hope you realize that it isn't easy, since I'm his friend as well as yours. In fact, Higuchi and I had a long argument with him last night, and he says he's leaving the dormitory. So I have to lose one friend on the account of another."

I took Nakamura's hand and gripped it hard. "I'm grateful for friends like you and Higuchi," I said, tears streaming from my eyes. Nakamura cried too. For the first time in my life I felt that I was really experiencing the warmth of human compassion. That was what I had been searching for while I was tormented by my sense of help-less isolation. No matter how vicious a thief I might be, I could never steal anything from Nakamura.

After a while I said: "To tell you the truth, I'm not worth the trouble I'm causing you. I can't stand by in silence and see you two lose such a good friend because of someone like me. Even though he doesn't trust me, I still respect him. He's a far better man than I am. I recognize his value as well as anyone. So why don't I move out instead, if it's come to that? Please — let *me* go, and you three can keep on living together. Even if I'm alone I'll feel better about it."

"But there's no reason for you to leave," said Nakamura, his voice charged with emotion. "I recognize his good points too, but you're the one that's being perse-cuted. I won't side with him when it's so unfair. If *you* leave, *we* ought to leave too. You know how stubborn he is — once he's made up his mind to go he's not apt to change it. Why not let him do as he pleases? We might as well wait for him to come to his senses and apologize. That shouldn't take very long anyway."

"But he'll never come back to apologize. He'll go on hating me forever."

Nakamura seemed to assume that I felt resentful toward Hirata. "Oh, I don't think so," he said quickly. "He'll stick to his word — that's both his strength and his weakness — but once he knows he's wrong he'll come and apologize, and make a clean breast of it. That's one of the likable things about him."

"It would be fine if he did. . . ," I said thoughtfully. "He may come back to you, but I don't believe he'll ever make friends with me again. . . . But you're right, he's really lik-able. I only wish he liked me too."

Nakamura put his hand on my shoulder as if to protect his poor friend, as we plodded listlessly along on the grass. It was evening and a light mist hung over the school grounds: we seemed to be on an island surrounded by endless gray seas. Now and then a few students walking the other way would glance at me and go on. They already know, I thought; they're ostracizing me. I felt an overwhelming loneliness.

THAT NIGHT Hirata seemed to have changed his mind; he showed no intention of moving. But he refused to speak to us — even to Higuchi and Nakamura. Yet for me to leave at this stage was impossible, I decided. Not only would I be disregarding the kindness of my friends, I would be making myself seem all the more guilty. I ought to wait a little longer.

"Don't worry," my two friends were forever telling me. "As soon as they catch him the whole business will clear up." But even after another week had gone by, the criminal was still at large and the thefts were as frequent as ever. At last even Nakamura and Higuchi lost some money and a few books.

"Well, you two finally got it, didn't you? But I have a feeling the rest of us won't be touched." I remember Hirata's taunting look as he made this sarcastic remark.

After supper Nakamura and Higuchi usually went to the library, and Hirata and I were left to confront each other. I found this so uncomfortable that I began spending my evenings away from the dormitory too, either going to the library or taking long walks. One night around nine-thirty I came back from a walk and looked into our study. Oddly enough, Hirata wasn't there, nor did the others seem to be back yet. I went to look in our bedroom, but it was empty too. Then I went back to the study and over to Hirata's desk. Quietly I opened his drawer and ferreted out the registered letter that had come to him from his home a few days ago. Inside the letter were three ten-yen money orders, one of which I leisurely removed and put in my pocket. I pushed the drawer shut again and sauntered out into the hall. Then I went down to the yard, cut across the tennis court, and headed for the dark weedy hollow where I always buried the things I stole. But at that moment someone yelled: "Thief!" and flew at me from behind, knocking me down with a blow to my head. It was Hirata.

"Come on, let's have it! Let's see what you stuck in your pocket!"

"All right, all right, you don't have to shout like that," I answered calmly, smiling at him. "I admit I stole your money order. If you ask for it I'll give it back to you, and if you tell me to come with you I'll go anywhere you say. So we understand each other, don't we? What more do you want?"

Hirata seemed to hesitate, but soon began furiously raining blows on my face. Somehow the pain was not wholly unpleasant. I felt suddenly relieved of the staggering burden I had been carrying.

"There's no use beating me up like this, when I fell right into your trap for you. I made that mistake because you were so sure of yourself—I thought: 'Why the devil can't I steal from *him?*' But now you've found me out, so that's all there is to it. Later on we'll laugh about it together."

I tried to shake Hirata's hand good-naturedly, but he grabbed me by the collar and dragged me off toward our room. That was the only time Hirata seemed contemptible in my eyes.

"Hey, you fellows, I've caught the thief! You can't say I was taken in by him!" Hirata swaggered into our room and shoved me down in front of Nakamura and Higuchi, who were back from the library. Hearing the commotion, the other boys in the dormitory came swarming around our doorway.

"Hirata's right!" I told my two friends, picking myself up from the floor. "I'm the thief." I tried to speak in my normal tone, as casually as ever, but I realized that my face had gone pale.

"I suppose you hate me," I said to them. "Or else you're ashamed of me.... You're both honest, but you're certainly gullible. Haven't I been telling you the truth over and over again? I even said: 'I'm not the person you think I am.

Hirata's the man to trust. He'll never be taken in.' But you didn't understand. I told you: 'Even if you become friendly with Hirata again, he'll never make friends with *me!*' I went as far as to say: 'I know better than anyone what a fine fellow Hirata is!' Isn't that so? I've never lied to you, have I? You may ask why I didn't come out and tell you the whole truth. You probably think I was deceiving you after all. But try looking at it from my position. I'm sorry, but stealing is one thing I can't control. Still, I didn't like to deceive you, so I told you the truth in a roundabout way. I couldn't be any more honest than that—it's your fault for not taking my hints. Maybe you think I'm just being perverse, but I've never been more serious. You'll probably ask why I don't quit stealing, if I'm so anxious to be honest. But that's not a fair question. You see, I was born a thief. I tried to be as sincere as I could with you under the circumstances. There was nothing else I could do. Even then my conscience bothered me—didn't I ask you to let *me* move out, instead of Hirata? I wasn't trying to fool you, I really wanted to do it for your sake. It's true that I stole from you, but it's also true that I'm your friend. I appeal to your friendship: I want you to understand that even a thief has feelings."

Nakamura and Higuchi stood there in silence, blinking with astonishment.

"Well, I can see you think I've got a lot of nerve. You just don't understand me. I guess it can't be helped, since you're of a different species." I smiled to conceal my bitterness, and added: "But since I'm your friend I'll warn you that this isn't the last time a thing like this will happen. So be on your guard! You two made friends with a thief because of your gullibility. You're likely to run into trouble when you go out in the world. Maybe you get better grades in school, but Hirata is a better man. You can't fool Hirata!"

W$_{HEN}$ I SINGLED HIM OUT for praise, Hirata made a wry face and looked away. At that moment he seemed strangely ill at ease.

Many years have passed since then. I became a professional thief and have been often behind bars; yet I cannot forget those memories — especially my memories of Hirata. Whenever I am about to commit a crime I see his face before me. I see him swaggering about as haughtily as ever, sneering at me: "Just as I suspected!" Yes, he was a man of character with great promise. But the world is mysterious. My prediction that the naïve Higuchi would "run into trouble" was wrong: partly through his father's influence, he has had a brilliant career — traveling abroad, earning a doctoral degree, and today holding a high position in the Ministry of Railways. Meanwhile nobody knows what has become of Hirata. It's no wonder we think life is unpredictable.

I assure my reader that this account is true. I have not written a single dishonest word here. And, as I hoped Nakamura and Higuchi would, I hope you will believe that delicate moral scruples can exist in the heart of a thief like me.

But perhaps you won't believe me either. Unless of course (if I may be pardoned for suggesting it) you happen to belong to my own species.

ABOUT **JUNICHIRO TANIZAKI**

Junichiro Tanizaki (jù nē chē⁄rô tä nē zä⁄kē; 1886–1965) grew up in Tokyo and moved at age thirty-seven to Kyoto, Japan's ancient capital. His early writing, which bore similarities to the writing of Edgar Allan Poe, eventually gave way to a more traditional Japanese style. Tanizaki wrote novels as well as short stories, and for many years worked on a translation of the classical Japanese masterpiece *The Tale of Genji* into modern Japanese.

RESPONDING

1. Personal Response How do you think the narrator would define "telling the truth"? How close is this to your definition?

2. *Literary Analysis* Do you think this story has a *surprise ending*, or were you alerted to the outcome throughout the narration? Explain.

3. *Multicultural Connection* In many Asian cultures it is a great disgrace to bring shame on your friends or family. Do you think the narrator has done this? Why or why not?

LANGUAGE WORKSHOP

Synonyms and Antonyms *Synonyms* are words that mean nearly the same thing. *Antonyms* are words whose meanings are nearly opposite. Write each of the following pairs of words, labeling them *S* for synonyms or *A* for antonyms: *confidential, public; lying, deceit; contempt, loathing; arrogance, shame; elite, outcast; hide, conceal; suspicion, doubt; prudent, careful.*

WRITER'S PORTFOLIO

What do you think happened to Hirata? Write a page of dialogue in which the narrator and Hirata meet after thirty years and tell each other of their careers. Before you begin, decide whether or not they would be truthful.

The Butcher

THE CALL TO NOON PRAYER was beat-
ing down from the sun. A laborer mutters his devotion in
the scant shade of a sapling.

Guide us along the straight path
The path of those You have favored
Not of those with whom You are angry
Not of those who are lost.

Enough playing and sightseeing at the marketplace.
Time to go home for lunch. I had spent the day watching
the grape flies at the fruitseller's shade. They float silently
in the fragrant air, their wings blurred around them like
halos. They read your mind. Try to grab one and it has
already drifted serenely out of the way. No hurry, no panic.
They know the future.

On the short walk home memories of the fruitseller's
paradise are already being bleached by the sun.

Guide us along the straight path. . .

Why do we need guiding along the straight path? I
wonder.

I reach the house, but the gate is locked. I don't feel like
knocking; there is an easier way. The neighbors are building
their house and there are piles of bricks everywhere. After

many trips back and forth I have enough bricks to make a step stool with which to climb the wall into the house. My arms are scraped pink by the effort. I sneak to the kitchen and try to startle my mother.

"You better go put those bricks back before the neighbor sees them," she says.

The next day I pass by the fruitseller's and go straight to the cobbler's tiny shop. A pair of my mother's shoes need mending. The cobbler flashes a "two" with his finger, and goes back to the shoe at hand. His hair and beard look just like the bristles he uses on the shoes.

"I will wait for them here," I say as I pull up a stool. He does not hear me. The walls are covered with unfinished shoes waiting to be soled. They look like faces with their mouths wide open.

"They are shouting at each other," I say, pointing to the walls. The cobbler cannot hear them; he is deaf-mute. He emphatically flashes two fingers again. Come back in two hours. So I walk next door to the butcher's shop to look at the ghastly picture on his window and try to figure out what it means. I hesitate to ask him. Some things are better left alone.

The butcher is a decent man. He has to be, for he is entrusted with doing all our killing. Even though we pass on the act, we are still responsible for the deaths we cause. The killing must be done mercifully and according to the rules of God. The killer must be pure of heart and without malice for the world.

Our butcher was a man of great physical and moral strength. My mother said he reminded her of the legendary champion, Rustam. Rustam was so strong that he asked God to take away some of his strength so that he would not make potholes wherever he walked. The butcher was very big. Every time he brought down the cleaver, I feared he might split the butcher's block. His burly hands carried the power of life

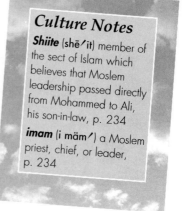

Culture Notes

Shiite (shē´it) member of the sect of Islam which believes that Moslem leadership passed directly from Mohammed to Ali, his son-in-law, p. 234

imam (i mäm´) a Moslem priest, chief, or leader, p. 234

and death. The carcasses hanging on the hooks and the smell of raw meat testified to this. Above the scales was a larger-than-life picture of the first Shiite imam, Ali, who supervised this Judgment-Day atmosphere with a stern but benevolent presence. Across Ali's lap lay his undefeated sword, Zulfaghar.

But the true object of my terror was the picture in the shop window.

A man was chopping off his own arm with a cleaver.

The artwork was eerie, as the man's face had no expression—he stared blankly at the viewer while the blood ran out. This was the butcher's logo. Underneath it the most common name for a butcher shop was beautifully calligraphed: *Javanmard* (man of integrity).

I had asked my mother what the mutilation signified. She had said it was a traditional symbol attesting the butcher's honesty, but she could not explain further.

"Is the butcher honest?" I had asked.

"Yes, he is very honest. We never have to worry about spoiled meat or bad prices."

"He would rather chop off his arm than be dishonest? Is that what his sign means?"

"Yes."

"What about other shopkeepers? What have they vowed to do in case they are dishonest?"

"I don't know."

"What about the cobbler? Did he do something dishonest? Is that what happened to him?"

"I don't know."

"Is that why people kill themselves? Because they have been very dishonest?"

"Look, it is just a picture. It's not worth having nightmares over. Next time you are there, you can ask him what it means."

I did not ask him about it until I was forced to by my conscience.

One day my mother sent me out to buy half a kilo of ground meat. She told me to tell the butcher that she wanted it without any fat. She knew it would be more expensive and gave me extra money to cover it. I got to the butcher shop at the busiest time of the day. One good thing about the butcher was that he, unlike other shopkeepers, helped the customers on a first-come, first-served basis. Status had no meaning for him and he could not be bribed. People knew this about him and respected it. When he asked whose turn it was, instead of the usual elbowing and jostling, he got a unanimous answer from the crowd. People do not lie to an honest man.

This gave great meaning to the picture of Ali above the scales. Ali, the Prophet's son-in-law and one-man army, is known for his uncompromising idealism. His guileless methods were interpreted as lack of political wisdom, and he was passed over three times for succession to Mohammad. When he did finally become caliph, he became an easy target for the assassin as he, like the Prophet, refused bodyguards for himself. Shiites regard him as the true successor to Mohammad and disregard the three caliphs that came before him.

W̲HEN MY TURN CAME UP, I asked for a half a kilo of ground meat with no fat. The butcher sliced off some meat from a carcass and ground it. Then he wrapped it in wax paper and wrapped that in someone's homework. Sometimes he used newspapers, but because of the Iranian habit of forcing students to copy volumes of text for homework, old notebook paper was as common as newsprint. He gave me the meat and I gave him the money and started to walk out, but he called me back and gave me some change. This was free money; my mother had not expected change. I took the money and immediately spent it on sweets.

When I went home, I did not tell her that she had given me too much money. I worried that she would know I had spent the change on candy and that she would yell at me for it.

Around noontime my mother called me into the kitchen. She asked me if I had told the butcher to put no fat in the meat. I said I had told him.

"I thought he was an honest man. He gave you meat with fat and charged you the higher price," she said sadly.

Now I knew where the extra money came from. In the heat of business he had forgotten about the "no fat" and had given me regular ground meat. But he had *not* charged me the higher price.

"We will go there now and straighten this out with him," she said sternly.

I thought about confessing, but I deluded myself into thinking the change had nothing to do with it. After all, *he* made the mistake. How much change had he given me anyway? Or maybe my mother was wrong about the quality of the meat. I was just a victim of the butcher's and my mother's stupidity.

It was still noontime as we set off to straighten out the butcher. The call to prayer was being sung. Across the neighborhood devout supplicants beseeched their maker.

Guide us along the straight path
The path of those You have favored
Not of those with whom You are angry
Not of those who are lost.

I was certainly lost. I was fighting the delusion like a drug, now dispelling it, now overwhelmed by it. When things were clear, I could see that I had done nothing wrong except fail to get permission to buy candy. The butcher made a mistake. I did not know about it, and I bought unauthorized candy. All I had to do was tell my mother and no crime would have been committed. The real crime was still a few minutes in the future, when I would endanger the reputation and livelihood of an honest man. I still had time to avert that.

Guide us along the straight path. . .

When delusion reigned, I felt I had committed a grave, irreversible sin that, paradoxically, others should be blamed for. The straight path was so simple, so forgiving; the other was harsh and muddled. How much more guidance did I need? The prayer did not say "chain us to the straight path." When we reached the shop, the butcher was cleaning the surfaces in preparation for lunch. He usually gathered with the cobbler and the fruitseller in front of the cobbler's shop. They spread their lunch cloth and ate a meal of bread and meat soup. In accordance with tradition, passersby were invited to join them, and in accordance with tradition, the invitation was declined with much apology and gratitude.

My mother told him that when she finished frying the meat, there was too much fat left over and she thought the wrong kind of meat had been sold. She asked if he remembered selling me the meat. The butcher was unclear. He remembered having to call me back to give me some change, but he was too busy at the time to remember more. My mother said that no change would have been involved as she had given me exact change. This confused the butcher and he decided that he did not remember the incident at all. His changing of his recollection added to my mother's suspicions. Meanwhile, Ali was glowering at me from the top of the scales, his Zulfaghar ready to strike. My face was hot and my fingers felt numb.

Finally, the butcher, who was not one to argue in the absence of evidence, ground the right amount of the right kind of meat, wrapped it in wax paper, wrapped that in someone's homework, and gave it to my mother. She offered to pay for it, but the butcher refused to accept the money and apologized for making the mistake. When we left, he was taking apart the meat grinder in order to clean it again.

On the way back I felt sleepy. My mother asked if I was all right.

"I'm fine," I said weakly.

"Your father will be home in a few more days," she reassured.

"Mother, do you think the butcher was dishonest?" I asked.

"No, I think he really made a mistake."

"How do you know that?"

"Because he gave us the new meat so willingly. If he was a greedy man, he would not have done that. He probably feels very bad."

A terrible thought occurred to me. "Bad enough to chop off his own arm?" I asked urgently.

"I don't think so," she said.

But I was not convinced. She did not know what awful things could happen off the straight path. "I have to go back," I said as I started to run.

"Where are you going, you crazy boy?"

"I have to ask him about the picture," I yelled.

"Ask him later, now is not the time. . . ." She gave up. I was already a whorl of dust.

I was panting and swallowing when I saw the butcher. He was having lunch with the cobbler and the fruitseller. What did I want now?

"Please, help yourself," said the butcher, inviting me to the spread. I just stood for a while.

"Why do you have a picture of the man chopping off his arm?" I finally asked. The cobbler was tapping the fruitseller on the back, asking what was going on. The fruitseller indicated a chopping motion over his own arm and pointed toward the butcher shop. The cobbler smiled and repeated the fruitseller's motions.

"That is the Javanmard," the butcher said. "He cheated Ali."

"Why?" I asked.

"Even when he was caliph, Ali did not believe in servants. One day a man came to the butcher's shop and bought some meat. The butcher put his thumb on the scale and so gave him less meat. Later he found out that the customer was Ali himself. The butcher was so distraught and ashamed that he got rid of the guilty thumb along with the arm," he said.

I was greatly relieved. One did not mutilate oneself for committing a wrong against just anybody. It had to be someone of Ali's stature. Our butcher was safe even if he was to blame himself for the mistake. But I had to be absolutely sure.

"So if one were to cheat someone not as holy as Ali, one would not have to feel so bad?" I asked. Looking back, I see that he interpreted this as a criticism of the moral of the parable. He was transfixed in thought for a long time. The cobbler was tapping the fruitseller again, but the fruitseller could not find the correct gestures; he kept shrugging irritably.

The butcher finally came to life again. "Ali was good at reminding us of the difference between good and bad," he explained.

I was glad I was not so gifted.

"Would he have killed the butcher with Zulfaghar?" I asked.

"No, in fact I think once he found out what the butcher had done, he went to him and healed the arm completely," he said, displaying his arms. I looked carefully at his arms, but there was not even a trace of an injury. "A miracle," he explained.

The fruitseller was able to translate this and the cobbler agreed vigorously. He had something to add to the story, but we could not understand him.

> **Culture Note**
>
> **chador** a large cloth used as a combination head covering, veil, and shawl, mostly among women in India and Iran, p. 239

During lunch I told my mother the butcher's story.

"Now why couldn't this wait until tomorrow?" she asked, collecting the dishes.

"Mother?"

"Yes?"

"If I were to get some change and not bring it back, what would you do?"

"Did you get change and not bring it back?" She smelled a guilty conscience.

"No, I was just wondering."

"It depends on what I had sent you to buy," she said deviously.

"Like meat for instance."

She pondered this while she did the dishes. When she was done, she donned her chador and asked me to put on my shoes.

"Where are we going?" I wondered.

"To the butcher's," she said curtly. "You are going to apologize and give him the money we owe him."

"It was *his* mistake," I protested guiltily.

"And you stood there all that time, under Ali's eyes, and watched him grind us the new meat without saying anything."

I followed her dolorously out the gate. I could tell she was upset because she was walking fast and did not care if her chador blew around. But halfway there she changed her mind and with a swish of her chador ordered me to follow her back home.

"Why are we going back, Mother?"

"If this gets out, they will never trust you at the market-place again," she said angrily.

"So we are not going to apologize?"

"Of course you will apologize. You are going to give him your summer homework so he can wrap his meat in it."

The summer homework filled two whole notebooks. The school had made us copy the entire second grade text. Completing it had been a torturous task and a major accomplishment. My mother had patiently encouraged me to get it out of the way early in the vacation so that it would not loom over me all summer.

"What will I tell the teacher?" I begged.

"You will either do the homework again or face whatever you get for not having it. Or maybe instead of the homework you can show her the composition you are going to write."

"We did not have to write any compositions," I whined.

"You are going to write one explaining why you don't have your homework."

So, for the fourth time that day I went to the butcher shop. It was still quiet at the marketplace; the butcher was taking a nap. He woke up to my shuffling and chuckled groggily when he saw me.

"I was looking for you in the skies but I find you on earth (long time no see)," he said.

I gave him my notebooks and told him that my mother said he could wrap meat in them. He thanked my mother and apologized again for the mistake. My mother had told me not to discuss that with him, so I left quickly.

Within a few days, scraps of my homework, wrapped around chunks of lamb, found their way into kitchens across the neighborhood.

I opted for writing the composition explaining the publication of my homework. My mother signed it. The teacher accepted it enthusiastically, and while other students were writing "How I spent my summer vacation," I was permitted to memorize the opening verses of the Koran. I had heard it many times before and knew the meaning, but I did not have it memorized. It goes:

Guide us along the straight path
The path of those You have favored. . .

A few summers later, the butcher became involved in the religious uprising against the Shah. He tacked a small picture of Khomeini next to Ali and Zulfaghar and would not take it down. His customers, including my mother, urged him not to be so foolish.

"Was Ali foolish to refuse body-guards?" he asked.

"You are not Ali, you are just a butcher. Khomeini is gone, exiled. At least hide his picture behind Ali's picture."

When he disappeared, we all worried that he would never come back. But a few days later, he opened his shop again and, as far as I know, never hid anything anywhere.

Culture Notes

Koran the sacred book of the Moslems, consisting of revelations of Allah to Mohammed, p. 241

uprising . . . Shah In early 1979, the West-supported government of Iran's shah was overthrown by the fundamentalist Moslem forces of Ayatollah Ruhollah Khomeini. p. 241

ABOUT **ARI B. SILETZ**

Ari B. Siletz (är′ē sī′lətz), who was born in 1953, grew up in Iran, attended school in England, and now lives with his family in California. In his collection *The Mullah with No Legs*, from which "The Butcher" comes, Siletz shows characters coming of age in Iran while encountering clashes between tradition and modernity.

RESPONDING

1. *Personal Response* Can you identify with the narrator's experience despite the unfamiliar setting and customs? Why or why not?

2. *Literary Analysis* What do you learn about life in Iran through Siletz's use of *local color* (the speech, dress, and customs of the locale)?

3. *Multicultural Connection* You would probably not find a butcher's logo like that described in the story in your community. You may, however, find other signs—for example, for a barbershop or pawnshop. Find out how these and other similar logos came about.

LANGUAGE WORKSHOP

Allusions An *allusion* is a reference to a historical or literary figure or event. It may refer to mythology, religion, or to any other aspect of ancient or modern culture. If people called you a Judas, for example, they would be making a biblical allusion comparing you to a traitor. What would it mean if someone were to call you a Romeo? the next Michael Jordan? another Mother Theresa?

Find three allusions in "The Butcher."

WRITER'S PORTFOLIO

"Guide us along the straight path," a line from the Koran, Islam's book of holy scriptures, appears five times in this story. Write a brief essay about the meaning this line has for the narrator.

Departure

Carolyn Forché

We take it with us, the cry
of a train slicing a field
leaving its stiff suture, a distant
tenderness as when rails slip
behind us and our windows
touch the field, where it seems
the dead are awake and so reach
for each other. Your hand
cups the light of a match
to your mouth, to mine, and I want
to ask if the dead hold
their mouths in their hands like this
to know what is left of them.
Between us, a tissue of smoke,
a bundle of belongings, luggage
that will seem to float beside us,
the currency we will change
and change again. Here is the name
of a friend who will take you in,
the papers of a man who vanished,
the one you will become when
the man you have been disappears.
I am the woman whose photograph
you will not recognize, whose face
emptied our eyes, whose eyes
were brief, like the smallest
of cities we slipped through.

The Chain

Christine Craig

I no longer care, keeping close my silence
has been a weight,
a lever pressing out my mind.
I want it told and said and printed down
the dry gullies,
circled through the muddy pools
outside my door.
I want it sung out high by thin-voiced elders,
front rowing murky churches.
I want it known by grey faces queuing under
greyer skies in countries waking
and sleeping with sleet and fog.
I want it known by hot faces pressed against
dust-streaked windows of country buses.

And you must know this now
I, me, I am a free black woman.
My grandmothers and their mothers
knew this and kept their silence
to compost up their strength,
kept it hidden
and played the game of deference
and agreement and pliant will.

It must be known now how that silent legacy
nourished and infused such a line,
such a close linked chain
to hold us until we could speak
until we could speak out
loud enough to hear ourselves
loud enough to hear ourselves
and believe our own words.

Afterglow

Jorge Luis Borges

Sunset is always disturbing
whether theatrical or muted,
but still more disturbing
is that last desperate glow
that turns the plain to rust
when on the horizon nothing is left
of the pomp and clamor of the setting sun.
How hard holding on to that light, so tautly drawn
    and different,
that hallucination which the human fear of the dark
imposes on space
and which ceases at once
the moment we realize its falsity,
the way a dream is broken
the moment the sleeper knows he is dreaming.

ABOUT **CAROLYN FORCHÉ**

Carolyn Forché (fôr shā⁄) was born in 1950 in Detroit, Michigan. She has taught at a variety of colleges and universities and worked as a journalist. Forché is recognized for her work as a human rights activist, particularly in Central America. "Departure" is from *The Country Between Us*, a collection of poems closely tied to her work in El Salvador in the late 1970s.

ABOUT **CHRISTINE CRAIG**

Christine Craig grew up in Jamaica. She writes poems, stories, training manuals, radio and television scripts, and children's books. A collection of her short stories, *Mint Tea*, was published in 1993. She has said, "I write, I am a feminist, I am a mother. I am a Jamaican woman. That's all the important things."

ABOUT **JORGE LUIS BORGES**

Jorge Luis Borges (hôr/hā lwēs bôr/hās) was born in Buenos Aires, Argentina, in 1899. After traveling in Europe as a youth, he returned to Buenos Aires in 1921 and began a career of writing essays, poems, character sketches, stories, and even detective novels. Often characterized by dreamlike settings, his works influenced many writers worldwide. Although blinded by an eye disease, Borges continued to write until his death in 1986.

RESPONDING

1. *Personal Response* Which of these poems are you most likely to remember? Why?

2. *Literary Analysis* These poems are full of memorable *images*—word pictures that appeal to the senses. Find an image from each poem and explain the sense(s) to which it appeals.

3. *Multicultural Connection* In which culture or under what circumstances would it be necessary to lose or hide one's identity? "The Chain" and "Departure" might provide some clues.

LANGUAGE WORKSHOP

Denotation and Connotation *Denotation* is a word's exact, literal meaning. *Connotation* is the associations that a word has apart from its literal meaning. For example, the denotation of *home* is a residence, a structure where one lives; but *home* may have connotations of cooking smells, spirited dinner conversation, outside street noises, and so on. Work with a partner to establish the connotations and denotations of the following words from the poems: *sunset, dream, chain, door, woman, free.*

WRITER'S PORTFOLIO

These poems are about secrets, deceptions, and dreams. Quick-write your associations with one of these words. Then use your ideas to write a brief poem.

One Word of Truth Outweighs the World

I THINK THAT WORLD LITERATURE has the power in these frightening times to help mankind see itself accurately despite what is advocated by partisans and by parties. It has the power to transmit the condensed experience of one region to another, so that different scales of values are combined, and so that one people accurately and concisely knows the true history of another with a power of recognition and acute awareness as if it had lived through that history itself — and could thus be spared repeating old mistakes. At the same time, perhaps we ourselves may succeed in developing our own WORLD-WIDE VIEW, like any man, with the center of the eye seeing what is nearby but the periphery of vision taking in what is happening in the rest of the world. We will make correlations and maintain world-wide standards.

Who, if not writers, are to condemn their own unsuccessful governments (in some states this is the easiest way to make a living; everyone who is not too lazy does it) as well as society itself, whether for its cowardly humiliation or for its self-satisfied weakness, or the lightheaded escapades of the young, or the youthful pirates brandishing knives?

We will be told: What can literature do against the pitiless onslaught of naked violence? Let us not forget that violence does not and cannot flourish by itself; it is inevitably intertwined with LYING. Between them there is the closest, the most profound and natural bond: nothing screens violence except lies, and the only way lies can hold out is by violence. Whoever has once announced violence as his METHOD must inexorably choose lying as his PRINCIPLE. At birth, violence behaves openly and even proudly. But as soon as it becomes stronger and firmly established, it senses the thinning of the air around it and cannot go on without befogging itself in lies, coating itself with lying's sugary oratory. It does not always or necessarily go straight for the gullet; usually it demands of its victims only allegiance to the lie, only complicity in the lie.

About Mass and Energy

the law . . . mass and energy This law states that mass and energy cannot be lost in a physical or chemical change. p. 249

The simple act of an ordinary courageous man is not to take part, not to support lies! Let *that* come into the world and even reign over it, but not through me. Writers and artists can do more: they can VANQUISH LIES! In the struggle against lies, art has always won and always will. Conspicuously, incontestably for everyone. Lies can stand up against much in the world, but not against art.

Once lies have been dispelled, the repulsive nakedness of violence will be exposed — and hollow violence will collapse.

That, my friends, is why I think we can help the world in its red-hot hour: not by the nay-saying of having no armaments, not by abandoning oneself to the carefree life, but by going into battle!

In Russian, proverbs about TRUTH are favorites. They persistently express the considerable, bitter, grim experience of the people, often astonishingly:

ONE WORD OF TRUTH OUTWEIGHS THE WORLD.

On such a seemingly fantastic violation of the law of the conservation of mass and energy are based both my own activities and my appeal to the writers of the whole world.

ABOUT **ALEXANDER SOLZHENITSYN**

Alexander Solzhenitsyn (sōl zhə nēt′sən) was born in southern Russia in 1918, the year after the Bolshevik Revolution. Awarded the Nobel Prize for Literature in 1970, he did not attend the ceremony in Stockholm for fear he would not be allowed to return home. In 1974, after foreign publication of *The Gulag Archipelago*, his history of Soviet prisons and labor camps, he was exiled from the Soviet Union and lived in Switzerland and the United States. In 1990, his Russian citizenship was restored. "One Word of Truth Outweighs the World" is part of his unpresented Nobel speech.

RESPONDING

1. *Personal Response* Solzhenitsyn writes, "Whoever has once announced violence as his METHOD must inexorably choose lying as his PRINCIPLE." What does he mean? Do you agree or disagree? Why?

2. *Literary Analysis* The *title* of this speech is based on a Russian proverb. What does it mean? How does it compare to another proverb, "The pen is mightier than the sword"?

3. *Multicultural Connection* Solzhenitsyn says that literature should enable one people to know the history of another people so that it can "be spared making old mistakes." Describe to your classmates a work of literature you have read that might prevent you from making mistakes.

LANGUAGE WORKSHOP

Persuasive Writing *Persuasive writing* is designed to convince others to accept an opinion by giving strong reasons in support of that opinion. Solzhenitsyn makes his point by using loaded words ("cowardly humiliation, self-satisfied weakness"), by using memorable images ("youthful pirates brandishing knives"), and by crafting strong topic sentences. Find five other examples of these techniques, along with any additional techniques that you think make his writing persuasive.

WRITER'S PORTFOLIO

Review the stories, poems, and nonfiction excerpts that you have read in this class so far. Which single selection strikes you as being best at vanquishing lies? Write a paragraph explaining why you settled on that particular piece.

Projects

SCRIPT FOR A FAMOUS DECEPTION

Working in small groups, research a historical or legendary deception that had personal, military, and/or political consequences. Possibilities include the incident of the Trojan horse, the Watergate scandal in the United States, or Iago's deceptions in *Othello*. Write a script for a reenactment of the moment at which the deception is discovered. In a five-minute presentation, live or on videotape, perform the reenactment for the class. Include enough background information about the deception to make its discovery dramatic and understandable.

EYE FOOLERS: PUZZLE KIT

Do some research on optical illusions or other things that deceive the eye, collecting art, objects, diagrams, puzzles, and tricks, along with explanations of how these things work. You might even want to interview a magician about sleight-of-hand techniques. Then make a puzzle kit, complete with artifacts, copies, and explanations. Decorate the box with eye-tricking designs. Present the puzzle box to classmates and let them explore its contents.

WRITING ABOUT TRUTH THROUGH LITERATURE

Alexander Solzhenitsyn observes that through reading literature, people can be spared from making mistakes others have made. Write an essay explaining what he means and whether or not you agree with him. Use some of the selections in this unit, along with other works of literature you have read to support your ideas.

Further Reading

The following titles provide good background reading for "Secrets and Deceptions," presenting characters who are inclined to conceal or expose the truth.

Achebe, Chinua and Innes, C. L. eds. *Contemporary African Short Stories.* Heinemann, 1992. Stories written since 1983 by both established and new African writers explore many facets of the human experience — from the ordinary to the supernatural.

Achebe, Chinua. *Things Fall Apart.* Fawcett, 1985. This novel's protagonist, Okonkwo, is an Ibo torn between the old and the new and between his inner uncertainties and the outer invasions of colonialism.

Craig, Christine. *Quadrille for Tigers.* Mina Press, 1984. Craig strips away stereotypes of the Caribbean people and lifestyles in these lyrical poems that touch on heritage, selfhood, and home.

Lessing, Doris. *The Real Thing.* HarperCollins, 1992. Eighteen sketches and stories focus on scenes of contemporary London and the darker side of human relationships.

Mrożek, Slawomir. *The Elephant.* Grove-Atlantic, 1985. Brief stories, usually with a moral, satirize human foibles and authoritarian regimes.

Orwell, George. *Animal Farm.* NAL-Dutton, 1983. This satiric fable about communism features rebelling farm animals, corrupted by power, who become tyrants that rule by deception.

Siletz, Ari. *The Mullah with No Legs and Other Stories: A Collection of Iranian Short Stories.* Intercultural Press, 1992. These stories, which are characterized by Siletz's wit and humor, present readers with a view of Iran "through the lens of American culture."

Youth
on the
Threshold

Imagine yourself poised in a
doorway, about to step forward. What are you moving
into? What are you leaving
behind? We have all crossed
the threshold between youth
and maturity — over and over
again. The characters in this
unit advance on the significant
passage toward adulthood not
in one move but in small incre-
ments, sometimes intentionally,
but more often because circumstances force them to do so.

Father's Help

LYING IN BED, Swami realized with a shudder that it was Monday morning. It looked as though only a moment ago it had been the last period on Friday; already Monday was here. He hoped that an earthquake would reduce the school building to dust, but that good building — Albert Mission School — had withstood similar prayers for over a hundred years now. At nine o'clock Swaminathan wailed, "I have a headache." His mother said, "Why don't you go to school in a jutka?"

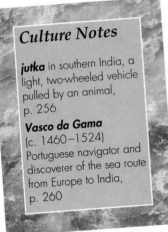

Culture Notes

jutka in southern India, a light, two-wheeled vehicle pulled by an animal, p. 256

Vasco da Gama (c. 1460–1524) Portuguese navigator and discoverer of the sea route from Europe to India, p. 260

"So that I may be completely dead at the other end? Have you any idea what it means to be jolted in a jutka?"

"Have you many important lessons today?"

"Important! Bah! That geography teacher has been teaching the same lesson for over a year now. And we have arithmetic, which means for a whole period we are going to be beaten by the teacher. . . . Important lessons!"

And Mother generously suggested that Swami might stay at home.

At 9:30, when he ought to have been shouting in the school prayer hall, Swami was lying on the bench in

Mother's room. Father asked him, "Have you no school today?"

"Headache," Swami replied.

"Nonsense! Dress up and go."

"Headache."

"Loaf about less on Sundays and you will be without a headache on Monday."

Swami knew how stubborn his father could be and changed his tactics. "I can't go so late to the class."

"I agree, but you'll have to; it is your own fault. You should have asked me before deciding to stay away."

"What will the teacher think if I go so late?"

"Tell him you had a headache and so are late."

"He will beat me if I say so."

"Will he? Let us see. What is his name?"

"Samuel."

"Does he beat the boys?"

"He is very violent, especially with boys who come late. Some days ago a boy was made to stay on his knees for a whole period in a corner of the class because he came late, and that after getting six cuts from the cane and having his ears twisted. I wouldn't like to go late to Samuel's class."

"If he is so violent, why not tell your headmaster about it?"

"They say that even the headmaster is afraid of him. He is such a violent man."

And then Swami gave a lurid account of Samuel's violence; how when he started caning he would not stop till he saw blood on the boy's hand, which he made the boy press to his forehead like a vermilion marking. Swami hoped that with this his father would be made to see that he couldn't go to his class late. But Father's behaviour took an unexpected turn. He became excited. "What do these swine mean by beating our children? They must be driven out of service. I will see. . . ."

The result was he proposed to send Swami late to his class as a kind of challenge. He was also going to send a letter with Swami to the headmaster. No amount of protest from Swami was of any avail: Swami had to go to school.

By the time he was ready Father had composed a long letter to the headmaster, put it in an envelope and sealed it.

"What have you written, Father?" Swaminathan asked apprehensively.

"Nothing for you. Give it to your headmaster and go to your class."

"Have you written anything about our teacher Samuel?"

"Plenty of things about him. When your headmaster reads it he will probably dismiss Samuel from the school and hand him over to the police."

"What has he done, Father?"

"Well, there is a full account of everything he has done in the letter. Give it to your headmaster and go to your class. You must bring an acknowledgement from him in the evening."

Swami WENT TO SCHOOL feeling that he was the worst perjurer on earth. His conscience bothered him: he wasn't at all sure if he had been accurate in his description of Samuel. He could not decide how much of what he had said was imagined and how much of it was real. He stopped for a moment on the roadside to make up his mind about Samuel: he was not such a bad man after all. Personally he was much more genial than the rest; often he cracked a joke or two centring around Swami's inactions, and Swami took it as a mark of Samuel's personal regard for him. But there was no doubt that he treated people badly. . . . His cane skinned people's hands. Swami cast his mind about for an instance of this. There was none within his knowledge. Years and years ago he was reputed to have skinned the knuckles of a boy in First Standard and made him smear the blood on his face. No one had actually seen it. But year after year the story persisted among the boys. . . . Swami's head was dizzy with confusion in regard to Samuel's character—whether he was good or bad, whether he deserved the allegations in the letter or not. . . . Swami felt an impulse to run home and beg his father to take back the letter. But Father was an obstinate man.

As he approached the yellow building he realized that he was perjuring himself and was ruining his teacher. Probably the headmaster would dismiss Samuel and then the police would chain him and put him in jail. For all this disgrace, humiliation and suffering, who would be responsible? Swami shuddered. The more he thought of Samuel, the more he grieved for him — the dark face, his small red-streaked eyes, his thin line of moustache, his unshaven cheek and chin, his yellow coat; everything filled Swami with sorrow. As he felt the bulge of the letter in his pocket, he felt like an executioner. For a moment he was angry with his father and wondered why he should not fling into the gutter the letter of a man so unreasonable and stubborn.

As he entered the school gate an idea occurred to him, a sort of solution. He wouldn't deliver the letter to the head-master immediately, but at the end of the day — to that extent he would disobey his father and exercise his independence. There was nothing wrong in it, and Father would not know anyway. If the letter was given at the end of the day there was a chance that Samuel might do something to justify the letter.

Swami stood at the entrance to his class. Samuel was teaching arithmetic. He looked at Swami for a moment. Swami stood hoping that Samuel would fall on him and tear his skin off. But Samuel merely asked, "Are you just coming to the class?"

"Yes, sir."

"You are half an hour late."

"I know it." Swami hoped that he would be attacked now. He almost prayed: "God of Thirupathi, please make Samuel beat me."

"Why are you late?"

Swami wanted to reply, "Just to see what you can do." But he merely said, "I have a headache, sir."

"Then why did you come to the school at all?"

A most unexpected question from Samuel. "My father said that I shouldn't miss the class, sir," said Swami.

This seemed to impress Samuel. "Your father is quite right; a very sensible man. We want more parents like him."

"Oh, you poor worm!" Swami thought. "You don't know what my father has done to you." He was more puzzled than ever about Samuel's character.

"All right, go to your seat. Have you still a headache?"

"Slightly, sir."

Swami went to his seat with a bleeding heart. He had never met a man so good as Samuel. The teacher was inspecting the home lessons, which usually produced (at least, according to Swami's impression) scenes of great violence. Notebooks would be flung at faces, boys would be abused, caned and made to stand up on benches. But today Samuel appeared to have developed more tolerance and gentleness. He pushed away the bad books, just touched people with the cane, never made anyone stand up for more than a few minutes. Swami's turn came. He almost thanked God for the chance.

"Swaminathan, where is your homework?"

"I have not done any homework, sir," he said blandly.

There was a pause.

"Why — headache?" asked Samuel.

"Yes, sir."

"All right, sit down." Swami sat down, wondering what had come over Samuel. The period came to an end, and Swami felt desolate. The last period for the day was again taken by Samuel. He came this time to teach them Indian history. The period began at 3:45 and ended at 4:30. Swaminathan had sat through the previous periods thinking acutely. He could not devise any means of provoking Samuel. When the clock struck four Swami felt desperate. Half an hour more. Samuel was reading the red text, the portion describing Vasco da Gama's arrival in India. The boys listened in half-languor. Swami suddenly asked at the top of his voice, "Why did not Columbus come to India, sir?"

"He lost his way."

"I can't believe it; it is unbelievable, sir."

"Why?"

"Such a great man. Would he have not known the way?"

"Don't shout. I can hear you quite well."

"I am not shouting, sir; this is my ordinary voice, which God has given me. How can I help it?"

"Shut up and sit down."

Swaminathan sat down, feeling slightly happy at his success. The teacher threw a puzzled, suspicious glance at him and resumed his lessons.

His next chance occurred when Sankar of the first bench got up and asked, "Sir, was Vasco da Gama the very first person to come to India?"

Before the teacher could answer, Swami shouted from the back bench, "That's what they say."

The teacher and all the boys looked at Swami. The teacher was puzzled by Swami's obtrusive behaviour today. "Swaminathan, you are shouting again."

"I am not shouting, sir. How can I help my voice, given by God?" The school clock struck a quarter-hour. A quarter more. Swami felt he must do something drastic in fifteen minutes. Samuel had no doubt scowled at him and snubbed him, but it was hardly adequate. Swami felt that with a little more effort Samuel could be made to deserve dismissal and imprisonment.

THE TEACHER came to the end of a section in the textbook and stopped. He proposed to spend the remaining few minutes putting questions to the boys. He ordered the whole class to put away their books, and asked someone in the second row, "What is the date of Vasco da Gama's arrival in India?"

Swaminathan shot up and screeched, "1648, December 20."

"You needn't shout," said the teacher. He asked, "Has your headache made you mad?"

"I have no headache now, sir," replied the thunderer brightly.

"Sit down, you idiot." Swami thrilled at being called an idiot. "If you get up again I will cane you," said the teacher. Swami sat down, feeling happy at the promise. The teacher then asked, "I am going to put a few questions on the Mughal period. Among the Mughal emperors, whom would you call the greatest, whom the strongest, and whom the most religious emperor?"

Swami got up. As soon as he was seen, the teacher said emphatically, "Sit down."

"I want to answer, sir."

"Sit down."

"No, sir; I want to answer."

"What did I say I'd do if you got up again?"

"You said you would cane me and peel the skin off my knuckles and make me press it on my forehead."

"All right; come here."

Swaminathan left his seat joyfully and hopped on the platform. The teacher took out his cane from the drawer and shouted angrily, "Open your hand, you little devil." He whacked three wholesome cuts on each palm. Swami received them without blenching. After half a dozen the teacher asked, "Will these do, or do you want some more?"

Swami merely held out his hand again, and received two more; and the bell rang. Swami jumped down from the platform with a light heart, though his hands were smarting. He picked up his books, took out the letter lying in his pocket and ran to the headmaster's room. He found the door locked.

He asked the peon, "Where is the headmaster?"

"Why do you want him?"

"My father has sent a letter for him."

"He has taken the afternoon off and won't come back for a week. You can give the letter to the assistant headmaster. He will be here now."

"Who is he?"

"Your teacher, Samuel. He will be here in a second."

Swaminathan fled from the place. As soon as Swami went home with the letter, Father remarked, "I knew you wouldn't deliver it, you coward."

"I swear our headmaster is on leave," Swaminathan began.

Father replied, "Don't lie in addition to being a coward. . . ."

Swami held up the envelope and said, "I will give this to the headmaster as soon as he is back. . . ." Father snatched it from his hand, tore it up and thrust it into the wastepaper basket under his table. He muttered, "Don't come to me for help even if Samuel throttles you. You deserve your Samuel."

ABOUT R. K. NARAYAN

R(asipuram) K(rishnaswami) Narayan (nä ri/yän), perhaps the best-known Indian today writing in English, was born in 1906 in Madras, India. The fictional town of Malgudi, where many of his works are set, is a microcosm of the world. Narayan's characters are more concerned about human relationships than about politics and social issues.

RESPONDING

1. *Personal Response* What do you think was in the letter from Swami's father to the headmaster? Why do you think so?

2. *Literary Analysis* The main character in a story is called the *protagonist;* the opposing character, the *antagonist.* Do you think that Samuel, the antagonist, fits the description of a story villain? Why or why not?

3. *Multicultural Connection* The practice of corporal punishment (physical discipline) in schools has been debated in many cultures. How do you think it would work at your school? Would your student culture — or the culture at large — benefit or suffer from it?

LANGUAGE WORKSHOP

Verb Tenses Three of the basic tenses are past, present, and future. Keep tenses in your writing consistent, unless there is a reason to shift them. For example, "When I *was* six, I first *realized* that fire *is* dangerous." (*Was* and *realized* denote a past condition, but *is* denotes a fact that is always true.) Choose the italicized expression that is in the best tense for each of these examples.

1. Samuel wants Swami to explain, but Swami (*said, says, will say*) nothing.
2. If Samuel will cane Swami for shouting, it (*made, makes, will make*) Swami feel better.
3. Although Samuel was kind to Swami, the boy (*feels, will feel, felt*) disappointed by this treatment.
4. Every schoolboy will learn that Vasco da Gama (*is, was, will be*) honored each year for finding a sea route from Europe to India.

WRITER'S PORTFOLIO

Think of the most elaborate excuse you could give for being late to school—one that will make your principal or teacher laugh. Now draft a note no longer than two paragraphs presenting your excuse.

Fathers and Daughters

Vietnam has had a long history of war and occupation. Conquered by the Chinese under the Han dynasty in the third century B.C., *the Vietnamese finally established and maintained an independent state from the tenth to the late nineteenth century when the French seized control. After World War II, the French were defeated by Ho Chi Minh, a Vietnamese Communist who became head of the Viet Minh. The country was divided into communist North Vietnam and noncommunist South Vietnam. In the late 1950s, rebels known as the Viet Cong, who were backed by North Vietnam, revolted against the South Vietnamese government. The war escalated and by 1965, the U.S. began sending ground combat troops to Vietnam and bombing North Vietnam. The following excerpt, taken from* When Heaven and Earth Changed Places, *describes growing up amidst this tumultuous background during the 1950s and early '60s.*

AFTER MY BROTHER BON WENT North, I began to pay more attention to my father.

He was built solidly—big-boned—for a Vietnamese man, which meant he probably had well-fed, noble ancestors. People said he had the body of a natural-born warrior. He was a year younger and an inch shorter than my mother, but just as good-looking. His face was round, like a

Khmer or Thai, and his complexion was brown as soy from working all his life in the sun. He was very easygoing about everything and seldom in a hurry. Seldom, too, did he say no to a request—from his children or his neighbors.

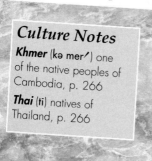

Culture Notes

Khmer (kə mer′) one of the native peoples of Cambodia, p. 266

Thai (ti) natives of Thailand, p. 266

Although he took everything in stride, he was a hard and diligent worker. Even on holidays, he was always mending things or tending to our house and animals. He would not wait to be asked for help if he saw someone in trouble. Similarly, he always said what he thought, although he knew, like most honest men, when to keep silent. Because of his honesty, his empathy, and his openness to people, he understood life deeply. Perhaps that is why he was so easygoing. Only a half-trained mechanic thinks everything needs fixing.

He loved to smoke cigars and grew a little tobacco in our yard. My mother always wanted him to sell it, but there was hardly ever enough to take to market. I think for her it was the principle of the thing: smoking cigars was like burning money. Naturally, she had a song for such gentle vices—her own habit of chewing betel nuts included:

> Get rid of your tobacco,
> And you will get a water buffalo.
> Give away your betel,
> And you will get more paddy land.

Despite her own good advice, she never abstained from chewing betel, nor my father from smoking cigars. They were rare luxuries that life and the war allowed them.

My father also liked rice wine, which we made; and enjoyed an occasional beer, which he purchased when there was nothing else we needed. After he'd had a few sips, he would tell jokes and happy stories and the village kids would flock around. Because I was his youngest daughter, I was entitled to listen from his knee—the place of honor. Sometimes he would sing funny songs about whoever threatened the village and we would feel better. For example, when the French or Moroccan soldiers were near, he would sing:

> There are many kinds of vegetables,
> Why do you like spinach?
> There are many kinds of wealth,
> Why do you use Minh money?
> There are many kinds of people,
> Why do you love terrorists?

We laughed because these were all the things the French told us about the Viet Minh fighters whom we favored in the war. Years later, when the Viet Cong were near, he would sing:

> There are many kinds of vegetables,
> Why do you like spinach?
> There are many kinds of money,
> Why do you use Yankee dollars?
> There are many kinds of people,
> Why do you disobey your ancestors?

This was funny because the words were taken from the speeches the North Vietnamese cadres delivered to shame us for helping the Republic. He used to have a song for when the Viet Minh were near too, which asked in the same way, "Why do you use francs?" and "Why do you love French traitors?" Because he sang these songs with a comical voice, my mother never appreciated them. She couldn't see the absurdity of our situation as clearly as we children. To her, war and real life were different. To us, they were all the same.

Even as a parent, my father was more lenient than our mother, and

Culture Notes

French or Moroccan former colonists who occupied Vietnam until the mid-twentieth century, p. 267

Viet Minh fighters against the French, p. 267

North Vietnamese cadres representatives of the communist half of Vietnam, p. 267

Republic South Vietnam, p. 267

we sometimes ran to him for help when she was angry. Most of the time, it didn't work and he would lovingly rub our heads as we were dragged off to be spanked. The village saying went: "A naughty child learns more from a whipping stick than a sweet stick." We children were never quite sure about that, but agreed the whipping stick was an eloquent teacher. When he absolutely had to punish us himself, he didn't waste time. Wordlessly, he would find a long, supple bamboo stick and let us have it behind our thighs. It stung, but he could have whipped us harder. I think seeing the pain in his face hurt more than receiving his halfhearted blows. Because of that, we seldom did anything to merit a father's spanking—the highest penalty in our family. Violence in any form offended him. For this reason, I think, he grew old before his time.

One of the few times my father ever touched my mother in a way not consistent with love was during one of the yearly floods, when people came to our village for safety from the lower ground. We sheltered many in our house, which was nothing more than a two-room hut with woven mats for a floor. I came home one day in winter rain to see refugees and Republican soldiers milling around outside. They did not know I lived there so I had to elbow my way inside. It was nearly supper time and I knew my mother would be fixing as much food as we could spare.

In the part of the house we used as our kitchen, I discovered my mother crying. She and my father had gotten into an argument outside a few minutes before. He had assured the refugees he would find something to eat for everyone and she insisted there would not be enough for her children if everyone was fed. He repeated his order to her, this time loud enough for all to hear. Naturally, he thought this would end the argument. She persisted in contradicting him, so he had slapped her.

This show of male power—we called it *do danh vo*— was usual behavior for Vietnamese husbands but unusual for my father. My mother could be as strict as she wished with his children and he would seldom interfere. Now, I discovered there were limits even to his great patience. I saw the glowing red mark on her cheek and asked if she was crying because it hurt. She said no. She said she was crying because her action had caused my father to lose face in front of strangers. She promised that if I ever did what she had done to a husband, I would have both cheeks glowing: one from his blow and one from hers.

ONCE, WHEN I WAS THE ONLY CHILD at home, my mother went to Danang to visit Uncle Nhu, and my father had to take care of me. I woke up from my nap in the empty house and cried for my mother. My father came in from the yard and reassured me, but I was still cranky and continued crying. Finally, he gave me a rice cookie to shut me up. Needless to say, this was a tactic my mother never used.

The next afternoon I woke up and although I was not feeling cranky, I thought a rice cookie might be nice. I cried a fake cry and my father came running in.

"What's this?" he asked, making a worried face. "Little Bay Ly doesn't want a cookie?"

I was confused again.

"Look under your pillow," he said with a smile.

I twisted around and saw that, while I was sleeping, he had placed a rice cookie under my pillow. We both laughed and he picked me up like a sack of rice and carried me outside while I gobbled the cookie.

In the yard, he plunked me down under a tree and told me some stories. After that, he got some scraps of wood and showed me how to make things: a doorstop for my mother and a toy duck for me. This was unheard of—a father doing these things with a child that was not a son! Where my mother would instruct me on cooking and cleaning and tell stories about brides, my father showed me the mystery of hammers and explained the customs of our people.

His knowledge of the Vietnamese went back to the Chinese Wars in ancient times. I learned how one of my distant ancestors, a woman named Phung Thi Chinh, led Vietnamese fighters against the Han. In one battle, even though she was pregnant and surrounded by Chinese, she delivered the baby, tied it to her back, and cut her way to safety wielding a sword in each hand. I was amazed at this warrior's bravery and impressed that I was her descendant. Even more, I was amazed and impressed by my father's pride in her accomplishments (she was, after all, a humble female), and his belief that I was worthy of her example. *"Con phai theo got chan co ta"* (Follow in her footsteps), he said. Only later would I learn what he truly meant.

Never again did I cry after my nap. Phung Thi women were too strong for that. Besides, I was my father's daughter and we had many things to do together.

On the eve of my mother's return, my father cooked a feast of roast duck. When we sat down to eat it, I felt guilty and my feelings showed on my face. He asked why I acted so sad.

"You've killed one of mother's ducks," I said. "One of the fat kind she sells at the market. She says the money buys gold which she saves for her daughters' weddings. Without gold for a dowry—*con o gia*——I will be an old maid!"

My father looked suitably concerned, then brightened and said, "Well, Bay Ly, if you can't get married, you will just have to live at home forever with me!"

I clapped my hands at the happy prospect.

My father cut into the rich, juicy bird and said, "Even so, we won't tell your mother about the duck, okay?"

I giggled and swore myself to secrecy.

The next day, I took some water out to him in the fields. My mother was due home any time and I used every opportunity to step outside and watch for her. My father stopped working, drank gratefully, then took my hand and led me to the top of a nearby hill. It had a good view of the village and the land beyond it, almost to the ocean. I thought he was going to show me my mother coming back, but he had something else in mind.

He said, "Bay Ly, you see all this here? This is the Vietnam we have been talking about. You understand that a country is more than a lot of dirt, rivers, and forests, don't you?"

I said, "Yes, I understand." After all, we had learned in school that one's country is as sacred as a father's grave.

"Good. You know, some of these lands are battlefields where your brothers and cousins are fighting. They may never come back. Even your sisters have all left home in search of a better life. You are the only one left in my house. If the enemy comes back, you must be both a daughter and a son. I told you how the Chinese used to rule our land. People in this village had to risk their lives diving in the ocean just to find pearls for the Chinese emperor's gown. They had to risk tigers and snakes in the jungle just to find herbs for his table. Their payment for this hardship was a bowl of rice and another day of life. That is why Le Loi, Gia Long, the Trung Sisters, and Phung Thi Chinh fought so hard to expel the Chinese. When the French came, it was the same old story. Your mother and I were taken to Danang to build a runway for their airplanes. We labored from sunup to sundown and well after dark. If we stopped to rest or have a smoke, a Moroccan would come up and whip our behinds. Our reward was a bowl of rice and another day of life. Freedom is never a gift, Bay Ly. It must be won and won again. Do you understand?"

I said that I did.

"Good." He moved his finger from the patchwork of brown dikes, silver water, and rippling stalks to our house at the edge of the village. "This land here belongs to me. Do you know how I got it?"

I thought a moment, trying to remember my mother's stories, then said honestly, "I can't remember."

He squeezed me lovingly. "I got it from your mother."

"What? That can't be true!" I said. Everyone in the family knew my mother was poor and my father's family was wealthy. Her parents were dead and she had to work like a slave for her mother-in-law to prove herself worthy. Such women don't have land to give away!

"It's true." My father's smile widened. "When I was a young man, my parents needed someone to look after their lands. They had to be very careful about who they chose as wives for their three sons. In the village, your mother had a reputation as the hardest worker of all. She raised herself and her brothers without parents. At the same time, I noticed a beautiful woman working in the fields. When my mother said she was going to talk to the matchmaker about this hard-working village girl she'd heard about, my heart sank. I was too attracted to this mysterious tall woman I had seen in the rice paddies. You can imagine my surprise when I found out the girl my mother heard about and the woman I admired were the same.

"WELL, WE WERE MARRIED and my mother tested your mother severely. She not only had to cook and clean and know everything about children, but she had to be able to manage several farms and know when and how to take the extra produce to the market. Of course, she was testing her other daughters-in-law as well. When my parents died, they divided their several farms among their sons, but you know what? They gave your mother and me the biggest share because they knew we would take care of it best. That's why I say the land came from her, because it did."

I suddenly missed my mother very much and looked down the road to the south, hoping to see her. My father noticed my sad expression.

"Hey." He poked me in the ribs. "Are you getting hungry for lunch?"

"No. I want to learn how to take care of the farm. What happens if the soldiers come back? What did you and Mother do when the soldiers came?"

My father squatted on the dusty hilltop and wiped the sweat from his forehead. "The first thing I did was to tell myself that it was my duty to survive—to take care of my family and my farm. That is a tricky job in wartime. It's as hard as being a soldier. The Moroccans were very savage. One day the rumor passed that they were coming to destroy the village. You may remember the night I sent you and your brothers and sisters away with your mother to Danang."

"You didn't go with us!" My voice still held the horror of the night I thought I had lost my father.

"Right! I stayed near the village—right on this hill—to keep an eye on the enemy and on our house. If they really wanted to destroy the village, I would save some of our things so that we could start over. Sure enough, that was their plan.

"The real problem was to keep things safe and avoid being captured. Their patrols were everywhere. Sometimes I went so deep in the forest that I worried about getting lost, but all I had to do was follow the smoke from the burning huts and I could find my way back.

"Once, I was trapped between two patrols that had camped on both sides of a river. I had to wait in the water for two days before one of them moved on. When I got out, my skin was shriveled like an old melon. I was so cold I could hardly move. From the waist down, my body was black with leeches. But it was worth all the pain. When your mother came back, we still had some furniture and tools to cultivate the earth. Many people lost everything. Yes, we were very lucky."

My father put his arms around me. "My brother Huong—your uncle Huong—had three sons and four daughters. Of his four daughters, only one is still alive. Of his three sons, two went north to Hanoi and one went south to Saigon. Huong's house is very empty. My other brother, your uncle Luc, had only two sons. One went north to Hanoi, the other was killed in the fields. His daughter is deaf and

Culture Notes

Hanoi (hä noi´) capital of North Vietnam, now capital of Vietnam, p. 273

Saigon (si´gän) capital of South Vietnam, now Ho Chi Minh City, p. 273

dumb. No wonder he has taken to drink, eh? Who does he have to sing in his house and tend his shrine when he is gone? My sister Lien had three daughters and four sons. Three of the four sons went to Hanoi and the fourth went to Saigon to find his fortune. The girls all tend their in-laws and mourn slain husbands. Who will care for Lien when she is too feeble to care for herself? Finally, my baby sister Nhien lost her husband to French bombers. Of her two sons, one went to Hanoi and the other joined the Republic, then defected, then was murdered in his house. Nobody knows which side killed him. It doesn't really matter."

My father drew me out to arm's length and looked me squarely in the eye. "Now, Bay Ly, do you understand what your job is?"

I squared my shoulders and put on a soldier's face. "My job is to avenge my family. To protect my farm by killing the enemy. I must become a woman warrior like Phung Thi Chinh!"

My father laughed and pulled me close. "No, little peach blossom. Your job is to stay alive — to keep an eye on things and keep the village safe. To find a husband and have babies and tell the story of what you've seen to your children and anyone else who'll listen. Most of all, it is to live in peace and tend the shrine of our ancestors. Do these things well, Bay Ly, and you will be worth more than any soldier who ever took up a sword."

ABOUT LE LY HAYSLIP

Le Ly Hayslip was born in 1949 into a close-knit Buddhist family and grew up in Central Vietnam during the long war between North and South Vietnam. Hayslip's autobiography, *When Heaven and Earth Changed Places*, was published in 1989 and made into a movie in 1993. Now living in California, the author has recently published another book, *Child of War, Woman of Peace*.

RESPONDING

1. *Personal Response* Why did Bay Ly's family remain in their village? Would you have done the same thing? Why or why not?

2. *Literary Analysis* Bay Ly's father describes the *setting* of the Vietnamese countryside as "more than a lot of

dirt, rivers, and forests." What does the land represent to him?

3. *Multicultural Connection* What have you learned about Vietnam and the Vietnamese people in this selection? What effects do you think that growing up in a war-torn country might have on a person of your age?

LANGUAGE WORKSHOP

Dialogue In direct quotations, quotation marks are placed before and after the speaker's exact words. If the direct quotation is interrupted, both parts are enclosed in quotation marks. Periods, commas, and usually question and exclamation marks are placed inside quotation marks. Note that a comma sets off the speaker from the words spoken in a sentence. Punctuate the *dialogue* in this passage from "Fathers and Daughters":

You've killed one of mother's ducks I said. One of the fat kind she sells at the market.

WRITER'S PORTFOLIO

Plan an interview with a parent and daughter you know. The purpose of the interview is to find out what wisdom the parent wants to pass on to the daughter and what things the daughter would like to learn from her parent. Write interview questions beforehand. Tape your interview or write it out.

From Behind the Veil

The STREET, although wide, was inconveniently full of strollers passing to and fro. The situation was not helped by the sleek swift cars, which sped by from time to time. They carried wealthy occupants, young women and ladies, who, protected from the curiosity of the outside world, displayed radiant faces. Their shining gaze roved across the street, smiling or frowning as they took in sights which pleased or displeased them.

Among the surging crowd was an amazing mixture of different clothes and contrasting shapes, which, if nothing else, serve to emphasize the varying tastes of these passers-by.

A European who had never been to the East before might be excused for thinking that its people were in the middle of a great festival. As time goes by, however, he is moved to say in amazement, "What long carnival celebrations you have in this country!" Our Western friend would think that people wear these amazing clothes for a festival, just as they would do in his own country.

You can also see women in the crowd, both veiled and unveiled. A man can be surprised to find himself turning involuntarily towards those figures, wearing long silk gowns, which give them such an enticing and alluring shape, and make the observer yearn to uncover the magic and the secrets which lie beneath them.

His desire is only increased when his gaze falls on the filmy veil. Behind it he can catch a fleeting glimpse of fine features and pencilled eyebrows, which serve to inflame the fires of his heart. It makes him want to devote the rest of his life to the exploration of this world full of shame-faced beauty.

Ihsan was one of those who would stroll along with the crowd displaying his smart and tasteful suit over his slim figure, patting his dark gleaming hair whenever he felt that the evening breezes had ruffled it, or spread a curl over his clear forehead.

This Ihsan was a young man of eighteen, good-looking with fine features which made him attractive to a number of women. Naturally he was aware of his appeal and attraction, and he had the youthful capacity to exploit it. That's why you can see him now, with his eyes wandering in search of a quarry.

Ihsan was not interested in chasing unveiled girls. They exuded poise, which he found unattractive, and they were always looking anxiously to avoid criticism so they never looked the passers-by directly in the face. They would walk by without turning their heads, paying no attention to the expressions of flattery which came their way from the gallants, who, after getting as much out of them as a dog gets out of barking at clouds, would give them no further attention.

This is the reason that makes Ihsan always sidle up to the girls with the long cloaks and the secret little movements which attract him: the burning sighs and the gentle laughter and the concealed glances.

Siham had gone out on the evening of that day as usual to take the air and stroll through the streets. This evening stroll had become a part of her life to such an extent that it was now indispensable. She couldn't remember exactly the date when she first set out to saunter through the street, and did not really know the reason why she kept up her evening appointments. If she did, she did not admit it. Whatever the case, no sooner had Siham seen the bustle in the middle of the street than she headed for the pavement. She looked cautiously left and right until she saw Ihsan in the distance, and suddenly she felt the blood coursing through her veins.

She found herself unconsciously moving towards him until she was almost parallel with him, saw him staring at her from top to bottom, and felt a tremor throughout her body. When she saw his burning stare almost penetrating the cloak which covered her slender body her heart beat violently. She was used to seeing him every day at this time, and she used to stare at him freely each time until she had memorized his face. Of late, she had begun to feel her heart pounding whenever she saw him, and her face flushed with confusion. There was nothing to stop her from feasting her eyes on him, however, because she knew that the veil covered her face and concealed the overwhelming attraction she felt for him.

We cannot be certain what it was that made this youth know that the girl was interested in him, and whether his first overture to her came in the course of one of his habitual overtures, which he made to any girl. Whatever it was, he went up to the girl boldly on that first day, and sidled up to her, greeted her, and saw her turning round to look at him cautiously before hurrying on her way.

He knew immediately that she was not angry with him, and emboldened, he carried on behind her and saw her going into one of the public parks. She knew that he was following her, and hastened on her way, trembling with conflicting emotions of joy, fear, and caution.

He followed her into the park for a short distance, until he saw her sitting on her own, behind a big tree. He went up to her and spoke to her smilingly.

"Good evening."

"Good evening," she replied shyly.

Then she raised her veil from her brown face and her dark eyes, and Ihsan was captivated by the long dark eyelashes which cast a shadow over her features.

The features of her face were fine, and inspired the beholder with the strongest feelings of awe and worship. She was fearful and breathless, turning from side to side like a timid gazelle. She knew that what she was doing amounted to an unpardonable crime, but drew comfort from one thing—the knowledge that this boy had not seen her before and did not know her. She was having an adventure, nothing more, and she was drawn into it by her youth and by the warm blood which coursed in her veins.

The boy's mind worked on some expressions of flattery and endearment. For his opening shot, he ventured: "I've seen you often, as you've passed by this street and then gone to walk among the trees. I wasn't able to talk to you because I respect you, and your whole appearance tells me that you are from a good family."

She replied, a little resentfully: "But I suppose you always try to talk with ordinary girls as well? Why don't you just chase the common girls, and satisfy your passions on them?"

"I'm sorry, really, I don't mean you any harm. But I'm alone, as you see, and I can't find a companion to share my walks with me. I saw that you were the only girl who found pleasure in these strolls, and so I felt that there was a link between us. Anyway, if you find my presence unpleasant in any way, I'll move off right now."

He made a move to get up, but she checked him and asked: "Do you know who I am?"

"I haven't the least idea, but this doesn't stop me from believing that I share your spirit," he replied softly.

"If you want to accompany me on these innocent walks, I don't see any objection," she mused. "There's no harm in strolling around with you for an hour or so, at intervals which we can agree on, on condition that you promise me that you won't try to follow me and try to find out who I am. I don't want you trying to contact me at any other times."

"I respect your wish and I shall honour it," he replied formally.

The two of them sat side by side on one of the stone benches, and a deep silence reigned over them, in which each felt the beating of their own hearts. This silence continued for a long time. Both of them had been overcome by the novelty of their strange and singular situation.

Ihsan, however, was a youth accustomed to flirtations, although he realized that this time he was faced with a girl who was pure and virtuous. There was something about her, a certain strength of purpose and character, which confused him, and stopped him from going too far. His mind worked to collect his thoughts and to rescue him from the situation into which he had unwittingly walked.

At length, he spoke, somewhat confused.

"What is your name, please?"

"Have you forgotten my condition that you should not try to identify me?"

"Of course. I'm sorry. But surely . . . in view of our future friendship. . . ?"

"Have you forgotten? We live in a society in which this situation is unforgivable. If my people knew anything of this they'd kill me. While society is like this, we must learn to deceive. We must use the follies of our society in order to break its shackles!"

"What a penetrating mind you have!" said Ihsan admiringly.

"Thank you. Time's getting on and I must be getting back to the house. I will see you again in two days."

As she said goodbye he tried to put his arm around her waist, but she rebuffed him sharply. Then she relented slightly, saying: "I don't know who you are. You might be one of those mean boys who take delight in trapping girls for their own pleasure and sport."

She went back to the house invigorated, but somewhat disturbed, for she had broken with the most binding and serious of traditions in one fell swoop. She didn't understand how it had begun and how it had ended, until it seemed to her that everything that had happened that day was a disturbing dream.

She threw her cloak on one side, and went to help her mother with the housework. She flattered her mother, made herself agreeable, and took delight in carrying out her orders and her arrangements. When her father returned home from work she welcomed him with smiling face, then she went to her room to get on with her studies.

She set about her work mechanically, with nervous high spirits, and had disturbing dreams at night.

The meetings went on longer, and the subjects of their conversations diversified. The relationship between them developed, and things became deeply involved. She no longer felt that there was anything strange or unusual about the meetings, but she kept her head, using her lively mind to conceal her relationship with this boy, and to prevent him from trying to find out who she was and getting in touch with her.

ONE DAY SIHAM was sitting with her father, talking to him after supper, while he was scanning the evening paper. His eye fell on a long article about women who had abandoned the veil, and, deciding to have his daughter's view, he read the article out aloud. No sooner had he finished than Siham roundly abused the author for trying to break with convention and introduce modern heresies. Her father felt a greatly increased regard for his intelligent, well-brought-up daughter, who obviously knew the value of traditions and respected them. Such a difference between her and the rest of her irresponsible scandalous friends, who, no sooner had they learned to read and write, went around throwing overboard society's conventions without shame or respect!

Impulsively, he moved towards his daughter and kissed her forehead.

"God preserve you as a treasure for your father."

When she reached her room Siham could barely stop herself from laughing out loud. She picked up her veil and danced with glee, then stopped in the middle of the room and began to whisper to the veil: "You black shroud, you know how I despise you and make use of you to keep him apart from me! I don't care about you, and I feel nothing for you. I defy you. But I love you too. These poor girls take refuge behind you in order to preserve their virginity, and their honour, and good morals. If they were more truthful they would say they love you because you hide faults and scandals. I love you because you help me to enjoy my life in a way that only those who wear the veil can appreciate. I pity those wretched unveiled women. I scorn them."

ABOUT **DHU'L NUN AYYOUB**

Born in 1908 in Iraq, Duh'l Nun Ayyoub (dül nun ā/yəb) is one of that country's most prominent fiction writers. His stories often portray bitter personal, political, or religious conflict and its aftermath, as well as the clash of traditional and modern forces in the Arab world.

RESPONDING

1. *Personal Response* Imagine that you wore a veil, or some other facial covering. Would it be easier to meet the people who interest you or to do other things? Would you feel more free? Explain.

2. *Literary Analysis* An *apostrophe* is a figure of speech in which an absent person, an abstract concept, or an inanimate object is directly addressed, as when Siham tells her veil, "I love you because you help me to enjoy my life in a way that only those who wear the veil can appreciate." What do you think she means? What else can the veil do, according to the final paragraph of the story?

3. *Multicultural Connection* What in your culture serves the purpose of a veil? If nothing does, what do you think could be made to serve that purpose? How?

LANGUAGE WORKSHOP

Drawing Conclusions When you draw a conclusion, you use evidence and clues to determine what something means. Based on your impression of the story, choose one of the following conclusions about what the relationship with Ihsan means to Siham. Then list pieces of evidence and clues from the story that support the conclusion.

1. Siham enjoys flirting with Ihsan but has no interest in a serious relationship with him.
2. Siham is in love with Ihsan. However, her social position means she cannot bring him home to meet

her family, and she must find other ways to spend time with him.
3. Siham uses Ihsan as an excuse to get out of the house and see the city.

WRITER'S PORTFOLIO

Would you want to have Siham as a friend, girlfriend, or acquaintance? In a journal entry, explain what qualities you look for in a friend or girlfriend. Then tell whether or not you think Siham measures up to your expectations.

Columbus in Chains

Outside, as usual, the sun shone, the trade winds blew; on her way to put some starched clothes on the line, my mother shooed some hens out of her garden; Miss Dewberry baked the buns, some of which my mother would buy for my father and me to eat with our afternoon tea; Miss Henry brought the milk, a glass of which I would drink with my lunch, and another glass of which I would drink with the bun from Miss Dewberry; my mother prepared our lunch; my father noted some perfectly idiotic thing his partner in housebuilding, Mr. Oatie, had done, so that over lunch he and my mother could have a good laugh.

The Anglican church bell struck eleven o'clock—one hour to go before lunch. I was then sitting at my desk in my classroom. We were having a history lesson—the last lesson of the morning. For taking first place over all the other girls, I had been given a prize, a copy of a book called *Roman Britain*, and I was made prefect of my class. What a mistake the prefect part had been, for I was among the worst-behaved in my class and did not at all believe in setting myself up as a good example, the way a prefect was supposed to do. Now I had to sit in the prefect's seat—the first seat in the front row, the seat from which I could stand up and survey quite easily my classmates. From where I sat I could see out the window. Sometimes when I looked out, I could see the sexton going over to the minister's house. The sexton's daughter, Hilarene, a disgusting model of good behavior and keen attention to scholarship, sat next to me, since she took second place. The minister's daughter, Ruth, sat in the last row, the row reserved for all the dunce girls. Hilarene, of course, I could not stand. A girl that good would never do for me. I would probably not have cared so much for first place if I could be sure it would not go to her. Ruth I liked, because she was such a dunce and came from England and had yellow hair. When I first met her, I used to walk her home and sing bad songs to her just to see her turn pink, as if I had spilled hot water all over her.

Our books, *A History of the West Indies*, were open in front of us. Our day had begun with morning prayers, then a geometry lesson, then it was over to the science building for a lesson in "Introductory Physics" (not a subject we cared much for), taught by the most dingy-toothed Mr. Slacks, a teacher from Canada, then precious recess, and now this, our history lesson. Recess had the usual drama: this time, I coaxed Gwen out of her disappointment at not being allowed to join the junior choir. Her father—how many times had I wished he would become a leper and so be banished to a leper colony for the rest of my long and happy life with Gwen—had forbidden it, giving as his reason that she lived too far away from church, where choir rehearsals were conducted, and that it would be dangerous for her, a young girl, to walk home alone at night in the dark. Of course, all the streets had lamplight, but it was useless to point that out to him. Oh, how it would have pleased us to press and rub our knees together as we sat in our pew while pretending to pay close attention to Mr. Simmons, our choirmaster, as he waved his baton up and down and across, and how it would have pleased us even more to walk home together, alone in the "early dusk" (the way Gwen had phrased it, a ready phrase always on her tongue), stopping, if there was a full moon, to lie down in a pasture and expose our bosoms in the moonlight. We had heard that full moonlight would make our breasts grow to a size we would like. Poor Gwen! When I first heard from her that she was one of ten children, right on the spot I told her that I would love only her, since her mother already had so many other people to love.

Our teacher, Miss Edward, paced up and down in front of the class in her usual way. In front of her desk stood a small table, and on it stood the dunce cap. The dunce cap was in the shape of a coronet, with an adjustable opening in the back, so that it could fit any head. It was made of cardboard with a shiny gold paper covering and the word "DUNCE" in shiny red paper on the front. When the sun shone on it, the dunce cap was all aglitter, almost as if you were being tricked into thinking it a desirable thing to wear. As Miss Edward paced up and down, she would pass between us and the dunce cap like an eclipse. Each Friday morning, we were given a small test to see how well we had learned the things taught to us all week. The girl who scored lowest was made to wear the dunce cap all day the following Monday. On many Mondays, Ruth wore it— only, with her short yellow hair, when the dunce cap was sitting on her head she looked like a girl attending a birthday party in *The Schoolgirl's Own Annual.*

It was Miss Edward's way to ask one of us a question the answer to which she was sure the girl would not know and then put the same question to another girl who she was sure would know the answer. The girl who did not answer correctly would then have to repeat the correct answer in the exact words of the other girl. Many times, I had heard my exact words repeated over and over again, and I liked it especially when the girl doing the repeating was one I didn't care about very much. Pointing a finger at Ruth, Miss Edward asked a question the answer to which was "On the third of November 1493, a Sunday morning, Christopher Columbus discovered Dominica." Ruth, of course, did not know the answer, as she did not know the answer to many questions about the West Indies. I could hardly blame her. Ruth had come all the way from England. Perhaps she

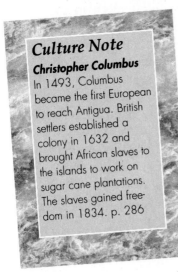

Culture Note

Christopher Columbus
In 1493, Columbus became the first European to reach Antigua. British settlers established a colony in 1632 and brought African slaves to the islands to work on sugar cane plantations. The slaves gained freedom in 1834. p. 286

did not want to be in the West Indies at all. Perhaps she wanted to be in England, where no one would remind her constantly of the terrible things her ancestors had done; perhaps she had felt even worse when her father was a missionary in Africa. I could see how Ruth felt from looking at her face. Her ancestors had been the masters, while ours had been the slaves. She had such a lot to be ashamed of, and by being with us every day she was always being reminded. We could look everybody in the eye, for our ancestors had done nothing wrong except just sit somewhere, defenseless. Of course, sometimes, what with our teachers and our books, it was hard for us to tell on which side we really now belonged—with the masters or the slaves—for it was all history, it was all in the past, and everybody behaved differently now; all of us celebrated Queen Victoria's birthday, even though she had been dead a long time. But we, the descendants of the slaves, knew quite well what had really happened, and I was sure that if the tables had been turned we would have acted differently; I was sure that if our ancestors had gone from Africa to Europe and come upon the people living there, they would have taken a proper interest in the Europeans on first seeing them, and said, "How nice," and then gone home to tell their friends about it.

I was sitting at my desk, having these thoughts to myself. I don't know how long it had been since I lost track of what was going on around me. I had not noticed that the girl who was asked the question after Ruth failed—a girl named Hyacinth—had only got a part of the answer correct. I had not noticed that after these two attempts Miss Edward had launched into a harangue about what a worthless bunch we were compared to girls of the past. In fact, I was no longer on the same chapter we were studying. I was way ahead, at the end of the chapter about Columbus's third voyage. In this chapter, there was a picture of Columbus that took up a whole page, and it was in color— one of only five color pictures in the book. In this picture, Columbus was seated in the bottom of a ship. He was wearing the usual three-quarter trousers and a shirt with enormous sleeves, both the trousers and shirt made of maroon-colored velvet. His hat, which was cocked up on one side of his head, had a gold feather in it, and his black shoes had huge bold buckles. His hands and feet were bound up in chains, and he was sitting there staring off into space, looking quite dejected and miserable. The picture had as a title "Columbus in Chains," printed at the bottom of the page. What had happened was that the usually quarrelsome Columbus had got into a disagreement with people who were even more quarrelsome, and a man named Bobadilla, representing King Ferdinand and Queen Isabella, had sent him back to Spain fettered in chains attached to the bottom of a ship. What just deserts, I thought, for I did not like Columbus. How I loved this picture—to see the usually triumphant Columbus, brought so low, seated at the bottom of a boat just watching things go by. Shortly after I first discovered it in my history book, I heard my mother read out loud to my father a letter she had received from her sister, who still lived with her mother and father in the very same Dominica, which is where my mother came from. Ma Chess was fine, wrote my aunt, but Pa Chess was not well. Pa Chess was having a bit of trouble with his limbs; he was not able to go about as he pleased; often he had to depend on someone else to do one thing or another for him. My mother read the letter in quite a state, her voice rising to a higher pitch with each sentence. After she read the part about Pa Chess's stiff limbs, she turned to my father and laughed as she said, "So the great man can no longer just get up and go. How I would love to see his face now!" When I next saw the picture of Columbus sitting there all locked up in his chains, I wrote under it the words "The Great Man Can No Longer Just Get Up and Go." I had written this out with my fountain pen, and in Old English lettering—a script I had recently mastered. As I sat there looking at the picture, I traced the words with my pen over and over, so that the letters grew big and you could read what I had written from not very far away. I don't know how long it was before I heard that my name, Annie John, was being said by this bellowing dragon in the form of Miss Edward bearing down on me.

I had never been a favorite of hers. Her favorite was Hilarene. It must have pained Miss Edward that I so often beat out Hilarene. Not that I liked Miss Edward and wanted her to like me back, but all my other teachers regarded me with much affection, would always tell my mother that I was the most charming student they had ever had, beamed at me when they saw me coming, and were very sorry when they had to write some version of this on my report card: "Annie is an unusually bright girl. She is well behaved in class, at least in the presence of her masters and mistresses, but behind their backs and outside the classroom quite the opposite is true." When my mother read this or something like it, she would burst into tears. She had hoped to display, with a great flourish, my report card to her friends, along with whatever prize I had won. Instead, the report card would have to take a place at the bottom of the old trunk in which she kept any important thing that had to do with me. I became not a favorite of Miss Edward's in the following way: Each Friday afternoon, the girls in the lower forms were given, instead of a last lesson period, an extra-long recess. We were to use this in ladylike recreation — walks, chats about the novels and poems we were reading, showing each other the new embroidery stitches we had learned to master in home class, or something just as seemly. Instead, some of the girls would play a game of cricket or rounders or stones, but most of us would go to the far end of the school grounds and play band. In this game, of which teachers and parents disapproved and which was sometimes absolutely forbidden, we would place our arms around each other's waist or shoulders, forming lines of ten or so girls, and then we would dance from one end of the school grounds to the other. As we danced, we would sometimes chant these words: "Tee la la la, come go. Tee la la la, come go." At other times we would sing a popular calypso song which usually had lots of unladylike words to it. Up and down the school-yard, away from our teachers, we would dance and sing. At the end of recess — forty-five minutes — we were missing ribbons and other ornaments from our hair, the pleats of our linen tunics became unset, the collars of our blouses were pulled out, and we were soaking wet all the way down to our bloomers. When the school bell rang, we would make a whooping sound, as if in a great panic, and then we would throw ourselves on top of each other as we laughed and shrieked. We would then run back to our classes, where we prepared to file into the auditorium for evening prayers. After that, it was home for the weekend. But how could we go straight home after all that excitement? No sooner were we on the street than we would form little groups, depending on the direction we were headed in. I was never keen on joining them on the way home, because I was sure I would run into my mother. Instead, my friends and I would go to our usual place near the back of the churchyard and sit on the tombstones of people who had been buried there way before slavery was abolished, in 1833. We would sit and sing bad songs, use forbidden words, and, of course, show each other various parts of our bodies. While some of us watched, the others would walk up and down on the large tombstones showing off their legs. It was immediately a popular idea; everybody soon wanted to do it. It wasn't long before many girls — the ones whose mothers didn't pay strict attention to what they were doing — started to come to school on Fridays wearing not bloomers under their uniforms but underpants trimmed with lace and satin frills. It also wasn't long before an end came to all that. One Friday afternoon, Miss Edward, on her way home from school, took a shortcut through the churchyard. She must have heard the commotion we were making, because there she suddenly was, saying, "What is the meaning of this?"—just the very thing someone like her would say if she came unexpectedly on something like us. It was obvious that I was the ringleader. Oh, how I wished the ground would open up and take her in, but it did not. We all, shamefacedly, slunk home, I with Miss Edward at my side. Tears came to my mother's eyes when she heard what I had done. It was apparently such a bad thing that my mother couldn't bring herself to repeat my misdeed to my father in my presence. I got the usual punishment of dinner alone, outside under the breadfruit tree, but added on to that, I was not allowed to go to the library on Saturday, and on Sunday, after Sunday school and dinner, I was not allowed to take a stroll in the botanical gardens, where Gwen was waiting for me in the bamboo grove.

THAT HAPPENED when I was in the first form. Now here Miss Edward stood. Her whole face was on fire. Her eyes were bulging out of her head. I was sure that at any minute they would land at my feet and roll away. The small pimples on her face, already looking as if they were constantly irritated, now ballooned into huge, on-the-verge-of-exploding boils. Her head shook from side to side. Her strange bottom, which she carried high in the air, seemed to rise up so high that it almost touched the ceiling. Why did I not pay attention, she said. My impertinence was beyond endurance. She then found a hundred words for the different forms my impertinence took. On she went. I was just getting used to this amazing bellowing when suddenly she was speechless. In fact, everything stopped. Her eyes stopped, her bottom stopped, her pimples stopped. Yes, she had got close enough so that her eyes caught a glimpse of what I had done to my textbook. The glimpse soon led to closer inspection. It was bad enough that I had defaced my schoolbook by writing in it. That I should write under the picture of Columbus "The Great Man. . ." etc. was just too much. I had gone too far this time, defaming one of the great men in history, Christopher Columbus, discoverer of the island that was my home. And now look at me. I was not even hanging my head in remorse. Had my peers ever seen anyone so arrogant, so blasphemous?

I was sent to the headmistress, Miss Moore. As punishment, I was removed from my position as prefect, and my place was taken by the odious Hilarene. As an added punishment, I was ordered to copy Books I and II of *Paradise Lost*, by John Milton, and to have it done a week from that day. I then couldn't wait to get home to lunch and the comfort of my mother's kisses and arms. I had nothing to worry about there yet; it would be a while before my mother and father heard of my bad deeds. What a terrible morning! Seeing my mother would be such a tonic—something to pick me up.

When I got home, my mother kissed me absent-mindedly. My father had got home ahead of me, and they were already deep in conversation, my father regaling her with some unusually outlandish thing the oaf Mr. Oatie had done. I washed my hands and took my place at table. My mother brought me my lunch. I took one smell of it, and I could tell that it was the much hated breadfruit. My mother said not at all, it was a new kind of rice imported from Belgium, and not breadfruit, mashed and forced through a ricer, as I thought. She went back to talking to my father. My father could hardly get a few words out of his mouth before she was a jellyfish of laughter. I sat there, putting my food in my mouth. I could not believe that she couldn't see how miserable I was and so reach out a hand to comfort me and caress my cheek, the way she usually did when she sensed that something was amiss with me. I could not believe how she laughed at everything he said, and how bitter it made me feel to see how much she liked him. I ate my meal. The more I ate of it, the more I was sure that it was breadfruit. When I finished, my mother got up to remove my plate. As she started out the door, I said, "Tell me, really, the name of the thing I just ate."

My mother said, "You just ate some breadfruit. I made it look like rice so that you would eat it. It's very good for you, filled with lots of vitamins." As she said this, she laughed. She was standing half inside the door, half outside. Her body was in the shade of our house, but her head was in the sun. When she laughed, her mouth opened to show off big, shiny, sharp white teeth. It was as if my mother had suddenly turned into a crocodile.

ABOUT JAMAICA KINCAID

Born in Antigua, Jamaica Kincaid immigrated to the United States at age seventeen. For nearly two decades she has been a staff writer at *The New Yorker.* The strong influence of the West Indies is reflected in her works of fiction — *At the Bottom of the River,* which was nominated for the PEN/Faulkner Award; *Annie John;* and *Lucy.*

RESPONDING

1. *Personal Response* At the end of the story, the narrator felt as if her mother "had suddenly turned into a crocodile." Why? Have you ever felt that way about a family member? Explain.

2. *Literary Analysis* What effect does Kincaid achieve through her use of *exaggeration* in the paragraph beginning "That happened when. . ." on page 291?

3. *Multicultural Connection* Given the history of the narrator and other Antiguans, why is her reaction to the picture of Columbus in chains significant?

LANGUAGE WORKSHOP

Underlining Underline titles of books, foreign words, and words to be emphasized. In printed matter such as this book, these items appear in italics. Find three examples of book titles italicized in this selection. Then explain which words should be underlined in the sentences below.
1. Didn't you hear her say help?
2. Annie John is a novel by Jamaica Kincaid.
3. They said shalom when they left.

WRITER'S PORTFOLIO

As editor of the school yearbook, choose a slogan, saying, and/or descriptive phrase to put beneath the picture of the narrator of "Columbus in Chains." List sports, activities, and clubs that she might join, given what you know about her from the story.

Sally

SALLY IS THE GIRL with eyes like Egypt and nylons the color of smoke. The boys at school think she's beautiful because her hair is shiny black like raven feathers and when she laughs, she flicks her hair back like a satin shawl over her shoulders and laughs.

Her father says to be this beautiful is trouble. They are very strict in his religion. They are not supposed to dance. He remembers his sisters and is sad. Then she can't go out. Sally I mean.

Sally, who taught you to paint your eyes like Cleopatra? And if I roll the little brush with my tongue and chew it to a point and dip it in the muddy cake, the one in the little red box, will you teach me?

I like your black coat and those shoes you wear, where did you get them? My mother says to wear black so young is dangerous, but I want to buy shoes just like yours, like your black ones made out of suede, just like those. And one day, when my mother's in a good mood, maybe after my next birthday, I'm going to ask to buy the nylons too.

Cheryl, who is not your friend anymore, not since last Tuesday before Easter, not since the day you made her ear bleed, not since she called you that name and bit a hole in your arm and you looked as if you were going to cry and everyone was waiting and you didn't, you didn't. Sally, not since then, you don't have a best friend to lean against the schoolyard fence with, to laugh behind your hands at what the boys say. There is no one to lend you her hairbrush.

The stories the boys tell in the coatroom, they're not true. You lean against the schoolyard fence alone with your eyes closed as if no one was watching, as if no one could see you standing there, Sally. What do you think about when you close your eyes like that? And why do you always have to go straight home after school? You become a different Sally. You pull your skirt straight, you rub the blue paint off your eyelids. You don't laugh, Sally. You look at your feet and walk fast to the house you can't come out from.

SALLY, do you sometimes wish you didn't have to go home? Do you wish your feet would one day keep walking and take you far away from Mango Street, far away and maybe your feet would stop in front of a house, a nice one with flowers and big windows and steps for you to climb up two by two upstairs to where a room is waiting for you? And if you opened the little window latch and gave it a shove, the windows would swing open, all the sky would come in. There'd be no nosy neighbors watching, no motorcycles and cars, no sheets and towels and laundry. Only trees and more trees and plenty of blue sky. And you could laugh, Sally. You could go to sleep and wake up and never have to think who likes and doesn't like you. You could close your eyes and you wouldn't have to worry what people said because you never belonged here anyway and nobody could make you sad and nobody would think you're strange because you like to dream and dream. And no one could yell at you if they saw you out in the dark leaning against a car, leaning against somebody without someone thinking you are bad, without somebody saying it is wrong, without the whole world waiting for you to make a mistake when all you wanted, all you wanted, Sally, was to love and to love and to love and to love, and no one could call that crazy.

First Frost

Andrei Voznesensky

A girl is freezing in a telephone booth,
huddled in her flimsy coat,
her face stained by tears
and smeared with lipstick.

She breathes on her thin little fingers.
Fingers like ice. Glass beads in her ears.

She has to beat her way back alone
down the icy street.

First frost. A beginning of losses.
The first frost of telephone phrases.

It is the start of winter glittering on her cheek,
the first frost of having been hurt.

ABOUT SANDRA CISNEROS

Sandra Cisneros (sēs ne′rōs) was born to parents of Mexican and American descent in Chicago in 1954. She began writing about her neighborhood in college. Her first work of fiction, *The House on Mango Street*, earned the American Book Award in 1985. Other works include a collection of stories, *Woman Hollering Creek*, and *My Wicked Wicked Ways*, a collection of poems.

ABOUT **ANDREI VOZNESENSKY**

Born in Moscow in 1933, Andrei Voznesensky (on′drä väz nə sen′skē) writes poems that have drawn both government censure and public praise. Youth is commonly recognized as Voznesensky's main theme.

RESPONDING

1. *Personal Response* Do Cisneros and Voznesensky seem to understand what it's like to be a teenager? Explain.

2. *Literary Analysis* Cisneros makes extensive use of *figurative* language in this selection. What does "eyes like Egypt" mean in the first paragraph? To what is her hair compared in this paragraph? Do you think these comparisons are good, or could you suggest others?

3. *Multicultural Connection* Do you think that young people are generally free to dress and look as they want to in your culture? Explain. Pick another culture and explain whether you think you would have more— or less—license to look the way you want.

LANGUAGE WORKSHOP

Style Style is the way a writer puts words together to achieve effects. Cisneros's style is poetic; in fact, her stories have been called prose poems. Her style is also conversational. What qualities in her writing make it seem like a poem? like a young girl's first-hand account?

WRITER'S PORTFOLIO

Choose a friend, family member, or acquaintance to describe. Jot down details about that person's physical appearance, manner of dress or speaking, or personal style. Then think of figurative comparisons to add to your description. Now incorporate your ideas into a paragraph or two, or a poem.

A Lesson for This Sunday

Derek Walcott

This growing idleness of summer grass
With its frail kites of furious butterflies
Requests the lemonade of simple praise
In scansion gentler than my hammock swings
And rituals no more upsetting than a
Black maid shaking linen as she sings
The plain notes of some Protestant hosanna —
Since I lie idling from the thought in things —

Or so they should, until I hear the cries
Of two small children hunting yellow wings,
Who break my Sabbath with the thought of sin.
Brother and sister, with a common pin,
Frowning like serious lepidopterists.
The little surgeon pierces the thin eyes.
Crouched on plump haunches, as a mantis prays
She shrieks to eviscerate its abdomen.
The lesson is the same. The maid removes
Both prodigies from their interest in science.
The girl, in lemon frock, begins to scream
As the maimed, teetering thing attempts its flight.
She is herself a thing of summery light,
Frail as a flower in this blue August air,
Not marked for some late grief that cannot speak.
The mind swings inward on itself in fear
Swayed towards nausea from each normal sign.
Heredity of cruelty everywhere,
And everywhere the frocks of summer torn,
The long look back to see where choice is born,
As summer grass sways to the scythe's design.

Words to Know

lepidopterists people who collect and study butterflies (butterflies and moths belong to the scientific order *Lepidoptera*), p. 298

mantis an insect having forelegs modified for capturing other insects, often lifted in a prayerlike manner, therefore praying mantis, p. 298

eviscerate to remove internal organs, or viscera, p. 298

ABOUT **DEREK WALCOTT**

Derek Walcott was born in 1930 on the island of St. Lucia, West Indies, and now divides his time between Boston, Massachusetts, and Trinidad. He has won a number of awards for his poetry and plays, including the Nobel Prize for Literature in 1992. Critics characterize Walcott's writing as dense with metaphor. His plays often deal with cultural ambiguities and racial tensions.

RESPONDING

1. *Personal Response* Do you think the children in this poem are cruel? Would their age be a factor in determining your answer? Explain.

2. *Literary Analysis* Explain the *theme* of this poem. What does this theme have to do with the idea of growing toward adulthood?

3. *Multicultural Connection* Compare Walcott's idea of growing up with the views presented in "From Behind the Veil," or with those from another selection in this unit.

LANGUAGE WORKSHOP

Sound Devices Poets use *sound devices* to relate words or ideas, to make a poem sound a certain way, or to influence the rhythm of their work. For example, Walcott uses some exact rhymes (*swings, sings, things, wings*), as well as repeated consonant sounds (*"frail kites of furious butterflies"*) and repeated vowel sounds (*"Since I lie idling"*). Reread "A Lesson for This Sunday" out loud, listening for patterns in sound. Then answer the following questions:

1. Is there a repeated rhyme pattern throughout the poem, or just within stanzas? What patterns do you find?

2. What sound devices do you find in the final line? What effect do they achieve?

WRITER'S PORTFOLIO

Write two paragraphs that describe this poem's main qualities and explain what it means. Analyze the imagery, tone, and overall message of the poem.

B. Wordsworth

T̶HREE BEGGARS CALLED punctually every day at the hospitable houses in Miguel Street. At about ten an Indian came in his dhoti and white jacket, and we poured a tin of rice into the sack he carried on his back. At twelve an old woman smoking a clay pipe came and she got a cent. At two a blind man led by a boy called for his penny.

Sometimes we had a rogue. One day a man called and said he was hungry. We gave him a meal. He asked for a cigarette and wouldn't go until we had lit it for him. That man never came again.

The strangest caller came one afternoon at about four o'clock. I had come back from school and was in my home clothes. The man said to me, "Sonny, may I come inside your yard?"

He was a small man and he was tidily dressed. He wore a hat, a white shirt, and black trousers.

I asked, "What do you want?"

He said, "I want to watch your bees."

We had four small gru-gru palm trees and they were full of uninvited bees.

I ran up the steps and shouted, "Ma, it have a man outside here. He say he want to watch the bees."

My mother came out, looked at the man and asked in an unfriendly way, "What you want?"

The man said, "I want to watch your bees."

Culture Notes

dhoti a loincloth, p. 301

congorees This may refer to large eels that are a source of food in the West Indies. p. 302

His English was so good, it didn't sound natural, and I could see my mother was worried.

She said to me, "Stay here and watch him while he watch the bees."

The man said, "Thank you, madam. You have done a good deed today."

He spoke very slowly and very correctly as though every word was costing him money.

We watched the bees, this man and I, for about an hour, squatting near the palm trees.

The man said, "I like watching bees. Sonny, do you like watching bees?"

I said, "I ain't have the time."

He shook his head sadly. He said, "That's what I do, I just watch. I can watch ants for days. Have you ever watched ants? And scorpions, and centipedes, and *congorees*—have you watched those?"

I shook my head.

I said, "What you does do, mister?"

He got up and said, "I am a poet."

I said, "A good poet?"

He said, "The greatest in the world."

"What your name, mister?"

"B. Wordsworth."

"B for Bill?"

"Black. Black Wordsworth. White Wordsworth was my brother. We share one heart. I can watch a small flower like the morning-glory and cry."

I said, "Why you does cry?"

"Why, boy? Why? You will know when you grow up. You're a poet, too, you know. And when you're a poet you can cry for everything."

I couldn't laugh.

He said, "You like your mother?"

"When she not beating me."

He pulled out a printed sheet from his hip pocket and said, "On this paper is the greatest poem about mothers and I'm going to sell it to you at a bargain price. For four cents."

I went inside and I said, "Ma, you want to buy a poetry for four cents?"

My mother said, "Tell that blasted man to haul his tail away from my yard, you hear."

I said to B. Wordsworth, "My mother say she ain't have four cents."

B. Wordsworth said, "It is the poet's tragedy."

And he put the paper back in his pocket. He didn't seem to mind.

I said, "Is a funny way to go round selling poetry like that. Only calypsonians do that sort of thing. A lot of people does buy?"

He said, "No one has yet bought a single copy."

"But why you does keep on going round, then?"

He said, "In this way I watch many things, and I always hope to meet poets."

I said, "You really think I is a poet?"

"You're as good as me," he said.

And when B. Wordsworth left, I prayed I would see him again.

Culture Notes

calypsonians popular outdoor singers who make up songs about current events, p. 303

Port of Spain the port and capital city of Trinidad, p. 303

About a week later, coming back from school one afternoon, I met him at the corner of Miguel Street.

He said, "I have been waiting for you a long time."

I said, "You sell any poetry yet?"

He shook his head.

He said, "In my yard I have the best mango tree in Port of Spain. And now the mangoes are ripe and red and very sweet and juicy. I have waited here for you to tell you this and to invite you to come and eat some of my mangoes."

He lived in Alberto Street in a one-roomed hut placed right in the center of the lot. The yard seemed all green.

There was the big mango tree. There was a coconut tree and there was a plum tree. The place looked wild, as though it wasn't in the city at all. You couldn't see all the big concrete houses in the street.

H<small>E WAS RIGHT</small>. The mangoes were sweet and juicy. I ate about six, and the yellow mango juice ran down my arms to my elbows and down my mouth to my chin and my shirt was stained.

My mother said when I got home, "Where you was? You think you is a man now and could go all over the place? Go cut a whip for me."

She beat me rather badly, and I ran out of the house swearing that I would never come back. I went to B. Wordsworth's house. I was so angry, my nose was bleeding.

B. Wordsworth said, "Stop crying, and we will go for a walk."

I stopped crying, but I was breathing short. We went for a walk. We walked down St. Clair Avenue to the Savannah and we walked to the racecourse.

Culture Note

Orion the Hunter the most conspicuous constellation in the heavens, represented by a man with belt and sword, p. 304

B. Wordsworth said, "Now, let us lie on the grass and look up at the sky, and I want you to think how far those stars are from us."

I did as he told me, and I saw what he meant. I felt like nothing, and at the same time I had never felt so big and great in all my life. I forgot all my anger and all my tears and all the blows.

When I said I was better, he began telling me the names of the stars, and I particularly remembered the constellation of Orion the Hunter, though I don't really know why. I can spot Orion even today, but I have forgotten the rest.

Then a light was flashed into our faces, and we saw a policeman. We got up from the grass.

The policeman said, "What you doing here?"

B. Wordsworth said, "I have been asking myself the same question for forty years."

We became friends, B. Wordsworth and I. He told me, "You must never tell anybody about me and about the mango tree and the coconut tree and the plum tree. You must keep that a secret. If you tell anybody, I will know, because I am a poet."

I gave him my word and I kept it.

I liked his little room. It had no more furniture than George's front room, but it looked cleaner and healthier. But it also looked lonely.

One day I asked him, "Mr. Wordsworth, why you does keep all this bush in your yard? Ain't it does make the place damp?"

He said, "Listen, and I will tell you a story. Once upon a time a boy and girl met each other and they fell in love. They loved each other so much they got married. They were both poets. He loved words. She loved grass and flowers and trees. They lived happily in a single room, and then one day, the girl poet said to the boy poet, "We are going to have another poet in the family." But this poet was never born, because the girl died, and the young poet died with her, inside her. And the girl's husband was very sad, and he said he would never touch a thing in the girl's garden. And so the garden remained, and grew high and wild."

I LOOKED AT B. WORDSWORTH, and as he told me this lovely story, he seemed to grow older. I understood his story.

We went for long walks together. We went to the Botanical Gardens and the Rock Gardens. We climbed Chancellor Hill in the late afternoon and watched the darkness fall on Port of Spain, and watched the lights go on in the city and on the ships in the harbor.

He did everything as though he were doing it for the first time in his life. He did everything as though he were doing some church rite.

He would say to me, "Now, how about having some ice cream?"

And when I said yes, he would grow very serious and say, "Now, which café shall we patronize?" As though it were a very important thing. He would think for some time about it, and finally say, "I think I will go and negotiate the purchase with that shop."

The world became a most exciting place.

One day, when I was in his yard, he said to me, "I have a great secret which I am now going to tell you."

I said, "It really secret?"

"At the moment, yes."

I looked at him, and he looked at me. He said, "This is just between you and me, remember. I am writing a poem."

"Oh." I was disappointed.

He said, "But this is a different sort of poem. This is the greatest poem in the world."

I whistled.

He said, "I have been working on it for more than five years now. I will finish it in about twenty-two years from now, that is, if I keep on writing at the present rate."

"You does write a lot, then?"

He said, "Not any more. I just write one line a month. But I make sure it is a good line."

I asked, "What was last month's good line?"

He looked up at the sky, and said, *"The past is deep."*

I said, "It is a beautiful line."

B. Wordsworth said, "I hope to distill the experiences of a whole month into that single line of poetry. So, in twenty-two years, I shall have written a poem that will sing to all humanity."

I was filled with wonder.

Our walks continued. We walked along the seawall at Docksite one day, and I said, "Mr. Wordsworth, if I drop this pin in the water, you think it will float?"

He said, "This is a strange world. Drop your pin, and let us see what will happen."

The pin sank.

I said, "How is the poem this month?"

But he never told me any other line. He merely said, "Oh, it comes, you know. It comes."

Or we would sit on the seawall and watch the liners come into the harbor.

But of the greatest poem in the world I heard no more.

I felt he was growing older.

"How does you live, Mr. Wordsworth?" I asked him one day.

He said, "You mean how I get money?"

When I nodded, he laughed in a crooked way.

He said, "I sing calypso in the calypso season."

"And that last you the rest of the year?"

"It is enough."

"But you will be the richest man in the world when you write the greatest poem?"

He didn't reply.

One day when I went to see him in his little house, I found him lying on his little bed. He looked so old and so weak, that I found myself wanting to cry.

He said, "The poem is not going well."

He wasn't looking at me. He was looking through the window at the coconut tree, and he was speaking as though I wasn't there. He said, "When I was twenty I felt the power within myself." Then, almost in front of my eyes, I could see his face growing older and more tired. He said, "But that — that was a long time ago."

And then — I felt it so keenly, it was as though I had been slapped by my mother. I could see it clearly on his face. It was there for everyone to see. Death on the shrinking face.

He looked at me, and saw my tears and sat up.

He said, "Come." I went and sat on his knees.

He looked into my eyes, and he said, "Oh, you can see it, too. I always knew you had the poet's eye."

He didn't even look sad, and that made me burst out crying loudly.

He pulled me to his thin chest, and said, "Do you want me to tell you a funny story?" and he smiled encouragingly at me.

But I couldn't reply.

He said, "When I have finished this story, I want you to promise that you will go away and never come back to see me. Do you promise?"

I nodded.

He said, "Good. Well, listen. That story I told you about the boy poet and the girl poet, do you remember that? That wasn't true. It was something I just made up. All this talk about poetry and the greatest poem in the world, that wasn't true, either. Isn't that the funniest thing you have heard?"

But his voice broke.

I left the house, and ran home crying, like a poet, for everything I saw.

I walked along Alberto Street a year later, but I could find no sign of the poet's house. It hadn't vanished, just like that. It had been pulled down, and a big two-storied building had taken its place. The mango tree and the plum tree and the coconut tree had all been cut down, and there was brick and concrete everywhere.

It was just as though B. Wordsworth had never existed.

The New Suit

Nidia Sanabria de Romero

Striped suit,
a terrific tie,
buttoned shoes
and brown socks —
my outfit
for the party.

And the recommendations
drove me crazy —
— Don't eat ice cream
because it might drip.
— Juice, drink it slowly
since it dribbles.
— And nothing about
chocolate bombs
that might explode!
Happy birthday!
Who's that stuffed breathless
inside a tight suit?

Next year will be different
I'll wear old clothes,
be ready to dribble,
and enjoy
ice cream, cake, and everything else.

ABOUT V. S. NAIPAUL

V(idiadhar) S(urajprasad) Naipaul (nā´pôl) was born in 1932 on the Caribbean island of Trinidad. A self-described person without roots, he writes, in addition to novels, non-fiction about traveling and exploring different cultures. In most of his settings, native cultures have given way to colonial or national rule, and people are striving to find a new national identity. Among his best-known works are *Miguel Street, A House for Mr. Biswas,* and *A Bend in the River.*

ABOUT NIDIA SANABRIA DE ROMERO

Nidia Sanabria de Romero (nē´dē ə sä nä´brē ə dā rō mä´rō) was born in Paraguay in 1928. She is involved in children's theater, and has founded the Iberoamericano High School in Paraguay, where she serves as principal.

RESPONDING

1. **Personal Response** If you were a parent, would you allow your child to associate with B. Wordsworth? Do you think the speaker in "The New Suit" would enjoy the company of B. Wordsworth? Why or why not?

2. **Literary Analysis** William Wordsworth (1770–1850) was a British Romantic poet famed for his poems about nature and his simplicity of expression. Why is it important to know this *allusion* when thinking about the title character?

3. **Multicultural Connection** Do you think that poets are appropriately honored in any culture? Explain. Why do you think leading sports figures are accorded more rewards than poets are in our culture? Is this fair?

LANGUAGE WORKSHOP

Characterization Naipaul uses details to make B. Wordsworth a memorable *character*. Make a list of six things B. Wordsworth says and does that distinguish him from other characters that you have read about. Does he fit your ideas of what a poet should be? Explain.

WRITER'S PORTFOLIO

Imagine you are an unemployed poet who is writing his or her job description in a want ad. The ad should draw attention to things a poet can do for specific people and for society in general. Think about what poets can do — from entertaining and writing for special occasions to offering reminders about the important things in life. Then write an ad.

Projects

COLLAGE OF GROWING UP

Choose a person from history, sports, entertainment, your family, or some other area who chose a career path early in life. Make a collage of this person's youth or entire life, using photos, drawings, small objects, and significant words and phrases. If you find items that illustrate a turning point or "threshold" in that person's life, use them as the central focus of the collage. Provide captions if you wish. Present your collage to the class.

EVALUATE ADVERTISING

For one week, keep a journal of advertisements you hear or see that are geared specifically toward people your age. Develop a list of the traits of your age group that the ads are designed to appeal to. What makes the ads appeal to you instead of to a first-grader or a teacher? What do advertisers seem to think people your age really want? Are they right? Bring your list to class and present your findings.

STEPS TO MATURITY

The characters who appear in this unit don't cross the threshold to adulthood in one move. Instead, they gain small insights and victories that advance them a few steps toward maturity. In several paragraphs, point out things that these characters have learned or done that will better equip them as adults.

Further Reading

The following books contain portraits of young people in the process of growing up.

Cisneros, Sandra. *The House on Mango Street.* Vintage Contemporaries, 1989. A series of brief poetic snapshots follow Esperanza Cordero as she grows up in an urban neighborhood.

Franklin, Miles. *My Brilliant Career.* Pocket, 1981 (originally published in 1901). An Australian teenager grows up in the country's wild rural region.

Hayslip, Le Ly. *When Heaven and Earth Changed Places.* Doubleday, 1989. A memoir of the author's girlhood and youth in war-torn Vietnam portrays growing up amid an exceptionally traumatic background.

Kincaid, Jamaica. *Annie John.* Penguin Books, 1983. The title character in this novel is a headstrong and rebellious adolescent growing up in Antigua.

Mehta, Ved. *Sound-Shadows of the New World.* Norton, 1987. A boy leaves his family in India to study at a school for the blind in Arkansas. This is one in a series of memoirs.

Walker, Scott, ed. *Stories from the Rest of the World.* Graywolf Press, 1989. The stories in this collection by contemporary non-Western authors explore universal themes.

Wright, Richard. *Black Boy.* Harper, 1945; HarperPerennial edition with notes, 1993. This autobiographical narrative of a young man's coming of age examines what it was like to be Southern, male, and African American in the United States between the world wars.

Between Generations

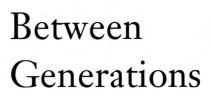

Special things can happen when you reach across generations! Has an older person, or someone much younger, taught you to value something or to see it in a new light? Think of times that you have turned to an older person for advice, insight, or help—or times when someone of another generation has turned to you in need. The characters in this unit show that communication between generations can be rewarding, instructive, and at times difficult—but well worth the effort.

From **Kaffir Boy**

"Education will open doors where none seem to exist."

WHEN MY MOTHER began dropping hints that I would soon be going to school, I vowed never to go because school was a waste of time. She laughed and said, "We'll see. You don't know what you're talking about." My philosophy on school was that of a gang of ten-, eleven- and twelve-year-olds whom I so revered that their every word seemed that of an oracle.

These boys had long left their homes and were now living in various neighbourhood junkyards, making it on their

About Apartheid

Mathabane was raised under South Africa's system of legalized racism known as *apartheid* (ə pärt'hāt; ə pärt'hĭt). Under this system, black people were denied the vote and experienced police brutality and the constant threat of deportation to tribal reserves. Through the efforts of many people, most notably Nelson Mandela, then head of the African National Congress, and F. W. de Klerk, then South Africa's president, who were jointly awarded the Nobel Peace Prize in 1993, apartheid no longer legally exists. In 1994, Nelson Mandela was elected president in the first multiracial election in South Africa's history. Racial unrest and riots, however, continue.

own. They slept in abandoned cars, smoked glue and benzene, ate pilchards and brown bread, sneaked into the white world to caddy and, if unsuccessful, came back to the township to steal beer and soda bottles from shebeens, or goods from the Indian traders on First Avenue. Their lifestyle was exciting, adventurous and full of surprises; and I was attracted to it. My mother told me that they were nogooders, that they would amount to nothing, that I should not associate with them, but I paid no heed. What does she know? I used to tell myself. One thing she did not know was that the gang's way of life had captivated me wholly, particularly their philosophy on school: they hated it and considered an education a waste of time.

They, like myself, had grown up in an environment where the value of an education was never emphasized, where the first thing a child learned was not how to read and write and spell, but how to fight and steal and rebel; where the money to send children to school was grossly lacking, for survival was first priority. I kept my membership in the gang, knowing that for as long as I was under its influence, I would never go to school.

One day my mother woke me up at four in the morning.

"Are they here? I didn't hear any noises," I asked in the usual way.

"No," my mother said. "I want you to get into that washtub over there."

"What!" I balked, upon hearing the word *washtub*. I feared taking baths like one feared the plague. Throughout seven years of hectic living the number of baths I had taken could be counted on one hand with several fingers missing. I simply had no natural inclination for water; cleanliness was a trait I still had to acquire. Besides, we had only one bathtub in the house, and it constantly sprung a leak.

"I said get into that tub!" My mother shook a finger in my face.

Reluctantly, I obeyed, yet wondered why all of a sudden I had to take a bath. My mother, armed with a scropbrush and a piece of Lifebuoy soap, purged me of years and years of grime till I ached and bled. As I howled, feeling pain

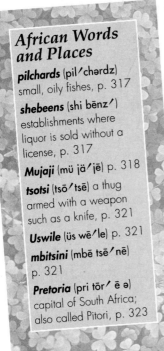

African Words and Places

pilchards (pil′chərdz) small, oily fishes, p. 317

shebeens (shi bēnz′) establishments where liquor is sold without a license, p. 317

Mujaji (mü jä′jē) p. 318

tsotsi (tsō′tsē) a thug armed with a weapon such as a knife, p. 321

Uswile (üs wē′le) p. 321

mbitsini (mbē tsē′nē) p. 321

Pretoria (pri tōr′ ē ə) capital of South Africa; also called Pitori, p. 323

shoot through my limbs as the thistles of the brush encountered stubborn callouses, there was a loud knock at the door.

Instantly my mother leaped away from the tub and headed, on tiptoe, toward the bedroom. Fear seized me as I, too, thought of the police. I sat frozen in the bathtub, not knowing what to do.

"Open up, Mujaji [my mother's maiden name]," Granny's voice came shrilling through the door. "It's me."

My mother heaved a sigh of relief; her tense limbs relaxed. She turned and headed to the kitchen door, unlatched it and in came Granny and Aunt Bushy.

"You scared me half to death," my mother said to Granny. "I had forgotten all about your coming."

"Are you ready?" Granny asked my mother.

"Yes—just about," my mother said, beckoning me to get out of the washtub.

She handed me a piece of cloth to dry myself. As I dried myself, questions raced through my mind: What's going on? What's Granny doing at our house this ungodly hour of the morning? And why did she ask my mother, "Are you ready?" While I stood debating, my mother went into the bedroom and came out with a stained white shirt and a pair of faded black shorts.

"Here," she said, handing me the togs, "put these on."

"Why?" I asked.

"Put them on I said!"

I put the shirt on; it was grossly loose-fitting. It reached all the way down to my ankles. Then I saw the reason why: it was my father's shirt!

"But this is Papa's shirt," I complained. "It don't fit me."

"Put it on," my mother insisted. "I'll make it fit."

"The pants don't fit me either," I said. "Whose are they anyway?"

"Put them on," my mother said. "I'll make them fit."

Moments later I had the garments on; I looked ridiculous. My mother started working on the pants and shirt to make them fit. She folded the shirt in so many intricate ways and stashed it inside the pants, they too having been folded several times at the waist. She then choked the pants at the waist with a piece of sisal rope to hold them up. She then lavishly smeared my face, arms and legs with a mixture of pig's fat and vaseline. "This will insulate you from the cold," she said. My skin gleamed like the morning star and I felt as hot as the centre of the sun and I smelled God knows like what. After embalming me, she headed to the bedroom.

"Where are we going, Gran'ma?" I said, hoping that she would tell me what my mother refused to tell me. I still had no idea I was about to be taken to school.

"Didn't your mother tell you?" Granny said with a smile. "You're going to start school."

"What!" I gasped, leaping from the chair where I was sitting as if it were made of hot lead. "I am not going to school!" I blurted out and raced toward the kitchen door.

My mother had just reappeared from the bedroom and guessing what I was up to, she yelled, "Someone get the door!"

Aunt Bushy immediately barred the door. I turned and headed for the window. As I leaped for the windowsill, my mother lunged at me and brought me down. I tussled, "Let go of me! I don't want to go to school! Let me go!" but my mother held fast onto me.

"It's no use now," she said, grinning triumphantly as she pinned me down. Turning her head in Granny's direction, she shouted, "Granny! Get a rope quickly!"

Granny grabbed a piece of rope nearby and came to my mother's aid. I bit and clawed every hand that grabbed me, and howled protestations against going to school; however, I was no match for the two determined matriarchs. In a jiffy they had me bound, hands and feet.

"What's the matter with him?" Granny, bewildered, asked my mother. "Why did he suddenly turn into an imp when I told him you're taking him to school?"

"You shouldn't have told him that he's being taken to school," my mother said. "He doesn't want to go there. That's why I requested you come today, to help me take him there. Those boys in the streets have been a bad influence on him."

As the two matriarchs hauled me through the door, they told Aunt Bushy not to go to school but stay behind and mind the house and the children.

THE SUN WAS BEGINNING TO RISE from beyond the veld when Granny and my mother dragged me to school. The streets were beginning to fill with their everyday traffic: old men and women, wizened, bent and ragged, were beginning their rambling; workless men and women were beginning to assemble in their usual coteries and head for shebeens in the backyards where they discussed how they escaped the morning pass raids and contemplated the conditions of life amidst intense beer drinking and vacant, uneasy laughter; young boys and girls, some as young as myself, were beginning their aimless wanderings along the narrow, dusty streets in search of food, carrying bawling infants piggyback.

As we went along some of the streets, boys and girls who shared the same fears about school as I were making their feelings known in a variety of ways. They were howling their protests and trying to escape. A few managed to break loose and make a mad dash for freedom, only to be recaptured in no time, admonished or whipped, or both, and ordered to march again.

As we made a turn into Sixteenth Avenue, the street leading to the tribal school I was being taken to, a short, chubby black woman came along from the opposite direction. She had a scuttle overflowing with coal on her *doek*-covered (cloth-covered) head. An infant, bawling deafeningly, was loosely swathed with a piece of sheepskin onto her back. Following closely behind the woman, and picking up pieces of coal as they fell from the scuttle and placing them in a small plastic bag, was a half-naked, pot-bellied and thumb-sucking boy of about four. The woman stopped abreast. For some reason we stopped too.

"I wish I had done the same to my oldest son," the strange woman said in a regretful voice, gazing at me. I was confounded by her stopping and offering her unsolicited opinion.

"I wish I had done that to my oldest son," she repeated, and suddenly burst into tears; amidst sobs, she continued, "before . . . the street claimed him . . . and . . . turned him into a *tsotsi*."

Granny and my mother offered consolatory remarks to the strange woman.

"But it's too late now," the strange woman continued, tears now streaming freely down her puffy cheeks. She made no attempt to dry them. "It's too late now," she said for the second time, "he's beyond any help. I can't help him even if I want to. *Uswile* [He is dead]."

"How did he die?" my mother asked in a sympathetic voice.

"He shunned school and, instead, grew up to live by the knife. And the same knife he lived by ended his life. That's why whenever I see a boy-child refuse to go to school, I stop and tell the story of my dear little *mbitsini* [heart-break]."

Having said that, the strange woman left as mysteriously as she had arrived.

"Did you hear what that woman said!" my mother screamed into my ears. "Do you want the same to happen to you?"

I dropped my eyes. I was confused.

"Poor woman," Granny said ruefully. "She must have truly loved her son."

Finally, we reached the school and I was ushered into the principal's office, a tiny cubicle facing a row of privies and a patch of yellowed grass.

"So this is the rascal we'd been talking about," the principal, a tall, wiry man, foppishly dressed in a black pinstriped suit, said to my mother as we entered. His austere, shiny face, inscrutable and imposing, reminded me of my father. He was sitting behind a brown table upon which stood piles of dust and cobweb-covered books and papers. In one upper pocket of his jacket was arrayed a variety of pens and pencils; in the other nestled a lily-white handkerchief whose presence was more decorative than utilitarian. Alongside him stood a disproportionately portly black woman, fashionably dressed in a black skirt and a white blouse. She had but one pen, and this she held in her hand. The room was hot and stuffy and buzzing with flies.

"Yes, Principal," my mother answered, "this is he."

"I see he's living up to his notoriety," remarked the principal, noticing that I had been bound. "Did he give you too much trouble?"

"Trouble, Principal," my mother sighed. "He was like an imp."

"He's just like the rest of them, Principal," Granny sighed. "Once they get out into the streets, they become wild. They take to the many vices of the streets like an infant takes to its mother's milk. They begin to think that there's no other life but the one shown them by the *tsotsis*. They come to hate school and forget about the future."

"Well," the principal said. "We'll soon remedy all that. Untie him."

"He'll run away," my mother cried.

"I don't think he's that foolish to attempt that with all of us here."

"He *is* that foolish, Principal," my mother said as she and Granny began untying me. "He's tried it before. Getting him here was an ordeal in itself."

The principal rose from his seat, took two steps to the door and closed it. As the door swung closed, I spotted a row of canes of different lengths and thicknesses hanging behind it. The principal, seeing me staring at the canes, grinned and said, in a manner suggesting that he had wanted me to see them, "As long as you behave, I won't have to use any of those on you."

Use those canes on me? I gasped. I stared at my mother—she smiled; at Granny—she smiled too. That made me abandon any inkling of escaping.

"So they finally gave you the birth certificate and the papers," the principal addressed my mother as he returned to his chair.

"Yes, Principal," my mother said, "they finally did. But what a battle it was. It took me nearly a year to get all them papers together." She took out of her handbag a neatly wrapped package and handed it to the principal. "They've been running us around for so long that there were times when I thought he would never attend school, Principal," she said.

"That's pretty much standard procedure, Mrs. Mathabane," the principal said, unwrapping the package. "But you now have the papers and that's what's important."

"As long as we have the papers," he continued, minutely perusing the contents of the package, "we won't be breaking the law in admitting your son to this school, for we'll be in full compliance with the requirements set by the authorities in Pretoria."

"Sometimes I don't understand the laws from Pitori," Granny said. "They did the same to me with my Piet and Bushy. Why, Principal, should our children not be allowed to learn because of some piece of paper?"

"The piece of paper you're referring to, Mrs. Mabaso [Granny's maiden name]," the principal said to Granny, "is as important to our children as a pass is to us adults. We all hate passes; therefore, it's only natural we should hate the regulations our children are subjected to. But as we have to live with passes, so our children have to live with the regulations, Mrs. Mabaso. I hope you understand, that is the law of the country. We would have admitted your grandson a long time ago, as you well know, had it not been for the papers. I hope you understand."

"I understand, Principal," Granny said, "but I don't understand," she added paradoxically.

One of the papers caught the principal's eye and he turned to my mother and asked, "Is your husband a Shangaan, Mrs. Mathabane?"

"No, he's not, Principal," my mother said. "Is there anything wrong? He's Venda and I'm Shangaan."

The principal reflected for a moment or so and then said, concernedly, "No, there's nothing seriously wrong. Nothing that we can't take care of. You see, Mrs. Mathabane, technically, the fact that your child's father is a Venda makes him ineligible to attend this tribal school because it is only for children whose parents are of the Shangaan tribe. May I ask what language the children speak at home?"

"Both languages," my mother said worriedly, "Venda and Shangaan. Is there anything wrong?"

The principal coughed, clearing his throat, then said, "I mean which language do they speak more?"

"It depends, Principal," my mother said, swallowing hard. "When their father is around, he wants them to speak only Venda. And when he's not, they speak Shangaan. And when they are out at play, they speak Zulu and Sisotho."

"Well," the principal said, heaving a sigh of relief. "In that case, I think an exception can be made. The reason for such an exception is that there's currently no school for Vendas in Alexandra. And should the authorities come asking why we took in your son, we can tell them that. Anyway, your child is half-half."

Everyone broke into a nervous laugh, except me. I was bewildered by the whole thing. I looked at my mother, and she seemed greatly relieved as she watched the principal register me; a broad smile broke across her face. It was as if some enormously heavy burden had finally been lifted from her shoulders and her conscience.

"Bring him back two weeks from today," the principal said as he saw us to the door. "There're so many children registering today that classes won't begin until two weeks hence. Also, the school needs repair and cleaning up after the holidays. If he refuses to come, simply notify us, and we'll send a couple of big boys to come fetch him, and he'll be very sorry if it ever comes to that."

As we left the principal's office and headed home, my mind was still against going to school. I was thinking of running away from home and joining my friends in the junkyard.

I didn't want to go to school for three reasons: I was reluctant to surrender my freedom and independence over to what I heard every school-going child call "tyrannous discipline." I had heard many bad things about life in tribal school—from daily beatings by teachers and mistresses who worked you like a mule to long school hours—and the sight of those canes in the principal's office gave ample credence to rumors that school was nothing but a torture chamber. And there was my allegiance to the gang.

But the thought of the strange woman's lamentations over her dead son presented a somewhat strong case for going to school: I didn't want to end up dead in the streets. A more compelling argument for going to school, however, was the vivid recollection of all that humiliation and pain my mother had gone through to get me the papers and the birth certificate so I could enroll in school. What should I do? I was torn between two worlds.

But later that evening something happened to force me to go to school.

I was returning home from playing soccer when a neighbour accosted me by the gate and told me that there had been a bloody fight at my home.

"Your mother and father have been at it again," the neighbour, a woman, said.

"And your mother left."

I was stunned.

"Was she hurt badly?"

"A little bit," the woman said. "But she'll be all right. We took her to your grandma's place."

I became hot with anger.

"Is anyone in the house?" I stammered, trying to control my rage.

"Yes, your father is. But I don't think you should go near the house. He's raving mad. He's armed with a meat cleaver. He's chased out your brother and sisters, also. And some of the neighbours who tried to intervene he's threatened to carve them to pieces. I have never seen him this mad before."

I brushed aside the woman's warnings and went. Shattered windows convinced me that there had indeed been a skirmish of some sort. Several pieces of broken bricks, evidently broken after being thrown at the door, were lying about the door. I tried opening the door; it was locked from the inside. I knocked. No one answered. I knocked again. Still no one answered, until, as I turned to leave:

"Who's out there?" my father's voice came growling from inside.

"It's me, Johannes," I said.

"Go away, you bastard!" he bellowed. "I don't want you or that whore mother of yours setting foot in this house. Go away before I come out there and kill you!"

"Let me in!" I cried. "Dammit, let me in! I want my things!"

"What things? Go away, you black swine!"

I went to the broken window and screamed obscenities at my father, daring him to come out, hoping that if he as much as ever stuck his black face out, I would pelt him with the half-a-loaf brick in my hand. He didn't come out. He continued launching a tirade of obscenities at my mother and her mother, calling them whores and bitches and so on. He was drunk, but I wondered where he had gotten the money to buy beer because it was still the middle of the week and he was dead broke. He had lost his entire wage for the past week in dice and had had to borrow bus fare.

"I'll kill you someday for all you're doing to my mother," I threatened him, overwhelmed with rage. Several nosey neighbours were beginning to congregate by open windows and doors. Not wanting to make a spectacle of myself, which was something many of our neighbours seemed to always expect from our family, I backtracked away from the door and vanished into the dark street. I ran, without stopping, all the way to the other end of the township where Granny lived. There I found my mother, her face swollen and bruised and her eyes puffed up to the point where she could scarcely see.

"What happened, Mama?" I asked, fighting to hold back the tears at the sight of her disfigured face.

"Nothing, child, nothing," she mumbled, almost apologetically, between swollen lips. "Your papa simply lost his temper, that's all."

"But why did he beat you up like this, Mama?" Tears came down my face. "He's never beaten you like this before."

MY MOTHER APPEARED reluctant to answer me. She looked searchingly at Granny, who was pounding millet with pestle and mortar and mixing it with sorghum and nuts for an African delicacy. Granny said, "Tell him, child, tell him. He's got a right to know. Anyway, he's the cause of it all."

"Your father and I fought because I took you to school this morning," my mother began. "He had told me not to, and when I told him that I had, he became very upset. He was drunk. We started arguing, and one thing led to another."

"Why doesn't he want me to go to school?"

"He says he doesn't have money to waste paying for you to get what he calls a useless white man's education," my mother replied. "But I told him that if he won't pay for your schooling, I would try and look for a job and pay, but he didn't want to hear that, also. 'There are better things for you to work for,' he said. 'Besides, I don't want you to work. How would I look to other men if you, a woman I owned, were to start working?' When I asked him why shouldn't I take you to school, seeing that you were now of age, he replied that he doesn't believe in schools. I told him that school would keep you off the streets and out of trouble, but still he was belligerent."

"Is that why he beat you up?"

"Yes, he said I disobeyed his orders."

"He's right, child," Granny interjected. "He paid *lobola* [bride price] for you. And your father ate it all up before he left me."

To which my mother replied, "But I desperately want to leave this beast of a man. But with his *lobola* gone I can't do it. That worthless thing you call your husband shouldn't have sold Jackson's scrawny cattle and left you penniless."

"Don't talk like that about your father, child," Granny said. "Despite all, he's still your father, you know. Anyway, he asked for *lobola* only because he had to get back what he spent raising you. And you know it would have been taboo for him to let you or any of your sisters go without asking for *lobola*."

"You and Papa seemed to forget that my sisters and I have minds of our own," my mother said. "We didn't need you to tell us whom to marry, and why, and how. If it hadn't been for your interference, I could have married that schoolteacher."

GRANNY DID NOT REPLY; she knew well not to. When it came to the act of "selling" women as marriage partners, my mother was vehemently opposed to it. Not only was she opposed to this one aspect of tribal culture, but to others as well, particularly those involving relations between men and women and the upbringing of children. But my mother's sharply differing opinion was an exception rather than the rule among tribal women. Most times, many tribal women questioned her sanity in daring to question well-established mores. But my mother did not seem to care; she would always scoff at her opponents and call them fools in letting their husbands enslave them completely.

Though I disliked school, largely because I knew nothing about what actually went on there, and the little I knew had painted a dreadful picture, the fact that a father would not want his son to go to school, especially a father who didn't go to school, seemed hard to understand.

"Why do you want me to go to school, Mama?" I asked, hoping that she might, somehow, clear up some of the confusion that was building in my mind.

"I want you to have a future, child," my mother said. "And, contrary to what your father says, school is the only means to a future. I don't want you growing up to be like your father."

The latter statement hit me like a bolt of lightning. It just about shattered every defense mechanism and every pretext I had against going to school.

"Your father didn't go to school," she continued, dabbing her puffed eyes to reduce the swelling with a piece of cloth dipped in warm water, "that's why he's doing some of the bad things he's doing. Things like drinking, gambling and neglecting his family. He didn't learn how to read and write; therefore, he can't find a decent job. Lack of any education has narrowly focused his life. He sees nothing beyond himself. He still thinks in the old, tribal way, and still believes that things should be as they were back in the old days when he was growing up as a tribal boy in Louis Trichardt. Though he's my husband, and your father, he doesn't see any of that."

"Why didn't he go to school, Mama?"

"He refused to go to school because his father led him to believe that an education was a tool through which white people were going to take things away from him, like they did black people in the old days. And that a white man's education was worthless insofar as black people were concerned because it prepared them for jobs they can't have. But I know it isn't totally so, child, because times have changed somewhat. Though our lot isn't any better today, an education will get you a decent job. If you can read or write you'll be better off than those of us who can't. Take my situation: I can't find a job because I don't have papers, and I can't get papers because white people mainly want to register people who can read and write. But I want things to be different for you, child. For you and your brother and sisters. I want you to go to school, because I believe that an education is the key you need to open up a new world and a new life for yourself, a world and life different from that of either your father's or mine. It is the only key that can do that, and only those who seek it earnestly and perseveringly will get anywhere in the white man's world. Education will open doors where none seem to exist. It'll make people talk to you, listen to you and help you; people who otherwise wouldn't bother. It will make you soar, like a bird lifting up into the endless blue sky, and leave poverty, hunger and suffering behind. It'll teach you to learn to embrace what's good and shun what's bad and evil. Above all, it'll make you a somebody in this world. It'll make you grow up to be a good and proud person. That's why I want you to go to school, child, so that education can do all that, and more, for you."

A long, awkward silence followed, during which I reflected upon the significance of my mother's lengthy speech. I looked at my mother; she looked at me.

Finally, I asked, "How come you know so much about school, Mama? You didn't go to school, did you?"

"No, child," my mother replied. "Just like your father, I never went to school." For the second time that evening, a mere statement of fact had a thunderous impact on me. All the confusion I had about school seemed to leave my mind, like darkness giving way to light. And what had previously been a dark, yawning void in my mind was suddenly transformed into a beacon of light that began to grow larger and larger, until it had swallowed up, blotted out, all the blackness. That beacon of light seemed to reveal things and facts, which, though they must have always existed in me, I hadn't been aware of up until now.

"But unlike your father," my mother went on, "I've always wanted to go to school, but couldn't because my father, under the sway of tribal traditions, thought it unnecessary to educate females. That's why I so much want you to go, child, for if you do, I know that someday I too would come to go, old as I would be then. Promise me, therefore, that no matter what, you'll go back to school. And I, in turn, promise that I'll do everything in my power to keep you there."

With tears streaming down my cheeks and falling upon my mother's bosom, I promised her that I would go to school "forever." That night, at seven and a half years of my life, the battlelines in the family were drawn. My mother on the one side, illiterate but determined to have me drink, for better or for worse, from the well of knowledge. On the other side, my father, he too illiterate, yet determined to have me drink from the well of ignorance. Scarcely aware of the magnitude of the decision I was making or, rather, the decision which was being emotionally thrusted upon me, I chose to fight on my mother's side, and thus my destiny was forever altered.

ABOUT **MARK MATHABANE**

Mark Mathabane (**ma´thä bān´**) was born in 1960 in Alexandra, a black ghetto of South Africa. Despite tremendous obstacles, he attended school, took up tennis, and in 1978, inspired by U.S. tennis star Arthur Ashe and aided by another U.S. tennis player, Stan Smith, he entered a U.S. college on a tennis scholarship. In 1986, he published *Kaffir Boy*. Other works include *Kaffir Boy in America: An Encounter with Apartheid*, and *Love in Black and White: The Triumph of Love over Prejudice and Taboo*, written with his wife Gail.

RESPONDING

1. *Personal Response* At the end of the selection, Mathabane observes "thus my destiny was forever altered." Do you think that your decisions about education are important enough to alter your destiny? Explain.

2. *Literary Analysis* The *conflict* in this selection comes mainly from the opposing views of education held by Mathabane's parents. Why do you think the narrator's mother and father feel as they do about his going to school?

3. *Multicultural Connection* Why might people in Mathabane's culture oppose getting a formal education? Before answering, you may want to reread the paragraph that begins, "He refused to go to school. . . ." (page 329)

LANGUAGE WORKSHOP

Word Origins Mathabane describes a black school in Africa under *apartheid*. This word, from Afrikaans, meaning "separate," refers to South Africa's system of legalized racism at the time he wrote. Under this system, he was known as a *Kaffir*. This word, of Arabic origin, is a derogatory term used by whites to refer to blacks. Use a dictionary to find out the meaning and origins of these words used by Mathabane: *austere, inscrutable, utilitarian, paradoxically, beacon, embalming, sorghum, wizened.*

WRITER'S PORTFOLIO

Write a brief motivational speech that Mark Mathabane might give to a youth group summarizing why he decided to attend and succeed at school.

The Conjurer Made Off with the Dish

THE TIME HAS COME for you to be useful," said my mother to me. And she slipped her hand into her pocket, saying, "Take this piaster and go off and buy some beans. Don't play on the way and keep away from the carts."

I took the dish, put on my clogs, and went out, humming a tune. Finding a crowd in front of the bean seller, I waited until I discovered a way through to the marble counter.

"A piaster's worth of beans, mister," I called out in my shrill voice.

He asked me impatiently, "Beans alone? With oil? With cooking butter?"

I did not answer, and he said to me roughly, "Make way for someone else."

I withdrew, overcome by embarrassment, and returned home defeated.

"Returning with an empty dish?" my mother shouted at me. "What did you do—spill the beans or lose the piaster, you naughty boy?"

"Beans alone? With oil? With cooking butter?—you didn't tell me," I protested.

"Stupid boy! What do you eat every morning?"

"I don't know."

"You good-for-nothing, ask him for beans with oil."

I went off to the man and said, "A piaster's worth of beans with oil, mister."

With a frown of impatience he asked, "Linseed oil? Vegetable oil? Olive oil?"

I was taken aback and again made no answer.

"Make way for someone else," he shouted at me.

I returned in a rage to my mother, who called out in astonishment, "You've come back empty-handed — no beans and no oil."

"Linseed oil? Vegetable oil? Olive oil? Why didn't you tell me?" I said angrily.

"Beans with oil means beans with linseed oil."

"How should I know?"

"You're a good-for-nothing, and he's a tiresome man — tell him beans with linseed oil."

Culture Notes

piaster a coin of Lebanon, Egypt, Syria, and the Sudan, worth several cents, p. 333

Koran the sacred book of the Moslems, consisting of revelations of Allah to Mohammed, p. 334

I went off quickly and called out to the man while still some yards from his shop, "Beans with linseed oil, mister."

"Put the piaster on the counter," he said, plunging the ladle into the pot.

I put my hand into my pocket but did not find the piaster. I searched for it anxiously. I turned my pocket inside out but found no trace of it. The man withdrew the ladle empty, saying with disgust, "You've lost the piaster — you're not a boy to be depended on."

"I haven't lost it," I said, looking under my feet and round about me. "It was in my pocket all the time."

"Make way for someone else and stop bothering me."

I returned to my mother with an empty dish.

"Good grief, are you an idiot, boy?"

"The piaster. . ."

"What of it?"

"It 's not in my pocket."

"Did you buy sweets with it?"

"I swear I didn't."

"How did you lose it?"

"I don't know."

"Do you swear by the Koran you didn't buy anything with it?"

"I swear."

"Is there a hole in your pocket?"

"No, there isn't."

"Maybe you gave it to the man the first time or the second."

"Maybe."

"Are you sure of nothing?"

"I'm hungry."

She clapped her hands together in a gesture of resignation.

"Never mind," she said. "I'll give you another piaster but I'll take it out of your money-box, and if you come back with an empty dish, I'll break your head."

I WENT OFF AT A RUN, dreaming of a delicious breakfast. At the turning leading to the alleyway where the bean-seller was, I saw a crowd of children and heard merry, festive sounds. My feet dragged as my heart was pulled toward them. At least let me have a fleeting glance. I slipped in among them and found the conjurer looking straight at me. A stupefying joy overwhelmed me; I was completely taken out of myself. With the whole of my being I became involved in the tricks of the rabbits and the eggs, and the snakes and the ropes. When the man came up to collect money, I drew back mumbling, "I haven't got any money."

He rushed at me savagely, and I escaped only with difficulty. I ran off, my back almost broken by his blow, and yet I was utterly happy as I made my way to the seller of beans.

"Beans with linseed oil for a piaster, mister," I said.

He went on looking at me without moving, so I repeated my request.

"Give me the dish," he demanded angrily.

The dish! Where was the dish? Had I dropped it while running? Had the conjurer made off with it?

"Boy, you're out of your mind!"

I retraced my steps, searching along the way for the lost dish. The place where the conjurer had been, I found empty, but the voices of children led me to him in a nearby lane. I moved around the circle. When the conjurer spotted me, he shouted out threateningly, "Pay up or you'd better scram."

"The dish!" I called out despairingly.

"What dish, you little devil?"

"Give me back the dish."

"Scram or I'll make you into food for snakes."

He had stolen the dish, yet fearfully I moved away out of sight and wept in grief. Whenever a passerby asked me why I was crying, I would reply, "The conjurer made off with the dish."

Through my misery I became aware of a voice saying, "Come along and watch!"

I looked behind me and saw a peep show had been set up. I saw dozens of children hurrying toward it and taking it in turns to stand in front of the peepholes, while the man began his tantalizing commentary to the pictures.

"There you've got the gallant knight and the most beautiful of all ladies, Zainat al-Banat."

My tears dried up, and I gazed up in fascination at the box, completely forgetting the conjurer and the dish. Unable to overcome the temptation, I paid over the piaster and stood in front of the peephole next to a girl who was standing in front of the other one, and enchanting picture stories flowed across our vision. When I came back to my own world I realized I had lost both the piaster and the dish, and there was no sign of the conjurer. However, I gave no thought to the loss, so taken up was I with the pictures of chivalry, love, and deeds of daring. I forgot my hunger. I forgot even the fear of what threatened me at home. I took a few paces back so as to lean against the ancient wall of what had once been a treasury and the chief cadi's seat of office, and gave myself up wholly to my reveries. For a long while I dreamed of chivalry, of Zainat al-Banat and the ghoul. In my dream I spoke aloud, giving

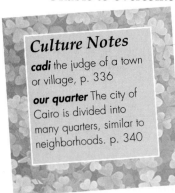

Culture Notes

cadi the judge of a town or village, p. 336

our quarter The city of Cairo is divided into many quarters, similar to neighborhoods. p. 340

meaning to my words with gestures. Thrusting home the imaginary lance, I said, "Take that, O ghoul, right in the heart!"

"And he raised Zainat al-Banat up behind him on the horse," came back a gentle voice.

I looked to my right and saw the young girl who had been beside me at the performance. She was wearing a dirty dress and colored clogs and was playing with her long plait of hair. In her other hand were the red-and-white sweets called "lady's fleas," which she was leisurely sucking. We exchanged glances, and I lost my heart to her.

"Let's sit down and rest," I said to her.

She appeared to go along with my suggestion, so I took her by the arm and we went through the gateway of the ancient wall and sat down on the step of its stairway that went nowhere, a stairway that rose up until it ended in a platform behind which there could be seen the blue sky and minarets. We sat in silence, side by side. I pressed her hand, and we sat in silence, not knowing what to say. I experienced feelings that were new, strange, and obscure. Putting my face close to hers, I breathed in the natural smell of her hair mingled with an odor of dust, and the fragrance of breath mixed with the aroma of sweets. I kissed her lips. I swallowed my saliva, which had taken on a sweetness from the dissolved "lady's fleas." I put my arm around her, without her uttering a word, kissing her cheek and lips. Her lips grew still as they received the kiss, then went back to sucking at the sweets. At last she decided to get up. I seized her arm anxiously. "Sit down," I said.

"I'm going," she replied simply.

"Where to?" I asked dejectedly.

"To the midwife Umm Ali," and she pointed to a house on the ground floor of which was a small ironing shop.

"Why?"

"To tell her to come quickly."

"Why?"

"My mother's crying in pain at home. She told me to go to the midwife Umm Ali and to tell her to come along quickly."

"And you'll come back after that?"

She nodded her head in assent and went off. Her mentioning her mother reminded me of my own, and my heart missed a beat. Getting up from the ancient stairway, I made my way back home. I wept out loud, a tried method by which I would defend myself. I expected she would come to me, but she did not. I wandered from the kitchen to the bedroom but found no trace of her. Where had my mother gone? When would she return? I was fed up with being in the empty house. A good idea occurred to me. I took a dish from the kitchen and a piaster from my savings and went off immediately to the seller of beans. I found him asleep on a bench outside the shop, his face covered by his arm. The pots of beans had vanished and the long-necked bottles of oil had been put back on the shelf and the marble counter had been washed down.

"Mister," I whispered, approaching.

Hearing nothing but his snoring, I touched his shoulder. He raised his arm in alarm and looked at me through reddened eyes.

"Mister."

"What do you want?" he asked roughly, becoming aware of my presence and recognizing me.

"A piaster's worth of beans with linseed oil."

"Eh?"

"I've got the piaster and I've got the dish."

"You're crazy, boy," he shouted at me. "Get out or I'll bash your brains in."

WHEN I DID NOT MOVE, he pushed me so violently I went sprawling onto my back. I got up painfully, struggling to hold back the crying that was twisting my lips. My hands were clenched, one on the dish and the other on the piaster. I threw him an angry look. I thought about returning home with my hopes dashed, but dreams of heroism and valor altered my plan of action. Resolutely I made a quick decision and with all my strength threw the dish at him. It flew through the air and struck him on the head, while I took to my heels, heedless of everything. I was convinced I had killed him, just as the knight had killed the ghoul. I didn't stop running till I was near the ancient wall. Panting, I looked behind me but saw no signs of any pursuit. I stopped to get my breath, then asked myself what I should do now that the second dish was lost? Something warned me not to return home directly, and soon I had given myself over to a wave of indifference that bore me off where it willed. It meant a beating, neither more nor less, on my return, so let me put it off for a time. Here was the piaster in my hand, and I could have some sort of enjoyment with it before being punished. I decided to pretend I had forgotten I had done anything wrong—but where was the conjurer, where was the peep show? I looked everywhere for them to no avail.

Worn out by this fruitless searching, I went off to the ancient stairway to keep my appointment. I sat down to wait, imagining to myself the meeting. I yearned for another kiss redolent with the fragrance of sweets. I admitted to myself that the little girl had given me lovelier sensations than I had ever experienced. As I waited and dreamed, a whispering sound came from behind me. I climbed the stairs cautiously, and at the final landing I lay down flat on my face in order to see what was beyond, without anyone being able to notice me. I saw some ruins surrounded by a high wall, the last of what remained of the treasury and the chief cadi's seat of office. Directly under the stairs sat a man and a woman, and it was from them that the whispering came. The man looked like a tramp; the woman like one of those Gypsies that tend sheep. A suspicious inner voice told me that their meeting was similar to the one I had had. Their lips and the looks they exchanged spoke of this, but they showed astonishing expertise in the unimaginable things they did. My gaze became rooted upon them with curiosity, surprise, pleasure, and a certain amount of disquiet. At last they sat down side by side, neither of them taking any notice of the other. After quite a while the man said, "The money!"

"You're never satisfied," she said irritably.

Spitting on the ground, he said, "You're crazy."

"You're a thief."

He slapped her hard with the back of his hand, and she gathered up a handful of earth and threw it in his face. Then, his face soiled with dirt, he sprang at her, fastening his fingers on her windpipe, and a bitter fight ensued. In vain she gathered all her strength to escape from his grip. Her voice failed her, her eyes bulged out of their sockets, while her feet struck out at the air. In dumb terror, I stared at the scene till I saw a thread of blood trickling down from her nose. A scream escaped from my mouth. Before the man raised his head, I had crawled backward. Descending the stairs at a jump, I raced off like mad to wherever my legs might carry me. I did not stop running till I was breathless. Gasping for breath, I was quite unaware of my surroundings, but when I came to myself I found I was under a raised vault at the middle of a crossroads. I had never set foot there before and had no idea of where I was in relation to our quarter. On both sides sat sightless beggars, and crossing from all directions were people who paid attention to no one. In terror I realized I had lost my way and that countless difficulties lay in wait for me before I found my way home. Should I resort to asking one of the passersby to direct me? What, though, would happen if chance should lead me to a man like the seller of beans or the tramp of the waste plot? Would a miracle come about whereby I would see my mother approaching so that I could eagerly hurry toward her? Should I try to make my own way, wandering about till I came across some familiar landmark that would indicate the direction I should take?

I told myself that I should be resolute and make a quick decision. The day was passing, and soon mysterious darkness would descend.

ABOUT NAGUIB MAHFOUZ

Naguib Mahfouz (nä gēb⁄ mäk füz⁄), winner of the Nobel Prize in Literature in 1988, has popularized the novel and short story genres in the Arab literary world, which has traditionally favored poetry. Despite the

difficulty of translating Arabic into English, some of Mahfouz's works, including *Cairo Trilogy* and *Miramar*, enjoy popularity among readers in English. Set mainly in Cairo, Mahfouz's works realistically portray social and political problems in Egypt.

RESPONDING

1. *Personal Response* If you were sending the narrator on another errand, what would you do to ensure that he completed the job?

2. *Literary Analysis* How old do you think the *narrator* is? What clues in the story lead to your answer?

3. *Multicultural Connection* What do you learn about things such as meals, customs, entertainment, street scenes, and other aspects of everyday life in Egypt from this story? Would you like to live in or visit a city like the one described?

LANGUAGE WORKSHOP

Mood *Mood,* which is the atmosphere in a literary work, can be described as happy, peaceful, sad, thoughtful, angry, humorous, and so forth. Think about the atmosphere that Mahfouz creates in his work and then answer the following questions.

1. What word would you use to describe the predominant mood in this story? Why did you choose this word?

2. How does the mood change in the last two paragraphs of the story? What words and details help establish this mood?

WRITER'S PORTFOLIO

When the narrator first encounters the conjurer, Mahfouz writes: "A stupefying joy overwhelmed me; I was completely taken out of myself." Write a short sketch describing a time when you felt like that.

Grandmother

Sameeneh Shirazie

I hadn't asked her much,
just how she felt,
and she told me all about her day,
and how she'd washed the sheets,
and how she could not understand
why the towel got so heavy
when it was wet.
She'd also sunned the mattresses,
such tired bones and so much to do,
and my eyes filled with tears
when I thought of how I was simply
going to say "Salaam" and walk away
and so many words would have been
trapped inside her.
I would have passed by as if
what lay between those bedclothes
was just old life
and not really my grandmother.

Mid-Term Break

Seamus Heaney

I sat all morning in the college sick bay
Counting bells knelling classes to a close.
At two o'clock our neighbours drove me home.

In the porch I met my father crying —
He had always taken funerals in his stride —
And Big Jim Evans saying it was a hard blow.

The baby cooed and laughed and rocked the pram
When I came in, and I was embarrassed
By old men standing up to shake my hand

And tell me they were "sorry for my trouble."
Whispers informed strangers I was the eldest,
Away at school, as my mother held my hand

In hers and coughed out angry tearless sighs.
At ten o'clock the ambulance arrived
With the corpse, stanched and bandaged by the
    nurses.

Next morning I went up into the room. Snowdrops
And candles soothed the bedside; I saw him
For the first time in six weeks. Paler now,

Wearing a poppy bruise on his left temple,
He lay in the four foot box as in his cot.
No gaudy scars, the bumper knocked him clear.

A four foot box, a foot for every year.

My Father and the Figtree

Naomi Shihab Nye

For other fruits my father was indifferent.
He'd point at the cherry trees and say,
"See those? I wish they were figs."
In the evenings he sat by my bed
weaving folktales like vivid little scarves.
They always involved a figtree.
Even when it didn't fit, he'd stick it in.
Once Joha was walking down the road and he saw
      a figtree.
Or, he tied his camel to a figtree and went to sleep.
Or, later when they caught and arrested him,
his pockets were full of figs.

At age six I ate a dried fig and shrugged.
"That's not what I'm talking about!" he said,
"I'm talking about a fig straight from the earth—
gift of Allah!—on a branch so heavy it touches the
      ground.
I'm talking about picking the largest fattest sweetest
      fig
in the world and putting it in my mouth."
(Here he'd stop and close his eyes.)

Years passed, we lived in many houses, none had
      figtrees.
We had lima beans, zucchini, parsley, beets.
"Plant one!" my mother said, but my father never
      did.
He tended garden half-heartedly, forgot to water,
let the okra get too big.
"What a dreamer he is. Look how many things he
      starts and doesn't finish."

The last time he moved, I got a phone call.
My father, in Arabic, chanting a song I'd never
    heard.
"What's that?" I said.
"Wait till you see!"
He took me out back to the new yard.
There, in the middle of Dallas, Texas,
a tree with the largest, fattest sweetest figs in the
    world.
"It's a figtree song!" he said,
plucking his fruits like ripe tokens,
emblems, assurance
of a world that was always his own.

ABOUT **SAMEENEH SHIRAZIE**

Sameeneh Shirazie (sə mē⁄nə shi räz⁄ē) lives in Karachi, Pakistan, with her daughter Noor, Arabic for "light." She holds a master's degree in English literature. Her poem, "Grandmother," appears in *This Same Sky*, a collection of poetry from sixty-eight countries around the world for young adult readers.

ABOUT **SEAMUS HEANEY**

Widely recognized as one of Ireland's finest poets, Seamus Heaney (shā⁄müs hē⁄nē) was born in 1939 in County Derry, Northern Ireland. He now teaches at Harvard University, is Professor of Poetry at Oxford University, and is officially a resident of Dublin, Ireland. Heaney's poetry depicts modern Northern Ireland and the civil strife  of its farms and cities. He uses language to portray "the music of what happens," as he says in one of his poems.

ABOUT **NAOMI SHIHAB NYE**

Born in 1952 to a Palestinian father and an American mother, Naomi Shihab Nye (nā ō′mē shē′häb nī) grew up in St. Louis, Missouri; Jerusalem; and San Antonio, Texas, her current home. She has published three books of poems: *Different Ways to Pray, Hugging the Jukebox,* and *Yellow Glove.* In addition to her own writing, Nye teaches writing workshops around the world.

RESPONDING

1. *Personal Response* Quick — say three words that you associate with poetry in general. Do these words apply to the poems that you have just read? If not, suggest other words that describe these poems.

2. *Literary Analysis* Are the *tones* of these poems similar or different? Explain.

3. *Multicultural Connection* Nye calls her father's figs "tokens, emblems, assurance of a world that was always his own." What does she mean by this figurative language?

LANGUAGE WORKSHOP

Assonance *Assonance* is a type of rhyme in which the same vowel sounds are repeated with different consonants. Note, for example, the repetition of the long *o* sound in *close, drove,* and *home* in the first stanza of "Mid-Term Break." Although the ends of lines don't rhyme exactly (*close/rose* or *home/dome*), assonance helps unify these lines. List four other examples of assonance in Heaney's poem.

WRITER'S PORTFOLIO

Think of several things — physical items or spiritual traditions — that you feel have special significance or value and should be passed down to future generations. Then write a letter to an imaginary grandchild, to be put into a time capsule and opened in two generations, explaining why these things are valuable and must be preserved.

A Devoted Son

WHEN THE RESULTS APPEARED in the morning papers, Rakesh scanned them, barefoot and in his pyjamas, at the garden gate, then went up the steps to the veranda where his father sat sipping his morning tea and bowed down to touch his feet.

"A first division, son?" his father asked, beaming, reaching for the papers.

"At the top of the list, Papa," Rakesh murmured, as if awed. "First in the country."

Bedlam broke loose then. The family whooped and danced. The whole day long visitors streamed into the small yellow house at the end of the road, to congratulate the parents of this *Wunderkind*, to slap Rakesh on the back and fill the house and garden with the sounds and colours of a festival. There were garlands and *halwa*, party clothes and gifts (enough fountain pens to last years, even a watch or two), nerves and temper and joy, all in a multicoloured whirl of pride and great shining vistas newly opened: Rakesh was the first son in the family to receive an education, so much had been sacrificed in order to send him to school and then medical college, and at last the fruits of their sacrifice had arrived, golden and glorious.

To everyone who came to him to say, "*Mubarak*, Varma-ji, your son has brought you glory," the father said, "Yes, and do you know what is the first thing he did when he saw the results this morning? He came and touched my feet. He bowed down and touched my feet." This moved many of the women in the crowd so much that they were seen to raise the ends of their saris and dab at their tears while the men reached out for the betel-leaves and sweetmeats that were offered around on trays and shook their heads in wonder and approval of such exemplary filial behaviour. "One does not often see such behaviour in sons any more," they all agreed, a little enviously perhaps. Leaving the house, some of the women said, sniffing, "At least on such an occasion they might have served pure *ghee* sweets," and some of the men said, "Don't you think old Varma was giving himself airs? He needn't think we don't remember that he comes from the vegetable market himself, his father used to sell vegetables, and he has never seen the inside of a school." But there was more envy than rancour in their voices and it was, of course, inevitable—not every son in that shabby little colony at the edge of the city was destined to shine as Rakesh shone, and who knew that better than the parents themselves?

And that was only the beginning, the first step in a great, sweeping ascent to the radiant heights of fame and fortune. The thesis he wrote for his M.D. brought Rakesh still greater glory, if only in select medical circles. He won a scholarship. He went to the USA (that was what his father learnt to call it and taught the whole family to say—not America, which was what the ignorant neighbours called it, but, with a grand familiarity, "the USA") where he pursued his career in the most prestigious of all hospitals and won encomiums from his American colleagues which were relayed to his admiring and glowing family. What was more, he came *back*, he actually returned to that small yellow house in the once-new but increasingly shabby colony, right at the end of the road where the rubbish vans tipped out their stinking contents for pigs to nose in and

> **Indian Delicacies**
>
> **halwa** (soojie halwa) flaky confections of sesame and honey, p. 348
>
> **ghee** semifluid clarified butter, p. 349
>
> **samosas** small fried turnovers filled with seasoned vegetables or meat, p. 357

rag-pickers to build their shacks on, all steaming and smoking just outside the neat wire fences and well-tended gardens. To this Rakesh returned and the first thing he did on entering the house was to slip out of the embraces of his sisters and brothers and bow down and touch his father's feet.

As for his mother, she gloated chiefly over the strange fact that he had not married in America, had not brought home a foreign wife as all her neighbours had warned her he would, for wasn't that what all Indian boys went abroad for? Instead he agreed, almost without argument, to marry a girl she had picked out for him in her own village, the daughter of a childhood friend, a plump and uneducated girl, it was true, but so old-fashioned, so placid, so complaisant that she slipped into the household and settled in like a charm, seemingly too lazy and too good-natured to even try and make Rakesh leave home and set up independently, as any other girl might have done. What was more, she was pretty — really pretty, in a plump, pudding way that only gave way to fat — soft, spreading fat, like warm wax — after the birth of their first baby, a son, and then what did it matter?

For some years Rakesh worked in the city hospital, quickly rising to the top of the administrative organization, and was made a director before he left to set up his own clinic. He took his parents in his car — a new, sky-blue Ambassador with a rear window full of stickers and charms revolving on strings — to see the clinic when it was built, and the large sign-board over the door on which his name was printed in letters of red, with a row of degrees and qualifications to follow it like so many little black slaves of the regent. Thereafter his fame seemed to grow just a little dimmer — or maybe it was only that everyone in town had grown accustomed to it at last — but it was also the beginning of his fortune for he now became known not only as the best but also the richest doctor in town.

However, all this was not accomplished in the wink of an eye. Naturally not. It was the achievement of a lifetime and it took up Rakesh's whole life. At the time he set up his clinic his father had grown into an old man and retired from his post at the kerosene dealer's depot at which he had worked for forty years, and his mother died soon after, giving up the ghost with a sigh that sounded positively happy, for it was her own son who ministered to her in her last illness and who sat pressing her feet at the last moment — such a son as few women had borne.

For it had to be admitted — and the most unsuccessful and most rancorous of neighbours eventually did so — that Rakesh was not only a devoted son and a miraculously good-natured man who contrived somehow to obey his parents and humour his wife and show concern equally for his children and his patients, but there was actually a brain inside this beautifully polished and formed body of good manners and kind nature and, in between ministering to his family and playing host to many friends and coaxing them all into feeling happy and grateful and content, he had actually trained his hands as well and emerged an excellent doctor, a really fine surgeon. How one man — and a man born to illiterate parents, his father having worked for a kerosene dealer and his mother having spent her life in a kitchen — had achieved, combined and conducted such a medley of virtues, no one could fathom, but all acknowledged his talent and skill.

It WAS A STRANGE FACT, however, that talent and skill, if displayed for too long, cease to dazzle. It came to pass that the most admiring of all eyes eventually faded and no longer blinked at his glory. Having retired from work and having lost his wife, the old father very quickly went to pieces, as they say. He developed so many complaints and fell ill so frequently and with such mysterious diseases that even his son could no longer make out when it was something of significance and when it was merely a peevish whim. He sat huddled on his string bed most of the day and developed an exasperating habit of stretching out suddenly and lying absolutely still, allowing the whole family to fly around him in a flap, wailing and weeping, and then suddenly sitting up, stiff and gaunt, and spitting out a big gob of betel-juice as if to mock their behaviour.

He did this once too often: there had been a big party in the house, a birthday party for the youngest son, and the celebrations had to be suddenly hushed, covered up and hustled out of the way when the daughter-in-law discovered, or thought she discovered, that the old man, stretched out from end to end of his string bed, had lost his pulse; the party broke up, dissolved, even turned into a band of mourners, when the old man sat up and the distraught daughter-in-law received a gob of red spittle right on the hem of her new organza sari. After that no one much cared if he sat up cross-legged on his bed, hawking and spitting, or lay down flat and turned grey as a corpse. Except, of course, for that pearl amongst pearls, his son Rakesh.

It was Rakesh who brought him his morning tea, not in one of the china cups from which the rest of the family drank, but in the old man's favourite brass tumbler, and sat at the edge of his bed, comfortable and relaxed with the string of his pyjamas dangling out from under his fine lawn night-shirt, and discussed or, rather, read out the morning news to his father. It made no difference to him that his father made no response apart from spitting. It was Rakesh, too, who, on returning from the clinic in the evening, persuaded the old man to come out of his room, as bare and desolate as a cell, and take the evening air out in the garden, beautifully arranging the pillows and bolsters on the *divan* in the corner of the open verandah. On summer nights he saw to it that the servants carried out the old man's bed onto the lawn and himself helped his father down the steps and onto the bed, soothing him and settling him down for a night under the stars.

All this was very gratifying for the old man. What was not so gratifying was that he even undertook to supervise his father's diet. One day when the father was really sick, having ordered his daughter-in-law to make him a dish of *soojie halwa* and eaten it with a saucerful of cream, Rakesh marched into the room, not with his usual respectful step but with the confident and rather contemptuous stride of the famous doctor, and declared, "No more *halwa* for you, Papa. We must be sensible, at your age. If you must have something sweet, Veena will cook you a little *kheer*, that's light, just a little rice and milk. But nothing fried, nothing rich. We can't have this happening again."

The old man who had been lying stretched out on his bed, weak and feeble after a day's illness, gave a start at the very sound, the tone of these words. He opened his eyes — rather, they fell open with shock — and he stared at his son with disbelief that darkened quickly to reproach. A son who actually refused his father the food he craved? No, it was unheard of, it was incredible. But Rakesh had turned his back to him and was cleaning up the litter of bottles and packets on the medicine shelf and did not notice while Veena slipped silently out of the room with a little smirk that only the old man saw, and hated.

Halwa was only the first item to be crossed off the old man's diet. One delicacy after another went — everything fried to begin with, then everything sweet, and eventually everything, everything that the old man enjoyed. The meals that arrived for him on the shining stainless steel tray twice a day were frugal to say the least — dry bread, boiled lentils, boiled vegetables and, if there were a bit of chicken or fish, that was boiled too. If he called for another help-ing — in a cracked voice that quavered theatrically — Rakesh himself would come to the door, gaze at him sadly and shake his head, saying "Now, Papa, we must be careful, we can't risk another illness, you know," and although the daughter-in-law kept tactfully out of the way, the old man could just see her smirk sliding merrily through the air. He tried to bribe his grandchildren into buying him sweets (and how he missed his wife now, that generous, indulgent and illiterate cook), whispering, "Here's fifty *paise*" as he stuffed the coins into a tight, hot fist. "Run down to the shop at the crossroads and buy me thirty *paise* worth of *jalebis*, and you can spend the remaining twenty *paise* on yourself. Eh? Understand? Will you do that?" He got away with it once or twice but then was found out, the conspira-tor was scolded by his father and smacked by his mother and Rakesh came storming into the room, almost tearing his hair as he shouted through compressed lips, "Now Papa, are you trying to turn my little son into a liar? Quite apart from spoiling your own stomach, you are spoiling him as well—you are encouraging him to lie to his own parents. You should have heard the lies he told his mother when she saw him bringing back those *jalebis* wrapped up in filthy newspaper. I don't allow anyone in my house to buy sweets in the bazaar, Papa, surely you know that. There's cholera in the city, typhoid, gastroenteritis—I see these cases daily in the hospital, how can I allow my own family to run such risks?" The old man sighed and lay down in the corpse position. But that worried no one any longer.

THERE WAS ONLY ONE PLEASURE left the old man now (his son's early morning visits and readings from the newspaper could no longer be called that) and those were visits from elderly neighbours. These were not frequent as his contemporaries were mostly as decrepit and helpless as he and few could walk the length of the road to visit him any more. Old Bhatia, next door, however, who was still spry enough to refuse, adamantly, to bathe in the tiled bathroom indoors and to insist on carrying out his brass mug and towel, in all seasons and usually at impossible hours, into the yard and bathe noisily under the garden tap, would look over the hedge to see if Varma were out on his verandah and would call to him and talk while he wrapped his *dhoti* about him and dried the sparse hair on his head, shivering with enjoyable exaggeration. Of course these conversations, bawled across the hedge by two rather deaf old men conscious of having their entire households overhearing them, were not very satisfactory but Bhatia occasionally came out of his yard, walked down the bit of road and came in at Varma's gate to collapse onto the stone plinth built under the temple tree. If Rakesh were at home he would help his father down the steps into the garden and arrange him on his night bed under the tree and leave the two old men to chew betelleaves and discuss the ills of their individual bodies with combined passion.

"At least you have a doctor in the house to look after you," sighed Bhatia, having vividly described his martyrdom to piles.

"Look after me?" cried Varma, his voice cracking like an ancient clay jar. "He—he does not even give me enough to eat."

"What?" said Bhatia, the white hairs in his ears twitching. "Doesn't give you enough to eat? Your own son?"

"My own son. If I ask him for one more piece of bread, he says no, Papa. I weighed out the *ata* myself and I can't allow you to have more than two hundred grams of cereal a day. He *weighs* the food he gives me, Bhatia—he has scales to weigh it on. That is what it has come to."

"Never," murmured Bhatia in disbelief. "Is it possible, even in this evil age, for a son to refuse his father food?"

"Let me tell you," Varma whispered eagerly. "Today the family was having fried fish—I could smell it. I called to my daughter-in-law to bring me a piece. She came to the door and said No. . ."

"Said No?" It was Bhatia's voice that cracked. A *drongo* shot out of the tree and sped away. "*No?*"

"No, she said no, Rakesh has ordered her to give me nothing fried. No butter, he says, no oil—"

"No butter? No oil? How does he expect his father to *live?*"

Old Varma nodded with melancholy triumph. "That is how he treats me—after I have brought him up, given him an education, made him a great doctor. Great doctor! This is the way great doctors treat their fathers, Bhatia," for the son's sterling personality and character now underwent a curious sea change. Outwardly all might be the same but the interpretation had altered: his masterly efficiency was nothing but cold heartlessness, his authority was only tyranny in disguise.

There was cold comfort in complaining to neighbours and, on such a miserable diet, Varma found himself slipping, weakening and soon becoming a genuinely sick man. Powders and pills and mixtures were not only brought in when dealing with a crisis like an upset stomach but became a regular part of his diet—became his diet, complained Varma, supplanting the natural foods he craved. There were pills to regulate his bowel movements, pills to bring down his blood pressure, pills to deal with his arthritis and, eventually, pills to keep his heart beating. In between there were panicky rushes to the hospital, some humiliating experiences with the stomach pump and enema, which left him frightened and helpless. He cried easily, shrivelling up on his bed, but if he complained of a pain or even a vague, grey fear in the night, Rakesh would simply open another bottle of pills and force him to take one. "I have my duty to you, Papa," he said when his father begged to be let off.

"Let me be," Varma begged, turning his face away from the pills on the outstretched hand. "Let me die. It would be better. I do not want to live only to eat your medicines."

"Papa, be reasonable."

"I leave that to you," the father cried with sudden spirit. "Let me alone, let me die now, I cannot live like this."

"Lying all day on his pillows, fed every few hours by his daughter-in-law's own hands, visited by every member of his family daily — and then he says he does not want to live 'like this'," Rakesh was heard to say, laughing, to someone outside the door.

"Deprived of food," screamed the old man on the bed, "his wishes ignored, taunted by his daughter-in-law, laughed at by his grandchildren — *that* is how I live." But he was very old and weak and all anyone heard was an incoherent croak, some expressive grunts and cries of genuine pain. Only once, when old Bhatia had come to see him and they sat together under the temple tree, they heard him cry, "God is calling me — and they won't let me go."

The quantities of vitamins and tonics he was made to take were not altogether useless. They kept him alive and even gave him a kind of strength that made him hang on long after he ceased to wish to hang on. It was as though he were straining at a rope, trying to break it, and it would not break, it was still strong. He only hurt himself, trying.

In the evening, that summer, the servants would come into his cell, grip his bed, one at each end, and carry it out to the verandah, there setting it down with a thump that jarred every tooth in his head. In answer to his agonized complaints they said the Doctor Sahib had told them he must take the evening air and the evening air they would make him take—thump. Then Veena, that smiling, hypocritical pudding in a rustling sari, would appear and pile up the pillows under his head till he was propped up stiffly into a sitting position that made his head swim and his back ache.

"Let me lie down," he begged. "I can't sit up any more."

"Try, Papa, Rakesh said you can if you try," she said, and drifted away to the other end of the verandah where her transistor radio vibrated to the lovesick tunes from the cinema that she listened to all day.

So THERE HE SAT, like some stiff corpse, terrified, gazing out on the lawn where his grandsons played cricket, in danger of getting one of their hardspun balls in his eye, and at the gate that opened onto the dusty and rubbish-heaped lane but still bore, proudly, a newly touched-up sign-board that bore his son's name and qualifications, his own name having vanished from the gate long ago.

At last the sky-blue Ambassador arrived, the cricket game broke up in haste, the car drove in smartly and the doctor, the great doctor, all in white, stepped out. Someone ran up to take his bag from him, others to escort him up the steps. "Will you have tea?" his wife called, turning down the transistor set, "or a Coca-Cola? Shall I fry you some *samosas?*" But he did not reply or even glance in her direction. Ever a devoted son, he went first to the corner where his father sat gazing, stricken, at some undefined spot in the dusty yellow air that swam before him. He did not turn his head to look at his son. But he stopped gobbling air with his uncontrolled lips and set his jaw as hard as a sick and very old man could set it.

"Papa," his son said, tenderly, sitting down on the edge of the bed and reaching out to press his feet.

Old Varma tucked his feet under him, out of the way, and continued to gaze stubbornly into the yellow air of the summer evening.

"Papa, I'm home."

Varma's hand jerked suddenly, in a sharp, derisive movement, but he did not speak.

"How are you feeling, Papa?"

Then Varma turned and looked at his son. His face was so out of control and all in pieces, that the multitude of expressions that crossed it could not make up a whole and convey to the famous man exactly what his father thought of him, his skill, his art.

"I'm dying," he croaked. "Let me die, I tell you."

"Papa, you're joking," his son smiled at him, lovingly. "I've brought you a new tonic to make you feel better. You must take it, it will make you feel stronger again. Here it is. Promise me you will take it regularly, Papa."

Varma's mouth worked as hard as though he still had a gob of betel in it (his supply of betel had been cut off years ago). Then he spat out some words, as sharp and bitter as poison, into his son's face. "Keep your tonic—I want none—I won't take any more of—of your medicines. None. Never," and he swept the bottle out of his son's hand with a wave of his own, suddenly grand, suddenly effective.

His son jumped, for the bottle was smashed and thick brown syrup had splashed up, staining his white trousers. His wife let out a cry and came running. All around the old man was hubbub once again, noise, attention.

He gave one push to the pillows at his back and dislodged them so he could sink down on his back, quite flat again. He closed his eyes and pointed his chin at the ceiling, like some dire prophet, groaning, "God is calling me—now let me go."

ABOUT **ANITA DESAI**

Daughter of a Bengali father and a German mother, Anita Desai (də sī′) was born in Mussoorie, India, in 1937. Her 1978 novel *Fire on the Mountain* won international awards and worldwide recognition. Desai has written novels for both

adults and young adults. She focuses on Indians' struggle to mesh modern lives with cultural traditions. Other major themes are family relationships, social changes, and the position and emotions of women.

RESPONDING

1. *Personal Response* Whom do you like better, Rakesh or his father? Which would you prefer to have living in your home? Why?

2. *Literary Analysis* Examine Desai's *characterization* of Rakesh's father, noting traits that disappear or become more obvious as he ages. Does Desai succeed in making you like or dislike the father? Do you think his behavior is understandable? Explain.

3. *Multicultural Connection* How do you think the United States compares with other countries in caring for its elderly? On what do you base your opinion?

LANGUAGE WORKSHOP

Fact and Opinion Statements of *fact* can be proven true or false. Statements of *opinion* cannot be proven either way. Based on evidence in the story, label the following statements either *F* for fact or *O* for opinion.
1. Rakesh is the first son in his family to receive an education.
2. Rakesh's successful career is highly praised by everyone.
3. Only ignorant people refer to America as "the USA."
4. Rakesh restricts his father's diet.
5. Varma is being mistreated by his son.
6. Rakesh's father is a selfish, mean-spirited man.

WRITER'S PORTFOLIO

What qualities do you think a "devoted" son or daughter would have? Do you think Rakesh fits this description? Would you like to have a son like him? Write your thoughts in a brief evaluation.

The Jay

SINCE DAYBREAK, the jay had been singing noisily. When they'd slid open the rain shutters, it had flown up before their eyes from a lower branch of the pine, but it seemed to have come back. During breakfast, there was the sound of whirring wings.

"That bird's a nuisance." The younger brother started to get to his feet.

"It's all right. It's all right." The grandmother stopped him. "It's looking for its child. Apparently the chick fell out of the nest yesterday. It was flying around until late in the evening. Doesn't she know where it is? But what a good mother. This morning she came right back to look."

"Grandmother understands well," Yoshiko said.

Her grandmother's eyes were bad. Aside from a bout with nephritis about ten years ago, she had never been ill in her life. But, because of her cataracts, which she'd had since girlhood, she could only see dimly out of her left eye. One had to hand her the rice bowl and the chopsticks. Although she could grope her way around the familiar interior of the house, she could not go into the garden by herself.

Sometimes, standing or sitting in front of the sliding-glass door, she would spread out her hands, fanning out her fingers against the sunlight that came through the glass, and gaze out. She was concentrating all the life that was left to her into that many-angled gaze.

At such times, Yoshiko was frightened by her grand-mother. Though she wanted to call out to her from behind, she would furtively steal away.

This nearly blind grandmother, simply from having heard the jay's voice, spoke as if she had seen everything. Yoshiko was filled with wonder.

When, clearing away the breakfast things, Yoshiko went into the kitchen, the jay was singing from the roof of the neighbor's house.

In the back garden, there was a chestnut tree and two or three persimmon trees. When she looked at the trees, she saw that a light rain was falling. It was the sort of rain that you could not tell was falling unless you saw it against the dense foliage.

The jay, shifting its perch to the chestnut tree, then fly-ing low and skimming the ground, returned again to its branch, singing all the while.

The mother bird could not fly away. Was it because her chick was somewhere around there?

Worrying about it, Yoshiko went to her room. She had to get herself ready before the morning was over.

In the afternoon, her father and mother were coming with the mother of Yoshiko's fiancé.

Sitting at her mirror, Yoshiko glanced at the white stars under her fingernails. It was said that, when stars came out under your nails, it was a sign that you would receive something, but Yoshiko remembered having read in the newspaper that it meant a deficiency of vitamin C or some-thing. The job of putting on her makeup went fairly pleas-antly. Her eyebrows and lips all became unbearably winsome. Her kimono, too, went on easily.

She'd thought of waiting for her mother to come and help her with her clothes, but it was better to dress by her-self, she decided.

Her father lived away from them. This was her second mother.

When her father had divorced her first mother, Yoshiko had been four and her younger brother two. The reasons given for the divorce were that her mother went around dressed in flashy clothes and spent money wildly, but Yoshiko sensed dimly that it was more than that, that the real cause lay deeper down.

Her brother, as a child, had come across a photograph of their mother and shown it to their father. The father hadn't said anything but, with a face of terrible anger, had suddenly torn the photograph to bits.

When Yoshiko was thirteen, she had welcomed the new mother to the house. Later, Yoshiko had come to think that her father had endured his loneliness for ten years for her sake. The second mother was a good person. A peaceful home life continued.

When the younger brother, entering upper school, began living away from home in a dormitory, his attitude toward his stepmother changed noticeably.

"Elder sister, I've met our mother. She's married and lives in Azabu. She's really beautiful. She was happy to see me."

Hearing this suddenly, Yoshiko could not say a word. Her face paled, and she began to tremble.

From the next room, her stepmother came in and sat down.

"It's a good thing, a good thing. It's not bad to meet your own mother. It's only natural. I've known for some time that this day would come. I don't think anything particular of it."

But the strength seemed to have gone out of her stepmother's body. To Yoshiko, her emaciated stepmother seemed pathetically frail and small.

Her brother abruptly got up and left. Yoshiko felt like smacking him.

"Yoshiko, don't say anything to him. Speaking to him will only make that boy go bad." Her stepmother spoke in a low voice.

Tears came to Yoshiko's eyes.

Her father summoned her brother back home from the dormitory. Although Yoshiko had thought that would settle the matter, her father had then gone off to live elsewhere with her stepmother.

It had frightened Yoshiko. It was as if she had been crushed by the power of masculine indignation and resentment. Did their father dislike even them because of their tie to their first mother? It seemed to her that her brother, who'd gotten to his feet so abruptly, had inherited the frightening male intransigence of his father.

And yet it also seemed to Yoshiko that she could now understand her father's sadness and pain during those ten years between his divorce and remarriage.

And so, when her father, who had moved away from her, came back bringing a marriage proposal, Yoshiko had been surprised.

"I've caused you a great deal of trouble. I told the young man's mother that you're a girl with these circumstances and that, rather than treating you like a bride, she should try to bring back the happy days of your childhood."

When her father said this kind of thing to her, Yoshiko wept.

I F YOSHIKO MARRIED, there would be no woman's hand to take care of her brother and grandmother. It had been decided that the two households would become one. With that, Yoshiko had made up her mind. She had dreaded marriage on her father's account, but, when it came down to the actual talks, it was not that dreadful after all.

When her preparations were completed, Yoshiko went to her grandmother's room.

"Grandmother, can you see the red in this kimono?"

"I can faintly make out some red over there. Which is it, now?" Pulling Yoshiko to her, the grandmother put her eyes close to the kimono and the sash.

"I've already forgotten your face, Yoshiko. I wish I could see what you look like now."

Yoshiko stifled a desire to giggle. She rested her hand lightly on her grandmother's head.

Wanting to go out and meet her father and the others, Yoshiko was unable just to sit there, vaguely waiting. She went out into the garden. She held out her hand, palm upward, but the rain was so fine that it didn't wet the palm. Gathering up the skirts of her kimono, Yoshiko assiduously searched among the little trees and in the bear-grass bamboo thicket. And there, in the tall grass under the bush clover, was the baby bird.

Her heart beating fast, Yoshiko crept nearer. The baby jay, drawing its head into its neck feathers, did not stir. It was easy to take it up into her hand. It seemed to have lost its energy. Yoshiko looked around her, but the mother bird was nowhere in sight.

Running into the house, Yoshiko called out, "Grandmother! I've found the baby bird. I have it in my hand. It's very weak."

"Oh, is that so? Try giving it some water."

Her grandmother was calm.

When she ladled some water into a rice bowl and dipped the baby jay's beak in it, it drank, its little throat swelling out in an appealing way. Then—had it recovered?—it sang out, "Ki-ki-ki, Ki-ki-ki. . . ."

The mother bird, evidently hearing its cry, came flying. Perching on the telephone wire, it sang. The baby bird, struggling in Yoshiko's hand, sang out again, "Ki-ki-ki. . . ."

"Ah, how good that she came! Give it back to its mother, quick," her grandmother said.

Yoshiko went back out into the garden. The mother bird flew up from the telephone wire but kept her distance, looking fixedly toward Yoshiko from the top of a cherry tree.

As if to show her the baby jay in her palm, Yoshiko raised her hand, then quietly placed the chick on the ground.

As Yoshiko watched from behind the glass door, the mother bird, guided by the voice of its child singing plaintively and looking up at the sky, gradually came closer. When she'd come down to the low branch of a nearby pine, the chick flapped its wings, trying to fly up to her. Stumbling forward in its efforts, falling all over itself, it kept singing.

Still the mother bird cautiously held off from hopping down to the ground.

Soon, however, it flew in a straight line to the side of its child. The chick's joy was boundless. Turning and turning its head, its outspread wings trembling, it made up to its mother. Evidently the mother had brought it something to eat.

Yoshiko wished that her father and stepmother would come soon. She would like to show them this, she thought.

ABOUT **YASUNARI KAWABATA**

In 1968, internationally acclaimed writer Yasunari Kawabata (yä sü nä′re kä wä bä′tä; 1899–1972) became the first Japanese ever to receive the Nobel Prize in Literature. His writing is characterized by a melancholy tone, sensual images, and a poetic style that has been compared to haiku. As a young boy he wanted to become a painter, and this interest in art is reflected in his writing, which at times resembles graceful brush strokes. *Snow Country* and *Thousand Cranes*, the first of his works translated into English, are among his best known works in the United States.

RESPONDING

1. *Personal Response* Do you think Yoshiko's father should have returned to her with a marriage proposal, or let her choose her own husband? Why?

2. *Literary Analysis* What do you think is the *theme* of this story? How does the title relate to the theme?

3. *Multicultural Connection* Yoshiko and her brother first live with their biological parents, then with their father and stepmother, and then with their grandmother. How do the family's changing arrangements compare to typical family arrangements in your society?

LANGUAGE WORKSHOP

Visualizing Kawabata "paints" his scenes by carefully

arranging details and creating word pictures for effect. You can appreciate the images in this story by *visualizing*, or forming mental pictures of the descriptions. For example, Grandmother is described this way: ". . . she would spread out her hands, fanning out her fingers against the sunlight that came through the glass, and gaze out." Discuss how an actress or an artist would communicate this description. Then find two other descriptions from the story and visualize them by acting them out, explaining them, or drawing them.

WRITER'S PORTFOLIO

Imagine you are Yoshiko's fiancé. How do you feel about your upcoming marriage and the prospect of living with Yoshiko's brother and grandmother? Write a letter to Yoshiko expressing your feelings.

EDWARD ALBEE

The Sandbox

CHARACTERS

Young Man, *a good-looking, well-built boy of twenty-five years in a bathing suit*
Mommy, *a well-dressed, imposing woman of fifty-five*
Daddy, *a small man, grey, thin, sixty years old*
Grandma, *a tiny, wizened woman with bright eyes, eighty-six*
Musician, *no particular age, but young would be nice*

Time. Eternally
Place. The beach

The action takes place on a bare stage with only the following: near the footlights far stage right, are two simple chairs set side by side, facing the audience; near the footlights, far left, there is a chair facing stage right, with a music stand before it; farther back, and center, slightly elevated and raked, is a large sandbox with a toy pail and shovel; the background is the sky, which alters from brightest day to deepest night.

At the beginning, it is brightest day; the Young Man *is alone on stage, to the rear of the sandbox, and to one side. He is doing calisthenics; he does calisthenics until the very end of the play. These calisthenics, employing the arms only, should suggest the beating and fluttering of wings. The* Young Man *is, after all, the Angel of Death.*

Mommy *(Mommy enters from left, followed by* Daddy. *Motioning to* Daddy.*)* Well, here we are: this is the beach.

Daddy *(whining).* I'm cold.

Mommy *(dismissing him with a little laugh).* Don't be silly; it's as warm as toast. Look at that nice young man over there: he doesn't think it's cold. *(Waves to the* Young Man*)* Hello!

Young Man *(with an endearing smile).* Hi!

Mommy *(looking around).* This will do perfectly. Don't you think so, Daddy? There's sand there, and the water beyond. What do you think, Daddy?

Daddy *(vaguely).* Whatever you say, Mommy.

Mommy *(with the same little laugh).* Well, of course, whatever I say . . . Then it's settled, is it?

Daddy *(shrugs).* She's *your* mother, not mine.

Mommy. I know she's my mother. What do you take me for? *(A pause)* All right, now; let's get on with it. *(She shouts into the wings, left.)* You! Out there! You can come in, now. *(The* Musician *enters, seats himself in the chair, left, places music on the music stand, and is ready to play.* Mommy *nods approvingly.)* Very nice; very nice. Are you ready, Daddy? Let's go get Grandma.

Daddy. Whatever you say, Mommy.

Mommy *(leading the way out, left).* Of course, whatever I say. *(To the* Musician*)* You can begin now.

(The Musician *begins.* Mommy *and* Daddy *exit; the* Musician *nods to the* Young Man, *still playing.)*

Young Man *(with the same endearing smile).* Hi!

(After a moment, Mommy *and* Daddy *re-enter, carrying* Grandma. *She is borne in by their hands under her armpits; she is quite rigid; her legs are drawn up; the expression on her ancient face is one of puzzlement and fear; her feet do not touch the ground.)*

Daddy. Where do we put her?

Mommy *(with her little laugh).* Wherever I say, of course. Let me see . . . well . . . All right, over there in the sandbox. Well, what are you waiting for, Daddy: the sandbox?

(Together they carry Grandma *over to the sandbox, and more or less dump her in.)*

Grandma *(righting herself to a sitting position; her voice is a cross between a baby's laugh and cry).* Ahhhh! Ah-haaaa! Graaaa!

Daddy *(dusting himself).* What do we do now?

Mommy *(to the* Musician*).* You can stop now. *(The* Musician *stops.) (To* Daddy*)* What do you mean, what do we do now? We go over there and sit down, of course. *(Pointing to right) (To the* Young Man*)* Hello there!

Young Man *(again smiling).* Hi!

(Mommy *and* Daddy *move to the chairs, right, and sit in them. A pause.)*

Grandma *(same as before).* Ahhh! Ah-haaa! Graaa!

Daddy. Do you think . . . Do you think she's — comfortable?

Mommy *(impatiently).* How would I know?

Daddy *(after a pause).* What do we do now?

Mommy *(as if remembering).* We . . . wait. We sit here . . . and we wait. That's what we do.

Daddy *(another pause).* Shall we talk to each other?

Mommy *(with that little laugh, picking something off her dress).* Well, *you* can talk, if you want to — if you can think of anything to say — if you think of anything *new.*

Daddy *(thinks).* No, I suppose not.

Mommy *(with a triumphant laugh).* Of course not!

Grandma *(banging the toy shovel against the pail).* Haaa! Ah-haaa!

Mommy *(speaking out over the audience).* Be quiet, Grandma! Just be quiet and wait. (Grandma *throws a shovel full of sand at* Mommy.) She's throwing sand at me! *(Still speaking out over the audience)* You stop that, Grandma! You stop throwing sand at Mommy! *(To* Daddy*)* She's throwing sand at me.

(Daddy *looks around at* Grandma, *who screams at him.)*

Grandma. GRAAA!

Mommy. Don't look at her! Just — sit — here. Be very still — and wait. *(To the* Musician*)* You — uh — you go ahead and do whatever it is that you do.

(The *Musician* plays, Mommy *and* Daddy *are fixed, staring beyond the audience.* Grandma *looks at them, looks at the* Musician, *looks at the sandbox, throws down the shovel.)*

Grandma. Ah-haaa! Graaa! *(She looks for reaction, gets none, speaks to the audience.)* Honestly! What a way to treat an old woman! Drag her out of the house, stick her in a car, bring her out here from the city, dump her in a pile of sand, and leave her there to set. I'm eighty-six years old. I was married when I was seventeen to a farmer. He died when I was thirty. *(To the* Musician*)* Will you stop that, please? *(The* Musician *stops playing.)* I'm a feeble old woman. How do you expect anybody to hear me over that peep! peep! peep? *(To herself)* There's no respect around here. *(To the* Young Man*)* No respect around here!

Young Man *(the same smile).* Hi!

(Grandma *gives him a look of mild approval, then continues, to the audience.)*

Grandma. My husband died when I was thirty, and I had to raise that big cow over there *(Indicates* Mommy*)* all by my lonesome. You can imagine what that was like. Lordy! *(To the* Young Man*)* Where'd they get *you?*

Young Man. Oh, I've been around for a while.

Grandma. I'll bet you have. Heh, heh, heh. Will you look at you!

Young Man *(flexing his muscles).* Isn't that something? *(He continues his calisthenics.)*

Grandma. Boy, oh boy; I'll say! Pretty good.

Young Man *(sweetly).* I'll say.

Grandma. What's your name, honey. Where ya from?

Young Man. Southern California.

Grandma *(nodding).* Figgers; figgers . . . *(To the audience)* Bright, too! *(To the* Young Man*)* Your name?

Young Man. I don't know. I mean—I mean, they haven't given me one yet—the studio.

Grandma *(looking him over).* You don't say . . . You don't say! Well, uh, I've got to talk some more . . . Don't you go 'way!

Young Man. Oh, no.

Grandma *(turning her attention back to the audience).* Fine; fine. *(Then once more, back to the* Young Man*)* You're— you're an actor, huh?

Young Man *(beaming)*. Yes, I am.

Grandma *(to the audience again; shrugs)*. I'm smart, too. Anyhow, I had to raise *that* over there all by my lonesome. And what's next to her there, that's what she married. Rich? I tell you: money, money, money. They took me off the farm—which was real decent of them—and moved me into the big townhouse with them, fixed a nice place for me under the stove, gave me an army blanket, and my own dish. My very own dish! So what have I got to complain about? Nothing, of course. I'm not complaining. *(She looks up to the sky, and speaks to someone offstage.)* Shouldn't it be getting dark now, dear?

    (The lights dim; night comes on. The Musician *begins to play; it becomes deepest night. Stars are out. There are lights on all the players, including the* Young Man, *who is, of course, continuing his calisthenics.)*

Daddy *(stirring)*. It's nighttime.

Mommy. Shhh! Be still. Wait!

Daddy *(whining)*. It's so hot.

Mommy. Shhh! Be still. Wait!

Grandma *(to herself)*. That's better: night. *(To the* Musician*)* Honey, do you play all through this party? *(The* Musician *nods.)* Well, keep it nice and soft; that's a good boy. *(The* Musician *nods again, plays softly.)* That's nice.

    (There is an offstage rumble.)

Daddy *(starting)*. What was that?

Mommy *(beginning to weep)*. It was nothing.

Daddy. It was—it was thunder, or a wave breaking—or something.

Mommy *(whispering, through her tears)*. It was an offstage rumble—and you know what that means.

Daddy. I forget.

Mommy *(barely able to talk)*. It means the time has come for poor Grandma—and I can't bear it!

Daddy *(vacantly)*. I suppose you've got to be brave.

Grandma *(mocking)*. That's right, kid, be brave! You'll bear up. You'll get over it.

    (Another offstage rumble, louder)

Mommy. Ohhh! Poor Grandma—poor Grandma. . .

Grandma (*to* Mommy). I'm fine. I'm all right. It hasn't happened yet.

(*A violent offstage rumble. All the lights go out except the spot on the* Young Man. *The* Musician *stops playing.*)

Mommy. Ohhh! Ohhh!

(*Silence*)

Grandma. Don't put the lights up yet! I'm not ready. I'm not quite ready. (*Silence*) I'm about done.

Mommy. Music!

(*The lights come on again, to brightest day. The* Musician *begins to play.* Grandma *is discovered still in the sandbox, lying on her side, propped up on an elbow, half covered, busily shoveling sand over herself.*)

Grandma. I don't know how I'm supposed to do anything with this goddamn toy shovel. . .

Daddy. Mommy, it's daylight!

Mommy (*brightly*). So it is! Well! Our long night is over. We must put away our tears, take off our mourning—and face the future. It's our duty.

Grandma (*still shoveling; mimicking*). "Take off our mourning—face the future." Lordy!

(Mommy *and* Daddy *rise, stretch.* Mommy *waves to the* Young Man.)

Young Man (*with that smile*). Hi!

(Grandma *plays dead,* Mommy *and* Daddy *go over to look at her. She is a little more than half buried in the sand; the toy shovel is in her hands, which are crossed on her breast.*)

Mommy (*by the sandbox, shakes her head*). Lovely! It's—it's hard to be sad. She looks so happy. (*With pride and conviction*) It pays to do things well. (*She and* Daddy *nod, and walk to the left.* Mommy *speaks to the* Musician.) All right: you can stop now, if you want to. I mean, stay around and have yourself a swim, or something; it's all right with us. (*The* Musician *stops playing.* Mommy *sighs heavily.*) Well, Daddy, off we go.

Daddy. Brave Mommy!

Mommy. Brave Daddy! (*They exit, left.*)

Grandma (*after they leave; lying quite still*). "It pays to do things well." Boy, oh boy! (*She tries to sit up.*) Well, kids

(But she finds she can't.) I—I can't get up. I—I can't move. *(The* Young Man *stops his calisthenics, nods to the* Musician, *who begins playing again. The* Young Man *walks over to* Grandma, *kneels down by the sandbox.)* I—I can't move.

Young Man. Shhh! Be very still.

Grandma. I—I can't move.

Young Man. Uh, ma'am, I have a line here.

Grandma. Oh, I'm sorry, sweetie. You go right ahead.

Young Man *(prepares; delivers the line like a real amateur).* I am the Angel of Death. I am . . . uh . . . come for you.

Grandma. What? Wha . . . ? *(Then, with resignation)* Ohhh, Ohhh, I see. *(The* Young Man *bends over, kisses* Grandma *gently on the forehead, then stands up.* Grandma's *eyes close, her hands folded on her breast again, the shovel between her hands, a sweet smile on her face.)* Well . . . that was very nice, dear.

Young Man. Shhh! Be still!

(Kneeling)

Grandma. What I meant was: you did that very well, dear.

Young Man *(blushing).* Oh. . .

Grandma. No, I mean it. You've got that . . . you've got a quality. . .

Young Man *(with his endearing smile).* Oh, thank you; thank you very much, ma'am.

Grandma *(slowly; softly—as the* Young Man *puts his hands over* Grandma). You're welcome, dear.

(The Musician *continues to play, as the curtain comes slowly down.)*

ABOUT **EDWARD ALBEE**

Edward Albee, born in 1928, garnered praise in
the 1960s for *Who's Afraid of Virginia
Woolf?*, which has become his most
frequently performed play. Like several
other of his works, this play presents a
scathing portrait of people in relationships
that thrive on verbal abuse and betrayal.
In 1975, his play *Seascape* won a Pulitzer
Prize but closed after only two months. Albee wrote *The Sandbox*
as a memorial to his grandmother when he was thirty-one years
old.

RESPONDING

1. *Personal Response* What point do you think Albee is
making in this play?

2. *Literary Analysis* A *foil* is someone or something that
serves as a contrast to another. How is Daddy a foil for
Mommy? How is the young man a foil for Grandma?

3. *Multicultural Connection* Compare the treatment of
Grandma in this play to the treatment of Varma in "A
Devoted Son," which appears in this unit. What cultural
insights do these two works provide about the treatment
of the elderly?

LANGUAGE WORKSHOP

Symbolism A *symbol* is something used to represent
something else. A symbol usually refers to something
concrete that designates an abstract quality or concept —
for example, a dove for peace, or a skull for death or
poison. In this play, the sandbox functions as a rather
complex symbol. With its shovel and sand for burial, the
sandbox represents a place where old people are left to
die. In broader terms, it represents the way our society
displaces and disposes of the elderly.

Tell what you think the following might symbolize:
a flag, a sunrise, a serpent, a light bulb.

WRITER'S PORTFOLIO

In several paragraphs, explain how Edward Albee has used satire to make his point in *The Sandbox*. Consider such elements of the play as the young actor doing calisthenics, the musician's role, Grandma's dialogue, and Mommy and Daddy's characters. Consider also the message that Albee is trying to get across.

Translations

Poetic translations are rarely exact. Translators have
many decisions to make. Two such decisions involve
whether or not to observe the original patterns of rhyme
and rhythm, as well as how close to adhere to the literal
meaning of the original. Note that in Mistral's
"Meciendo," the second and fourth lines of each stanza
have at least approximate rhymes, and the last line of
each stanza is the same.

 As you read, think about why these translators
might have chosen the words and rhythms they did.

Meciendo ("Rocking")
Gabriela Mistral

El mar sus millares de olas
mece, divino.
Oyendo a los mares amantes,
mezo a mi niño.

El viento errabundo en la noche
mece a los trigos.
Oyendo a los vientos amantes,
mezo a mi niño.

Dios Padre sus miles de mundos
mece sin ruido.
Sintiendo su mano en la sombra,
mezo a mi niño.

Rocking

Doris Dana (translator)

The sea rocks her thousands of waves.
The sea is divine.
Hearing the loving sea
I rock my son.

The wind wandering by night
rocks the wheat.
Hearing the loving wind
I rock my son.

God, the Father, soundlessly rocks
His thousands of worlds.
Feeling His hand in the shadow
I rock my son.

Rocking

Muriel Kittel (translator)

With divine rhythm the ocean
rocks its myriad waves.
Listening to the waters' love,
I rock this child of mine.

The night-wandering wind
rocks the fields of wheat.
Listening to the winds' love,
I rock this child of mine.

Silently God the Father
rocks his numerous worlds.
Feeling his hand in the darkness,
I rock this child of mine.

ABOUT GABRIELA MISTRAL

Gabriela Mistral (gä´brē ā´lä mēs träl´; 1889–1957) is the pen-name of Lucila Godoy Alcayaga, the daughter of two Chilean schoolteachers. She received the Nobel Prize in Literature in 1945, the first Latin American to do so. For many years she worked as a teacher and school director. Mistral's poetry, which is lyrical and simple, has been compared to a mountain stream. Her first book was said to have been inspired by the suicide of a man she once planned to marry. Many of her works focus on love and families.

RESPONDING

1. *Personal Response* Which translation of the poem do you think would be more soothing to a small child? Read both translations out loud before you decide. What made you choose this translation?

2. *Literary Analysis* A *lyric* poem has a musical quality and reflects a particular emotion. Why do you think "Meciendo" and its translations are classified as lyrics?

3. *Multicultural Connection* Note how different translators can come up with different versions of a poem. What are some differences and some similarities between the Dana and the Kittel translations? Which do you prefer? Why? Do you think that a language such as Spanish is more musical than another language such as English? Explain.

LANGUAGE WORKSHOP

Connotation The *connotation* of a word is its meaning over and above its literal, dictionary meaning. For example, although a dictionary defines *turkey* as a large American bird, you might associate the word with the

rituals and festivities on Thanksgiving. What connotations do you attach to the following words from these translations?
1. love
2. shadow
3. sea

WRITER'S PORTFOLIO

Try your hand at translating "Meciendo." Use your own knowledge of Spanish, enlist a Spanish-speaking friend, or find a Spanish dictionary to decipher the words. Then make choices and use your own creativity to compose a translation of "Rocking" that is true to Mistral's original but uniquely your own.

Projects

ART EXHIBIT

Work in small groups to illustrate three of the selections in this unit. Think about a scene, character, or mood to portray from each work, as well as media that would best complement the writers' various styles. For example, the selection from *Kaffir Boy* might suggest broad strokes in charcoal, while Kawabata's delicate style might be suited to fine brush strokes and pastels. You may feel that some selections lend themselves to photographs, computer art, or other forms. When you're done, show your illustrations to the class and ask them to try to match each illustration with a work. Discuss how the art is suited to the work. Then exhibit your art on a bulletin board.

FIELD TRIP

Work with your teacher to arrange a visit to either a day-care center or a nursing home. When you have decided on a destination, discuss your upcoming visit with an administrator there and determine what you could do to assist the staff and to entertain the clients. As part of the program, read a short work or develop a dramatic presentation, perhaps one based on a selection in *World Writers Today*. You may want to use props or make adaptations, especially for a younger audience. Think of ways to follow up on your visit.

WRITING A FABLE

Write a short fable, using animals as the main characters, that illustrates relationships among at least three generations in the same neighborhood or culture. You might base your animal-characters on characters in this unit or those elsewhere in the book, focusing on their traits. Give the fable a simple plot and present a moral at the end.

Further Reading

Many authors have examined relationships among generations, especially within families. The following titles are samples from a rich literature that spans eras and age groups.

Alvarez, Julia. *How the García Girls Lost Their Accents.* Penguin Books, 1991. Comprised of fifteen interconnected stories, this novel recounts the adjustments the García family makes when they move to New York City from the Dominican Republic.

Anaya, Rudolfo. *Bless Me, Ultima.* TQS Publications, 1972. Antonio Márez comes of age as he learns to reconcile elements of the natural world with his Hispanic culture and religion — under the tutelage of his wise grandmother Ultima.

Bell-Scott, Patricia, et al., eds. *Double Stitch: Black Women Write about Mothers and Daughters.* Beacon Press, 1991. With a foreword by Maya Angelou and a preface by Johnnetta Cole, this collection of over fifty stories, poems, critical essays, and memoirs addresses questions of identity, history, and the tensions and affections between generations.

Halter, Marek. *The Book of Abraham.* Dell, 1987. One hundred generations of a Jewish family, from the destruction of Jerusalem to the Warsaw Ghetto, are followed in this long novel.

Mathabane, Mark. *Kaffir Boy.* Plume, 1987. Born in South Africa, Mark Mathabane received an education and escaped apartheid largely through the inspiraton and sacrifice of an unusual mother.

Nye, Naomi Shihab. *This Same Sky.* Four Winds Press, 1992. This international collection of poetry, "from places where it is tomorrow or even yesterday," joins generations from sixty-eight countries.

Many
Shapes of
Love

What is the shape of love? Does it look like a sunset, sound like a waterfall, or taste like fiery salsa? No matter how you see love, one thing is certain: Love in its many guises is everywhere. The selections in this unit explore simple and complex love, dark and bright love, and the love trapped inside the hearts of certain characters.

Two Words

SHE WENT BY THE NAME OF BELISA Crepusculario, not because she had been baptized with that name or given it by her mother, but because she herself had searched until she found the poetry of "beauty" and "twilight" and cloaked herself in it. She made her living selling words. She journeyed through the country from the high cold mountains to the burning coasts, stopping at fairs and in markets where she set up four poles covered by a canvas awning under which she took refuge from the sun and rain to minister to her customers. She did not have to peddle her merchandise because from having wandered far and near, everyone knew who she was. Some people waited for her from one year to the next, and when she appeared in the village with her bundle beneath her arm, they would form a line in front of her stall. Her prices were fair. For five centavos she delivered verses from memory; for seven she improved the quality of dreams; for nine she wrote love letters; for twelve she invented insults for irreconcilable enemies. She also sold stories, not fantasies but long, true stories she recited at one telling, never skipping a word. This is how she carried news from one town to another. People paid her to add a line or two: our son was born; so-and-so died; our children got married; the crops burned in the field. Wherever she went a small crowd gathered around to listen as she began to speak, and that was how they learned about each other's doings, about distant relatives, about what was going on in the civil war. To anyone who paid her fifty centavos in trade, she gave the gift of a secret word to drive away melancholy. It was not the same word for everyone, naturally, because that would have been collective deceit. Each person received his or her own word, with the assurance that no one else would use it that way in this universe or the Beyond.

Belisa Crepusculario had been born into a family so poor they did not even have names to give their children. She came into the world and grew up in an inhospitable land where some years the rains became avalanches of water that bore everything away before them and others when not a drop fell from the sky and the sun swelled to fill the horizon and the world became a desert. Until she was twelve, Belisa had no occupation or virtue other than having withstood hunger and the exhaustion of centuries. During one interminable drought, it fell to her to bury four younger brothers and sisters; when she realized that her turn was next, she decided to set out across the plains in the direction of the sea, in hopes that she might trick death along the way. The land was eroded, split with deep cracks, strewn with rocks, fossils of trees and thorny bushes, and skeletons of animals bleached by the sun. From time to time she ran into families who, like her, were heading south, following the mirage of water. Some had begun the march carrying their belongings on their back or in small carts, but they could barely move their own bones, and after a while they had to abandon their possessions. They dragged themselves along painfully, their skin turned to lizard hide and their eyes burned by the reverberating glare. Belisa greeted them with a wave as she passed, but she did not stop, because she had no strength to waste in acts of compassion. Many people fell by the wayside, but she was so stubborn that she survived to cross through that hell and at long last reach the first trickles of water, fine, almost invisible threads that fed spindly vegetation and farther down widened into small streams and marshes.

Belisa Crepusculario saved her life and in the process accidentally discovered writing. In a village near the coast, the wind blew a page of newspaper at her feet. She picked up the brittle yellow paper and stood a long while looking at it, unable to determine its purpose, until curiosity overcame her shyness. She walked over to a man who was washing his horse in the muddy pool where she had quenched her thirst.

"What is this?" she asked.

"The sports page of the newspaper," the man replied, concealing his surprise at her ignorance.

The answer astounded the girl, but she did not want to seem rude, so she merely inquired about the significance of the fly tracks scattered across the page.

"Those are words, child. Here it says that Fulgencio Barba knocked out El Negro Tiznao in the third round."

That was the day Belisa Crepusculario found out that words make their way in the world without a master, and that anyone with a little cleverness can appropriate them and do business with them. She made a quick assessment of her situation and concluded that aside from becoming a prostitute or working as a servant in the kitchens of the rich there were few occupations she was qualified for. It seemed to her that selling words would be an honorable alternative. From that moment on, she worked at that profession, and was never tempted by any other. At the beginning, she offered her merchandise unaware that words could be written outside of newspapers. When she learned otherwise, she calculated the infinite possibilities of her trade and with her savings paid a priest twenty pesos to teach her to read and write; with her three remaining coins she bought a dictionary. She poured over it from *A* to *Z* and then threw it into the sea, because it was not her intention to defraud her customers with packaged words.

ONE AUGUST MORNING several years later, Belisa Crepusculario was sitting in her tent in the middle of a plaza, surrounded by the uproar of market day, selling legal arguments to an old man who had been trying for sixteen years to get his pension. Suddenly she heard yelling and thudding hoofbeats. She looked up from her writing and saw, first, a cloud of dust, and then a band of horsemen come galloping into the plaza. They were the Colonel's men, sent under orders of El Mulato, a giant known throughout the land for the speed of his knife and his loyalty to his chief. Both the Colonel and El Mulato had spent their lives fighting in the civil war, and their names were ineradicably linked to devastation and calamity. The rebels swept into town like a stampeding herd, wrapped in noise, bathed in sweat, and leaving a hurricane of fear in their trail. Chickens took wing, dogs ran for their lives, women and children scurried out of sight, until the only living soul left in the market was Belisa Crepusculario. She had never seen El Mulato and was surprised to see him walking toward her.

"I'm looking for you," he shouted, pointing his coiled whip at her; even before the words were out, two men rushed her—knocking over her canopy and shattering her inkwell—bound her hand and foot, and threw her like a sea bag across the rump of El Mulato's mount. Then they thundered off toward the hills.

Hours later, just as Belisa Crepusculario was near death, her heart ground to sand by the pounding of the horse, they stopped, and four strong hands set her down. She tried to stand on her feet and hold her head high, but her strength failed her and she slumped to the ground, sinking into a confused dream. She awakened several hours later to the murmur of night in the camp, but before she had time to sort out the sounds, she opened her eyes and found herself staring into the impatient glare of El Mulato, kneeling beside her.

"Well, woman, at last you've come to," he said. To speed her to her senses, he tipped his canteen and offered her a sip of liquor laced with gunpowder.

She demanded to know the reason for such rough treatment, and El Mulato explained that the Colonel needed her sei .ices. He allowed her to splash water on her face, and then led her to the far end of the camp where the most feared man in all the land was lazing in a hammock strung between two trees. She could not see his face, because he lay in the deceptive shadow of the leaves and the indelible shadow of all his years as a bandit, but she imagined from the way his gigantic aide addressed him with such humility that he must have a very menacing expression. She was surprised by the Colonel's voice, as soft and well-modulated as a professor's.

"Are you the woman who sells words?" he asked.

"At your service," she stammered, peering into the dark and trying to see him better.

The Colonel stood up, and turned straight toward her. She saw dark skin and the eyes of a ferocious puma, and she knew immediately that she was standing before the loneliest man in the world.

"I want to be President," he announced.

The Colonel was weary of riding across that godforsaken land, waging useless wars and suffering defeats that no subterfuge could transform into victories. For years he had been sleeping in the open air, bitten by mosquitoes, eating iguanas and snake soup, but those minor inconveniences were not why he wanted to change his destiny. What truly troubled him was the terror he saw in people's eyes. He longed to ride into a town beneath a triumphal arch with bright flags and flowers everywhere; he wanted to be cheered, and be given newly laid eggs and freshly baked bread. Men fled at the sight of him, children trembled, and women miscarried from fright; he had had enough, and so he had decided to become President. El Mulato had suggested that they ride to the capital, gallop up to the Palace, and take over the government, the way they had taken so many other things without anyone's permission. The Colonel, however, did not want to be just another tyrant; there had been enough of those before him and, besides, if he did that, he would never win people's hearts. It was his aspiration to win the popular vote in the December elections.

"To do that, I have to talk like a candidate. Can you sell me the words for a speech?" the Colonel asked Belisa Crepusculario.

She had accepted many assignments, but none like this. She did not dare refuse, fearing that El Mulato would shoot her between the eyes, or worse still, that the Colonel would burst into tears. There was more to it than that, however; she felt the urge to help him because she felt a throbbing warmth beneath her skin, a powerful desire to touch that man, to fondle him, to clasp him in her arms.

ALL NIGHT AND A GOOD PART of the following day, Belisa Crepusculario searched her repertory for words adequate for a presidential speech, closely watched by El Mulato, who could not take his eyes from her firm wanderer's legs and virginal breasts. She discarded harsh, cold words, words that were too flowery, words worn from abuse, words that offered improbable promises, untruthful and confusing words, until all she had left were words sure to touch the minds of men and women's intuition. Calling upon the knowledge she had purchased from the priest for twenty pesos, she wrote the speech on a sheet of paper and then signaled El Mulato to untie the rope that bound her ankles to a tree. He led her once more to the Colonel, and again she felt the throbbing anxiety that had seized her when she first saw him. She handed him the paper and waited while he looked at it, holding it gingerly between thumbs and fingertips.

"What the hell does this say?" he asked finally.

"Don't you know how to read?"

"War's what I know," he replied.

She read the speech aloud. She read it three times, so her client could engrave it on his memory. When she finished, she saw the emotion in the faces of the soldiers who had gathered round to listen, and saw that the Colonel's eyes glittered with enthusiasm, convinced that with those words the presidential chair would be his.

"If after they've heard it three times, the boys are still standing there with their mouths hanging open, it must mean the thing's damn good, Colonel," was El Mulato's approval.

"All right, woman. How much do I owe you?" the leader asked.

"One peso, Colonel."

"That's not much," he said, opening the pouch he wore at his belt, heavy with proceeds from the last foray.

"The peso entitles you to a bonus. I'm going to give you two secret words," said Belisa Crepusculario.

"What for?"

She explained that for every fifty centavos a client paid, she gave him the gift of a word for his exclusive use. The Colonel shrugged. He had no interest at all in her offer, but he did not want to be impolite to someone who had served him so well. She walked slowly to the leather stool where he was sitting, and bent down to give him her gift. The man smelled the scent of a mountain cat issuing from the woman, a fiery heat radiating from her hips, he heard the terrible whisper of her hair, and a breath of sweetmint murmured into his ear the two secret words that were his alone.

"They are yours, Colonel," she said as she stepped back. "You may use them as much as you please."

El Mulato accompanied Belisa to the roadside, his eyes as entreating as a stray dog's, but when he reached out to touch her, he was stopped by an avalanche of words he had never heard before; believing them to be an irrevocable curse, the flame of his desire was extinguished.

DURING THE MONTHS of September, October, and November the Colonel delivered his speech so many times that had it not been crafted from glowing and durable words it would have turned to ash as he spoke. He traveled up and down and across the country, riding into cities with a triumphal air, stopping in even the most forgotten villages where only the dump heap betrayed a human presence, to convince his fellow citizens to vote for him. While he spoke from a platform erected in the middle of the plaza, El Mulato and his men handed out sweets and painted his name on all the walls in gold frost. No one paid the least attention to those advertising ploys; they were dazzled by the clarity of the Colonel's proposals and the poetic lucidity of his arguments, infected by his powerful wish to right the wrongs of history, happy for the first time in their lives. When the Candidate had finished his speech, his soldiers would fire their pistols into the air and set off firecrackers, and when finally they rode off, they left behind a wake of hope that lingered for days on the air, like the splendid memory of a comet's tail. Soon the Colonel was the favorite. No one had ever witnessed such a phenomenon: a man who surfaced from the civil war, covered with scars and speaking like a professor, a man whose fame spread to every corner of the land and captured the nation's heart. The press focused their attention on him. Newspapermen came from far away to interview him and repeat his phrases, and the number of his followers and enemies continued to grow.

"We're doing great, Colonel," said El Mulato, after twelve successful weeks of campaigning.

But the Candidate did not hear. He was repeating his secret words, as he did more and more obsessively. He said them when he was mellow with nostalgia; he murmured them in his sleep; he carried them with him on horseback; he thought them before delivering his famous speech; and he caught himself savoring them in his leisure time. And every time he thought of those two words, he thought of Belisa Crepusculario, and his senses were inflamed with the memory of her feral scent, her fiery heat, the whisper of her hair, and her sweetmint breath in his ear, until he began to go around like a sleepwalker, and his men realized that he might die before he ever sat in the presidential chair.

"What's got hold of you, Colonel," El Mulato asked so often that finally one day his chief broke down and told him the source of his befuddlement: those two words that were buried like two daggers in his gut.

"Tell me what they are and maybe they'll lose their magic," his faithful aide suggested.

"I can't tell them, they're for me alone," the Colonel replied.

Saddened by watching his chief decline like a man with a death sentence on his head, El Mulato slung his rifle over his shoulder and set out to find Belisa Crepusculario. He followed her trail through all that vast country, until he found her in a village in the far south, sitting under her tent reciting her rosary of news. He planted himself, spraddle-legged, before her, weapon in hand.

"You! You're coming with me," he ordered.

She had been waiting. She picked up her inkwell, folded the canvas of her small stall, arranged her shawl around her shoulders, and without a word took her place behind El Mulato's saddle. They did not exchange so much as a word in all the trip; El Mulato's desire for her had turned into rage, and only his fear of her tongue prevented his cutting her to shreds with his whip. Nor was he inclined to tell her that the Colonel was in a fog, and that a spell whispered into his ear had done what years of battle had not been able to do. Three days later they arrived at the encampment, and immediately, in view of all the troops, El Mulato led his prisoner before the Candidate.

"I brought this witch here so you can give her back her words, Colonel," El Mulato said, pointing the barrel of his rifle at the woman's head. "And then she can give you back your manhood."

The Colonel and Belisa Crepusculario stared at each other, measuring one another from a distance. The men knew then that their leader would never undo the witch-craft of those accursed words, because the whole world could see the voracious-puma eyes soften as the woman walked to him and took his hand in hers.

ABOUT ISABEL ALLENDE

Isabel Allende (ä yen´dä), who was born in Lima, Peru, in 1942, grew up in Chile and now lives in the United States. Her father was a Chilean diplomat, and her uncle Salvador Allende was president of Chile until his assassination in 1973.

Allende's first novel, *The House of the Spirits,* which brought her worldwide fame, has been made into a movie. Her works often explore the subjects of political violence and women's role in society. Marked by magical realism, Allende's style has been compared to that of Gabriel García Márquez.

RESPONDING

1. *Personal Response* What do you think the two words were that Belisa gave the Colonel? Why?

2. *Literary Analysis* Some writers use *hyperbole,* or exaggeration, to make points about a character. For example, the Colonel is described as "the loneliest man in the world." Find one other example of hyperbole in this story and describe what it tells you about the related character.

3. *Multicultural Connection* Do you think that a love story such as this could take place in the United States? Why or why not?

LANGUAGE WORKSHOP

Imagery Allende uses unusual *imagery,* or word pictures, to convey strong emotions. Examine the following passage and explain the senses to which the various images appeal. "And every time he thought of those two words, he thought of Belisa Crepusculario, and his senses were inflamed with the memory of her feral scent, her fiery heat, the whisper of her hair, and her sweetmint breath in his ear, until he began to go around like a sleepwalker."

WRITER'S PORTFOLIO

Spend some time thinking about which two words you consider the most powerful in the world. Then write an explanation of why you have chosen these particular words.

On Meeting My 100 Percent Woman One Fine April Morning

ONE FINE APRIL MORNING, I passed my 100 percent woman on a Harajuku back street.

She wasn't an especially pretty woman. It wasn't that she was wearing fine clothes, either. In the back, her hair still showed how she'd slept on it; and her age must already have been close to thirty. Nonetheless, even from fifty meters away, I knew it: she is the 100 percent woman for me. From the moment her figure caught my eye, my chest shook wildly; my mouth was parched dry as a desert.

Maybe you have a type of woman that you like. For example, you think, women with slender ankles are good; or, all in all, it's women with big eyes; or it's definitely women with pretty fingers; or, I don't understand it, but I'm attracted to women who take a lot of time to eat a meal—something like that. Of course, I have that kind of preference. I've even been distracted, eating at a restaurant, by the shape of a woman's nose at the next table.

But no one can "typify" the 100 percent woman at all.

I absolutely cannot even remember what her nose looked like—not even whether she had a nose or not, only that she wasn't especially beautiful. How bizarre!

I tell someone, "Yesterday I passed my 100 percent woman on the street."

"Hmm," he replies, "was she a beauty?"

"No, it wasn't that."

"Oh, she was the type you like?"

"That I don't remember. What shape her eyes were or whether her breasts were big or small. I don't remember anything at all about that."

"That's strange, isn't it?"

"Really strange."

"So," he said, sounding bored, "did you do anything, speak to her, follow her, huh?"

"I didn't do anything," I said. "Only just passed her."

She was walking from east to west and I was heading west to east. It was a very happy April morning.

I think I would have liked to have a talk with her, even thirty minutes would have been fine. I would have liked to hear about her life; I would have liked to open up about mine. And, more than anything, I think I'd like to clear up the facts about the kind of fate that led us to pass on a Harajuku back street one fine morning in April 1981. No doubt there's some kind of tender secret in there, just like the ones in the souls of old-time machines.

After that talk we would have lunch somewhere, maybe see a movie, go to a hotel lounge and drink cocktails or something. If everything went well, after that I might even be able to sleep with her.

Opportunity knocks on the door of my heart.

The distance separating her and myself is already closing down to only fifteen meters.

Now, how in the world should I speak up to her?

"Good morning. Would you please speak with me for just thirty minutes?"

That's absurd. It sounds like an insurance come-on.

"Excuse me, is there a twenty-four-hour cleaning shop around here?"

This is absurd, too. First of all, I'm not carrying a laundry basket, am I? Maybe it would be best to speak out sincerely. "Good morning. You really are my 100 percent woman."

She probably wouldn't believe that confession. Besides, even if she believed it, she might think she didn't want to talk to me at all. Even if I'm your 100 percent woman, you really are not my 100 percent man, she might say. If it should come to that, no doubt I'd just end up completely flustered. I'm already thirty-two, and when you get down to it, that's what getting older is like.

In front of a flower shop, I pass her. A slight, warm puff of air touches my skin. Water is running on the asphalt sidewalk; the smell of roses is in the air. I can't speak out to her. She is wearing a white sweater, she's carrying an envelope that isn't stamped yet in her right hand. She's written someone a letter. Since she has extremely sleepy eyes, maybe she spent all night writing it. And all of her secrets might be carried inside that envelope.

After walking on a few more steps, when I turned around, her figure had already disappeared into the crowd.

*　　*　　*

OF COURSE, NOW I KNOW exactly how I should have spoken up to her then. But, no matter what, it's such a long confession I know I wouldn't have been able to say it well. I'm always thinking of things like this that aren't realistic.

Anyway, that confession starts, "once upon a time," and ends, "isn't that a sad story?"

Once upon a time, in a certain place, there was a young boy and a young girl. The young boy was eighteen; the young girl was sixteen. He was not an especially handsome boy; she was not an especially pretty girl, either. They were an average young man and young woman, just like lonely people anywhere. But they believed firmly, without doubt, that somewhere in this world their perfect 100 percent partners really existed.

One day it happened that the two suddenly met at a street corner. "What a surprise! I've been looking for you for a long time. You might not believe this, but you are the 100 percent woman for me," the man says to the young woman.

The young woman says to the young man, "You yourself are my 100 percent man, too. In every way you are what I imagined. This really seems like a dream!"

The couple sat on a park bench, and they continued talking without ever getting tired. The two were no longer lonely. How wonderful to claim a 100 percent partner and be claimed as one too!

However, a tiny, really tiny, doubt drifted across their hearts; could it really be all right for a dream to come completely true this simply?

When the conversation happened to pause, the young man spoke like this.

"Well, shall we give this another try? If we're really, truly the 100 percent lovers for each other, surely, no doubt, we can meet again sometime, somewhere. And this next time we meet, if we're really each other's 100 percent, then let's get married right away, OK?"

"OK," the young woman said.

And the two parted.

However, if the truth be told, it wasn't really necessary to give it another try. That's because they were really and truly the 100 percent lovers for each other. Now, it came to pass that the two were tossed about in the usual waves of fate.

One winter, the two caught a bad flu that was going around that year. After wandering on the borderline of life and death for several weeks, they ended up having quite lost their old memories. When they came to, the insides of their heads, like D. H. Lawrence's childhood savings bank, were empty.

But since the two were a wise and patient young man and young woman, piling effort upon effort, they put new knowledge and feeling into themselves again, and they were able to return to society splendidly. In fact, they even became able to do things like transfer on the subway or send a special-delivery letter at the post office. And they were even able to regain 75 percent or 85 percent of their ability to fall in love.

In that way, the young man became thirty-two, the young woman became thirty. Time went by surprisingly fast.

And one fine April morning, in order to have breakfast coffee, the young man was headed from west to east on a Harajuku back street, and in order to buy a special-delivery stamp the young woman was headed from east to west on the same street. In the middle of the block the couple passed. A weak light from their lost memories shone out for one instant in their hearts.

She is the 100 percent woman for me.

He is the 100 percent man for me.

However, the light of their memories was too weak, and their words didn't rise as they had fourteen years ago. The couple passed without words, and they disappeared like that completely into the crowd.

Isn't that a sad story?

That's what I should have tried to tell her.

Coils the Robot

Floria Herrero Pinto

Coils the robot
named by some scientists
is the smallest one in school.
They sent him to learn
to cope with numbers,
letters and things
but Coils the robot
only understands poetry.
His square tiny tummy
glows in the sun
and rings like a bell
when he dances and sings.
He enlightens his eyes,
his hands are of wire,
his little antenna twinkles magically.
Coils needs love,
oily light, silvery
with the sparkles of sunlight;
deep down inside
his little heart glitters and throbs.

ABOUT **HARUKI MURAKAMI**

Manager of a Tokyo jazz bar for seven years, Haruki Murakami (hä rü/kē mėr ä kä/mē) began receiving literary awards in his thirties. He was born in 1949 in Kobe, Japan, a city tucked between mountains and the sea. His novels, which include *Dance, Dance, Dance* and *A Wild Sheep Chase,* are tangled adventures into bizarre worlds.

ABOUT **FLORIA HERRERO PINTO**

Floria Herrero Pinto (flôr/ē ə hə rä/rō pēn/tō) was born in Costa Rica in 1943. She has published several books of children's literature in Costa Rica and Venezuela. "Coils the Robot" appears in an international collection of poems titled *This Same Sky.*

RESPONDING

1. *Personal Response* What conversation starter would you suggest that the narrator use to become acquainted with his 100 percent woman when he encounters her on the street?

2. *Literary Analysis* How does the *flashback* about the teenage couple serve to explain the narrator's attraction to the 100 percent woman he encounters fourteen years later?

3. *Multicultural Connection* Coils the Robot and the narrator of "On Meeting My 100 Percent Woman . . ." are both searching for love. Compare this poem and story to a work of literature on the same theme by an American writer. What are the similarities and differences between these works?

LANGUAGE WORKSHOP

Sequence Writers sometimes rearrange the *sequence* of events in a plot for dramatic effect. Place the following

events from this selection in chronological order.
1. The teenage couple claim each other as 100 percent partners.
2. The narrator cannot muster up the courage to speak to the woman.
3. The narrator starts on a walk one April morning.
4. The teenage couple get the flu.
5. The narrator meets a woman who appears to be about thirty.
6. The teenage couple regain most of their memory.

WRITER'S PORTFOLIO

Write a want ad for your 100 percent partner, listing the qualifications you're looking for. Write a second ad, listing your own qualifications that you think would appeal to a prospective 100 percent partner.

From Like Water for Chocolate

Ingredients:

1   can of sardines
¹/₂ chorizo sausage
1   onion
    oregano
1   can of chiles serranos
10 hard rolls

About Food

chorizo sausage a highly seasoned pork sausage usually containing cayenne pepper, p. 402

Preparation:

Take care to chop the onion fine. To keep from crying when you chop it (which is so annoying!), I suggest you place a little bit on your head. The trouble with crying over an onion is that once the chopping gets you started and the tears begin to well up, the next thing you know you just can't stop. I don't know whether that's ever happened to you, but I have to confess it's happened to me, many times. Mama used to say it was because I was especially sensitive to onions, like my great-aunt, Tita.

Tita was so sensitive to onions, any time they were being chopped, they say she would just cry and cry; when she was still in my great-grandmother's belly her sobs were so loud that even Nacha, the cook, who was half-deaf, could hear them easily. Once her wailing got so violent that it brought on an early labor. And before my great-grandmother could let out a word or even a whimper, Tita made her entrance into this world, prematurely, right there on the kitchen table amid the smells of simmering noodle soup, thyme, bay leaves, and cilantro, steamed milk, garlic, and, of course, onion. Tita had no need for the usual slap on the bottom, because she was already crying as she emerged; maybe that was because she knew then that it would be her lot in life to be denied marriage. The way Nacha told it, Tita was literally washed into this world on a great tide of tears that spilled over the edge of the table and flooded across the kitchen floor.

That afternoon, when the uproar had subsided and the water had been dried up by the sun, Nacha swept up the residue the tears had left on the red stone floor. There was enough salt to fill a ten-pound sack — it was used for cooking and lasted a long time. Thanks to her unusual birth, Tita felt a deep love for the kitchen, where she spent most of her life from the day she was born.

When she was only two days old, Tita's father, my great-grandfather, died of a heart attack and Mama Elena's milk dried up from the shock. Since there was no such thing as powdered milk in those days, and they couldn't find a wet nurse anywhere, they were in a panic to satisfy the infant's hunger. Nacha, who knew everything about cooking — and much more that doesn't enter the picture until later — offered to take charge of feeding Tita. She felt she had the best chance of "educating the innocent child's stomach," even though she had never married or had children. Though she didn't know how to read or write, when it came to cooking she knew everything there was to know. Mama Elena accepted her offer gratefully; she had enough to do between her mourning and the enormous responsibility of running the ranch — and it was the ranch that would provide her children the food and education they deserved — without having to worry about feeding a newborn baby on top of everything else.

From that day on, Tita's domain was the kitchen, where she grew vigorous and healthy on a diet of teas and thin corn gruels. This explains the sixth sense Tita developed about everything concerning food. Her eating habits, for example, were attuned to the kitchen routine: in the morning, when she could smell that the beans were ready; at midday, when she sensed the water was ready for plucking the chickens; and in the afternoon, when the dinner bread was baking, Tita knew it was time for her to be fed.

Sometimes she would cry for no reason at all, like when Nacha chopped onions, but since they both knew the cause of those tears, they didn't pay them much mind. They made them a source of entertainment, so that during her childhood Tita didn't distinguish between tears of laughter and tears of sorrow. For her laughing was a form of crying.

Likewise for Tita the joy of living was wrapped up in the delights of food. It wasn't easy for a person whose knowledge of life was based on the kitchen to comprehend the outside world. That world was an endless expanse that began at the door between the kitchen and the rest of the house, whereas everything on the kitchen side of that door, on through the door leading to the patio and the kitchen and herb gardens was completely hers—it was Tita's realm.

HER SISTERS were just the opposite: to them, Tita's world seemed full of unknown dangers, and they were terrified of it. They felt that playing in the kitchen was foolish and dangerous. But once, Tita managed to convince them to join her in watching the dazzling display made by dancing water drops dribbled on a red hot griddle.

While Tita was singing and waving her wet hands in time, showering drops of water down on the griddle so they would "dance," Rosaura was cowering in the corner, stunned by the display. Gertrudis, on the other hand, found this game enticing, and she threw herself into it with the enthusiasm she always showed where rhythm, movement, or music were involved. Then Rosaura had tried to join them—but since she barely moistened her hands and then shook them gingerly, her efforts didn't have the desired effect. So Tita tried to move her hands closer to the griddle.

Rosaura resisted, and they struggled for control until Tita became annoyed and let go, so that momentum carried Rosaura's hands onto it. Tita got a terrible spanking for that, and she was forbidden to play with her sisters in her own world. Nacha became her playmate then. Together they made up all sorts of games and activities having to do with cooking. Like the day they saw a man in the village plaza twisting long thin balloons into animal shapes, and they decided to do it with sausages. They didn't just make real animals, they also made up some of their own, creatures with the neck of a swan, the legs of a dog, the tail of a horse, and on and on.

Then there was trouble, however, when the animals had to be taken apart to fry the sausage. Tita refused to do it. The only time she was willing to take them apart was when the sausage was intended for the Christmas rolls she loved so much. Then she not only allowed her animals to be dismantled, she watched them fry with glee.

The sausage for the rolls must be fried over very low heat, so that it cooks thoroughly without getting too brown. When done, remove from the heat and add the sardines, which have been deboned ahead of time. Any black spots on the skin should also have been scraped off with a knife. Combine the onions, chopped chiles, and the ground oregano with the sardines. Let the mixture stand before filling the rolls.

Tita enjoyed this step enormously; while the filling was resting, it was very pleasant to savor its aroma, for smells have the power to evoke the past, bringing back sounds and even other smells that have no match in the present. Tita liked to take a deep breath and let the characteristic smoke and smell transport her through the recesses of her memory.

It was useless to try to recall the first time she had smelled one of those rolls—she couldn't, possibly because it had been before she was born. It might have been the unusual combination of sardines and sausages that had called to her and made her decide to trade the peace of ethereal existence in Mama Elena's belly for life as her daughter, in order to enter the De la Garza family and share their delicious meals and wonderful sausage.

On Mama Elena's ranch, sausage making was a real ritual. The day before, they started peeling garlic, cleaning chiles, and grinding spices. All the women in the family had to participate: Mama Elena; her daughters, Gertrudis, Rosaura, and Tita; Nacha, the cook; and Chencha, the maid. They gathered around the dining-room table in the afternoon, and between the talking and the joking the time flew by until it started to get dark. Then Mama Elena would say:

"That's it for today."

For a good listener, it is said, a single word will suffice, so when they heard that, they all sprang into action. First they had to clear the table; then they had to assign tasks: one collected the chickens, another drew water for breakfast from the well, a third was in charge of wood for the stove. There would be no ironing, no embroidery, no sewing that day. When it was all finished, they went to their bedrooms to read, say their prayers, and go to sleep. One afternoon, before Mama Elena told them they could leave the table, Tita, who was then fifteen, announced in a trembling voice that Pedro Muzquiz would like to come and speak with her. . . .

After an endless silence during which Tita's soul shrank, Mama Elena asked:

"And why should this gentleman want to come talk to me?"

Tita's answer could barely be heard:

"I don't know."

Mama Elena threw her a look that seemed to Tita to contain all the years of repression that had flowed over the family, and said:

"If he intends to ask for your hand, tell him not to bother. He'll be wasting his time and mine too. You know perfectly well that being the youngest daughter means you have to take care of me until the day I die."

With that Mama Elena got slowly to her feet, put her glasses in her apron, and said in a tone of final command:

"That's it for today."

Tita knew that discussion was not one of the forms of communication permitted in Mama Elena's household, but even so, for the first time in her life, she intended to protest her mother's ruling.

"But in my opinion . . ."

"You don't have an opinion, and that's all I want to hear about it. For generations, not a single person in my family has ever questioned this tradition, and no daughter of mine is going to be the one to start."

Tita lowered her head, and the realization of her fate struck her as forcibly as the tears struck the table. From then on they knew, she and the table, that they could never have even the slightest voice in the unknown forces that fated Tita to bow before her mother's absurd decision, and the table to continue to receive the bitter tears that she had first shed on the day of her birth.

STILL TITA DID NOT SUBMIT. Doubts and anxieties sprang to her mind. For one thing, she wanted to know who started this family tradition. It would be nice if she could let that genius know about one little flaw in this perfect plan for taking care of women in their old age. If Tita couldn't marry and have children, who would take care of her when she got old? Was there a solution in a case like that? Or are daughters who stay home and take care of their mothers not expected to survive too long after the parent's death? And what about women who marry and can't have children, who will take care of them? And besides, she'd like to know what kind of studies had established that the youngest daughter and not the eldest is best suited to care for their mother. Had the opinion of the daughter affected by the plan ever been taken into account? If she couldn't marry, was she at least allowed to experience love? Or not even that?

Tita knew perfectly well that all these questions would have to be buried forever in the archive of questions that have no answers. In the De la Garza family, one obeyed—immediately. Ignoring Tita completely, a very angry Mama Elena left the kitchen, and for the next week she didn't speak a single word to her.

What passed for communication between them resumed when Mama Elena, who was inspecting the clothes each of the women had been sewing, discovered that Tita's creation, which was the most perfect, had not been basted before it was sewed.

"Congratulations," she said, "your stitches are perfect—but you didn't baste it, did you?"

"No," answered Tita, astonished that the sentence of silence had been revoked.

"Then go and rip it out. Baste it and sew it again and then come and show it to me. And remember that the lazy man and the stingy man end up walking their road twice."

"But that's if a person makes a mistake, and you yourself said a moment ago that my sewing was . . ."

"Are you starting up with your rebelliousness again? It's enough that you have the audacity to break the rules in your sewing."

"I'm sorry, Mami. I won't ever do it again."

Wɪᴛʜ ᴛʜᴀᴛ Tɪᴛᴀ sᴜᴄᴄᴇᴇᴅᴇᴅ in calming Mama Elena's anger. For once she had been very careful; she had called her "Mami" in the correct tone of voice. Mama Elena felt that the word *Mama* had a disrespectful sound to it, and so, from the time they were little, she had ordered her daughters to use the word *Mami* when speaking to her. The only one who resisted, the only one who said the word without the proper deference was Tita, which had earned her plenty of slaps. But how perfectly she had said it this time! Mama Elena took comfort in the hope that she had finally managed to subdue her youngest daughter.

Unfortunately her hope was short-lived, for the very next day Pedro Muzquiz appeared at the house, his esteemed father at his side, to ask for Tita's hand in marriage. His arrival caused a huge uproar, as his visit was completely unexpected. Several days earlier Tita had sent Pedro a message via Nacha's brother asking him to abandon his suit. The brother swore he had delivered the message to Pedro, and yet, there they were, in the house. Mama Elena received them in the living room; she was extremely polite and explained why it was impossible for Tita to marry.

"But if you really want Pedro to get married, allow me to suggest my daughter Rosaura, who's just two years older than Tita. *She* is one hundred percent available, and ready for marriage. . . ."

At that Chencha almost dropped right onto Mama Elena the tray containing coffee and cookies, which she had carried into the living room to offer don Pascual and his son. Excusing herself, she rushed back to the kitchen, where Tita, Rosaura, and Gertrudis were waiting for her to fill them in on every detail about what was going on in the living room. She burst headlong into the room, and they all immediately stopped what they were doing, so as not to miss a word she said.

They were together in the kitchen making Christmas Rolls. As the name implies, these rolls are usually prepared around Christmas, but today they were being prepared in honor of Tita's birthday. She would soon be sixteen years old, and she wanted to celebrate with one of her favorite dishes.

"Isn't that something? Your ma talks about being ready for marriage like she was dishing up a plate of enchiladas! And the worse thing is, they're completely different! You can't just switch tacos and enchiladas like that!"

Chencha kept up this kind of running commentary as she told the others — in her own way, of course — about the scene she had just witnessed. Tita knew Chencha sometimes exaggerated and distorted things, so she held her aching heart in check. She would not accept what she had just heard. Feigning calm, she continued cutting the rolls for her sisters and Nacha to fill.

It is best to use homemade rolls. Hard rolls can easily be obtained from a bakery, but they should be small; the larger ones are unsuited for this recipe. After filling the rolls, bake for ten minutes and serve hot. For best results, leave the rolls out overnight, wrapped in a cloth, so that the grease from the sausage soaks into the bread.

When Tita was finishing wrapping the next day's rolls, Mama Elena came into the kitchen and informed them that she had agreed to Pedro's marriage—to Rosaura.

Hearing Chencha's story confirmed, Tita felt her body fill with a wintry chill: in one sharp, quick blast she was so cold and dry her cheeks burned and turned red, red as the apples beside her. That overpowering chill lasted a long time, and she could find no respite, not even when Nacha told her what she had overheard as she escorted don Pascual Muzquiz and his son to the ranch's gate. Nacha followed them, walking as quietly as she could in order to hear the conversation between father and son. Don Pascual and Pedro were walking slowly, speaking in low, controlled, angry voices.

"Why did you do that, Pedro? It will look ridiculous, your agreeing to marry Rosaura. What happened to the eternal love you swore to Tita? Aren't you going to keep that vow?"

"Of course I'll keep it. When you're told there's no way you can marry the woman you love and your only hope of being near her is to marry her sister, wouldn't you do the same?"

Nacha didn't manage to hear the answer; Pulque, the ranch dog, went running by, barking at a rabbit he mistook for a cat.

"So you intend to marry without love?"

"No, Papa. I am going to marry with a great love for Tita that will never die."

Their voices grew less and less audible, drowned out by the crackling of dried leaves beneath their feet. How strange that Nacha, who was quite hard of hearing by that time, should have claimed to have heard this conversation. Still, Tita thanked Nacha for telling her—but that did not alter the icy feelings she began to have for Pedro. It is said that the deaf can't hear but can understand. Perhaps Nacha only heard what everyone else was afraid to say. Tita could not get to sleep that night; she could not find the words for what she was feeling. How unfortunate that black holes in space had not yet been discovered, for then she might have understood the black hole in the center of her chest, infinite coldness flowing through it.

W HENEVER SHE CLOSED HER EYES she saw scenes from last Christmas, the first time Pedro and his family had been invited to dinner; the scenes grew more and more vivid, and the cold within her grew sharper. Despite the time that had passed since that evening, she remembered it perfectly: the sounds, the smells, the way her new dress had grazed the freshly waxed floor, the look Pedro gave her . . . That look! She had been walking to the table carrying a tray of egg-yolk candies when she first felt his hot gaze burning her skin. She turned her head, and her eyes met Pedro's. It was then she understood how dough feels when it is plunged into boiling oil. The heat that invaded her body was so real she was afraid she would start to bubble—her face, her stomach, her heart, her breasts—like batter, and unable to endure his gaze she lowered her eyes and hastily crossed the room, to where Gertrudis was pedaling the player piano, playing a waltz called "The Eyes of Youth." She set her tray on a little table in the middle of the room, picked up a glass of Noyo liquor that was in front of her, hardly aware of what she was doing, and sat down next to Paquita Lobo, the De la Garza's neighbor. But even that distance between herself and Pedro was not enough; she felt her blood pulsing, searing her veins. A deep flush suffused her face and no matter how she tried she could not find a place for her eyes to rest. Paquita saw that something was bothering her, and with a look of great concern, she asked:

"That liquor is pretty strong, isn't it?"
"Pardon me?"
"You look a little woozy, Tita. Are you feeling all right?"
"Yes, thank you."

"You're old enough to have a little drink on a special occasion, but tell me, you little devil, did your mama say it was okay? I can see you're excited — you're shaking — and I'm sorry but I must say you'd better not have any more. You wouldn't want to make a fool of yourself."

That was the last straw! To have Paquita Lobo think she was drunk. She couldn't allow the tiniest suspicion to remain in Paquita's mind or she might tell her mother. Tita's fear of her mother was enough to make her forget Pedro for a moment, and she applied herself to convincing Paquita, any way she could, that she was thinking clearly, that her mind was alert. She chatted with her, she gossiped, she made small talk. She even told her the recipe for this Noyo liquor which was supposed to have had such an effect on her. The liquor is made by soaking four ounces of peaches and a half pound of apricots in water for twenty-four hours to loosen the skin; next, they are peeled, crushed, and steeped in hot water for fifteen days. Then the liquor is distilled. After two and half pounds of sugar have been completely dissolved in the water, four ounces of orange-flower water are added, and the mixture is stirred and strained. And so there would be no lingering doubts about her mental and physical well-being, she reminded Paquita, as if it were just an aside, that the water containers held 2.016 liters, no more and no less.

So when Mama Elena came over to ask Paquita if she was being properly entertained, she replied enthusiastically.

"Oh yes, perfectly! You have such wonderful daughters. Such fascinating conversation!"

Mama Elena sent Tita to the kitchen to get something for the guests. Pedro "happened" to be walking by at that moment and he offered his help. Tita rushed off to the kitchen without a word. His presence made her extremely uncomfortable. He followed her in, and she quickly sent him off with one of the trays of delicious snacks that had been waiting on the kitchen table.

She would never forget the moment their hands accidentally touched as they both slowly bent down to pick up the same tray.

That was when Pedro confessed his love.

"Señorita Tita, I would like to take advantage of this opportunity to be alone with you to tell you that I am deeply in love with you. I know this declaration is presumptuous, and that it's quite sudden, but it's so hard to get near you that I decided to tell you tonight. All I ask is that you tell me whether I can hope to win your love."

"I don't know what to say . . . give me time to think."

"No, no, I can't! I need an answer now: you don't have to think about love; you either feel it or you don't. I am a man of few words, but my word is my pledge. I swear that my love for you will last forever. What about you? Do you feel the same way about me?"

"Yes!"

Yes, A THOUSAND TIMES. From that night on she would love him forever. And now she had to give him up. It wasn't decent to desire your sister's future husband. She had to try to put him out of her mind somehow, so she could get to sleep. She started to eat the Christmas Roll Nacha had left out on her bureau, along with a glass of milk; this remedy had proven effective many times. Nacha, with all her experience, knew that for Tita there was no pain that wouldn't disappear if she ate a delicious Christmas Roll. But this time it didn't work. She felt no relief from the hollow sensation in her stomach. Just the opposite, a wave of nausea flowed over her. She realized that the hollow sensation was not hunger but an icy feeling of grief. She had to get rid of that terrible sensation of cold. First she put on a wool robe and a heavy cloak. The cold still gripped her. Then she put on felt slippers and another two shawls. No good. Finally she went to her sewing box and pulled out the bedspread she had started the day Pedro first spoke of marriage. A bedspread like that, a crocheted one, takes about a year to complete. Exactly the length of time Pedro and Tita had planned to wait before getting married. She decided to use the yarn, not to let it go to waste, and so she worked on the bedspread and wept furiously, weeping and working until dawn, and threw it over herself. It didn't help at all. Not that night, nor many others, for as long as she lived, could she free herself from that cold.

ABOUT **LAURA ESQUIVEL**

Laura Esquivel (**e skē vel ⁄**) was born in 1950 in Mexico, where she still lives with her husband and children. She began her career as a screenwriter, a talent she has used in turning her work into performance pieces. Her play *Chido One* was nominated for the Ariel Award by the Mexican Academy of Motion Pictures. In 1992, the film version of *Like Water for Chocolate (Como agua para chocolate)* won eleven awards from the Mexican Academy, including the award for best screenplay. The film enjoyed popularity both in Mexico and in the United States.

RESPONDING

1. *Personal Response* If you were Tita or Pedro, what would you do after the selection ends?

2. *Literary Analysis* What do you consider the *climax* of this story? What, if anything, is resolved?

3. *Multicultural Connection* Judging from this story, what seems to be the relationship between love and marriage? Are married men and women expected to love each other, for instance, or to take equal responsibility in their relationship? How can you tell?

LANGUAGE WORKSHOP

Dramatic Effect Throughout this story, descriptions of love and food are juxtaposed for *dramatic effect*. When Tita first encounters Pedro in the kitchen, her eyes meet his and "she understood how dough feels when it is plunged into boiling oil." What does this comparison suggest about her feelings? Find three other comparisons between love and food.

WRITER'S PORTFOLIO
Write an advertisement for some kind of food, suggesting that it will help you find romance, be a better athlete, enjoy happiness, be more popular, or in some way improve your life. Use some figurative comparisons.

At the Bridge

THEY HAVE PATCHED UP MY LEGS and given me a job I can do sitting down: I count the people crossing the new bridge. They get such a kick out of it, documenting their efficiency with figures, that senseless nothing made up of a few numbers goes to their heads, and all day long, all day long, my soundless mouth ticks away like clockwork, piling number on number, just so I can present them each evening with the triumph of a figure.

They beam delightedly when I hand over the result of my day's labors, the higher the figure the broader their smiles, and they have every reason to hug themselves when they climb into bed, for many thousands of pedestrians cross their new bridge every day. . . .

But their statistics are wrong. I am sorry, but they are wrong. I am an untrustworthy soul, although I have no trouble giving an impression of sterling integrity.

Secretly it gives me pleasure to do them out of one pedestrian every so often, and then again, when I feel sorry for them, to throw in a few extra. I hold their happiness in the palm of my hand. When I am mad at the world, when I have smoked all my cigarettes, I just give them the average, sometimes less than the average; and when my spirits soar, when I am in a good mood, I pour out my generosity in a five-digit number. It makes them so happy! They positively snatch the sheet from my hand, their eyes light up, and they pat me on the back. How blissfully ignorant they are! And then they start multiplying, dividing, working out percentages, God knows what all. They figure out how many people crossed the bridge per minute today, and how many will have crossed the bridge in ten years. They are in love with the future-perfect tense, the future-perfect is their specialty—and yet I can't help being sorry that the whole thing is a fallacy.

When my little sweetheart crosses the bridge—which she does twice a day—my heart simply stops beating. The tireless ticking of my heart just comes to a halt until she has turned into the avenue and disappeared. And all the people who pass by during that time don't get counted. Those two minutes are mine, all mine, and nobody is going to take them away from me. And when she returns every evening from her ice-cream parlor, when she walks along on the far side, past my soundless mouth which must count, count, then my heart stops beating again, and I don't resume counting until she is out of sight. And all those who are lucky enough to file past my unseeing eyes during those minutes will not be immortalized in statistics: shadow-men and shadow-women, creatures of no account, they are barred from the parade of future-perfect statistics.

Needless to say, I love her. But she hasn't the slightest idea, and I would rather she didn't find out. I don't want her to suspect what havoc she wreaks in all those calculations. I want her to walk serenely off to her ice-cream parlor, unsuspecting and innocent with her long brown hair and slender feet, and to get lots of tips. I love her. It must surely be obvious that I love her.

NOT LONG AGO they checked up on me. My mate, who sits across the street and has to count the cars, gave me plenty of warning, and that day I was a lynx-eyed devil. I counted like crazy, no speedometer could do better. The chief statistician, no less, posted himself across the street for an hour, and then compared his tally with mine. I was only one short. My little sweetheart had walked past, and as long as I live I won't allow that adorable child to be whisked off into the future-perfect tense, they're not going to take my little sweetheart and multiply her and divide her and turn her into a meaningless percentage. It made my heart bleed to have to go on counting without turning round to watch her, and I am certainly grateful to my mate across the street who has to count the cars. It might have cost me my job, my very existence.

The chief statistician clapped me on the shoulder and said I was a good fellow, trustworthy and loyal. "To be out one in one hour," he said, "really makes no odds. We allow for a certain margin of error anyway. I'm going to apply for your transfer to horse-drawn vehicles."

Horse-drawn vehicles are, of course, money for jam. There's nothing to it. There are never more than a couple of dozen horse-drawn vehicles a day, and to tick over the next number in your brain once every half hour — what a cinch!

Horse-drawn vehicles would be terrific. Between four and eight they are not allowed across the bridge at all, and I could walk to the ice-cream parlor, feast my eyes on her or maybe walk her part-way home, my little uncounted sweetheart. . . .

ABOUT **HEINRICH BÖLL**

Heinrich Böll (hīn′riH bōl; 1917–1985) is one of a generation of German writers who reflect the social and individual calamities resulting from World War II. His writings are a blend of horror and compassion, and his characters are often bewildered pawns manipulated by faceless authorities. In 1972, a decade after he had published his most popular novel, *The Clown*, he was awarded the Nobel Prize for Literature.

RESPONDING

1. *Personal Response* What do you think the speaker means by the phrase "soundless mouth"?

2. *Literary Analysis* What do you think is the *setting*— time and place—of this story? What details from the story and from Böll's biography support your answer?

3. *Multicultural Connection* This story was written nearly three decades ago in Germany. Do you think it has relevance in the United States in the 1990s? Explain.

LANGUAGE WORKSHOP

Theme Which of the following do you think best expresses the *theme* of "At the Bridge"? Feel free to state another theme if you wish. Then explain why you have chosen this theme.

This is a story about (a) the plight of the disabled war veteran; (b) the lone individual fighting a war against the machine age and bureaucracy; (c) unrequited love.

WRITER'S PORTFOLIO

Imagine the narrator in his future occupation as a counter of horse-drawn vehicles. He finally declares his love to his sweetheart at the ice-cream parlor. Describe what you think her reaction would be.

The Needle

MY GOOD PEOPLE, nowadays all marriages are arranged by Mr. Love. Young folks fall in love and begin to date. They go out together until they start to quarrel and hate each other. In my time we relied on father and mother and the matchmaker. I myself did not see my Todie until the wedding ceremony, when he lifted the veil from my face. There he stood with his red beard and disheveled sidelocks. It was after Pentecost, but he wore a fur coat as if it were winter. That I didn't faint dead away was a miracle from heaven. I had fasted through the long summer day. Still, I wish my best friends no worse life than I had with my husband; he should intercede for me in the next world. Perhaps I shouldn't say this, but I can't wait until our souls are together again.

"Yes, love-shmuv. What does a young boy or girl know about what is good for them? Mothers used to know the signs. In Krasnostaw there lived a woman called Reitze Leah, and when she was looking for brides for her sons she made sure to drop in on her prospective in-laws early in the morning. If she found that the bed linens were dirty and the girl in

Culture Notes

sidelocks . . . Pentecost
Sidelocks, locks of hair that are long on the side of the head, are worn by Jewish male Hasidim, members of a mystical religious movement founded in the 1700s in Poland. Pentecost was originally a Jewish holiday commemorating the revelation of the Law at Mt. Sinai and later a wheat festival. p. 420

question came to the door with uncombed hair, wearing a sloppy dressing gown, that was it. Before long everybody in the neighboring villages was onto her, and when she was seen in the marketplace early in the morning, all the young girls made sure their doors were bolted. She had six able sons. None of the matches she made for them was any good, but that is another story. A girl may be clean and neat before the wedding, but afterwards she becomes a slattern. Everything depends on luck.

"But let me tell you a story. In Hrubyeshow there lived a rich man, Reb Lemel Wagmeister. In those days we didn't use surnames, but Reb Lemel was so rich that he was always called Wagmeister. His wife's name was Esther Rosa, and she came from the other side of the Vistula. I see her with my own eyes: a beautiful woman, with a big-city air. She always wore a black-lace mantilla over her wig. Her face was as white and smooth as a girl's. Her eyes were dark. She spoke Russian, Polish, German, and maybe even French. She played the piano. Even when the streets were muddy, she wore high-heeled patent-leather shoes. One autumn I saw her hopping from stone to stone like a bird, lifting her skirt with both hands, a real lady. They had an only son, Ben Zion. He was as like his mother as two drops of water. We were distant relatives, not on her side but on her husband's. Ben Zion—Benze, he was called—had every virtue: he was handsome, clever, learned. He studied the Torah with the rabbi in the daytime, and in the evening a teacher of secular subjects took over. Benze had black hair and a fair complexion, like his mother. When he took a walk in the summertime wearing his elegant gaberdine with a fashionable slit in the back, and his smart kid boots, all the girls mooned over him through the windows. Although it is the custom to give dowries only to daughters, Benze's

Culture Notes

ten thousand roubles at the time of this story, an amount in Russian money worth about five thousand dollars in U.S. currency, p. 422

Talmud scholar someone who makes a career of studying the Talmud, or the tradition and interpretation of Jewish law, p. 423

father set aside for his son a sum of ten thousand roubles. What difference did it make to him? Benze was his only heir. They tried to match him with the richest girls in the province, but Esther Rosa was very choosy. She had nothing to do, what with three maids, a manservant, and a coachman in addition. So she spent her time looking for brides for Benze. She had already inspected the best-looking girls in half of Poland, but not one had she found without some defect. One wasn't beautiful enough; another, not sufficiently clever. But what she was looking for most was nobility of character. 'Because,' she said, 'if a woman is coarse, it is the husband who suffers. I don't want any woman to vent her spleen on my Benze.' I was already married at the time. I married when I was fifteen. Esther Rosa had no real friend in Hrubyeshow and I became a frequent visitor to her house. She taught me how to knit and embroider and do needlepoint. She had golden hands. When the fancy took her, she could make herself a dress or even a cape. She once made me a dress, just for the fun of it. She had a good head for business as well. Her husband hardly took a step without consulting her. Whenever she told him to buy or sell a property, Reb Lemel Wagmeister immediately sent for Lippe the agent and said: 'My wife wants to buy or sell such-and-such.' She never made a mistake.

"Well, Benze was already nineteen, and not even engaged. In those days nineteen was considered an old bachelor. Reb Lemel Wagmeister complained that the boy was being disgraced by his mother's choosiness. Benze developed pimples on his forehead—because he needed a woman, it was said. We called them passion pimples.

"One day I came to see Esther Rosa to borrow a ball of yarn. And she said to me: 'Zeldele, would you like to ride to Zamosc with me?'

"'What will I do in Zamosc?' I asked.

"'What difference does it make?' she replied. 'You'll be my guest.'

"Esther Rosa had her own carriage, but this time she went along with someone else who was going to Zamosc. I guessed that the journey had something to do with looking over a bride, but Esther Rosa's nature was such that one didn't ask questions. If she were willing to talk, well and good. If not, you just waited. To make it short, I went to tell my mother about the trip. No need to ask my husband. He sat in the study house all day long. When he came home in the evening, my mother served him his supper. In those days a young Talmud scholar barely knew he had a wife. I don't believe that he would have recognized me if he met me on the street. I packed a dress and a pair of bloomers — I beg your pardon — and I was ready for the trip. We were traveling in a nobleman's carriage and he did the driving himself. Two horses like lions. The road was dry and smooth as a table. When we arrived in Zamosc, he let us off not at the marketplace but on a side street where the Gentiles live. Esther Rosa thanked him and he tipped his hat and waved his whip at us good-naturedly. It all looked arranged.

"As a rule, when Esther Rosa travelled any place she dressed as elegantly as a countess. This time she wore a simple cotton dress, and a kerchief over her wig. It was summer and the days were long. We walked to the marketplace and she inquired for Berish Lubliner's dry-goods store. A large store was pointed out to us. Nowadays in a dry-goods store you can only buy yard goods, but in those days they sold everything: thread, wool for knitting, and odds and ends. What didn't they sell? It was a store as big as a forest, filled with merchandise to the ceiling. At a high desk-stand a man sat writing in a ledger, as they do in big cities. I don't know what he was, the cashier or a book-keeper. Behind a counter stood a girl with black eyes that burned like fire. We happened to be the only customers in the store, and we approached her. 'What can I do for you?' she asked. 'You seem to be strangers.'

"'Yes, we are strangers,' said Esther Rosa.

"'What would you like to see?' the girl asked.

"'A needle,' said Esther Rosa.

"The moment she heard the word 'needle,' the girl's face changed. Her eyes became angry. 'Two women for one needle,' she said.

Merchants believe that a needle is unlucky. Nobody ever dared to buy a needle at the beginning of the week, because they knew it meant the whole week would be unlucky. Even in the middle of the week the storekeepers did not like to sell needles. One usually bought a spool of thread, some buttons, and the needle was thrown in without even being mentioned. A needle costs only half a groschen and it was a nuisance to make such small change.

"'Yes,' said Esther Rosa. 'All I need is a needle.'

"The girl frowned but took out a box of needles. Esther Rosa searched through the box and said: 'Perhaps you have some other needles.'

"'What's wrong with these?' the girl asked impatiently.

"'Their eyes are too small,' Esther Rosa said. 'It will be difficult to thread them.'

"'These are all I have,' the girl said angrily. 'If you can't see well, why don't you buy yourself a pair of eyeglasses.'

"Esther Rosa insisted. 'Are you sure you have no others? I must have a needle with a larger eye.'

"The girl reluctantly pulled out another box and slammed it down on the counter. Esther Rosa examined several needles and said: 'These too have small eyes.'

"The girl snatched away the box and screamed: 'Why don't you go to Lublin and order yourself a special needle with a big eye?'

"The man at the stand began to laugh. 'Perhaps you need a sackcloth needle,' he suggested. 'Some nerve,' the girl chimed in, 'to bother people over a half-groschen sale.'

"Esther Rosa replied: 'I have no use for sackcloth or for girls who are as coarse as sackcloth.' Then she turned to me and said: 'Come, Zeldele, they are not our kind.'

"The girl turned red in the face and said loudly, 'What yokels! Good riddance!'

"We went out. The whole business had left a bad taste in my mouth. A woman passed by and Esther Rosa asked her the way to Reb Zelig Izbitzer's drygoods store. 'Right across the street,' she said, pointing. We crossed the market-place and entered a store that was only a third of the size of the first one. Here too there was a young saleswoman. This one wasn't dark; she had red hair. She was not ugly but she had freckles. Her eyes were as green as gooseberries. Esther Rosa asked if she sold needles. And the girl replied, 'Why not? We sell everything.'

"'I'm looking for a needle with a large eye, because I have trouble threading needles,' Esther Rosa said.

"'I'll show you every size we have and you can pick the one that suits you best,' the girl replied.

"I had already guessed what was going on and my heart began to beat like a thief's. The girl brought out about ten boxes of needles. 'Why should you stand?' she said. 'Here is a stool. Please be seated.' She also brought a stool for me. It was perfectly clear to me that Esther Rosa was going to test her too.

"'Why are the needles all mixed together?' Esther Rosa complained. 'Each size should be in a different box.'

"'When they come from the factory, they are all sorted out,' the girl said apologetically. 'But they get mixed up.' I saw Esther Rosa was doing her best to make the girl lose her temper. 'I don't see too well,' Esther Rosa said. 'It's dark here.'

"'Just a moment, and I'll move the stools to the door. There is more light there,' the girl replied.

"'Does it pay you to make all this effort just to sell a half-penny needle?' Esther Rosa asked. And the girl answered: 'First of all; a needle costs only a quarter of a penny, and then as the Talmud says, the same law applies to a penny as it does to a hundred guilders. Besides, today you buy a needle and tomorrow you may be buying satins for a trousseau.'

"'Is that so? Then how come the store is empty?' Esther Rosa wanted to know. 'Across the street, Berish Lubliner's store is so full of customers you can't find room for a pin between them. I bought my materials there but I decided to come here for the needle.'

THE GIRL BECAME SERIOUS. I was afraid that Esther Rosa had overdone it. Even an angel can lose patience. But the girl said, 'Everything according to God's will.' Esther Rosa made a move to carry her stool to the door, but the girl stopped her. 'Please don't trouble yourself. I'll do it.' Esther Rosa interrupted. 'Just a moment. I want to tell you something.'

"'What do you want to tell me?' the girl said, setting down the stool.

"'My daughter, Mazel Tov!' Esther Rosa called out.

"The girl turned white as chalk. 'I don't understand,' she said.

"'You will be my daughter-in-law,' Esther Rosa announced. 'I am the wife of Reb Lemel Wagmeister of Hrubyeshow. I have come here to look for a bride for my son. Not to buy a needle. Reb Berish's daughter is like a straw mat and you are like silk. You will be my Benze's wife, God willing.'

"That the girl didn't faint dead away was a miracle from heaven. Everybody in Zamosc had heard of Reb Lemel Wagmeister. Zamosc is not Lublin. Customers came in and saw what was happening. Esther Rosa took a string of amber beads out of her basket. 'Here is your engagement gift. Bend your head.' The girl lowered her head submissively and Esther Rosa placed the beads around her neck. Her father and mother came running into the store. There was kissing, embracing, crying. Someone immediately rushed to tell the story to Reb Berish's daughter.

Culture Notes

a hundred guilders about twenty dollars, p. 425

Mazel Tov (mä′zəl tôv′) congratulations, p. 426

yeshiva (yə shē′və) a school for advanced study of the Talmud, p. 427

leech one who applies leeches, bloodsucking worms, to draw blood from wounds, p. 428

When she heard what had happened, she burst into tears. Her name was Itte. She had a large dowry and was known as a shrewd saleswoman. Zelig Izbitzer barely made a living.

"My good people, it was a match. Esther Rosa wore the pants in the family. Whatever she said went. And as I said, in those days young people were never asked. An engagement party was held and the wedding soon after. Zelig Izbitzer could not afford a big wedding. He barely could give his daughter a dowry, for he also had two other daughters and two sons who were studying in the yeshiva. But, as you know, Reb Lemel Wagmeister had little need for her dowry. I went to the engagement party and I danced at the wedding. Esther Rosa dressed the girl like a princess. She became really beautiful. When good luck shines, it shows on the face. Whoever did not see that couple standing under the wedding canopy and later dancing the virtue dance will never know what it means to have joy in children. Afterwards they lived like doves. Exactly to the year, she bore a son.

"From the day Itte discovered that Esther Rosa had come to test her, she began to ail. She spoke about the visit constantly. She stopped attending customers. Day and night she cried. The matchmakers showered her with offers, but first she wouldn't have anyone else and second what had happened had given her a bad name. You know how people exaggerate. All kinds of lies were invented about her. She had insulted Esther Rosa in the worst way, had spat in her face, had even beaten her up. Itte's father was stuffed with money and in a small town everybody is envious of his neighbour's crust of bread. Now his enemies had their revenge. Itte had been the real merchant and without her the store went to pieces. After a while she married a man from Lublin. He wasn't even a bachelor. He was divorced. He came to Zamosc and took over his father-in-law's store. But he was as much a businessman as I am a musician.

"That is how things are. If luck is with you, it serves you well. And when it stops serving you, everything goes topsy-turvy. Itte's mother became so upset she developed gallstones, or maybe it was jaundice. Her face became as yellow as saffron. Itte no longer entered the store. She became a stay-at-home. It was hoped that when she became pregnant and had a child, she would forget. But twice she miscarried. She became half crazy, went on cursing Frieda Gittel—that is what Benze's wife was called—and insisted that the other had connived against her. Who knows what goes on in a madwoman's head? Itte also foretold that Frieda Gittel would die and that she, Itte, would take her place. When Itte became pregnant for the third time, her father took her to a miracle-worker. I've forgotten to mention that by this time her mother was already dead. The miracle-worker gave her potions and talismans, but she miscarried again. She began to run to doctors and to imagine all kinds of illnesses.

"Now listen to this. One evening Itte was sitting in her room sewing. She had finished her length of thread and wanted to rethread her needle. While getting the spool she placed the needle between her lips. Suddenly she felt a stab in her throat and the needle vanished. She searched all over for it, but—what is the saying—'who can find a needle in a haystack?' My dear people, Itte began to imagine that she had swallowed the needle. She felt a pricking in her stomach, in her breast, her legs. There is a saying: 'A needle wanders.' She visited the leech, but what does a leech know? She went to the doctors in Lublin and even in Warsaw. One doctor said one thing; another, something different. They poked her stomach but could find no needle. God preserve us. Itte lay in bed and screamed that the needle was pricking her. The town was in a turmoil. Some said that she had swallowed the needle on purpose to commit suicide. Others, that it was a punishment from God. But why should she have been punished? She had already suffered enough for her rudeness. Finally she went to Vienna to a great doctor. And he found the way out. He put her to sleep and made a cut in her belly. When she woke up he showed her the needle that he was supposed to have removed from her insides. I wasn't there. Perhaps he really found a needle, but that's not what people said. When she returned from Vienna, she was her former self again. The store had gone to ruin. Her father was already in the other world. Itte, however, opened a new store. In the new store she succeeded again, but she never had any children.

"I've forgotten to mention that after what happened between Esther Rosa and the two girls, the salesgirls of Zamosc became the souls of politeness, not only to strangers, but even to their own townspeople. For how could one know whether a customer had come to buy or to test? The book peddler did a fine trade in books on etiquette, and when a woman came to buy a ball of yarn, she was offered a chair.

"I can't tell you what happened later, because I moved away from Zamosc. In the big cities one forgets about everything, even about God. Reb Lemel Wagmeister and Esther Rosa have long since passed away. I haven't heard from Benze or his wife for a long time. Yes, a needle. Because of a rooster and a chicken a whole town was destroyed in the Holy Land, and because of a needle a match was spoiled. The truth is that everything is fated from heaven. You can love someone until you burst, but if it's not destined, it will come to naught. A boy and a girl can be keeping company for seven years, and a stranger comes along and breaks everything up. I could tell you a story of a boy who married his girl's best friend out of spite, and she, to spite him kept to her bed for twenty years. Tell me? It's too late. If I were to tell you all the stories I know, we'd be sitting here for seven days and seven nights."

Culture Note

Because . . . Holy Land

According to an ancient Jewish custom, a chicken and a rooster were carried in the wedding procession to signify a fruitful union. According to the Talmud, when Roman soldiers came upon such a scene in a town near Jerusalem, a skirmish took place and was reported to Roman authorities as a rebellion. Consequently, Roman forces destroyed the town. p. 429

ABOUT ISAAC BASHEVIS SINGER

Isaac Bashevis (bə shev′əs) Singer (1904–1991) was born in Radzymin, Poland, when Poland was part of the Russian Empire. He was educated at the Warsaw Rabbinical Seminary but preferred writing to being a rabbi. In 1935 he fled the Nazis, and he became a U.S. citizen in 1942. Singer, who received the Nobel Prize in Literature in 1978, supervised the translations of his works from the original Yiddish. An old-fashioned storyteller in a modern age, Singer is best known for his short stories, which appear in collections such as *Gimpel the Fool, A Crown of Feathers,* and *Old Love.*

RESPONDING

1. *Personal Response* The narrator says, "You can love someone until you burst, but if it's not destined, it will come to naught." Explain whether or not you agree.

2. *Literary Analysis* A *simile* is a comparison using the words *like* or *as*. Find five similes in "The Needle." Then propose new similes that describe the following people: Itte, Esther Rosa, Frieda Gittel, and Benze.

3. *Multicultural Connection* What role do parents play in marriages in your culture? How do their roles compare with those portrayed in "The Needle"?

LANGUAGE WORKSHOP

Idiom An *idiom* is an expression that means something different from the ordinary meanings of the words that make it up. For example, someone who is "bursting with joy" is happy, not literally bursting. Explain what the following idioms from "The Needle" mean.
1. "I don't want any woman to vent her spleen on my Benze."
2. "The whole business had left a bad taste in my mouth."
3. "Esther Rosa wore the pants in the family."

WRITER'S PORTFOLIO

Write an engagement announcement for Frieda and Benze. Use models from your local newspaper if you like. Include details about the happy couple.

The Damask Drum

CHARACTERS

Iwakichi (ē wä kē chē), *an old janitor*
Kayoko (kä yô kô), *a girl of about 20, a clerk*
Shunnosuke Fujima (shùn nô sù ke fù jē mä),
a teacher of Japanese dance
Toyama (tô yä mä), *a young man*
Kaneko (kä ne kô), *a member of the Ministry of
Foreign Affairs*
Madame, *owner of a fashionable dressmaking establishment*
Shop Assistant, *a girl*
Hanako Tsukioka (hä nä kô tsù kē ô kä)

About the No Play

The *No* play developed from traditional religious festivals in the four-teenth and fifteenth centuries in Japan. Highly stylized and dancelike, this type of drama is staged with music (flute and drum), little scenery, and few props. Performed by all-male casts wearing symbolic masks and magnificent costumes, *No* plays usually are tragedies. The moments of "no action" between the dancing and music are enjoyable because they convey an actor's inner strength.

The center of the stage is a street between buildings. Windows and signboards face each other on the third floors of the buildings on either side.

Stage-right is a third-floor law office. A musty-looking room. A room in good faith, a forthright room. There is a potted laurel tree.

Stage-left is a third-floor couturier. A room in the most modern style. A room in bad faith, a deceitful room. There is a large mirror.

Spring. Evening.

(In the room to the right)

Iwakichi *(He is sweeping the room with a broom. He sweeps up to the window.)* Out of the way, out of the way. You act as if you're trying to protect the dirt around your feet.

Kayoko *(She takes a mirror from her cheap handbag and stands in the light applying a fresh coating of lipstick.)* Just a minute. I'll be finished in just one minute now. *(Iwakichi pushes up* Kayoko's *skirt from behind with his broom.)* Oh-h-h— you're dreadful. Really. The old men these days are getting to be horrible lechers. *(She finally moves aside.)*

Iwakichi *(sweeping).* And what about the young ladies? A girl of nineteen or twenty looks better when her lips aren't covered with all the paint. I'll bet your boy friend thinks so too.

Kayoko *(glancing at her watch).* I can't afford expensive clothes. Lipstick's the best I can do. *(She looks at her watch again.)* Oh, I'm really sick of it. I wonder why he and I can't both get off from work at the same time. Heaven help me if I tried to kill time waiting for him anywhere outside the office. The first thing you know it'd cost money.

Iwakichi. I've never once set foot in any of those fashionable drinking places. But they know my face in all the counter restaurants. If you want to know where the bean soup is good, just ask me. *(Pointing at the desk)* Once I invited the boss and he said it was first rate. I couldn't have been more pleased if he'd praised the bean soup in my own house.

Kayoko. Business has not been good for the boss lately.

Iwakichi. There're too many laws. That's why there're more lawyers than anybody knows what to do with.

Kayoko. I wonder—when he's got such a stylish place for an office.

Iwakichi. The boss hates anything crooked. I'm sure of that. *(Looking at a picture on the wall)* It bothers him even if that picture frame is a quarter of an inch crooked. That's why I've decided to spend the rest of my days working for him.

Kayoko *(opening the window)*. The wind's died down since evening.

Iwakichi *(approaching the window)*. I can't stand that dusty wind that blows at the beginning of spring. . . . The calm of evening. Oh, there's a good smell coming from somewhere.

Kayoko. It's from the Chinese restaurant on the ground floor.

Iwakichi. The prices are too high for me.

Kayoko. Look at the beautiful sunset. It's reflected in the windows of all the buildings.

Iwakichi. Those are pigeons from the newspaper office. Look at them scatter. Now they've formed a circle again. . . .

Kayoko. I'm glad you're in love too. It's made you young again.

Iwakichi. Don't be silly. My love is a one-sided affair, not like yours.

Kayoko. You're in love with a great lady whose name you don't even know.

Iwakichi. She's the princess of the laurel, the tree that grows in the garden of the moon.

Kayoko *(pointing at the potted tree)*. That's the tree you mean, isn't it? There's nothing so wonderful about a laurel.

Iwakichi. Oh! I've forgotten to water my precious laurel. *(Exits)*

Kayoko. Isn't he the sly one? Running off to cover his embarrassment.

Iwakichi *(enters with a watering can).* Laurel, I'm sorry I forgot to water you. One more effort now and you'll be covered with glossy leaves. *(As he waters the plant he strokes the leaves fondly.)* Poets often talk about hair glossy as leaves. . . .

Kayoko. You still haven't got any answer?

Iwakichi. Mmmm.

Kayoko. I call that disgusting. It makes me sick. Not to have the decency to send you an answer. Nobody else but me would go on being your messenger. How many letters has it been? Thirty, isn't it? Today makes exactly thirty.

Iwakichi. If you count in all the love letters I wrote without sending them, it'd make seventy more. For seventy days—every day I wrote her one and every day I burned it. That's what it was like before you were kind enough to take pity on me and become my postman. Let's see, that makes a total of. . . *(Thinks)*

Kayoko. A hundred, of course. Can't you count any more?

Iwakichi. Unrequited love is a bitter thing.

Kayoko. You haven't the sense to give up.

Iwakichi. Sometimes I think I'll try to forget. But I know now that trying to forget is worse than being unable to. I mean, even if being unable to forget is painful in the same way, it's still better.

Kayoko. How did you ever get into such a state, I wonder. *(As she speaks a light is lit in the room to the left.)*

Iwakichi. They've switched on the light. Every day at the same time . . . when this room dies that one comes to life again. And in the morning when this room returns to life, that one dies. . . . It was three months ago. I'd finished sweeping and I just happened to look at the room over there, with nothing particular on my mind. . . . Then I saw her for the first time. She came into the room with her maid. The Madame was showing her the way. . . . She was wearing a coat of some kind of golden fur, and when she took it off, her dress was all black. Her hat was black too. And her hair, of course, it was black, black as the night sky. If I tried to describe to you how beautiful her face was—It was like the moon, and everything around it was shining. . . . She said a few words, then she smiled. I trembled all over. . . . She smiled. . . . I stood behind the window staring at her until she went into the fitting-room. . . . That's when it began.

Kayoko. But she's not all that beautiful. It's her clothes— they're exquisite.

Iwakichi. Love's not that sort of thing. It's something that shines on the one you love from the mirror of your own ugliness.

Kayoko. In that case, even I qualify.

Iwakichi. There's nothing for you to worry about! You look like a great beauty to your boy friend.

Kayoko. Does that mean there's a moon for every woman in the world?

Iwakichi. Some women are fat, and some are thin. . . . That's why there's both a full moon and a crescent.
(Three men appear in the room to the left: Fujima, Toyama, Kaneko.*)*

Iwakichi. It'll be time soon. I've got to finish the rest of today's love letter.

Kayoko. Hurry, won't you? I'll read a book while I wait.
(Iwakichi *goes to the desk and finishes his letter.* Kayoko *sits and begins to read.)*

(In the room to the left)

Fujima *(He carries a parcel wrapped in a purple square of cloth).* I am Shunnosuke Fujima. Very pleased to meet you.

Toyama. How do you do? My name is Toyama. And this is Mr. Kaneko from the Ministry of Foreign Affairs. *(Introduces the men)* Mr. Fujima.

Kaneko. How do you do?

Fujima. You and Mr. Kaneko seem to be old friends.

Toyama. Yes. He was at the same school, but ahead of me.

Fujima. Oh, really? . . . My pupils are about to put on a dance-play. *(Hands them leaflets)* Please take these. . . . Mrs. Tsukioka said she would buy a hundred tickets.

Toyama (*jealously*). Mrs. Tsukioka wouldn't do that unless she were sure of making a profit.

Kaneko. No, she's not like you. She's the kind who makes losses, never a profit.

Fujima. Yes, that's the kind of person she really is.

Kaneko (*firmly*). I am perfectly well aware what kind of person she is.

Fujima (*changing the subject*). The plot of the dance-play is charming, if I must say so myself.

Toyama (*looking at his watch*). She's late, isn't she? Summoning people here like that. . . . It's bad taste to keep a man waiting in a dress shop.

Kaneko. In the reign of Louis XIV they used to receive men in their boudoirs. And when a man wanted to compliment a woman he'd say something like "Who does the shading under your eyes?" (*He says it in French.*)

Fujima. Excuse me? What was that?

(Kaneko *translates word for word.* Toyama *looks the other way.*)

Fujima. Shading under a woman's eyes is a lovely thing, isn't it? Like clouds hovering under the moon, you might say.

Kaneko (*interested only in what he himself has to say*). That's the secret of all diplomacy. To ask who did the shading under a woman's eyes when you know perfectly well she did it herself.

Toyama. Mr. Kaneko is about to become an ambassador.

Fujima (*bowing*). Congratulations.

(*In the room to the right*)

Iwakichi. I've written it. It's done. And very good this time.

Kayoko. It must be a terrific strain always thinking up new things to say.

Iwakichi. This is one of the more agreeable hardships of love.

Kayoko. I'll leave it on my way home.

Iwakichi. Sorry to bother you, Kayoko. Please don't lose it.

Kayoko. You talk as if it wasn't just across the street. I couldn't lose it even if I wanted to. . . . Good night.

Iwakichi. Good night, Kayoko.

Kayoko (*waving the letter as she stands in the door*). Maybe I will forget about the letter after all. I'm in a big hurry myself, you know.

Iwakichi. You mustn't tease an old man like that.

(*In the room to the left*)

Kaneko. She certainly is late.

Toyama (*He stands in front of the mirror and fiddles with his necktie.*) Mrs. Tsukioka's taste in neckties always runs to something like this. I really hate loud ties.

Fujima. This is a tobacco case Mrs. Tsukioka gave me when I succeeded as head of the company. The netsuke is more valuable than the case itself. Just have a look at it. (*He holds it up to the light.*) You'd never think it was made entirely of wood, would you? It's exactly like ivory, isn't it?

Kaneko. We civil servants must refuse all presents. There's always the suspicion of bribery. I envy artists.

Fujima. Everybody says that.

Toyama (*in a tearful voice*). Damned old woman! Why should she have invited everybody except me?

Kayoko (*out of breath*). Oh, excuse me. Is the Madame here?

Toyama. She went to the shop a couple of minutes ago. I think she had some business to do.

Kayoko. Now what am I going to do?

Toyama. Is it something urgent?

Kayoko. Yes. It's a letter. I give one to Madame every day, at somebody's request. . . .

Kaneko (*haughtily*). I'll take care of it.

Kayoko (*hesitantly*). It's very kind of you. . . .

Kaneko. I'll accept responsibility.

> ## Culture Notes
>
> **Louis XIV** (1638–1715), King of France from 1643 to 1715, called Louis the Great or the Sun King, p. 436
>
> **netsuke** (net′sə kē) a small piece of sculpture fastened onto a pouch or case, p. 437

Kayoko. I'm much obliged. Please. *(Exits)*

Toyama. What a terrific hurry that girl is in!

Kaneko *(He reads the address on the envelope.)* Well, I never! It says "To the princess of the laurel of the moon."

Fujima. Very romantic, isn't it?

Kaneko. You didn't write it yourself, by any chance?

Fujima. You're joking. When a dancing teacher has the time to write love letters, he holds hands instead.

Kaneko. The sender is one Iwakichi.

Fujima. He writes a very good hand, whoever he is.

Toyama. Just imagine—calling the Madame a "princess of the laurel of the moon"! I don't think I've ever seen a laurel. Is it a very big tree?

Fujima. Only around the middle, I think.

Toyama. No accounting for tastes, is there? Let's see— there's a French expression something like that—

Madame *(Enters. She is unusually tall.)* It's so good to find you all here.

Toyama. A love letter's come for you.

Madame. I wonder who it can be from. There are five or six gentlemen who might be sending me one.

Kaneko. Your affairs are touch-and-go, I take it?

Madame. Yes, that's right. I never forget my defenses.

Toyama. Your armor must take a lot of material.

Madame. Darling boy! You always say such amusing things.

Fujima *(dramatically).* "The princess of the laurel of the moon," I presume?

Madame. Oh, is *that* the love letter you're talking about? In that case, it's not for me.

Kaneko. Don't try to fool us.

Madame. You're quite mistaken. It's for Mrs. Tsukioka.

All. What?

Madame *(sitting).* These letters are driving me simply frantic. They're from the janitor who works in the building across the street. An old man almost seventy. He's fallen in love with Mrs. Tsukioka, from having seen her through the window.

Kaneko. That doesn't surprise me. They say that the aged tend to be farsighted. *(He laughs, amused at his own joke.)* I can't wait to grow old. It must be very convenient being farsighted.

Madame. The old man has sent her dozens—no, hundreds—of letters.

Toyama. If he sent out all his letters to different women, one of them might have been successful.

Kaneko. There's something in what you say. But if, after all, love were a question of probability, the probability for one woman might be the same as the probability for innumerable women.

Fujima. Have you shown her the letters? Mrs. Tsukioka, I mean.

Madame. How could I possibly show them to her? I've used them all as comb wipers.

Toyama. Do combs get as dirty as all that?

Madame. They're for my dogs' combs. I have five wire-haired fox terriers. They shut their eyes in positive rapture when I comb them.

Kaneko. Which runs faster—a lover or a dog?

Fujima. Which gets dirty faster?

Madame. It makes me quite giddy to talk with such enchanting men.

Kaneko. Sidetracked again. What's happened to the love letters?

Madame. This is what has happened. The one who's been delivering the letters is that sweet girl from the office across the way.

Toyama. The girl who was just here? What's sweet about her?

Madame. She's a well-behaved, good girl, and I've become so fond of her that I've been accepting the letters every day. But I've never dreamed of giving one to Mrs. Tsukioka.

Kaneko. If the girl knew that, she'd never give you another one.

Madame. You'll have to excuse me. Just put yourself in my place. If Mrs. Tsukioka should read them and get upset—

(Knock at the door)

Madame. Now what shall I do? It's Mrs. Tsukioka.
Kaneko. Attention. *(Hanako enters.)* Salute!
Toyama *(clutching her).* It's cruel of you. To be late again.
Fujima. We were expecting you at any minute.
Madame. You always look lovely, no matter how often I see you.
(Hanako does not answer. She smilingly removes her gloves.)
Madame *(trying to take the initiative).* Everybody's been waiting so impatiently I don't want to waste another minute. We'll start the fitting at once. *(She examines Hanako from the front and from behind.)* A dressy model really suits your naturally elegant line best, Mrs. Tsukioka. But in a spring suit, you know, I think we should try for a different effect. With your figure you can carry off something sporty. This time I've been really daring in the cut. The lines are simple, divinely simple. Just the barest of pleats on the sides of the waist, as you suggested. Very effective in bringing out the accents. . . . And now, would you mind stepping into the fitting-room? We can have a leisurely cup of coffee afterward.
Kaneko. A love letter came for you, Mrs. Tsukioka. Guess how old the man is who sent it. Twenty? Thirty? Older?

(Hanako holds up one finger.)

Toyama. No, no. He's not a high-school student.
(Hanako with a smile holds up two fingers. The others shake their heads. She holds up one more finger each time until finally, with a look of incredulity on her face, she holds up seven.)
Kaneko. You've guessed it, at last. A blushing seventy. I'm told he's the janitor in the building across the street.
(The Madame, flustered, lowers the blinds. Iwakichi, in the room to the right, stares fixedly at the shut window. During

the interval Kaneko *hands the letter to* Hanako. *She opens it. The others stand behind her and read over her shoulder.)*

Toyama *(reads).* "Please read this thirtieth expression of my love, and take it to your heart," it says. Madame's been lying again. She said there were hundreds of letters. You know, Mrs. Tsukioka, the Madame has embezzled all the previous letters.

Kaneko *(reads).* "My love grows only the stronger as the days go by. To heal the scars of the whip of love which torments my aged body from morn to night, I ask for one, for just one kiss." Isn't that touching? All he wants is one little kiss.

(They all burst into laughter.)

Toyama. Just one kiss? He's very modest in his demands.

Fujima. It really surprises me. The old men nowadays are younger at heart than we are.

Madame. Is that the sort of thing he's been writing? I confess I haven't read any of his other efforts. *(The letter is passed to her.)* Oh, dear. *(Reads)* "That which we call love is an eternal, unending sorrow." Trite, isn't it? He might just as well say: "That which we call vinegar, unlike honey, is an unending source of bitterness."

Kaneko. This old man thinks he's the only one who's suffering. Such conceit is detestable. All of us are suffering in exactly the same way. The only difference is that some people talk about it and others don't.

Fujima. That's because we have self-respect, isn't it?

Toyama. Even I can understand that much. I can't bear that tone which implies that he's the only one who knows real love, and the rest of us are all frivolous and fickle.

Kaneko. I'd be glad to show anyone who's willing to be shown how much repeated suffering we have to endure just in order to fool ourselves, all of us who are living in these depraved times.

Fujima. There's nothing you can do about people who are set in their ways. He must think there are special reserved seats for love.

Toyama. A romanticist.

Madame. Little boys should not interfere in the conversation of grown-ups. The argument has become serious. *(She rings a bell.)* Isn't it enchanting, Mrs. Tsukioka, how heated men get over an argument?

Kaneko *(as if he were delivering a speech).* I believe I may state without fear of contradiction that we are convinced that entities like this old man are abhorrent, and that such entities cannot further be tolerated by us — entities, that is, who believe in genuine feelings. There is not a village, no matter how remote, where the genuine and original Nagasaki sponge cake is not sold. I despise any shopkeeper who would really believe such nonsense and fatuously sell the cake as the genuine article. It is far better to sell it knowing all along that it is fake. That makes the sale a cheat and a fraud, the splendid product of a conscious human mind. We have tongues to recognize the taste of the sponge cake. Our loves begin from the tongue.

Madame. How erotic!

Kaneko. The tongue admits the existence of no "genuine," of no "original." What it depends on is the sense of taste common to all men. The tongue can say: "This tastes good." Its natural modesty forbids it to say more. The "Genuine and original" is merely a label people paste on the wrapping. The tongue confines itself to determining whether or not the sponge cake tastes good.

Shop Assistant *(enters).* Did you ring?

Madame. It wasn't for sponge cake. What was it? Oh yes, please bring five cups of coffee immediately.

Assistant. Yes, Madame.

Kaneko. All questions are relative. Love is the architecture of the emotion of disbelief in genuine articles. That old man, on the other hand, is impure, polluted — he's making fools of us. He is delighted with himself, inflated with pride.

Fujima. I'm afraid what you say is much too difficult for someone like myself, who's never had an education, to follow, but I was told by my teacher that all disputes about who was the senior member of a company or which was the oldest tradition in a dance have nothing whatsoever to do with art. He said that the only true atmosphere for the dance is one where the gesture to the front and the gesture to the rear can be performed in absolute freedom. . . . That old man is so anxious to found a school for himself that he *(Mimes dance action)* . . . one and two and over to the side . . . neglects the free, unconfined realms of the ecstasy of love.

Toyama. And what do you think about all this, Mrs. Tsukioka? It isn't very nice of you to keep so silent. But I suppose it isn't entirely distasteful to receive love letters even from such an old man. Isn't that the case? Say something, laurel of the moon.

Madame. Mrs. Tsukioka had a refined upbringing, and I'm sure she dislikes arguments.

Toyama. But she's very fond of tormenting people all the same.

Madame. That's a taste common to all beautiful women.

Fujima. And one which only becomes beautiful women, they say.

Madame. When it comes to colors, the ones which suit her best are the difficult ones like green.

Kaneko. Those, of course, are the colors she doesn't wear in public. She saves them for her nightgowns, and pretends she doesn't know they become her.

Toyama. I can testify that Mrs. Tsukioka never wears green nightgowns.

Kaneko. You've become increasingly cheeky of late.

Madame. Come, come.

(The Assistant *enters with the coffee. They all drink unhurriedly.)*

(In the room to the right)

Iwakichi. I wonder what's the matter. Why don't they open the curtains? Oh, the suspense. All I could get was just the barest glimpse of her. . . . And I was so sure that tonight she would take pity on me and at least stand at the window and smile at me, like a picture in a frame. . . . But I'm still not giving up hope. . . . No, I won't give up hope.

(In the room to the left)

Kaneko. Well, now.

Fujima. Oops. *(He spills coffee on his lap and wipes it.)*

Kaneko. What is it?

Fujima. Just now as I was drinking my coffee, a fine idea came to me.

Kaneko. I have also been considering what we might do to teach that old man a little lesson. What do you say, Mrs. Tsukioka? In general . . .

Fujima. My plan was . . .

Kaneko *(paying him no attention).* In general, such entities are incapable of seeing the light unless they have once been administered a sound thrashing. We need show him no pity simply because he's an old man. It is essential to make him realize that where he lives is a little room nobody will enter.

Toyama. You mean, human beings won't go in a dog's house?

Kaneko *(recovering his good mood).* Yes, exactly.

Fujima. My plan is this. *(He unfolds the parcel wrapped in purple silk, revealing a small hand drum.)* Do you see this?

Madame. It's a drum, isn't it?

Fujima. It's a prop for my forthcoming dance-play. Oh, since I mentioned the play, I must thank you, Mrs. Tsukioka . . . the tickets. . . . At any rate, about the drum. Shall I beat it for you? *(He beats it.)* You see, it doesn't make the least sound. It looks exactly like a real drum, but instead of a skin, which is essential of course, it's covered with damask.

Toyama. You mean they've invented a drum that doesn't make any noise?

Fujima. No, as I was saying, it's a prop.

Kaneko. And what do you propose to do with it?

Fujima. To attach a note to this drum and throw it into the old man's room. I've had the most wonderful idea about what to write in the note.

Madame. That sounds fascinating. Tell us.

Fujima. In the note we should write: "Please beat this drum." Do you follow me? "Please beat this drum. If the sound of your drum can be heard in this room above the street noises, I will grant your wish." That's all.

Toyama. Excellent idea! That will take the old man down a peg or two.

Kaneko. Don't you think you ought to add: "If the sound doesn't reach me, your wish will not be granted"?

Fujima. There's such a thing as an implied meaning.

Kaneko. In diplomatic correspondence you can't be too careful.

Fujima *(excitedly).* Don't you think it's a good plan, Mrs. Tsukioka? I'll be glad to sacrifice this prop to protect you.

Toyama. For a customer who buys a hundred tickets, what's one drum?

Fujima. I'll thank you not to interpret it in that way. Mrs. Tsukioka, you do agree, don't you? *(Hanako nods smilingly.)*

Madame. It will be a great relief to me too. This will probably be the last day the old man will bother us.

Fujima. Let's have some paper and a pen.

(They set about their preparations with animation. Fujima writes a note to attach to the drum. The Madame *draws the curtains. Hanako is led to the window, which* Kaneko *opens.)*

Kaneko. His room is pitch dark. Are you sure the old man is there?

Madame. The girl who comes as his messenger says that he stares at this window until Mrs. Tsukioka leaves.

Kaneko. Still, I wonder if our voices will reach him.

Toyama. That'll be my responsibility. Oh, doesn't it look pretty up here to see the neon lights everywhere?

Fujima. Who will throw the drum?

Kaneko. I will. I was quite a renowned pitcher in my high-school days.

(He limbers his arm by way of preparation.)

Toyama. Hey! Iwakichi! Open your window!

(The window opens. Iwakichi timidly shows himself.)

Toyama. Can you hear me? We're going to throw you something. Be sure to catch it.

(Iwakichi nods. Kaneko throws the drum. Iwakichi barely gets it. He takes the drum to the desk.)

Iwakichi. What can this mean? She's sent me a drum. She's standing at the window looking at me. It's strange, when she looks straight this way it's all I can do to keep from hiding myself. I wonder if she's always hidden herself from me because I stared too much. . . . Oh, there's a note attached. *(Reads)* At last my wish will be granted! What carries better than the sound of a drum, even above the traffic noise? It must be her elegant way of saying things — she can't pronounce a simple yes, but has to say it in some roundabout manner. . . . Oh, my heart hurts. It's never known such joy before. It's weak, like the stomach of a poor man's child before a feast. It hurts because it's been struck by happiness. . . . They're all waiting in the window over there. It must be for the fun of it. They think it will be amusing to hear an old man play the drum for the first time. . . . Ah, I've a good idea. I'll hang the drum on my laurel tree and beat it there. *(He kneels before the tree.)* Laurel, lovely, dear laurel, forgive me. I'm going to hang the drum in your green hair. Heavy, is it? Just be patient for a while. It becomes you. It becomes you very well, like a big beautiful ornament that has fallen from heaven into your hair. . . . It's all right, isn't it? Even when I begin to beat the drum, I won't shake your leaves. I've never before been so happy before you. Whenever I've seen you I've thought: My unhappiness has made you more beautiful, has made you put forth your leaves more abundantly. And it's true, my laurel, it's true.

Toyama. Hurry up and beat the drum. We're standing in the cold waiting for you.

Iwakichi. All right! I'm going to beat it now, so listen! *(He strikes the drum. It makes no sound. He strikes the other side. It is also silent. He strikes frantically but to no avail.)* It doesn't make a noise. They've given me a drum that doesn't make a noise! I've been made a fool of. I've been played with. (*He sinks to the floor and weeps.*) What shall I do? What shall I do? A refined lady like that—to play such a low trick on me. It's something that should never have happened. It couldn't have happened. (*The people at the window to the left laugh. The window is slammed shut.*) Laugh! Go ahead and laugh! Laugh all you like! . . . You'll still be laughing when you die. You'll be laughing when you rot away. That won't happen to me. People who are laughed at don't die just like that. . . . People who are laughed at don't rot away. (*He opens the window at the back. Climbs out on the window sill. He sits there motionlessly for a minute, sadly staring below. Then he pushes himself over the edge in a crumbling gesture. Shouts from below. Inarticulate cries from the crowd continue awhile.*)

No Mask

Masks, like this one of a young monk dating from the fourteenth century, were worn in No plays.

(*In the room to the left they are all chatting and laughing. They cannot see the window from which the old man committed suicide, and they are unaware what has happened. Suddenly the door opens.*)

Assistant. The janitor from the building across the way has just jumped out of the window and killed himself. (*They get up with confused outcries. Some rush to the window, others run toward the stairs.* Hanako *stands alone rigidly in the center of the stage.*)

(*Late at night. The sky between the two buildings is now full of stars. A clock on a shelf in the room to the left gives forth two delicate chimes. The room is pitch dark. Presently there is a scratching sound of a key in the door. The door opens. A flashlight beam shines in.* Hanako *enters. She wears a half-length coat thrown over the shoulders of her evening gown. In one hand she holds a key, in the other a flashlight. She puts the key in her handbag. She goes to the window, opens it, and stares motionlessly at the window on the right.)*

Hanako *(Her voice is low. She talks as if to someone present.)* I've come. You told me to come and I've come. I slipped out of a party, even though it was the middle of the night. . . . Answer me, please. Aren't you there?
(The window at the back of the room to the right opens. The ghost of Iwakichi *climbs in the window from which he jumped. He walks to the left. The window facing left gradually opens as he approaches it.)*

Hanako. You've come. . . . You've really come.

Iwakichi. I've been going back and forth between your dreams and this room.

Hanako. You summoned me and I am here. But you still do not know me. You don't know how I was able to come.

Iwakichi. Because I drew you here.

Hanako. No. Without human strength no door opens for human beings to pass through.

Iwakichi. Do you intend to deceive even a ghost?

Hanako. Where would I get the strength? My strength was enough only to kill a pitiful old man. And even in that all I did was to nod. I did nothing else. *(Iwakichi does not answer.)* Can you hear me? *(Iwakichi nods.)* My voice carries even when I speak as low as this. But when I talk to people they can't hear me unless I shout. . . . It would have been better if voices had not carried between this room and yours.

Iwakichi. The sky is full of stars. You can't see the moon. The moon has become covered with mud and fallen to earth. I was following the moon when I jumped. You might say that the moon and I committed suicide together.

Hanako *(looking down at the street).* Can you see the corpse of the moon anywhere? I can't. Only the all-night taxis cruising in the streets. There's a policeman walking there. He's stopped. But I don't think that means he's found a corpse. The policeman won't meet anything except the policeman who comes from the opposite direction. Is he a mirror, I wonder?

Iwakichi. Do you think that ghosts meet only ghosts, and the moon meets only the moon?

Hanako. In the middle of the night that's true of everything. *(She lights a cigarette.)*

Iwakichi. I'm not a phantom any more. While I was alive I was a phantom. Now all that remains is what I used to dream about. Nobody can disappoint me any more.

Hanako. From what I can see, however, you still aren't precisely the incarnation of love. I don't mean to criticize your growth of beard or your janitor's uniform or your sweaty undershirt—There's something lacking, something your love needs before it can assume a form. There's insufficient proof that your love in this world was real, if that was the only reason why you died.

Iwakichi. Do you want proof from a ghost? *(He empties his pockets.)* Ghosts don't own anything. I've lost every possession which might have served as proof.

Hanako. I am teeming with proofs. A woman simply crawls with proofs of love. When she has produced the last one, she is full of proofs that the love is gone. It's because women have the proofs that men can make love empty-handed.

Iwakichi. Please don't show me such things.

Hanako. A little while ago I opened the door and came in, didn't I? Where do you suppose I got the key to the door?

Iwakichi. Please don't ask me such things.

Hanako. I stole the key from Madame's pocket. My fingers are very nimble, you know. It gave me great pleasure to discover my skill at pickpocketing has still not left me.

Iwakichi. I understand now. You're afraid of my tenacity, and you're trying to make me hate you. That must be it.

Hanako. Then shall I show you? You gave me a very appropriate name, princess of the moon. I used otherwise to be known by the nickname of Crescent, from a tattoo on my belly. The tattoo of a crescent.

Iwakichi. Ah-h-h.

Hanako. It wasn't that I asked to have it tattooed myself. A man did it, violently. When I drink the crescent turns a bright red, but usually it is pale as a dead man's face.

Iwakichi. Whore! You've made a fool of me twice. Once wasn't enough.

Hanako. Once wasn't enough. Yes, that's right, it wasn't. For our love to be fulfilled, or for it to be destroyed.

Iwakichi. You were poisoned by men who were untrue.

Hanako. That's not so. Men who were untrue molded me.

Iwakichi. I was made a fool of because I was true.

Hanako. That's not so. You were made a fool of because you were old.

(The room to the right becomes red with the wrath of the ghost. The laurel tree on which the drum had been hung appears in the glow.)

Iwakichi. Don't you feel ashamed of yourself? I'll place a curse on you.

Hanako. That doesn't frighten me in the least. I'm strong now. It's because I've been loved.

Iwakichi. By whom?

Hanako. By you.

Iwakichi. Was it the strength of my love that made you tell the truth?

Hanako. Look at me. It's not the real me you love. *(She laughs.)* You tried to place a curse on me. Clumsy men are all like that.

Iwakichi. No, no. I am in love with you, passionately. Everybody in the world of the dead knows it.

Hanako. Nobody knows it in this world.

Iwakichi. Because the drum didn't sound?

Hanako. Yes, because I couldn't hear it.

Iwakichi. It was the fault of the drum. A damask drum makes no noise.

Hanako. It wasn't the fault of the drum that it didn't sound.

Iwakichi. I yearn for you, even now.

Hanako. Even now! You've been dead all of a week.

Iwakichi. I yearn for you. I shall try to make the drum sound.

Hanako. Make it sound. I have come to hear it.

Iwakichi. I will. My love will make a damask drum thunder. *(The ghost of* Iwakichi *strikes the drum. It gives forth a full sound.)* It sounded! It sounded! You heard it, didn't you?

Hanako *(smiling slyly).* I can't hear a thing.

Iwakichi. You can't hear this? It's not possible. Look. I'll strike it once for every letter I wrote you. Once, twice, you can hear it, I know, three, four, the drum has sounded. *(The drum sounds.)*

Hanako. I can't hear it. Where is a drum sounding?

Iwakichi. You can't hear it? You're lying. You can't hear this? Ten, eleven. You can't hear this?

Hanako. I can't. I can't hear any drum.

Iwakichi. It's a lie. *(In a fury)* I won't let you say it—that you can't hear what I can. Twenty, twenty-one. It's sounded.

Hanako. I can't hear it. I can't hear it.

Iwakichi. Thirty, thirty-one, thirty-two. . . . You can't say you don't hear it. The drum is beating. A drum that never should have sounded is sounding.

Hanako. Ah, hurry and sound it. My ears are longing to hear the drum.

Iwakichi. Sixty-six, sixty-seven. . . . Could it possibly be that only my ears can hear the drum?

Hanako *(in despair, to herself).* Ah, he's just the same as living men.

Iwakichi *(in despair, to himself).* Who can prove it—that she hears the drum?

Hanako. I can't hear it. I still can't hear it.

Iwakichi *(weakly).* Eighty-nine, ninety, ninety-one. . . . It will soon be over. Have I only imagined I heard the sound of the drum? *(The drum goes on sounding.)* It's useless. A waste of time. The drum won't sound at all, will it? Beat it and beat it as I may, it's a damask drum.

Hanako. Hurry, strike it so I can hear. Don't give up. Hurry, so it strikes my ears. *(She stretches her hand from the window.)* Don't give up!

Iwakichi. Ninety-four, ninety-five. . . . Completely useless. The drum doesn't make a sound. What's the use of beating a drum that is silent? . . . Ninety-six, ninety-seven. . . .

Farewell, my laurel princess, farewell. . . . Ninety-eight, ninety-nine. . . . Farewell, I've ended the hundred strokes. . . . Farewell.
(The ghost disappears. The beating stops. Hanako *stands alone, an empty look on her face.* Toyama *rushes in excitedly.)*
Toyama. Is that where you've been? Oh, I'm so relieved. . . . We've all been out searching for you. What happened to you? Running off like that in the middle of the night. What happened to you? *(He shakes her.)* Get a hold on yourself.
Hanako *(as in a dream).* I would have heard if he had only struck it once more.

CURTAIN

ABOUT **YUKIO MISHIMA**

Yukio Mishima (yŭ⁄kē ô mē shē⁄mä; 1925–1970) began to write and publish fiction while studying law at Tokyo University. His work explores the sordid side of human nature. He wrote a number of plays, including several *No* dramas, which are highly stylized theatrical presentations that are as much dances as plays. Like his other *No* plays, *The Damask Drum* is based on an earlier play. Mishima's version, however, introduces modern settings and characters and contemporary psychological insights.

RESPONDING

1. *Personal Response* What is your reaction to this play? How does it compare to plays that you have seen or read?

2. *Literary Analysis* In a tragedy, the main character, or *protagonist*, suffers disaster after a significant struggle, but faces his downfall in a noble, heroic way. Does

Iwakichi fit this description of a tragic hero? Why or why not?

3. *Multicultural Connection* Do you think that an informed American audience can appreciate *The Damask Drum* in the same way that a Japanese audience can? (Before answering, you might want to reread the Note on the *No* play on page 431 to review qualities of this kind of drama.) Give reasons for your answer.

LANGUAGE WORKSHOP

Stage Directions *Stage directions,* indicated in italics, provide information about characters and settings in plays. What factual information about time and place do the stage directions that begin "The center of the stage" and end "Evening" (page 432) provide?
1. What additional information about the contrasting settings do these directions provide?
2. How do these two settings reflect the differences between the two main "lovers" in the play?

WRITER'S PORTFOLIO

Write a stage bill for *The Damask Drum* describing its dramatic qualities, its plot, and its theme. You may want to design a cover based on what you think one of the symbolic masks worn by the actors would look like.

Sunday Greens

Rita Dove

She wants to hear
wine pouring.
She wants to taste
change. She wants
pride to roar through
the kitchen till it shines
like straw, she wants

lean to replace
tradition. Ham knocks
in the pot, nothing
but bones, each
with its bracelet
of flesh.

The house stinks
like a zoo in summer,
while upstairs
her man sleeps on.
Robe slung over
her arm and
the cradled hymnal,

she pauses, remembers
her mother in a slip
lost in blues,
and those collards,
wild-eared,
singing.

Sinful City

Jaroslav Seifert

The city of factory owners, boxers, millionaires,
the city of inventors and of engineers,
the city of generals, merchants and patriotic poets
with its black sins has exceeded the bounds of
    God's wrath:
God was enraged.
A hundred times he'd threatened vengeance on the
    town,
a rain of sulphur, fire, thunderbolts hurled down,
and a hundred times he'd taken pity.
For he always remembered what once he had
    promised:
that even for two just men he'd not destroy his city,
and a god's promise should retain its power:

just then two lovers walked across the park,
breathing the scent of hawthorn shrubs in flower.

ABOUT **RITA DOVE**

When she was named Poet Laureate of the United States in 1993, Rita Dove became the first African American to hold the post. Her book-length poem *Thomas and Beulah,* loosely based on the lives of her grandparents, won a Pulitzer Prize in 1987. Born
and raised in Akron, Ohio, she is presently Commonwealth Professor of English at the University of Virginia in Charlottesville. Quoted in *Time* magazine, Dove said, "I think that when a poem moves you, it moves you in a way that leaves you speechless."

ABOUT **JAROSLAV SEIFERT**

A lifelong resident of Prague, Czechoslovakia, Jaroslav Seifert (yä′rô släf′ sī′fĕrt; 1901–1986) worked as a journalist before turning to poetry full-time. He received the Nobel Prize for Literature in 1984, in recognition of his creative genius as well as his resistance to political repression. His life — and over thirty volumes of poems — spanned the eras of Nazi, Stalinist, and communist governments in his native land.
In his eighties he said, "I'm being laughed at for being old and still writing love poems, but I shall write them until the end."

RESPONDING

1. *Personal Response* Which of these poems seems closer to how you feel about love? Explain.

2. *Literary Analysis* *Style* is characterized by, among other things, a writer's tone, word choice, and images. Note that a word like *stinks* suits Dove's poem and "a rain of sulphur" serves Seifert's purpose. Find details in each poem that serve to characterize these poets' different styles.

3. *Multicultural Connection* What does "Sunday Greens" reveal about the speaker's culture?

LANGUAGE WORKSHOP

Alliteration and Onomatopoeia Writers, especially poets, often choose words for the way they sound. *Alliteration*, the repetition of consonant sounds (*berries, boxes, benefit*), and *onomatopoeia*, a word that imitates the sound associated with the thing described (*crackles, hisses, buzz*) are two sound devices. Examine the poems, especially "Sunday Greens," to find alliteration and onomatopoeia. Then tell what the effects of two such sound devices are.

WRITER'S PORTFOLIO

Dove uses images from the kitchen—ham bones knocking in a pot and wild-eared collards. Write a poem, using details from a particular setting. Remember that a gym, a mall, a movie, a bus, or a basketball court can provide a vivid setting for a poem.

Projects

INTERVIEW

With three classmates, conduct an imaginary interview with three characters that appear in this unit to find out their ideas about love. Brainstorm five questions designed to elicit views about subjects such as the best way to meet a partner, arranged marriages, the roles of males and females in marriage, and thwarted love. One of you will take the role of the interviewer, with the other three acting as the characters. Those acting as characters should answer each question the way they think that character would answer, keeping in mind what the selection reveals about that person.

LOVE MOBILE

Prepare a mobile featuring different aspects of love. Include pictures, small objects, cards, captions, song titles, items you have made yourself—and anything else that suggests a facet of love. Add several items suggested by the selections in this unit. Present your mobile to the class. You might want to use appropriate background music for your presentation.

WRITING ABOUT LOVE

Keep a log for one week of all the images relating to love that you encounter. Record images in things you read such as advertisements, signs, greeting cards, and billboards, as well as images from songs, television, or movies. After the week is over, sit down with your log and make some generalizations about love as it is portrayed by the media. Describe your findings in several paragraphs. Include illustrations, if you wish.

Further Reading

Love is one of the most popular topics for writers of all cultures. The works below are samples of the international literature of love.

Alter, Stephen and Dissanayake, Wimal, eds. *The Penguin Book of Modern Indian Short Stories.* Penguin Books, 1989. This is a richly diverse collection of Indian short stories, including some, like "The Weed" by Amrita Pritam, that focus on love.

Esquivel, Laura. *Like Water for Chocolate: A Novel in Monthly Installments, with Recipes, Romances, and Home Remedies.* Doubleday, 1992. Find out what happens to Tita and her unusual family in this novel featuring food as a backdrop for a story of thwarted love.

García Márquez, Gabriel. *Love in the Time of Cholera.* Knopf, 1988. Two memorable characters whose love is postponed until late in their lives prove in this novel that true love never dies and late love is sometimes the best.

McCullough, Frances, ed. *Love Is Like the Lion's Tooth.* HarperCollins, 1984. This international collection for teenagers includes love poems from many cultures and eras that run the gamut from romance, jealousy, and pain to ecstasy.

Neruda, Pablo. *100 Love Sonnets.* University of Texas Press, 1988. Poems written for the poet's wife explore various manifestations and shadings of love.

Wharton, Edith. *Ethan Frome.* Macmillan, 1987. First published in 1911, this classic novel, set against a stark New England background, chronicles a tragic love triangle.

The Triumph of the Spirit

There are many kinds of triumphs. The dramatic ones — the winning of a Nobel Prize or the overthrow of a dictator — become international news. But the everyday triumphs are chronicled on a smaller scale — in family albums, in diaries, through anecdotes, or simply in proud recollections. Big or small, these triumphs bear testimony that the human spirit can not only survive obstacles but overcome them.

The Rebellion of the Magical Rabbits

WHEN THE WOLVES conquered the land of the rabbits, the first thing the leader of the pack did was to proclaim himself King. The second was to announce that the rabbits had ceased to exist. Now and forever it would be forbidden to even mention their name.

Just to be on the safe side, the new Wolf King went over every book in his realm with a big black pencil, crossing out words and tearing out pictures of cottontails until he was satisfied that not a trace of his enemies remained.

But an old gray fox who was his counselor brought bad news.

"The birds, Your Wolfiness, insist that they have seen some . . . some of those creatures. From on high."

"So how come I don't see anything from way up here, on my throne?" asked the Wolf.

"In times like these," answered the fox, "people have got to see to believe."

"Seeing is believing? Bring me that monkey who takes photos, the one who lives nearby. I'll teach those birds a lesson."

The monkey was old and weak.

"What can the Wolf of all Wolves want with me?" he asked, looking at his wife and daughter.

The little girl had an answer. "He must want you to take a picture of the rabbits, Dad."

"Quiet, quiet," said her mother. "Rabbits don't exist."

But the little monkey knew that rabbits did exist. It was true that, since the howling wolves had invaded the country, the rabbits no longer came to visit her as they had before. But in her dreams she continued hearing the green rain of their voices singing nearby, reflecting in her head as if she were a pond under the moonlight, and when she awoke there was always a small gift beside her bed. Walls and closed doors were like water for the rabbits.

"That's why I sleep well," said the little girl. "That's why that General Wolf must need the photo. To keep nightmares away. You'll bring me a picture of them someday, won't you, Dad?"

The monkey felt fear crawl up and down his fur. "'Send this little girl to her room,'" he told his wife, "until she understands that there are certain things we just don't talk about."

The King of the Wolves was not in the best of moods when the monkey came in. "You're late. And I'm in a hurry. I need photographs of each important act in my life. And all my acts, let me tell you, are supremely important. . . . Can you guess what we're going to do with those pictures? You can't? We're going to put one on every street, inside every bush, in every home. I'll be there, watching each citizen with my very own eyes. You'd better pity those who don't have the latest events of my life hung up on their walls. And you know who is going to distribute each picture? You don't know?"

The monkey was trembling so hard that no words came out.

"The birds, ugly monkey. Now they'll bite their own beaks before they twitter around with any nonsense about rabbits. And we'll tie an endless cord to their legs, so they can't escape. Understand?"

The monkey understood so well that his trembling paw immediately clicked the shutter of the camera, taking the first picture.

"Go," roared the Wolf, "and develop it. I want it on every wall in the kingdom."

But when the photographer returned some minutes later, he did not dare to enter the throne room, and asked one of the soldiers to call the counselor. Without a word, the monkey passed him the picture he had just taken.

The fox blinked once, and then blinked again. In a corner of the photo, far from the muscular, ferocious figure of the King — who had both arms up in the air as if he had just won a boxing championship — appeared what was without any doubt the beginning of an ear, the ear of someone who had insolently come to spy on the whole ceremony.

"You blind monkey!" fumed the fox. "How come you didn't notice that this . . . this thing was there? Can't you focus that camera of yours?"

"If it could get into the picture," the monkey answered, "it was because you and your guards let it get close."

"It won't happen again," the counselor promised. "Rub out that . . . ear before his Wolfishness finds out."

From his bag, the monkey took out a special liquid that he used to erase any detail that might bother a client. The intruding ear began to disappear as if it had never existed.

THE KING OF THE WOLVES was pleased with the portrait and ordered it sent all over the realm. Two hours later he personally went on an inspection tour to make sure that not a window was without a picture of his large, gleaming, dangerous grin. "Not bad," he said, "but this photo is already getting old. People should see my latest deeds. Take another. Quick. Show me scaring these pigeons — right away. And bring it to me immediately. You took too long last time."

But the monkey wasn't able to comply this time either. Once again he had the counselor called secretly.

"Again?" asked the fox. "It happened again?"

Except that now it was worse than an indiscreet ear. A whole corner of the new picture was filled with the unmistakable face of . . . yes, there was no denying it, of a rabbit winking an eye in open defiance of the nearby guards.

"We've got to tighten security," muttered the fox. "Meanwhile, erase that invader."

"Wonderful," shouted the King Wolf when finally he was given the picture. "Look at the frightened faces of the pigeons trying to escape. I want a million copies. I want them on milk cartons and on the coupons inside cereals. . . . Onward. Onward. Let's go and smash up a dam. Come on, monkey. Fame awaits us both."

The beavers had been working summer and winter for three years on a beautiful dam that would allow them to irrigate a distant valley.

The Wolf of Wolves climbed a tree. "I want you to shoot the precise moment when my feet crash into the middle of the dam, monkey. If you miss the shot, next time I'll fall on top of you and then I'll have to get myself another photographer. Are you ready?"

Not only was the monkey ready, so was the counselor. The fox was breathing down the old monkey's back, peering over his shoulder, watching, listening. Nothing could escape those vigilant, darting eyes. Not a fuzzy ear would dare to make its appearance.

So neither the monkey nor the fox could believe it when, a bit later, they saw at the bottom of the picture a rabbit lolling on his side as if he were relaxing at a picnic. Next to him, another rabbit had raised her paw and was boldly thumbing her nose.

"This is an epidemic," said the fox. "And let me tell you, our lives are in danger."

"Let's start erasing," the monkey said wearily.

"You erase. I'll get a squadron of buzzards and hawks. They see all animals, even the quick and the small."

His Wolfhood the King yelped with pleasure when he saw the picture. It portrayed him at the exact moment he was breaking the backbone of the beavers' dam. In the distance, families of beavers could be seen fleeing. There was not a single shadow of a rabbit.

"Send it out! A strong country is an educated country, a country that always is tuned in to the latest news. What are we going to do now for some fun?"

"We could rest," the monkey suggested, his paws peeling from the harsh erasing fluid.

The Wolf looked at him as if he were a stone.

"And who asked you for an opinion? I'm in charge here. That's why I was born with these teeth, and you'd better pray you never have to feel them crunching your bones. Onward. We are the future, the morrow, the dawn! We'll go on until there's no more light."

BUT IN EACH NEW PHOTO, the rabbits became more plentiful, audacious, and saucy. His Wolfinity the King destroyed sugar mills, shook squirrels out of their trees and hid their nuts, stripped ducks of their feathers, drove sheep off cliffs, drilled holes in the road so that horses would break their legs, unveiled new cages and old dungeons . . . and the more his frightening yellow eyes flickered, the more innumerable were the rabbits of every color that frolicked in the margins of the photographs. Even the clouds seemed full of fur and whiskers and cottontails.

"Hey, birdie," jeered the Supreme Wolf, grabbing a swallow about to fly off with a bag overflowing with pictures, "what tune are you singing now, featherhead? Who's that in the center of the picture, huh? Who's the King?"

The bird held his beak tight, so that not even a peep could come out.

"Lights, camera, action, monkey!" the Monarch demanded. "Call this: WOLF KING RECEIVES HOMAGE FROM A MESSENGER."

The monkey obeyed, but could hardly hide his despair. Though nobody ever saw the rebels when the photos were taken, they were always there when it was time to show them, nibbling lettuce at the very feet of the biggest and baddest of wolves.

"Exterminate them," hissed the fox, who had ordered a stronger, more acid liquid. "Don't leave even a twitch of a nose."

But the pictures were beginning to look defective. There were blank spaces everywhere. The monkey knew that the only solution was to convince His Wolfiness to sit up high on an elevated throne. Since rabbits live underground, they wouldn't be able to wiggle their way into the frame of the photograph.

The King, fortunately, was delighted with the idea. "I'll look more impressive up here. And I can keep an eye on those birds. What a surprise for my subjects when they find my new picture at breakfast, right? So get here early, monkey, do you hear?"

When the exhausted monkey dragged himself home, his fingers hurting from the terrible liquid, the latest photograph of the King had just been plastered on the front door of his house. Just at that moment, a soldier was leaving.

"No cause for alarm, Mr. Monkey," the soldier laughed. "Just a routine inspection to see if anybody is sabotaging his Wolfhood's pictures."

The monkey rushed inside. "Our daughter? Is she all right? Did she say anything?"

"I'm fine, Dad," the little girl said. "Those wolves are gone, aren't they? And you brought me that special photo — you know, the one I asked you for?"

The monkey felt as if from all four walls, from all four pictures on the four walls, the eight eyes of the Biggest of Wolves were watching each word he might say.

"Let your father rest," said her mother. "The only pictures he's taken are the ones we've put up in the house, like good citizens."

But the next morning, the monkey was awakened by his child's kiss. She put her lips near his ears and whispered something so softly that only he could hear it: "Thank you. It's the best present you could ever give me. You're a magical dad."

"Thanks? Thanks for what?"

She motioned almost imperceptibly toward the wall from which the photo of the Wolf King ruled. Her father opened his eyes wide. In one of the corners of that picture, like the sun rising over the mountains, he could just glimpse, in the act of making their gradual but glorious appearance, a pair of, yes, of course, a pair of soft, pink, pointed ears.

The monkey jumped out of bed. The liquid he had applied did not work permanently. The rabbits had needed the whole night to sneak back into the pictures, but somehow they had managed it.

"I think they knew I was scared," the little girl murmured, "and came to see me while I slept."

Her father dressed in less time than it takes a chill to run up a spine and scurried to the palace without stopping for breakfast. Was this happening only at their house or could the same invasion have taken place everywhere in the kingdom? If so, how could the rabbits be removed from so many portraits?

His Wolfiness was still in bed, but the counselor was already pacing about, biting the tip of his tail. "It's a plague," he said, "but, fortunately, it is already under control. The offending pictures have been burned. As for you . . ."

"I swear that I—"

"Not a word from you, interrupted the fox. "It's lucky those creatures don't exist. Imagine the damage they'd cause if they really existed. But enough talk. What we need now is a new photo to replace the ones that are contaminated."

They rushed to the new throne, which was now set up on top of four colossal wooden legs, out of reach of the spreading virus of the mischievous ears.

"I want two shots," His Wolfhood demanded, "one of me ascending my throne and another of me sitting on it, enjoying the fresh air. And send them abroad too, so those silly foreign papers will stop attacking me."

This time, when the photos were developed, there was no trouble. Not so much as a carrot of a sign of a rabbit.

"Didn't I tell you? Didn't I tell you they don't exist?" The counselor was jubilant. "It was just a matter of your focusing the camera properly."

FOR THE NEXT FEW DAYS, there were no more unpleasant surprises. The Wolf of Wolves felt happy, high above the heads of the multitude. He let his lieutenants run things while he posed for pictures giving commands, delivering speeches, signing laws. He examined the shots carefully, however. "Congratulations," he said. "You're being more careful, monkey. It seems you're learning your trade just by being near me. I don't see any more of those whitish spots that spoiled my first pictures."

But one morning, the monkey was again awakened by his daughter's voice. "They're back, Dad," she whispered in his ears. "Those pictures you took sure are magical."

In one set of photos, at the foot of the towering throne, a small army of rabbits was biting, chewing, and splintering the wooden legs. Their teeth worked patiently, and they stopped their work only now and again to wave to the spectators.

The counselor was waiting. The monkey could see his fur ruffling and swelling like a swarm of bees.

"How many this time?" the monkey asked.

"The photos are being taken care of," the fox said grimly. "But the birds have got wind of what happened, and now they're telling everyone that those . . . those awful animals exist. And his Wolfinity is beginning to suspect something. 'Why are those birds so happy, so shrill?' he asks. I told him they're just a bunch of featherbrains, full of hot air."

"What did he answer?" asked the monkey.

The King had announced that balloons are full of hot air too and that they could be popped. If those birds didn't keep quiet, he would make them disappear.

But the counselor had another idea: The Wolf of All Wolves should tie a recording of one of his latest speeches around the necks of the birds. They would have to carry not only the photos, but also the King's words, all over his kingdom. Nobody would be able to hear any of their songs.

"Hearing is believing," trumpeted his Wolfiness. "We'll give them a taste of some hymns, some military marches, some lessons in history, economics, and ethics."

The old monkey's life became unbearable. Not even the recorded howls of the King and his chorus of warlike beasts could stop the timid appearance, in the next photo, of an inquisitive nose, a pair of furry ears, some white whiskers, and something hungry gnawing away at the legs of the throne.

The fox replaced the chief officer of the royal guard with a boa constrictor straight from the jungle of a neighboring country. He put small, hundred-eyed spiders in strategic places throughout the Wolfdom. One day he ordered half the population to shave off their shiny fur so that no spy could hide in it. To punish the cows, accused of uttering subversive moos, he commanded that their milk be soured. And finally, he raised the volume of the King's broadcasts. But in spite of these efforts, there began to be heard a persistent, rowdy, merry sound, the clicking of thousands of tiny teeth, the burbling of an underground stream.

The monkey felt dizzy.

The rhythm was maddening. During the night, the legs of the throne, spindlier by the minute, were reinforced grudgingly by woodpeckers who would have much preferred to take the throne apart. The monkey had to rely on every photographic trick of the trade, now erasing, now trimming with scissors, disguising ears so they looked like shadows and shadows so they looked like wallpaper. He even began using old portraits of the King, trying to make them seem like recent ones.

Until one night, when it was very late, the old monkey was awakened by an angry hand that shook him from his slumber. It was the counselor, flanked by a fierce escort of soldiers. The Lord Wolf had sent for him.

The whole house was up by now. The little girl watched her father begin dressing.

"Say hello to his Foxcellency," said the monkey.

"Dad," she said, and it was astonishing that she did not speak in a low, fearful voice anymore, as if the armed guards were not even there, "today you've got to bring me that picture I asked for."

"A picture?" The counselor showed interest. "A picture of what, of whom?"

The child continued to ignore him. "Today you'll bring me a photo of the rabbits, right, Dad? For my wall?"

The mother monkey touched the girl's head as if she had fever. "Hasn't your father told you that rabbits don't exist? Haven't we shut you up in your room for telling lies?"

"They exist," the girl announced. "Everybody knows they exist."

"Just as I suspected," said the counselor. "Let's go."

The Wolfiest of Wolves was waiting for them atop his throne. Around each leg, hundreds of guards and snakes kept watch.

"Monkey, you are a traitor," thundered the King. "Your photos are being used by people who say that strange and malicious creatures—who are nonexistent as everyone knows—are conspiring this very night to overthrow my rule. They say my throne trembles and my dynasty will topple. Is there any evidence that my throne trembles? Does anybody dare say so?" And he yowled like a hundred jet fighters in the air. "We'll start by making a recording of that sound. And you, you monkey, you're going to help me stamp out these rumors. Touching is believing. You are going to make me a wide-angle, three-dimensional picture that will cover all walls. In color. Because I am going to crown myself Emperor of the Wolves, the Supreme Wolferor. And if a single wretched rabbit shows its snout, I will make you eat the photos, one by one, a million of them, and then I'll eat you and not only you, but your wife and your daughter, and all the monkeys in this country. Now. Take that picture."

The monkey stuck his quaking head under the black cloth behind his camera and focused on the throne. He let out a little moan. Up till then, the rabbits had appeared only later, when the picture was developed. But here they were now, directly in front of his lens, ungovernable and carefree, gnawing away, biting not only the wood of the throne, but also the swords of the astonished guards and the very rattles of the rattlesnakes.

"What's the matter?" bellowed the future Wolferor, who was not looking downward so his profile would be perfect for posterity.

The monkey moved the camera nearer the throne, hoping the rabbit army would not come out in the picture. The rabbits moved faster than he did. They were clambering up the legs, one on top of the other as if they were monkeys or birds. The soldiers tried to frighten them away in silence, unwilling to attract the attention of the King, but the invaders were too agile. The Wolves kept bumping into one another and hitting each other over the head. The monkey realized that a contingent of birds had arrived from above, winging freely through the air, without a cord tied to them or a recording.

"Hurry up!" ordered the Wolf of all Wolves.

The monkey closed his eyes very tightly. It was better not to witness what was going to happen. At the very moment he clicked the shutter, he heard a deafening noise. He knew what he was going to see when he opened his eyes, but still could not believe it: Like an old elm tree rotten to the core, the throne had come crashing to the ground along with the King of Wolves, guards, snakes, counselor, and all. The monkey blinked. There at the foot of his tripod lay the Biggest, Baddest, the Most Boastful Wolf in the Universe. His ribs were broken, his black fur was torn by the fall, his yellow eyes were reddened, and he was wailing in pain.

"Monkey," squeaked the would-be Wolferor of the World, "this picture . . . you have my permission not to publish it."

At that moment, all the lights in the palace went out. The monkey was paralyzed. He did not know where to go. Then, as if someone in the darkness were suddenly shining a light on a pathway, he knew what he must do. He grabbed his camera and his bag, and clutching them to his chest like a treasure, he fled.

His daughter was waiting for him at the door of the house.

"Wait," he said to her. "Wait, I've brought you something." And without another word, he raced into his darkroom to develop the last picture as quickly as possible.

When he came out a few minutes later, his daughter and wife were standing on chairs, taking down the pictures of the Wolf King.

"Here," the old monkey said to his daughter, blinking in the bright light. "Here, this is the picture you've been asking for all this time. I've finally brought you your present."

"Thanks, Dad," the little girl said. "But I don't need it anymore."

She pointed around the room and toward the street and across the fields where the sun was beginning to rise.

The world was full of rabbits.

ABOUT **ARIEL DORFMAN**

Ariel Dorfman, an acclaimed Chilean author and human rights activist, is Research Professor of Literature and Latin American Studies at Duke University. Many of his works, including *The Empire's Old Clothes* and *Máscara*, have been translated into English. Plays such as *Death and the Maiden* have been presented in the United States.

RESPONDING

1. *Personal Response* What do you think the rabbits represent in this story?

2. *Literary Analysis* This story is a *fable*. Do you think that the lesson it teaches would have been more effective or less so had Dorfman written an essay instead? Explain.

3. *Multicultural Analysis* This story describes the events that led to the fall of a dictatorship. Mention real-life parallels of fallen dictators and tell what caused their downfall.

LANGUAGE WORKSHOP

Direct Address In *direct address,* the name of the person spoken to is set off from the rest of the sentence with commas: "No cause for alarm, Mr. Monkey. . . ." "The birds, Your Wolfiness, insist they have seen. . . ." Add commas where needed in the following sentences.

1. "He must want you to take a picture of the rabbits Dad."
2. "Come on Monkey."
3. "So get here early Monkey do you hear?"

WRITER'S PORTFOLIO

Think about a problem or injustice that exists in the world, such as hunger, unemployment, homelessness, war, or censorship. Then think of a possible solution to this problem and consider how you could present your ideas in a fable. Make a brief outline and write your fable in several paragraphs.

Elegy for the Giant Tortoises

Margaret Atwood

Let others pray for the passenger pigeon,
the dodo, the whooping crane, the eskimo:
everyone must specialize.

I will confine myself to a meditation
upon the giant tortoises
withering finally on a remote island.

I concentrate in subway stations,
in parks, I can't quite see them,
they move to the peripheries of my eyes

but on the last day they will be there;
already the event
like a wave travelling shapes vision:

on the road where I stand they will materialize,
plodding past me in a straggling line
awkward without water

their small heads pondering
from side to side, their useless armour
sadder than tanks and history,

in their closed gaze ocean and sunlight paralysed,
lumbering up the steps, under the archways
toward the square glass altars

where the brittle gods are kept,
the relics of what we have destroyed,
our holy and obsolete symbols.

Still I Rise

Maya Angelou

You may write me down in history
With your bitter, twisted lies,

You may trod me in the very dirt
But still, like dust, I'll rise.

Does my sassiness upset you?
Why are you beset with gloom?
'Cause I walk like I've got oil wells
Pumping in my living room.

Just like moons and like suns,
With the certainty of tides,
Just like hopes springing high,
Still I'll rise.

Did you want to see me broken?
Bowed head and lowered eyes?
Shoulders falling down like teardrops,
Weakened by my soulful cries.

Does my haughtiness offend you?
Don't you take it awful hard
'Cause I laugh like I've got gold mines
Diggin' in my own back yard.

You may shoot me with your words,
You may cut me with your eyes,
You may kill me with your hatefulness,
But still, like air, I'll rise.

Out of the huts of history's shame
I rise

Up from a past that's rooted in pain
I rise
I'm a black ocean, leaping and wide,
Welling and swelling I bear in the tide.

Leaving behind nights of terror and fear
I rise
Into a daybreak that's wondrously clear
I rise
Bringing the gifts that my ancestors gave,
I am the dream and the hope of the slave.
I rise
I rise
I rise.

Women on the Road
to Pine Gap

Wendy Poussard

Australia's best-kept dead-end road
leads through the desert
to a barbed wire fence.
Around the corner, past the gates,
inside a clutch of giant perspex balls,
space war computers
keep the deadly secrets
of another country.
A grid prevents the entry
of unauthorised cows
and lines of police
stand on the alert,
anticipating an attack on war
by women.

Women on the dead-end road
with drums and banners

dance for survival
in the face of violence.
Women disturb the orderly conduct
of the earth's destruction,
singing "no more war!"

ABOUT **MARGARET ATWOOD**

Born in Ottawa, Ontario, in 1939,
Margaret Atwood is a prolific novelist and
poet whose works explore, among other
things, the tensions between art and life.
Some of her best-known works, including
The Handmaid's Tale, focus on women —
their suffering and isolation, along with their resourceful measures
to improve their lives.

ABOUT **MAYA ANGELOU**

Born in St. Louis in 1928, Maya Angelou (än′jə lü) has been a
poet, playwright, composer, singer, and stage performer, among
other things. For her outstanding contribu-
tions to American literature, she has
received many honorary degrees and
the applause of the whole nation on
January 20, 1993, when she delivered
her poem, "On the Pulse of Morning," at
President Clinton's inauguration. Angelou
is currently Reynolds Professor at Wake Forest University in
Winston-Salem, North Carolina. Her autobiography, *I Know Why
the Caged Bird Sings,* has become a classic.

ABOUT **WENDY POUSSARD**

Wendy Poussard was born in 1943 in Melbourne, Australia.
She has been executive officer of the International Women's

Development Agency, which sponsors
women's political and community activities
in many nations. Poussard has written for
television and radio as well as print media.
Along with her poetry, she writes articles
and songs.

RESPONDING

1. *Personal Response* Which poem do you think best
expresses the theme "Triumph of the Spirit"? Why?

2. *Literary Analysis* Compare the *tone* in each of these
poems.

3. *Multicultural Connection* Angelou and Poussard both
include cultural and historical details in their poems. In
what respects can women influence historical events,
according to these poems?

LANGUAGE WORKSHOP

Compound Words All three poets use *compound words*
such as *gold mines, dead-end,* and *archways.* Note that
such words may be written as two separate words,
hyphenated, or one word. When you are unsure how
to write a compound word, consult a dictionary.

Think of two compound words that are written as
two words like *gold mine,* two that are written with a
hyphen such as *dead-end,* and two that are written as
one word such as *archways.* Check a dictionary to see if
you have written these compounds correctly.

WRITER'S PORTFOLIO

One of the poets observes that women who oppose war
"disturb the orderly conduct of the earth's destruction."
Do you think that women are more opposed to war than
men are? Do you consider it more "natural" for men to
partake in combat than women? Who should be allowed
to fight? Write an essay expressing your thoughts.

The Miracle

LIKE ALL PEOPLE who have nothing, I
lived on dreams. With nothing but my longing for love, I
burned my way through stone walls till I got to America.
And what happened to me when I became an American is
more than I can picture before my eyes, even in a dream.

I was a poor Melamid's daughter in Savel, Poland. In
my village, a girl without a dowry was a dead one. The only
kind of a man that would give a look on a girl without
money was a widower with a dozen children, or someone
with a hump or on crutches.

There was the village water-carrier with red, teary eyes,
and warts on his cracked lip. There was the janitor of the
bath-house, with a squash nose, and long, black nails with
all the dirt of the world under them. Maybe one of these
uglinesses might yet take pity on me and do me the favor to
marry me. I shivered and grew cold through all my bones at
the thought of them.

Like the hunger for bread was my hunger for love. My
life was nothing to me. My heart was empty. Nothing I did
was real without love. I used to spend nights crying on my
pillow, praying to God: "I want love! I want love! I can't
live—I can't breathe without love!"

And all day long I'd ask myself: "Why was I born?
What is the use of dragging on day after day, wasting
myself eating, sleeping, dressing? What is the meaning of
anything without love?" And my heart was so hungry I

couldn't help feeling and dreaming that somehow, somewhere, there must be a lover waiting for me. But how and
where could I find my lover was the one longing that
burned in my heart by day and by night.

Then came the letter from Hanneh Hayyeh, Zlata's
daughter, that fired me up to go to America for my lover.

"America is a lover's land," said
Hanneh Hayyeh's letter. "In America
millionaires fall in love with poorest
girls. Matchmakers are out of style,
and a girl can get herself married to a
man without the worries for a dowry."

"God from the world!" began
knocking my heart. "How grand to
live where the kind of a man you get
don't depend on how much money your father can put
down! If I could only go to America! There—there waits
my lover for me."

That letter made a holiday all over Savel. The butcher,
the grocer, the shoemaker, everybody stopped his work and
rushed to our house to hear my father read the news from
the Golden Country.

"Stand out your ears to hear my great happiness,"
began Hanneh Hayyeh's letter. "I, Hanneh Hayyeh, will
marry myself to Solomon Cohen, the boss from the shirtwaist factory, where all day I was working sewing on buttons. If you could only see how the man is melting away his
heart for me! He kisses me after each step I walk. The only
wish from his heart is to make me for a lady. Think only, he
is buying me a piano! I should learn piano lessons as if I
were from millionaires."

Fire and lightning burst through the crowd. "Hanneh
Hayyeh a lady!" They nudged and winked one to the other
as they looked on the loose fatness of Zlata, her mother, and
saw before their eyes Hanneh Hayyeh, with her thick, red
lips, and her shape so fat like a puffed-out barrel of yeast.

"In America is a law called 'ladies first,' " the letter
went on. "In the cars the men must get up to give their seats
to the women. The men hold the babies on their hands and

carry the bundles for the women, and even help with the dishes. There are not enough women to go around in America. And the men run after the women, and not like in Poland, the women running after the men."

Gewalt! What an excitement began to burn through the whole village when they heard of Hanneh Hayyeh's luck!

The ticket agents from the ship companies seeing how Hanneh Hayyeh's letter was working like yeast in the air for America, posted up big signs by all the market fairs: "Go to America, the New World. Fifty rubles a ticket."

"Fifty rubles! Only fifty rubles! And there waits your lover!" cried my heart.

Oi weh! How I was hungering to go to America after that! By day and by night I was tearing and turning over the earth, how to get to my lover on the other side of the world.

"Nu, Zalmon?" said my mother, twisting my father around to what I wanted. "It's not so far from sense what Sara Reisel is saying. In Savel, without a dowry, she had no chance to get a man, and if we got to wait much longer she will be too old to get one anywhere."

"But from where can we get together the fifty rubles?" asked my father. "Why don't it will itself in you to give your daughter the moon?"

I could no more think on how to get the money than they. But I was so dying to go, I felt I could draw the money out from the sky.

One night I could not fall asleep. I lay in the darkness and stillness, my wild, beating heart on fire with dreams of my lover. I put out my hungry hands and prayed to my lover through the darkness: "Oh, love, love! How can I get the fifty rubles to come to you?"

In the morning I got up like one choking for air. We were sitting down to eat breakfast, but I couldn't taste nothing. I felt my head drop into my hands from weakness.

Culture Notes

Saifer Torah and the candlesticks Torah refers to the first five books of the Hebrew scriptures; the candlesticks are lighted for Sabbath services. p. 483

Sabbath the seventh day of the week, Saturday, observed as the day of rest and religious observance among the Jews (and some Christian groups), p. 483

"Why don't you try to eat something?" begged my mother, going over to me.

"Eat?" I cried, jumping up like one mad. "How can I eat? How can I sleep? How can I breathe in this deadness? I want to go to America. I *must* go, and I *will* go!"

My mother began wringing her hands. "Oi weh! Mine heart! The knife is on our neck. The landlord is hollering for the unpaid rent, and it wills itself in you America?"

"Are you out of your head?" cried my father.

"What are you dreaming of golden hills on the sky? How can we get together the fifty rubles for a ticket?"

I stole a look at Yosef, my younger brother. Nothing that was sensible ever laid in his head to do; but if there was anything wild, up in the air that willed itself in him, he could break through stone walls to get it. Yosef gave a look around the house. Everything was old and poor, and not a thing to get money on—nothing except father's Saifer Torah—the Holy Scrolls—and mother's silver candlesticks, her wedding present from our grandmother.

"Why not sell the Saifer Torah and the candlesticks?" said Yosef.

Nobody but my brother would have dared to breathe such a thing.

"What? A Jew sell the Saifer Torah or the Sabbath candlesticks?" My father fixed on us his burning eyes like flaming wells. His hands tightened over his heart. He couldn't speak. He just looked on the Saifer Torah, and then on us with a look that burned like live coals on our naked bodies. "What?" he gasped. "Should I sell my life, my soul from generation and generation? Sell my Saifer Torah? Not if the world goes under!"

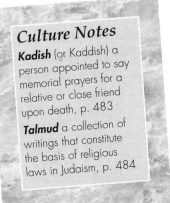

There was a stillness of thunder about to break. Everybody heard everybody's heart beating.

"Did I live to see this black day?" moaned my father, choking from quick breathing. "Mine own son, mine Kadish—mine Kadish tells me to sell the Holy Book that our forefathers shed rivers of blood to hand down to us."

"What are you taking it so terrible?" said my brother. "Doesn't it stand in the Talmud that to help marry his daughter a man may sell the holiest thing—even the Holy Book?"

"*Are there miracles in America?* Can she yet get there a man at her age and without a dowry?"

"If Hanneh Hayyeh, who is older than Sara Reisel and not half as good-looking," said my brother, "could get a boss from a factory, then whom cannot Sara Reisel pick out? And with her luck all of us will be lifted over to America."

My father did not answer. I waited, but still he did not answer.

At last I burst out with all the tears choking in me for years: "Is your old Saifer Torah that hangs on the wall dearer to you than I should marry? The Talmud tells you to sell the holiest thing to help marry your daughter, but you—you love yourself more than your own child!"

Then I turned to my mother. I hit my hands on the table and cried in a voice that made her tremble and grow frightened: "Maybe you love your silver candlesticks more than your daughter's happiness? To whom can I marry myself here, I ask you, only—to the bath janitor, to the water-carrier? I tell you I'll kill myself if you don't help me get away! I can't stand no more this deadness here. I must get away. And you must give up everything to help me get away. All I need is a chance. I can do a million times better than Hanneh Hayyeh. I got a head. I got brains. I feel I can marry myself to the greatest man in America."

My mother stopped crying, took up the candlesticks from the mantelpiece and passed her hands over them. "It's like a piece from my flesh," she said. "We grew up with this, you children and I, and my mother and my mother's mother. This and the Saifer Torah are the only things that shine up the house for the Sabbath."

She couldn't go on, her words choked in her so. I am seeing yet how she looked, holding the candlesticks in her hands, and her eyes that she turned on us. But then I didn't see anything but to go to America.

She walked over to my father, who sat with his head in his hands, stoned with sadness. "Zalmon!" she sobbed. "The blood from under my nails I'll give away, only my child should have a chance to marry herself well. I'll give away my candlesticks — "

Even my brother Yosef's eyes filled with tears, so he quick jumped up and began to whistle and move around. "You don't have sell them," he cried, trying to make it light in the air. "You can pawn them by Moisheh Itzek, the usurer, and as soon as Sara Reisel will get herself married, she'll send us the money to get them out again, and we'll yet live to take them over with us to America."

I never saw my father look so sad. He looked like a man from whom the life is bleeding away. "I'll not-stand myself against your happiness," he said, in a still voice. "I only hope this will be your luck and that you'll get married quick, so we could take out the Saifer Torah from the pawn."

IN LESS THAN A WEEK the Saifer Torah and the candlesticks were pawned and the ticket bought. The whole village was ringing with the news that I am going to America. When I walked in the street people pointed on me with their fingers as if I were no more the same Sara Reisel.

Everybody asked me different questions.

"Tell me how it feels to go to America? Can you yet sleep nights like other people?"

"When you'll marry yourself in America, will you yet remember us?"

God from the world! That last Friday night before I went to America! Maybe it is the last time we are together was in everybody's eyes. Everything that happened seemed so different from all other times. I felt I was getting ready to tear my life out from my body.

Without the Saifer Torah the house was dark and empty. The sun, the sky, the whole heaven shined from that Holy Book on the wall, and when it was taken out it left an aching emptiness on the heart, as if something beautiful passed out of our lives.

I yet see before me my father in the Rabbi's cap, with eyes that look far away into things; the way he sang the prayer over the wine when he passed around the glass for every one to give a sip. The tears rolled out from my little sister's eyes down her cheeks and fell into the wine. On that my mother, who was all the time wiping her tears, burst out crying. "Shah! Shah!" commanded my father, rising up from his chair and beginning to walk around the room. "It's Sabbath night, when every Jew should be happy. Is this the way you give honor to God on His one day that He set aside for you?"

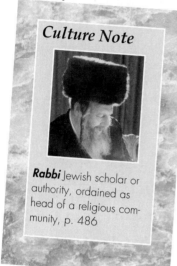

Culture Note

Rabbi Jewish scholar or authority, ordained as head of a religious community, p. 486

On the next day, that was Sabbath, father as if held us up in his hands, and everybody behaved himself. A stranger coming in couldn't see anything that was going on, except that we walked so still and each one by himself, as if somebody dying was in the air over us.

On the going-away morning, everybody was around our house waiting to take me to the station. Everybody wanted to give a help with the bundles. The moving along to the station was like a funeral. Nobody could hold in their feelings any longer. Everybody fell on my neck to kiss me, as if it was my last day on earth.

"Remember you come from Jews. Remember to pray every day," said my father, putting his hands over my head, like in blessing on the day of Atonement.

"Only try that we should be together soon again," were the last words from my mother as she wiped her eyes with the corner of her shawl.

"Only don't forget that I want to study, and send for me as quick as you marry yourself," said Yosef, smiling good-bye with tears in his eyes.

As I saw the train coming, what wouldn't I have given to stay back with the people in Savel forever! I wanted to cry out: "Take only away my ticket! I don't want any more America! I don't want any more my lover!"

But as soon as I got into the train, although my eyes were still looking back to the left-behind faces, and my ears were yet hearing the good-byes and the partings, the thoughts of America began stealing into my heart. I was thinking how soon I'd have my lover and be rich like Hanneh Hayyeh. And with my luck, everybody was going to be happy in Savel. The dead people will stop dying and all the sorrows and troubles of the world will be wiped away with my happiness.

I didn't see the day. I didn't see the night. I didn't see the ocean. I didn't see the sky. I only saw my lover in America, coming nearer and nearer to me, till I could feel eyes bending on me so near that I got frightened and began to tremble. My heart ached so with the joy of his nearness that I quick drew back and turned away, and began to talk to the people that were pushing and crowding themselves on the deck.

Nu, I got to America.

Ten hours I pushed a machine in a shirtwaist factory, when I was yet lucky to get work. And always my head was drying up with saving and pinching and worrying to send home a little from the little I earned. All that my face saw all day long was girls and machines — and nothing else. And

Culture Note

day of Atonement
Yom Kippur, a major Jewish holy day observed by fasting and prayers of repentance, p. 486

even when I came already home from work, I could only talk to the girls in the working-girls' boarding-house, or shut myself up in my dark, lonesome bedroom. No family, no friends, nobody to get me acquainted with nobody! The only men I saw were what passed me by in the street and in cars.

"Is this 'lovers' land'?" was calling in my heart. "Where are my dreams that were so real to me in the old country?"

Often in the middle of the work I felt like stopping all the machines and crying out to the world the heaviness that pressed on my heart. Sometimes when I walked in the street I felt like going over to the first man I met and cry out to him: "Oh, I'm so lonely! I'm so lonely!"

One day I read in the Jewish "Tageblatt" the advertisement from Zaretzky, the matchmaker. "What harm is it if I try my luck?" I said to myself. "I can't die away an old maid. Too much love burns in my heart to stand back like a stone and only see how other people are happy. I want to tear myself out from my deadness. I'm in a living grave. I've got to lift myself up. I have nobody to try for me, and maybe the matchmaker will help."

As I walked up Delancey Street to Mr. Zaretzky, the street was turning with me. I didn't see the crowds. I didn't see the pushcart peddlers with their bargains. I didn't hear the noises or anything. My eyes were on the sky, praying: Gottuniu! Send me only the little bit of luck!"

"Nu? Nu? What need you?" asked Mr. Zaretzky when I entered.

I got red with shame in the face the way he looked at me. I turned up my head. I was too proud to tell him for what I came. Before I walked in I thought to tell him everything. But when I looked on his face and saw his hard eyes, I couldn't say a word. I stood like a yok unable to move my tongue. I went to the matchmaker with my heart, and I saw before me a stone. The stone was talking to me—but—but—he was a stone!

"Are you looking for a shidduch?" he asked.

"Yes," I said, proud, but crushed.

"You know I charge five dollars for the stepping in," he bargained.

It got cold by my heart. I wasn't only to give him the five dollars, nearly a whole week's wages, but his thick-skinness for being only after the money. But I couldn't help myself — I was like in his fists hypnotized. And I gave him the five dollars.

I let myself go to the door, but he called me back.

"Wait, wait. Come in and sit down. I didn't question you yet."

"About what?"

"I got to know how much money you got saved before I can introduce you to anybody."

"Oh — h — h! Is it only depending on the *money*?"

"Certainly. No move in this world without money," he said, taking a pinch of snuff in his black, hairy fingers and sniffing it up in his nose.

I glanced on his thick neck and greasy, red face. "And to him people come looking for love," I said to myself, shuddering. Oh, how it burned in my heart, but I still went on. "Can't I get a man in America without money?"

He gave a look on me with his sharp eyes. Gottuniu! What a look! I thought I was sinking into the floor.

"There are plenty of *young* girls with money that are begging themselves the men to take them. So what can you expect? *Not young, not lively, and without money, too?* But, anyhow, I'll see what I can do for you."

He took out a little book from his vest-pocket and looked through the names.

"What trade do you go on your hands?" he asked, turning to me. "Sometimes a dressmaker or a hairdresser that can help make a living for a man, maybe — "

I couldn't hear any more. It got black before my eyes, my voice stopped inside of me.

"If you want to listen to sense from a friend, so I have a good match for you," he said, following me to the door. "I have on my list a widower with not more than five or six children. He has a grand business, a herring-stand on Hester Street. He don't ask for no money, and he don't make an objection if the girl is in years, so long as she knows how to cook well for him."

How I got myself back to my room I don't know. But for two days and for two nights I lay still on my bed, unable to move. I looked around on my empty walls, thinking, thinking, "Where am I? Is this the world? Is this America?"

Suddenly I sprang up from bed. "What can come from pitying yourself?" I cried. "If the world kicks you down and makes nothing of you, you bounce yourself up and make something of yourself." A fire blazed up in me to rise over the world because I was downed by the world.

"Make a person of yourself," I said. "Begin to learn English. Make yourself for an American if you want to live in America. American girls don't go to matchmakers. American girls don't run after a man: if they don't get a husband they don't think the world is over; they turn their mind to something else.

"Wake up!" I said to myself, "You want love to come to you? Why don't you give it out to other people? Love the women and children, everybody in the street and the shop. Love the rag-picker and the drunkard, the bad and the ugly. All those whom the world kicks down you pick up and press to your heart with love."

As I said this I felt wells of love that choked in me all my life flowing out of me and over me. A strange, wonderful light like a lover's smile melted over me, and the sweetness of lover's arms stole around me.

The first night I went to school I felt like falling on everybody's neck and kissing them. I felt like kissing the books and the benches. It was such great happiness to learn to read and write the English words.

Because I started a few weeks after the beginning of the term, my teacher said I might stay after the class to help me catch up with my back lessons. The minute I looked on him I felt that grand feeling: "Here is a person! Here is America!" His face just shined with high thoughts. There was such a beautiful light in his eyes that it warmed my heart to steal a look on him.

At first, when it came my turn to say something in the class, I got so excited the words stuck and twisted in my mouth and I couldn't give out my thoughts. But the teacher didn't see my nervousness. He only saw that I had something to say, and he helped me say it. How or what he did I don't know. I only felt his look of understanding flowing into me like draughts of air to one who is choking.

Long after I already felt free and easy to talk to him alone after the class, I looked at the books on his desk. "Oi weh!" I said to him, "If I only knew half of what is in your books, I couldn't any more sit still in the chair like you. I'd fly in the air with the joy of so much knowledge."

"Why are you so eager for learning?" he asked me.

"Because I want to make a person of myself," I answered. "Since I got to work for low wages and I can't be young any more, I'm burning to get among people where it's not against a girl if she is in years and without money."

His hand went out to me. "I'll help you," he said. "But you must first learn to get hold of yourself."

SUCH A BEAUTIFUL KINDNESS went out of his heart to me with his words! His voice, and the goodness that shone from his eyes, made me want to burst out crying, but I choked back my tears till I got home. And all night long I wept on my pillow: "Fool! What is the matter with you? Why are you crying? But I said, "I can't help it. He is so beautiful!"

My teacher was so much above me that he wasn't a man to me at all. He was a God. His face lighted up the shop for me, and his voice sang itself in me everywhere I went. It was like healing medicine to the flaming fever within me to listen to his voice. And then I'd repeat to myself his words and live in them as if they were religion.

Often as I sat at the machine sewing the waists I'd forget what I was doing. I'd find myself dreaming in the air. "Ach!" I asked myself, "what was that beautifulness in his eyes that made the lowest nobody feel like a somebody? What was that about him that when his smile fell on me I felt lifted up to the sky away from all the coldness and the ugliness of the world? Gottuniu!" I prayed, "if I could only always hold on to the light of high thoughts that shined from him. If I could only always hear in my heart the sound of his voice I would need nothing more in life. I would be happier than a bird in the air."

"Friend," I said to him once, "if you could but teach me how to get cold in the heart and clear in the head like you are!"

He only smiled at me and looked far away. His calmness was like the sureness of money in the bank. Then he turned and looked on me, and said: "I am not so cold in the heart and clear in the head as I make-believe. I am bound. I am a prisoner of convention."

"You make-believe—you bound?" I burst out. "You who do not have foreladies or bosses—you who do not have to sell yourself for wages—you who only work for love and truth—you a prisoner?"

"True, I do not have bosses just as you do," he said. "But still I am not free. I am bound by formal education and conventional traditions. Though you work in a shop, you are really freer than I. You are not repressed as I am by the fear and shame of feeling. You could teach me more than I could teach you. You could teach me how to be natural."

"I'm not so natural like you think," I said. "I'm afraid."

He smiled at me out of his eyes. "What are you afraid of?"

"I'm afraid of my heart," I said, trying to hold back the blood rushing to my face. "I'm burning to get calm and sensible like the born Americans. But how can I help it? My heart flies away from me like a wild bird. How can I learn to keep myself down on earth like the born Americans?"

"But I don't want you to get down on earth like the Americans. That is just the beauty and the wonder of you. We Americans are too much on earth; we need more of your power to fly. If you would only know how much you can teach us Americans. You are the promise of the centuries to come. You are the heart, the creative pulse of America to be."

I WALKED HOME ON WINGS. My teacher said that I could help him; that I had something to give to Americans. "But how could I teach him?" I wondered; "I who had never had a chance to learn anything except what he taught me. And what had I to give to the

Americans, I who am nothing but dreams and longings and hunger for love?"

When school closed down for vacation, it seemed to me all life stopped in the world. I had no more class to look forward to, no more chance of seeing my teacher. As I faced the emptiness of my long vacation, all the light went out of my eyes, and all the strength out of my arms and fingers.

For nearly a week I was like without air. There was no school. One night I came home from the shop and threw myself down on the bed. I wanted to cry, to let out the heavy weight that pressed on my heart, but I couldn't cry. My tears felt like hot, burning sand in my eyes.

"Oi-i-i! I can't stand it no more, this emptiness," I groaned. "Why don't I kill myself? Why don't something happen to me? No consumption, no fever, no plague or death ever comes to save me from this terrible world. I have to go on suffering and choking inside myself till I grow mad."

I jumped up from the bed, threw open the window, and began fighting with the deaf-and-dumb air in the air-shaft.

"What is the matter with you?" I cried. "You are going out of your head. You are sinking back into the old ways from which you dragged yourself out with your studies. Studies! What did I get from all my studies? Nothing. Nothing. I am still in the same shop with the same shirtwaists. A lot my teacher cares for me once the class is over."

A fire burned up in me that he was already forgetting me. And I shot out a letter to him:

"You call yourself a teacher? A friend? How can you go off in the country and drop me out of your heart and out of your head like a read-over book you left on the shelf of your shut-down classroom? How can you enjoy your vacation in the country while I'm in the sweatshop? You learned me nothing. You only broke my heart. What good are all the books you ever gave me? They don't tell me how to be happy in a factory. They don't tell me how to keep alive in emptiness, or how to find something beautiful in the dirt and ugliness in which I got to waste away. I want life. I want people. I can't live inside my head as you do."

I sent the letter off in the madness in which I wrote it, without stopping to think; but the minute after I dropped it in the mail-box my reason came again to my head. I went back tearing my hair. "What have I done? Meshugeneh!"

Walking up the stairs I saw my door open. I went in. The sky is falling to the earth! Am I dreaming? There was my teacher sitting on my trunk? My teacher come to see me? Me, in my dingy room? For a minute it got blind before my eyes, and I didn't know where I was any more.

"I had to come," he said, the light of heaven shining on me out of his eyes. "I was so desolate without you. I tried to say something to you before I left for my vacation, but the words wouldn't come. Since I have been away I have written you many letters, but I did not mail them, for they were like my old self from which I want to break away."

He put his cool, strong hand into mine. "You can save me," he said. "You can free me from the bondage of age-long repressions. You can lift me out of the dead grooves of sterile intellectuality. Without you I am the dry dust of hopes unrealized. You are fire and sunshine and desire. You make life changeable and beautiful and full of daily wonder."

I couldn't speak. I was so on fire with his words. Then, like whirlwinds in my brain, rushed out the burning words of the matchmaker: "Not young, not lively, and without money, too!"

"You are younger than youth," he said, kissing my hands. "Every day of your unlived youth shall be relived with love, but such a love as youth could never know."

And then how it happened I don't know; but his arms were around me. "Sara Reisel, tell me, do you love me," he said, kissing me on my hair and on my eyes and on my lips.

I could only weep and tremble with joy at his touch. "The miracle!" cried my heart; "the miracle of America come true!"

ABOUT **ANZIA YEZIERSKA**

Born in a village in the Russian part of Poland, Anzia Yezierska (än′zyə ye zyėr′ skä; 1885?–1970) immigrated to New York as a young girl. She worked in a sweatshop and began to learn

English at a vocational school. Soon she was writing short stories and gaining a literary reputation. Her best-known work, an autobiographical novel titled *Bread Givers* (1925), portrays a young woman who must defy her father and culture to pursue the American dream.

RESPONDING

1. *Personal Response* Do you consider this a realistic story or a fairy tale? Explain.

2. *Literary Analysis* What do you consider the *theme* of this story? Do you think the story belongs in a unit titled "Triumph of the Spirit"? Why or why not?

3. *Multicultural Connection* In this story, what Jewish customs, objects, and practices are mentioned? How important are they to Sara's family?

LANGUAGE WORKSHOP

Homonyms Do not confuse *homonyms*, words that sound alike but have different meanings and usually different spellings. The narrator *bares* (not *bears*) her *soul* (not *sole*) to her teacher.
Choose the correct word in each sentence below.
1. Sara was a (*border, boarder*) with other working girls in a dingy house with (*worn, warn*) carpeting.
2. Being open-minded to all cultures is a (*principal, principle*) that she espoused.
3. "Don't (*loose, lose*) your ideals," was (*their, they're, there*) (*advise, advice*).

WRITER'S PORTFOLIO

Sara Reisel finds out how to get a job and how to apply for a night school class. Both might have required either a résumé or a letter of application. Prepare a data sheet listing your achievements, talents, experience, and/or interests. Then use this information to write a résumé for a job or a letter of application for a college.

Just Lather, That's All

HE SAID NOTHING when he entered. I was passing the best of my razors back and forth on a strop. When I recognized him I started to tremble. But he didn't notice. Hoping to conceal my emotion, I continued sharpening the razor. I tested it on the meat of my thumb, and then held it up to the light.

At that moment he took off the bullet-studded belt that his gun holster dangled from. He hung it up on a wall hook and placed his military cap over it. Then he turned to me, loosening the knot of his tie, and said, "It's hot as hell. Give me a shave." He sat in the chair.

I estimated he had a four-day beard—the four days taken up by the latest expedition in search of our troops. His face seemed reddened, burned by the sun. Carefully, I began to prepare the soap. I cut off a few slices, dropped them into the cup, mixed in a bit of warm water, and began to stir with the brush. Immediately the foam began to rise. "The other boys in the group should have this much beard, too," he remarked. I continued stirring the lather.

"But we did all right, you know. We got the main ones. We brought back some dead, and we got some others still alive. But pretty soon they'll all be dead."

"How many did you catch?" I asked.

"Fourteen. We had to go pretty deep into the woods to find them. But we'll get even. Not one of them comes out of this alive, not one."

He leaned back on the chair when he saw me with the lather-covered brush in my hand. I still had to put the sheet on him. No doubt about it, I was upset. I took a sheet out of a drawer and knotted it around his neck. He wouldn't stop talking. He probably thought I was in sympathy with his party.

"The town must have learned a lesson from what we did," he said.

"Yes," I replied, securing the knot at the base of his dark, sweaty neck.

"That was a fine show, eh?"

"Very good," I answered, turning back for the brush.

The man closed his eyes with a gesture of fatigue and sat waiting for the cool caress of the soap. I had never had him so close to me. The day he ordered the whole town to file into the patio of the school to see the four rebels hanging there, I came face to face with him for an instant. But the sight of the mutilated bodies kept me from noticing the face of the man who had directed it all, the face I was now about to take into my hands.

It was not an unpleasant face, and the beard, which made him look a bit older than he was, didn't suit him badly at all. His name was Torres—Captain Torres. A man of imagination, because who else would have thought of hanging the naked rebels and then holding target practice on their bodies?

I began to apply the first layer of soap. With his eyes closed, he continued. "Without any effort I could go straight to sleep," he said, "but there's plenty to do this afternoon."

I stopped the lathering and asked with a feigned lack of interest, "A firing squad?"

"Something like that, but a little slower."

I got on with the job of lathering his beard. My hands started trembling again. The man could not possibly realize it, and this was in my favor. But I would have preferred that he hadn't come. It was likely that many of our faction had seen him enter. And an enemy under one's roof imposes certain conditions.

I would be obliged to shave that beard like any other one, carefully, gently, like that of any customer, taking pains to see that no single pore emitted a drop of blood. Being careful to see that the little tufts of hair did not lead the blade astray. Seeing that his skin ended up clean, soft, and healthy, so that passing the back of my hand over it I couldn't feel a hair. Yes, I was secretly a rebel, but I was also a conscientious barber, and proud of the precision required of my profession.

I TOOK THE RAZOR, opened up the two protective arms, exposed the blade, and began the job — from one of the sideburns downward. The razor responded beautifully. His beard was inflexible and hard, not too long, but thick. Bit by bit the skin emerged. The razor rasped along, making its customary sound as fluffs of lather, mixed with bits of hair, gathered along the blade.

I paused a moment to clean it, then took up the strop again to sharpen the razor, because I'm a barber who does things properly. The man, who had kept his eyes closed, opened them now, removed one of his hands from under the sheet, felt the spot on his face where the soap had been cleared off, and said, "Come to the school today at six o'clock."

"The same thing as the other day?" I asked, horrified.

"It could be even better," he said.

"What do you plan to do?"

"I don't know yet. But we'll amuse ourselves." Once more he leaned back and closed his eyes. I approached with the razor poised.

"Do you plan to punish them all?" I ventured timidly.

"All."

The soap was drying on his face. I had to hurry. In the mirror I looked towards the street. It was the same as ever — the grocery store with two or three customers in it. Then I glanced at the clock — 2:20 in the afternoon.

The razor continued on its downward stroke. Now from the other sideburn down. A thick, blue beard. He should have let it grow like some poets or priests do. It would suit him well. A lot of people wouldn't recognize him. Much to his benefit, I thought, as I attempted to cover the neck area smoothly.

There, surely, the razor had to be handled masterfully, since the hair, although softer, grew into little swirls. A curly beard. One of the tiny pores could open up and issue forth its pearl of blood, but a good barber prides himself on never allowing this to happen to a customer.

How many of us had he ordered shot? How many of us had he ordered mutilated? It was better not to think about it. Torres did not know that I was his enemy. He did not know it nor did the rest. It was a secret shared by very few, precisely so that I could inform the revolutionaries of what Torres was doing in the town and of what he was planning each time he undertook a rebel-hunting excursion.

So it was going to be very difficult to explain that I had him right in my hands and let him go peacefully—alive and shaved.

The beard was now almost completely gone. He seemed younger, less burdened by years than when he had arrived. I suppose this always happens with men who visit barber shops. Under the stroke of my razor Torres was being rejuvenated—rejuvenated because I am a good barber, the best in the town, if I may say so.

How hot it is getting! Torres must be sweating as much as I. But he is a calm man, who is not even thinking about what he is going to do with the prisoners this afternoon. On the other hand I, with this razor in my hands—I stroking and restroking this skin, can't even think clearly.

Damn him for coming! I'm a revolutionary, not a murderer. And how easy it would be to kill him. And he deserves it. Does he? No! What the devil! No one deserves to have someone else make the sacrifice of becoming a murderer. What do you gain by it? Nothing. Others come along and still others, and the first ones kill the second ones, and they the next ones—and it goes on like this until everything is a sea of blood.

I could cut his throat just so—*zip, zip*! I wouldn't give him time to resist and since he has his eyes closed he wouldn't see the glistening blade or my glistening eyes. But I'm trembling like a real murderer. Out of his neck a gush of blood would spout onto the sheet, on the chair, on my hands, on the floor. I would have to close the door. And the blood would keep inching along the floor, warm, ineradicable, uncontainable, until it reached the street, like a little scarlet stream.

I'm sure that one solid stroke, one deep incision, would prevent any pain. He wouldn't suffer. But what would I do with the body? Where would I hide it? I would have to flee, leaving all I have behind, and take refuge far away. But they would follow until they found me. "Captain Torres' murderer. He slit his throat while he was shaving him — a coward."

And then on the other side. "The avenger of us all. A name to remember. He was the town barber. No one knew he was defending our cause."

Murderer or hero? My destiny depends on the edge of this blade. I can turn my hand a bit more, press a little harder on the razor, and sink it in. The skin would give way like silk, like rubber. There is nothing more tender than human skin and the blood is always there, ready to pour forth.

But I don't want to be a murderer. You came to me for a shave. And I perform my work honorably . . . I don't want blood on my hands. Just lather, that's all. You are an executioner and I am only a barber. Each person has his own place in the scheme of things.

Now his chin had been stroked clean and smooth. The man sat up and looked into the mirror. He rubbed his hands over his skin and felt it fresh, like new.

"Thanks," he said. He went to the hanger for his belt, pistol, and cap. I must have been very pale; my shirt felt soaked. Torres finished adjusting the buckle, straightened his pistol in the holster, and after automatically smoothing down his hair, he put on the cap. From his pants pocket he took out several coins to pay me for my services and then headed for the door.

In the doorway he paused for a moment and said, "They told me that you'd kill me. I came to find out. But killing isn't easy. You can take my word for it." And he turned and walked away.

ABOUT **HERNANDO TÉLLEZ**

Hernando Téllez (tā⁄yez; 1908–1966), an essayist and short story writer, was born in Bogotá, Colombia. Along with his writing, he was involved in politics, serving as consul in Marseilles, France, and as a senator in his own country. His essays on many

themes are numerous, but it is his short stories, primarily "Just Lather, That's All," that have earned him a reputation.

RESPONDING

1. *Personal Response* Do you think that the narrator is a hero or a coward? Explain.

2. *Literary Analysis* What *mood* does the author create in the first four paragraphs? What details help create this mood?

3. *Multicultural Connection* What kind of government or laws would there be in a country where a situation like this could occur?

LANGUAGE WORKSHOP

Characterization *Characters* are seldom all good or all bad in a story. Even heroes and villains, in the hands of skilled writers, have complexities to their characters that make them interesting and three-dimensional. Cite at least five details from the story that reveal these two men are three-dimensional individuals rather than types.

WRITER'S PORTFOLIO

In your journal, explain whether you agree or disagree with the following observation: "This story illustrates two codes of honor: one man kills to reinforce his principles; the other man refuses to kill, according to his principles."

Babi Yar

Yevgeny Yevtushenko

There are no memorials at Babi Yar—
The steep slope is the only gravestone.
I am afraid.
Today I am as old as the Jewish people.
It seems to me now that I am a Jew.
Now I am wandering in Ancient Egypt.
And now, crucified on the cross, I die
And even now I bear the marks of the nails.
It seems to me that I am Dreyfus.
The worthy citizenry denounces me and judges me.
I am behind prison bars.
I am trapped, hunted, spat upon, reviled
And good ladies in dresses flounced with Brussels
        lace
Shrieking, poke umbrellas in my face.
It seems to me that I am a boy in Byelostok,
Blood flows and spreads across the floor.
Reeking of onion and vodka
The leading lights of the saloon

Culture Notes

Babi Yar a ravine in Kiev where 140,000 of the city's residents, mostly Jews, were buried after being murdered by Nazi troops during World War II, p. 502

Dreyfus Alfred Dreyfus (1859–1935), French army officer of Jewish descent convicted in 1894 of treason but later proved innocent, p. 502

Byelostok city in Poland that suffered a racial attack in 1906, p. 502

pogrom an authorized attack on minorities, particularly Jews. In Russia, such attacks were incited by the czarist regime to provide an outlet for the discontent of the masses. p. 503

Are on the rampage.
Booted aside, I am helpless:
I plead with the pogrom thugs
To roars of "Beat the Yids, and save Russia,"
A shopkeeper is beating up my mother.
O my Russian people!
You are really international at heart.
But the unclean
Have often loudly taken in vain
Your most pure name.
I know how good is my native land
And how vile is that, without a quiver,
The anti-Semites styled themselves with pomp
"The union of the Russian people."
It seems to me that I am Anne Frank,
As frail as a twig in April.
And I am full of love
And I have no need of empty phrases.
I want us to look at each other,
How little we can see or smell,
Neither the leaves on the trees nor the sky.
But we can do a lot.
We can tenderly embrace in a dark room.
Someone is coming? Don't be afraid—
It is the noise of spring itself.
Come to me, give me your lips.
Someone is forcing the door.
No, it is the breaking up of the ice...

Culture Notes

Yids a derogatory term for Jews, p. 503

Anne Frank a Jewish girl of Amsterdam who, with her family and several friends, was driven into hiding by the Nazis. Anne died in the Bergen-Belsen concentration camp, but her diary recounting her experiences survived. p. 503

"Internationale" the Russian anthem until 1944, p. 504

Wild grasses rustle over Babi Yar.
The trees look down sternly, like judges.
Everything here shrieks silently
And, taking off my cap,
I sense that I am turning gray.
And I myself am nothing but a silent shriek,
Over the thousands and thousands buried in
 this place.
I am every old man who was shot here.
I am every boy who was shot here.
No part of me will ever forget any of this.
Let the "Internationale" ring out
When the last anti-Semite on earth is buried.
There is no Jewish blood in mine,
But I am hated by every anti-Semite as a Jew,
And for this reason,
I am a true Russian.

Nobel Acceptance Speech

Following is the prepared text of the acceptance speech by Elie Wiesel, the winner of the 1986 Nobel Peace Prize, at a ceremony in Oslo yesterday, as made available by an aide:

The New York Times, December 11, 1986

IT IS WITH A PROFOUND SENSE OF humility that I accept the honor you have chosen to bestow upon me. I know: your choice transcends me. This both frightens and pleases me.

It frightens me because I wonder: do I have the right to represent the multitudes who have perished? Do I have the right to accept this great honor on their behalf? I do not. That would be presumptuous. No one may speak for the dead, no one may interpret their mutilated dreams and visions.

It pleases me because I may say that this honor belongs to all the survivors and their children, and through us, to the Jewish people with whose destiny I have always identified.

I remember: it happened yesterday or eternities ago. A young Jewish boy discovered the kingdom of night. I remember his bewilderment, I remember his anguish. It all happened so fast. The ghetto. The deportation. The sealed cattle car. The fiery altar upon which the history of our people and the future of mankind were meant to be sacrificed.

I remember: he asked his father: "Can this be true? This is the 20th century, not the Middle Ages. Who would allow such crimes to be committed? How could the world remain silent?"

And now the boy is turning to me: "Tell me," he asks. "What have you done with my future? What have you done with your life?"

And I tell him that I have tried. That I have tried to keep memory alive, that I have tried to fight those who would forget. Because if we forget, we are guilty, we are accomplices.

And then I explained to him how naïve we were, that the world did know and remain silent. And that is why I swore never to be silent whenever and wherever human beings endure suffering and humiliation. We must always take sides. Neutrality helps the oppressor, never the victim. Silence encourages the tormentor, never the tormented.

Sometimes we must interfere. When human lives are endangered, when human dignity is in jeopardy, national borders and sensitivities become irrelevant. Wherever men or women are persecuted because of their race, religion or political views, that place must—at that moment—become the center of the universe.

Of course, since I am a Jew profoundly rooted in my people's memory and tradition, my first response is to Jewish fears, Jewish needs, Jewish crises. For I belong to a traumatized generation, one that experienced the abandonment and

Culture Notes

Apartheid (ə pärt′hāt) government policy of racial segregation, p. 507

anti-Semitism hatred of Jewish people, p. 507

Andrei Sakharov . . . imprisonment references to leaders who were imprisoned or in forced isolation because of their resistance to government policies and their pursuit of human rights. These dissidents have all been freed since Wiesel's speech was delivered. Walesa and Mandela have since been elected presidents of Poland and South Africa, respectively. p. 507

solitude of our people. It would be unnatural for me not to make Jewish priorities my own: Israel, Soviet Jewry, Jews in Arab lands.

But there are others as important to me. Apartheid is, in my view, as abhorrent as anti-Semitism. To me, Andrei Sakharov's isolation is as much of a disgrace as Iosif Begun's imprisonment. As is the denial of Solidarity and its leader Lech Walesa's right to dissent. And Nelson Mandela's interminable imprisonment.

There is so much injustice and suffering crying out for our attention: victims of hunger, or racism and political persecution, writers and poets, prisoners in so many lands governed by the left and by the right. Human rights are being violated in every continent. More people are oppressed than free.

And then, too, there are the Palestinians to whose plight I am sensitive but whose methods I deplore. Violence and terrorism are not the answer. Something must be done about their suffering, and soon. I trust Israel, for I have faith in the Jewish people. Let Israel be given a chance, let hatred and danger be removed from her horizons, and there will be peace in and around the Holy Land.

> **Culture Notes**
>
> **Palestinians** people displaced by the establishment of modern Israel in 1948 or in later shifts of Israel's boundaries, p. 507
>
> **Raoul Wallenberg . . . Albert Schweitzer** Wallenberg, a Swedish diplomat who saved Jews by intervening with the Nazis, died in a Russian prison. Schweitzer, an Alsatian physician and missionary, was awarded the Nobel Peace Prize in 1952. p. 507

Yes, I have faith. Faith in God and even in His creation. Without it no action would be possible. And action is the only remedy to indifference: the most insidious danger of all. Isn't this the meaning of Alfred Nobel's legacy? Wasn't his fear of war a shield against war?

There is much to be done, there is much that can be done. One person—a Raoul Wallenberg, an Albert Schweitzer, one person of integrity, can make a difference, a difference of life and death. As long as one dissident is in prison, our freedom will not be true. As long as one child is hungry, our lives will be filled with anguish and shame.

What all these victims need above all is to know that they are not alone; that we are not forgetting them, that when their voices are stifled we shall lend them ours, that while their freedom depends on ours, the quality of our freedom depends on theirs.

This is what I say to the young Jewish boy wondering what I have done with his years. It is in his name that I speak to you and that I express to you my deepest gratitude. No one is as capable of gratitude as one who has emerged from the kingdom of night.

We know that every moment is a moment of grace, every hour an offering; not to share them would mean to betray them. Our lives no longer belong to us alone; they belong to all those who need us desperately.

Thank you Chairman Aarvik. Thank you, members of the Nobel Committee. Thank you, people of Norway, for declaring on this singular occasion that our survival has meaning for mankind.

ABOUT **YEVGENY YEVTUSHENKO**

Yevgeny Yevtushenko (also Evgeni Evtushenko; yev ge′nē yef tu shen′ko) was born in 1933 in Siberia, where one of his grandfathers had been exiled. He has long been concerned with anti-Semitism in his native country, and "Babi Yar," first published in 1961, has been both lauded and attacked for its sympathetic attitude toward Jewish people.

Although he still lives in Russia, Yevtushenko travels internationally, giving passionate readings that expose brutality and injustices.

ABOUT **ELIE WIESEL**

Elie(zer) Wiesel (el′ē wē zel′) received the Nobel Peace Prize in 1986 for his written works about the Nazi Holocaust during World War II. He and two of his sisters were the only members of their family to survive internment at Auschwitz, a concentration camp. Born in Sighet, Romania, in 1928, Wiesel became a naturalized American citizen in 1963. It was not until the mid-1950s that Wiesel decided to "bear witness" to the deaths of millions of people in the camps. His semi-autobiographical novel, *Night,* tells the story of a boy who has survived the Holocaust.

RESPONDING

1. *Personal Response* Speaking of the Holocaust, Wiesel says "if we forget, we are guilty, we are accomplices." Do you agree? Explain.

2. *Literary Analysis* A *symbol* is something used to represent something else — for example, a heart for love. What does night represent in Wiesel's speech?

3. *Multicultural Connection* Where in the world today do you see conditions that call out for Wiesel's kind of "interference" and Yevtushenko's remembrance? What do you think should be done?

LANGUAGE WORKSHOP

An *allusion* is a reference to a historical or literary figure or event. It may refer to myth, religion, or to any other aspect of ancient or modern culture. For example, there is an allusion in "Babi Yar" to Dreyfus, a French army officer of Jewish descent who was unjustly convicted of treason. How does this allusion reinforce Yevtushenko's theme? Find five other allusions in these works by Yevtushenko and Wiesel and explain how each reinforces the author's point.

WRITER'S PORTFOLIO

Compare Wiesel's speech to the speech of Alexander Solzhenitsyn (Unit 4) or Toni Morrison (Unit 3). Discuss the speeches in terms of their style, subject matter, and tone in a composition of several paragraphs.

Last Night

WHEN HANG FONG TOY FINALLY awakens, she can't tell if the rhythmic pounding is one of her headaches or just the water pipes banging again. She looks around the room, listening. The street light falls through the Venetian blinds; the slanting lines make the room seem larger.

You Thin Toy sleeps curled toward the wall, a brush stroke on the wide bed. He's a retired merchant marine and has sailed the world. Now he spends afternoons at Portsmouth Square, playing chess and telling stories about himself as a young man. "Like a seagull," he says, "I went everywhere, saw everything."

His old-timer friends like to tease him. "So, why do you sit around the Square now?"

"Curiosity," he says. "I want to see how you fleabags have been living."

You Thin knows all the terms for docking a ship; Hang Fong can name the parts and seams of a dress the way a doctor can name bones.

Hang Fong sews in a garment shop. She's only been outside Chinatown for official business: immigration, unemployment and social security. When the children were young, they took her to Market Street, the Emporium and J. C. Penney's, but now, without translators, she's not an adventuress.

There was a time when her desire to return to China was a sensation in her belly, like hunger. Now she only dreams of it, almost tasting those dishes she loved as a young girl. Sometimes she says to You Thin before falling asleep, maybe a visit, eh?

After raising their children, Chinatown has become their world. They feel lucky to have an apartment on Salmon Alley. Louie's Grocery is around the corner on Taylor, and Hang Fong's sewing shop is just down the block. Their apartment is well situated in the back of the alley, far from the traffic fumes of Pacific Avenue.

Hang Fong and You Thin like their landlord, an old Italian lady, and her mute son so much that they have given them Chinese names. Fay-Poah, Manager Lady, and Ah-Boy, Mute-Son. Manager Lady wears printed pastel dresses that Hang Fong, a sewing lady, admires very much. Ah-Boy, a big man with a milky smell, works as a porter at the Oasis Club, but during the day he works around the building. When Hang Fong hears his broom on the stairs or the garbage cans rattling in the airshaft, she feels safe. It's good to have a strong man like Ah-Boy nearby. She tells You Thin, Ah-Boy is a good son, and You Thin nods. He likes to think that the anchor tattoo on Ah-Boy's arm makes them comrades of sorts.

HANG FONG THINKS maybe Manager Lady left her window open. But then the sound becomes erratic and sharp. Hang Fong gets up, leans toward the wall. You Thin lets out a long breath.

Hang Fong presses her ear against the wall, listening. Her eyes are wide open. Suddenly she rushes toward her sleeping husband and shakes him. "Get up! Get up! It's the Manager Lady, she's in trouble!"

You Thin stretches out and props himself up on one elbow. He rubs his eyes, trying to wake up. The banging comes again, and the old couple stare at each other. Outside, a car screeches to an urgent stop. They listen to the faint bubbly hum of the fish tank in the other room, and then hear the rumbling icebox motor shut off with a final click. You Thin and Hang Fong look at each other; the silence feels big.

The pounding comes again. Once. Twice.

"Something's wrong! Manager Lady is trying to tell us that!" Hang Fong throws off her covers. In one motion, her legs whip out and her slippers make a swishing noise as she moves across the room. The overhead fluorescent light flickers and snaps and then is quiet. The room is bright, glaring.

You Thin squints, reaches over, and raps sharply, one-two-three on the wall.

A sound knocks back in return.

Hang Fong slaps the wall with her open palm; the sound is flat and dull. She presses palm and cheek into the wall, and shouts, "Manager, Manager, are you all right? Nothing's wrong, is there?"

"SSHHH!!!" You Thin yanks her away. "Don't talk loud like that, she don't know what you say, maybe she thinks that you yell at her."

You Thin is out of bed, pacing. Hang Fong sits; she pulls her sweater closer around her neck. The sleeves hang limply at her sides.

"Let's see . . . wait a minute, where's Ah-Boy?"

"It's Tuesday; he's got the night shift."

"Oh. Tuesday. Right."

Last week, when You Thin was at Manager Lady's paying the rent, he looked out her kitchen window while waiting for her to come back with the receipt. He saw a Chinese pot beneath a pile of chipped plates. So the next day he returned with a blue vase, its floral pattern similar to many of Manager Lady's dresses.

"I see?" he asked, pointing out the window.

Manager Lady opened her mouth wide, as her hand fluttered toward the window.

"Oh. Si, si," she said.

You Thin pulled the window open. He moved the cream-colored plates and lifted the pot for Manager Lady to see. She nodded, cradling the blue vase to her bosom.

With both hands, You Thin carried the pot back across the hall. Under the running faucet, Hang Fong scrubbed hard. Red, green and yellow, the palace ladies and plum blossoms came clean. You Thin scraped away the last of the dirt with a toothpick. The characters came clear. Good Luck and Long Life. You Thin and Hang Fong laughed, feeling lucky.

"Worth a lot of money, in time," You Thin said.

"Something to pass on to the children," Hang Fong added.

You Thin told everyone on the Square that the pot belonged to a hard-working old-timer who died alone. Hang Fong said that it was a good omen that they were chosen to house this valuable object. "It's very old," she told her sewing-lady friends.

S O, SHOULD WE CALL the Rescue Car?" Hang Fong asks.

You Thin looks out the window, distracted. He shakes his head. "Even if they get here in two minutes, best we could do is stand in front of the door with our mouths open."

Hang Fong knows that he wants to climb the fire escape and get inside Manager Lady's apartment. It's risky, she thinks. You Thin isn't a young man and his step isn't always steady. She won't say anything, because the long years of marriage have taught her one thing: he likes his way.

"Well, what do we do?" Hang Fong asks. On the fire escape, a pigeon sleeps, its beak in its chest feathers. Hang Fong watches it. She hears the big engines of the garbage trucks churning up the hill. Foghorns sound in the distance, like help on the way.

You Thin asks, "Well, you think I could make that big step across to their fire escape?"

Hang Fong shrugs her shoulders. "Don't know; how do you feel?"

You Thin raises the window, looks out and snaps back in. Before Hang Fong can speak, he's run to the bathroom and clattered his way out carrying the long wooden board they use as a shelf over the bathtub.

"This is how. . ." He slaps the board. "This will reach from our fire escape to theirs. You hold this end, just in case, and the rest I can do."

Hang Fong grips hard, but she keeps a harder eye on him. Inside, she repeats over and over, "Be careful . . . be safe . . . be careful . . . be safe. . . " You Thin is a brave man, she thinks; You Thin is a good man.

One leg, then the other, and he is over there. He peers through the window, knocks, and then tries to lift it open. Shut tight. He has to pull hard, two, three times before it comes open.

You Thin feels along the wall for the light switch. All along the way, he speaks to Manager Lady, softly, in Chinese, "You're all right, nothing's wrong, don't be frightened..." You Thin believes in the power of the voice: a well-meaning word spoken in the face of ill fortune can turn luck around.

Manager Lady is a wide figure on the floor. Everything around her speaks of her age: the faded covers, the cluttered nightstand, the bottles of lotions and pills. You Thin takes her hands; he's happy hers are warm.

Hang Fong knocks in quick, urgent raps, and You Thin opens the door for her. She moves quickly through the entryway, kneels and takes Manager Lady's head onto her lap, whispering, "Don't be scared, don't be scared." Manager Lady's eyes open. She says something in Italian; the long vowels reach forth and hang heavy in the air. Hang Fong and You Thin look at each other. They understand.

You Thin says, "I go. Go to get Ah-Boy."

"You know where it is then?"

"Uh, let me think . . . where Lee's Rice Shop used to be?"

"No! Across from Chong's Imports."

"Yes, right, I know, I know."

THE AIR OUTSIDE IS SHARP. The street lamps cast an orange glow to the empty alley. You Thin moves quickly through Salmon Alley. But when he turns onto Pacific, he rests a moment. The long road before him is marked with globes of light. He runs his hand along the walls for support. On the steep hill, his legs feel strangely heavy when they land on the pavement and oddly light when they bounce off. He chants to himself, "Hurry. Important. Faster."

When he reaches Powell, he leans against the fire hydrant for a moment, glad that he's halfway there. He can see Broadway; it's still brightly lit. He's breathing hard by the time he gets to The Oasis. This late, it's been long closed. You Thin stands outside, banging on the big wooden doors and rapping on the windows. He cups his hands to the barred window, trying to see in. But with the glare from the street lamps, it's like looking into a mirror.

He takes a deep breath. "Ah-Boy, AAHHH-Boy-AAAHH! . . ."

Silence. Then the sound of flapping slippers, and Ah-Boy opens the door, mop in hand.

You Thin throws his arms about, waving toward Pacific. He slaps the restaurant wall, shouting, "Mah-mah. Be sick. Be sick."

Ah-Boy opens his mouth; his head jerks back and forth, but there is no sound. He lets his broom fall with a clatter. The heavy door slams shut.

Ah-Boy is a big man and You Thin can't keep up for long. At Pacific, You Thin waves him on.

You Thin watches for a moment as Ah-Boy moves up the hill. Yes, he nods. Ah-Boy is a good son.

WHEN You Thin gets to the apartment, Ah-Boy is sitting on the floor with his mother's head on his lap, her gray hair loosened from its bun. She is speaking to Ah-Boy in a low voice.

You Thin and Hang Fong stand under the door frame, watching. "Just like last year," Hang Fong says, "just like Old Jue."

On the phone You Thin speaks loud. He pronounces the syllables as if each sound were a single character. "Numbah Two. Sah-moon Alley. Old Lady. Sick. You be the come.

Now, sabei? I stand by downdaire, sabei? Numbah Two, Sah-moon Alley."

Hang Fong stands next to him, listening hard. She whispers something to him.

You Thin raises his head, and speaks even louder. "One minute. You know, Old Lady, she be . . . uh, uh . . . Old Lady she be come from Italy. You sabei? Lady not from China."

At the square the next day, You Thin challenges the Newspaper Man to a chess game. You Thin plays with one leg raised on the cement stool. "My Car over your lousy paper Gun, and you're eaten." The Newspaper Man's children fold *The Chinese Times* on the next table. Lame-Leg Fong tries to tell You Thin which pieces to move. The #15 Kearney bus inches down Clay, its brakes squeaking and hissing. Cars honk.

You Thin tells his story about last night in between chess moves. He describes the distance between Salmon Alley and Broadway. His running motions make his blue sleeves go vlop-vlop in the wind. He repeats all the English words he used, tries to use the ones he'd heard, and makes all the faces Ah-Boy made. He walks the line on the ground to show what he did in midair. Little boys run by on their way to the water fountain.

Hang Fong tells the story without looking up. The ladies listen with rounded backs and moving hands. Sheets of fabric run from the machines to the floor. Clumps of thread knot around the chair legs; spools of color ripple above the ladies' bent heads. The overlock machines click; the steam irons hiss. Some ladies sing along with the drum and gong beat of the Cantonese opera playing on the radio. A voice booms over the intercom system, "LAST CHANCE TO HAND IN THOSE TICKETS, RIGHT NOW!" No one looks up. Some ladies cluck their tongues and roll their eyes. Others shake their heads and curse under their breath.

Many of the sewing ladies want to hear Hang Fong's story, but missing a sentence here or there, they can't follow the drama. Is it a story or is it real? The women become heavy-footed; the needles stamp urgent stitches into the fabric. Trousers fly over the work tables; the colorful mounds of clothing clutter the floor.

Eventually the grumble of the machines drowns out the story. A young girl runs in to ask her mother for money as the fish peddler arrives, singing out her catch in a breath as long as thread.

ABOUT FAE MYENNE NG

Fae Myenne Ng (fā myən əng) is a native San Franciscan, born in 1956, whose short works include an award-winning collection of stories about old-timers in San Francisco's Chinatown. Her first novel, *Bone*, published in 1993, explores the hopes, griefs, and quarrels of two generations of Chinese Americans in San Francisco. A recurrent theme in Ng's writing is the difficulty of maintaining old traditions in a new country.

RESPONDING

1. *Personal Response* Do Hang Fong and You Thin fit your image of good neighbors, or do their acts go beyond neighborliness? Explain.

2. *Literary Analysis* Find details about the *setting* that reveal what everyday life is like in this Chinatown community.

3. *Multicultural Connection* This is a story about Chinese and Italian people who manage to interact despite the fact that they are unable to speak each other's language. Why are these details important in the story?

LANGUAGE WORKSHOP

Writing a Descriptive Paragraph Ng gives a memorable glimpse of life at the square in Chinatown in the *descriptive paragraph* that begins, "At the square the next day" (page 516). Reread this paragraph. What images appeal to sight? to sound? Now write your own description of a place familiar to you, using at least three images that appeal to various senses.

WRITER'S PORTFOLIO

You Thin believes that "a well-meaning word spoken in the face of ill fortune can turn luck around." Devise a simple story plot that illustrates this saying. Then write a paragraph that could serve as the opening of this story.

Glory and Hope

In addition to bringing an end to white monopoly government in South Africa, the inauguration of Nelson Mandela on May 11, 1994, signaled the end of unparalleled international pressure on the country to change its racist policies. The elections in 1994 were marked by bloody dissension, particularly on the part of supporters of the Zulu Inkatha Freedom Party. Mandela refers to the national and the international climates in his inauguration speech, which follows.

YOUR MAJESTIES, your royal highnesses, distinguished guests, comrades and friends:

Today, all of us do, by our presence here, and by our celebrations in other parts of our country and the world, confer glory and hope to newborn liberty.

Out of the experience of an extraordinary human disaster that lasted too long must be born a society of which all humanity will be proud.

Our daily deeds as ordinary South Africans must produce an actual South African reality that will reinforce humanity's belief in justice, strengthen its confidence in the nobility of the human soul and sustain all our hopes for a glorious life for all.

All this we owe both to ourselves and to the peoples of the world who are so well represented here today.

To my compatriots, I have no hesitation in saying that each one of us is as intimately attached to the soil of this beautiful country as are the famous jacaranda trees of Pretoria and the mimosa trees of the bushveld.

Each time one of us touches the soil of this land, we feel a sense of personal renewal. The national mood changes as the seasons change.

We are moved by a sense of joy and exhilaration when the grass turns green and the flowers bloom.

That spiritual and physical oneness we all share with this common homeland explains the depth of the pain we all carried in our hearts as we saw our country tear itself apart in terrible conflict, as we saw it spurned, outlawed and isolated by the peoples of the world, precisely because it has become the universal base of the pernicious ideology and practice of racism and racial oppression.

We, the people of South Africa, feel fulfilled that humanity has taken us back into its bosom, that we, who were outlaws not so long ago, have today been given the rare privilege to be host to the nations of the world on our own soil.

We thank all our distinguished international guests for having come to take possession with the people of our country of what is, after all, a common victory for justice, for peace, for human dignity.

We trust that you will continue to stand by us as we tackle the challenges of building peace, prosperity, nonsexism, nonracialism and democracy.

We deeply appreciate the role that the masses of our people and their democratic, religious, women, youth, business, traditional and other leaders have played to bring about this conclusion. Not least among them is my Second Deputy President, the Honorable F. W. de Klerk.

We would also like to pay tribute to our security forces, in all their ranks, for the distinguished role they have played in securing our first democratic elections and the transition to democracy, from bloodthirsty forces which still refuse to see the light.

The time for the healing of the wounds has come.

The moment to bridge the chasms that divide us has come.

The time to build is upon us.

We have, at last, achieved our political emancipation. We pledge ourselves to liberate all our people from the continuing bondage of poverty, deprivation, suffering, gender and other discrimination.

We succeeded to take our last steps to freedom in conditions of relative peace. We commit ourselves to the construction of a complete, just and lasting peace.

We have triumphed in the effort to implant hope in the breasts of the millions of our people. We enter into a covenant that we shall build the society in which all South Africans, both black and white, will be able to walk tall, without any fear in their hearts, assured of their inalienable right to human dignity—a rainbow nation at peace with itself and the world.

As a token of its commitment to the renewal of our country, the new Interim Government of National Unity will, as a matter of urgency, address the issue of amnesty for various categories of our people who are currently serving terms of imprisonment.

We dedicate this day to all the heroes and heroines in this country and the rest of the world who sacrificed in many ways and surrendered their lives so that we could be free.

Their dreams have become reality. Freedom is their reward.

We are both humbled and elevated by the honor and privilege that you, the people of South Africa, have bestowed on us, as the first President of a united, democratic, nonracial and nonsexist South Africa, to lead our country out of the valley of darkness.

We understand it still that there is no easy road to freedom.

We know it well that none of us acting alone can achieve success.

We must therefore act together as a united people, for national reconciliation, for nation building, for the birth of a new world.

Let there be justice for all.

Let there be peace for all.

Let there be work, bread, water and salt for all.

Let each know that for each the body, the mind and the soul have been freed to fulfill themselves.

Never, never and never again shall it be that this beautiful land will again experience the oppression of one by another and suffer the indignity of being the skunk of the world.

The sun shall never set on so glorious a human achievement!

Let freedom reign. God bless Africa!

ABOUT **NELSON MANDELA**

Nelson Rolihlahla Mandela (män del′ə), elected President of South Africa in the country's first all-race elections in 1994, was born into a royal African family in 1918. In 1993 Mandela shared the Nobel Peace Prize with F. W. de Klerk, then South Africa's President and Mandela's main white opponent in the 1994 elections. For twenty-seven years Mandela served a  life sentence for attempting to overthrow the government he now leads. Upon his release in 1990, he began working with the white government to initiate democratic reforms in the country long dominated by apartheid.

RESPONDING

1. *Personal Response* Which paragraph of Mandela's speech do you find the most powerful? Why do you think it affects you this way?
2. *Literary Analysis* What *figurative language* does Mandela use to emphasize the changes taking place in South Africa?

3. *Multicultural Connection* In the 1994 election, Mandela's African National Congress won 252 of the 400 seats available in South Africa's National Assembly, formerly an all-white governing body. Based on what you know of South Africa's recent history, or on information provided in *Kaffir Boy*, page 316, how do you think such a change could influence the country?

LANGUAGE WORKSHOP

Adjectives Mandela's use of *adjectives* adds to the power of his speech. He contrasts the *terrible* conflicts of the past with the *glorious* life he envisions for the future. Explain which of the following adjectives would fit his hopeful vision for South Africa's future: *democratic, nonsexist, pernicious, nonracial, bloodthirsty*. Now think of two more adjectives that could be included in his vision.

WRITER'S PORTFOLIO

Imagine you were able to attend Mandela's inauguration in Pretoria, South Africa. Compose a journal entry about your experiences and emotions on that day.

Projects

TESTIMONIAL DINNER

You are master/mistress of ceremonies at a testimonial dinner at which awards will be presented. Think of characters, groups, and writers appearing in selections in this unit who have triumphed despite obstacles. Present five such candidates with an award, delivering a speech that highlights specific triumphs for each one.

INTERVIEW

Working with a partner, find someone in your school, neighborhood, or community who has triumphed over some obstacle—perhaps a tragedy such as a fire, a difficult goal, or a challenging class in school. Try to choose someone who would be willing and available to be an interview subject. Then plan your questions and set up an appointment to conduct your interview. If possible, record the interview on tape. Then present the interview to classmates.

WRITING ABOUT TRIUMPHS

Life's little triumphs—a new friend made, a puzzle solved, a good performance for your team—often go unrecorded. The act of charity performed by the Chinese couple in "Last Night," for example, seems insignificant when compared to something as dramatic as the overthrow of a dictator in "The Rebellion of the Magical Rabbits." How much credit is due someone like Sara Reisel, who decides to take control of her fate when life seems impossible? Write an essay about three authors or characters in this unit, explaining how each has triumphed. Then tell whose triumphs you consider most impressive.

Further Reading

The following books chronicle the struggles of people who overcome obstacles and triumph.

Angelou, Maya. *I Know Why the Caged Bird Sings.* Random House, 1970. This autobiography, which has become a classic, recounts the first sixteen years of Angelou's life.

Brönte, Emily. *Wuthering Heights.* Bantam, 1983. Set on the Yorkshire moors, this novel explores the relationship of Heathcliff and Catherine, whose fated love extends beyond the grave.

Carlson, Lori M. and Venture, Cynthia L., eds. *Where Angels Glide at Dawn.* J. B. Lippincott, New York, 1992. This collection of tales by modern Latin American writers mixes humor, poetry, politics, and imagination.

Dangarembga, Tsitsi. *Nervous Conditions.* The Seal Press, 1989. Two girls coming of age in Africa witness the destructive forces of colonization by another culture and learn to recognize the power of friendship and education.

Hansberry, Lorraine. *A Raisin in the Sun.* New American Library, 1988. In this drama, a family who seeks to move out of a Chicago ghetto maintains its dignity and dreams despite tremendous obstacles.

Wiesel, Elie. *Night.* Bantam, 1982. A Jewish boy who witnesses his family's death in Auschwitz survives to tell his story, in the hope of preventing the horrible incidents from recurring.

Yezierska, Anzia. *How I Found America.* Persea Books, 1991. This collection, which contains virtually all of Yezierska's fiction, provides keen insights into the immigrant experience and the obstacles immigrants had to overcome in this land.

Glossary

abhorrent (ab hôr′ənt), *adj.* causing horror and disgust; detestable

ablution (ab lü′shən), *n.* a washing or cleansing as a religious ceremony of purification

abortive (ə bôr′tiv), *adj.* unsuccessful

abstain (ab stān′), *v.* hold oneself back voluntarily; refrain

abstraction (ab strak′shən), *n.* anything concerned with ideas and concepts rather than actual particulars or instances

absurd (ab sèrd′), *adj.* plainly not logical or sensible; ridiculous

abyss (ə bis′), *n.* anything too deep or great to be measured; chasm

accompaniment (ə kum′pə nē mənt), *n.* a subsidiary instrumental part to support or enrich the melody

accomplice (ə kom′plis), *n.* a person who knowingly aids another in committing a crime or other wrong act

adamant (ad′ə mənt), *adj.* firm and unyielding

admonishing (ad mon′ish ing), *adj.* gentle scolding

adversary (ad′vər ser′ē), *n.* opponent

agitation (aj′ə tā′shən), *n.* a violent moving or shaking; a disturbed, upset, or troubled state

airshaft (er′shaft′), *n.* a ventilating shaft or well in a building; a narrow space in a building that allows air to flow through

Allah (al′ə), *n.* the Moslem name of the one Supreme Being, or God

allegation (al′ə gā′shən), *n.* an assertion; a charge undertaken to be proved

allocate (al′ə kāt), *v.* set or lay aside for a special purpose; divide and distribute in parts or shares

alluring (ə lùr′ing), *adj.* strongly attracting

alternating (ôl′tər nāt ing), *adj.* succeeding each other by turns; taking turns

amalgam (ə mal′gəm), *n.* a mixture or blend of different things

amateur (am′ə chər), *n.* person who does something for pleasure, not for money or as a profession; person who does something rather poorly

amber (am′bər), *n.* a hard, translucent, yellow or yellowish-brown fossil resin, easily polished and used for jewelry

amiable (ā′mē ə bəl), *adj.* having a good-natured and friendly disposition

amnesty (am′nə stē), *n.* a general pardon or conditional offer of pardon for past offenses against a government

annihilation (ə nī′ə lā′shən), *n.* complete destruction

apartheid (ə pärt′hāt), *n.* racial segregation, especially the former legalized segregation in the Republic of South Africa

apostasy (ə pos′tə sē), *n.* abandonment of one's principles

appalling (ə pô′ling), *adj.* dismaying; terrifying

archive (är′kīv), *n.* place where public records or historical documents are kept

arroyo (ə roi′ō), *n.* a dry gulch

assent (ə sent′), *n.* agreement

assiduously (ə sij′ü əs lē), *adj.* carefully; diligently

assimilate (ə sim′ə lāt), *v.* take in and make part of oneself

attune (ə tün′), *v.* put in harmony or agreement

audacious (ô dā′shəs), *adj.* recklessly daring; bold

audacity (ô das′ə tē), *n.* reckless daring; boldness

avail (ə vāl), *n.* use; help

avalanche (av′ə lanch), *n.* a large mass of snow or ice, or of dirt and rocks, loosened from a mountainside and descending swiftly into the valley below; anything that moves like an avalanche

avenger (ə venj′ər), *n.* one who takes revenge for or on behalf of; one who does harm in return for a wrong done

avert (ə vèrt′), *v.* keep from happening

awning (ô′ning), *n.* a roof-like cover extending over a place for protection from sun or rain

balustrade (bal′ə strād), *n.* row of short posts or columns supporting the railing of a staircase and the railing on them

baste (bāst), *v.* sew with long, loose stitches to hold the cloth until the final sewing

bazaar (bə zär′), *n.* a marketplace consisting of a street or streets full of small shops and booths

bemused (bi myüzd′), *adj.* confused; bewildered

benefactor (ben′ə fak′tər), *n.* person who has helped others by some kind act

benevolent (bə nev′ə lənt), *adj.* kindly

benzene (ben′zēn′), *n.* a colorless, volatile, flammable liquid obtained chiefly from coal tar

bereft (bi reft′), *adj.* left desolate and alone; deprived

betel (bē′tl), *n.* a climbing pepper plant of the East Indies, India, and Southeast Asia, whose leaves and a little lime are wrapped around its nuts and chewed

bizarre (bə zär′), *adj.* strikingly odd in appearance or style

blasphemous (blas′fə məs), *adj.* showing of abuse or contempt for sacred things; profane

blench (blench), *v.* draw back; flinch

blinker (bling′kər), *n.* either of two leather flaps on a horse's bridle to keep the horse from seeing sideways; blinder

bloomers (blü′mərz), *n. pl.* loose underwear, gathered at the knee

blues (blüz), *n. pl.* a slow, melancholy song with jazz rhythm that originated among American Negroes; in low spirits; sad; gloomy

blunderbuss (blun′dər bus), *n.* a short gun with a wide muzzle and large bore

borne (bôrn), *v.* taken from one place to another; carried

boudoir (bü′dwär), *n.* a lady's private bedroom, dressing room, or sitting room

bountiful (boun′tə fəl), *adj.* plentiful; abundant; generous

bout (bout), *n.* a period spent in some particular way

brilliant (bril′yənt), *adj.* splendid; having great ability

brink (bringk), *n.* edge at the top of a steep place; edge

bureaucratic (byùr′ə krat′ik), *adj.* having to do with a system of administration marked by red tape and officialism

bushveld (bùsh′felt′), *n.* southern African veld characterized by abundant shrubby and often thorny vegetation

caddy (caddie) (cad′ē), *v.* help a golf player by carrying golf clubs, finding balls, etc.

calcified (kal′sə fid), *adj.* made hard by the deposits of calcium salts; hardened

calisthenics (kal′is then′iks), *n. pl.* exercises to develop a strong and graceful body, carried out by moving the body, without the use of special equipment

calligraphed (kal′ə grafd), *v.* written by hand

callus (kal′əs), *v.* to develop a hard, thickened place on the skin

calypso (kə lip′sō), *n.* type of improvised song, usually about some matter of current interest, that originated in the West Indies

cannery (kan′ər ē), *n.* factory where food is canned

caress (kə res′), *n.* tender touch or stroke

caste (kast), *n.* an exclusive social group; distinct class

cataclysmic (kat′ə kliz′mik), *adj.* extremely sudden and violent

cataract (kat′ə rakt), *n.* an opaque condition in the lens of the eye that may cause partial or total blindness

caul (kôl), *n.* a portion of the membrane enclosing a child in the womb; a net lining in the back of a woman's cap or hat; a net or covering

certificate (sər tif′ə kit), *n.* an official written statement that declares something to be a fact; a stock certificate shows ownership of a specified number of shares of stock

character (kar′ik tər), *n.* letter, mark, or sign used in writing and printing; symbol

chasm (kaz′əm), *n.* any marked gap or break; a wide difference of feelings or interests between people or groups

check (chek), *v.* stop suddenly; restrain

cheeky (chē′kē), *adj.* saucy; impudent

chivalry (shiv′əl rē), *n.* rules and customs of knights in the Middle Ages — bravery, honor, etc.

chuck (chuk), *v.* throw or toss

churn (chėrn), *v.* move as if agitated or shaken; bounce along with grinding or rattling

cinch (sinch), *n.* something sure and easy (slang)

clairvoyance (kler voi′əns), *n.* the supposed power of seeing or knowing about things that are out of sight; exceptional insight

clamor (klam′ər), *n.* loud noise or continual uproar

classical (klas′ə kəl), *adj.* acquainted with or having to do with works of literature or art of the highest rank or quality; (in music) of high artistic quality and enjoyed especially by serious students of music

clatter (klat′ər), *n.* a confused noise like that of many plates being struck together; a rattling sound

clinical (klin′ə kəl), *adj.* coldly impersonal; unemotional

clutch (kluch), *n.* group of people or things

cockerel (kok′ər əl), *n.* a young rooster, not more than a year old

cognition (kog nish′ən), *n.* act of knowing; awareness

collards (kol′ərdz), *n. pl.* the fleshy leaves of the kale (collard) plant, cooked as greens

commissar (kom′ə sär), *n.* an official in charge of the supply of food, stores, and transport for soldiers; deputy

commodity (kə mod′ə tē), *n.* anything that is bought and sold; a useful thing

compassion (kəm pash′ən), *n.* pity, sympathy

compatriot (kəm pā′trē ət), *n.* another person born or living in one's own country

compensate (kom′pən sāt), *v.* make up (for)

complaisant (kəm plā′snt), *adj.* obliging, gracious

complicity (kəm plis′ə tē), *n.* partnership in wrongdoing

comply (kəm plī′), *v.* act in agreement with a request or demand

compost (kom′pōst), *v.* pile or build up a heap of vegetable matter in a special way so it decays for fertilizer; to build up

compromised (kom′prə mīzd), *adj.* exposed to suspicion, danger, etc.

comrade (kom′rad), *n.* companion or friend; fellow member of a union

conceit (kən sēt′), *n.* a fanciful notion; vanity

confidence man (kon′fə dəns), *n.* swindler who persuades his victim to trust him

confidential (kon′fə den′shəl), *adj.* told or written as a secret

conjurer (kon′jər ər), *n.* person who performs tricks with quick, deceiving movements of the hands

connive (kə nīv′), *v.* avoid noticing something wrong; cooperate secretly

conniving (kə nīv′ing), *adj.* cooperating secretly

connoisseur (kon′ə sėr′), *n.* a critical judge of art or of matters of taste; expert

constituency (kən stich′ü ən sē), *n.* a district

consumption (kən sump′shən), *n.* a wasting disease of the body, especially tuberculosis of the lungs

contempt (kən tempt′), *n.* the feeling that a person is mean, low, or worthless; scorn

contemptuous (kən temp′chü əs), *adj.* scornful; disgraceful

contingent (kən tin′jənt), *n.* group that is part of a larger group

convention (kən ven′shən), *n.* custom or practice approved by general agreement

conviction (kən vik′shən), *n.* firm belief; certainty

coronet (kôr′ə net′), *n.* a small crown

corral (kə ral′), *n.* pen for keeping or for capturing horses, cattle, etc.

coterie (kō′tər ē), *n.* set or circle of close acquaintances

counselor (koun′sə lər), *n.* a person who gives advice

countenance (koun′tə nəns), *v.* approve; sanction

court (kôrt), *v.* act so as to get; seek

courtyard (kôrt′yärd′), *n.* space enclosed by walls in or near a large building

couturier (kü tur′ē ər), *n.* a shop where dresses are made or designed

covenant (kuv′ə nənt), *n.* a solemn agreement between two or more persons or groups to do or not to do a certain thing

cower (kou′ər), *v.* crouch in fear

crane (krān), *n.* machine with a long, swinging arm, for lifting and moving heavy weights

credence (krēd′ns), *n.* belief; credit

crescent (kres′nt), *n.* shape of the moon in its first or last quarter; shape having one convex and one concave edge

crestfallen (krest′fô′lən), *adj.* dejected; discouraged

crinoline (krin′l ən), *n.* a full stiff skirt or underskirt

crocheted (krō shād′), *v.* made by crocheting

crocheting (krō shā′ing), *n.* needlework done by looping thread or yarn into links with a single hooked needle

crossbeam (krôs′bēm′), *n.* a large piece of timber that crosses another or extends from wall to wall

crossbow (krôs′bō), *n.* a weapon for shooting arrows, stones, etc.

cultivate (kul′tə vāt), *v.* loosen and break up soil for growing plants

curio (kyùr′ē ō), *n.* a strange, rare, or novel object

cutworm (kut′wèrm′), *n.* any of several night-feeding moth larvae that cut off the stalks of young plants near or below the ground

damask (dam′əsk), *n.* a firm, shiny, reversible linen, silk, or cotton fabric with woven designs

debase (di bās′), *v.* lessen in value

deceit (di sēt′), *n.* cheating

declaim (di klām′), *v.* speak in a loud and emotional manner

decorum (di kôr′əm), *n.* proper behavior; good taste in conduct

deference (def′ər əns), *n.* great respect; respect for the judgment, opinion, wishes, etc., of another

defiance (di fi′əns), *n.* challenge to do something

deformity (di fôr′mə tē), *n.* part that is not properly formed

defraud (di frôd′), *v.* cheat

delirium tremens (di lir′ē əm trē′mənz), *n.* violent tremblings and terrifying hallucinations, caused by prolonged and excessive drinking of alcoholic liquor

delude (di lüd′), *v.* trick or deceive

demagogue (dem′ə gog), *n.* a leader who makes use of popular prejudices and false claims and promises in order to gain power

denounce (di nouns′), *v.* condemn publicly; express strong disapproval of

deportation (dē′pôr tā′shən), *n.* removal from a country by banishment or expulsion

depraved (di prāvd′), *adj.* made morally bad; corrupted

deprivation (dep′rə vā′shən), *n.* condition of being kept from having or doing

derelict (der′ə likt), *n.* a penniless person who is homeless, jobless, and abandoned by others

desolate (des′ə lit), *adj.* unhappy; wretched

desolation (des′ə lā′shən), *n.* a ruined, lonely, or deserted condition

destitute (des′tə tüt), *adj.* lacking necessary things such as food, clothing, and shelter

detestable (di tes′tə bəl), *adj.* hateful

devotion (di vō′shən), *n.* an act of prayer

devour (di′vour), *v.* eat like an animal; eat very hungrily

diffident (dif′ə dənt), *n.* lacking in self-confidence; shy

diligent (dil′ə jənt), *adj.* hard-working; industrious

dim sum (dim′sum′), *n.* small dumplings, usually steamed or fried and filled with meat, seafood, or vegetables, etc. (Chinese cooking)

dingy (din′jē), *adj.* lacking brightness or freshness; dirty-looking

diplomacy (də plō′mə sē), *n.* skill in dealing with others; tact

directive (də rek′tiv), *n.* a general instruction on how to proceed or act

discreet (dis krēt′), *adj.* wisely cautious; sensible

discreetly (dis creet′lē), *adv.* with wise caution

dismantle (dis man′tl), *v.* take apart

dissident (dis′ə dənt), *n.* person who disagrees or thinks differently

distraught (dis trôt′), *adj.* in a state of mental conflict and confusion

divan (dī′van), *n.* a long, low, soft couch or sofa

diversify (də vèr′sə fi), *v.* vary

divine (də vīn′), *adj.* like God or a god; heavenly

divulge (də vulj′), *v.* reveal

dock (dok), *n.* the place where an accused person stands or sits in a court of law

dolorously (dol′ər əs lē), *adv.* mournfully

domain (dō mān′), *n.* sphere of activity

dossier (dos′ē ā), *n.* collection of documents or papers about some subject or person

dowry (dou′rē), *n.* money or property that a woman brings to the man she marries; a gift of money or property by a man to or for his bride

draught (draft), *n.* current of air, especially in a confined space, as a room or a chimney

drouth (drought) (drout), *n.* a long period of dry weather; continued lack of rain

duct (dukt), *n.* tube in the body for carrying a bodily fluid, such as tears

dumbfoundment (dum′found′mənt), *n.* state of amazement and inability to speak; confusion

dunce (duns), *n.* person who is stupid or slow to learn

eclipse (i klips′), *n.* the passing into the shadow of a heavenly body

economize (i kon′ə mīz), *v.* use to the best advantage; cut down expenses

ecstasy (ek′stə sē), *n.* condition of great joy

egalitarian (ē gal′ə tər′ē ən), *adj.* believing that all people are equal

egret (ē′gret), *n.* any of various herons which in mating season grow tufts of beautiful long plumes

eloquence (el′ə kwəns), *n.* flow of speech that has grace and force

eloquent (el′ə kwənt), *adj.* very expressive

eloquently (el′ə kwənt lē), *adv.* very expressively; with vivid revelation

elude (i lüd′), *v.* baffle

emaciated (i mā′shē āt əd), *adj.* condition of being unnaturally thin

embalm (em bäm′), *v.* to treat a dead body to protect it from decay; cover with a balm (ointment) to protect the skin

embezzle (em bez′əl), *v.* steal (money, securities, etc., entrusted to one's care)

embroider, *v.* ornament (cloth, leather, etc.) with a raised design or pattern of stitches

embroidered (em broi′dərd), *adj.* ornamented with needlework

embroidery (em broi′dər ē), *n.* the act or art of embroidering

empathy (em′pə thē), *n.* the quality of entering fully, through imagination, into another's feelings; sympathy

en masse (en mas′), *adv.* in a group; all together

encomium (en kō′mē əm), *n.* a formal expression of high praise

endearing (en dir′ing), *adj.* that inspires or creates affection for

endgame (end′gām), *n.* the stage of a chess game following a serious reduction of forces

enthusiasm (en thü′zē az′əm), *n.* eager interest

entice (en tis′), *v.* tempt; coax

enticing (en tis′ing), *adj.* tempting

epidemic (ep′ə dem′ik), *n.* the rapid spread of an idea, fashion, etc.

equestrian (i kwes′trē ən), *adj.* on horseback

erotic (i rot′ik), *adj.* of or having to do with sexual passion or love

errant (er′ənt), *adj.* wandering; roving

escarpment (e skärp′mənt), *n.* ground made into a steep slope as part of a fortification; a steep slope

ethereal (i thir′ē əl), *adj.* not of the earth; heavenly

ethics (eth′iks), *n. pl.* the study of standards of right and wrong

etiquette (et′ə ket), *n.* the customary rules for conduct or behavior in polite society

evanescence (ev′ə nes′ns), *n.* a fading away; vanishing

evolution (ev′ə lü′shən), *n.* a process of change or gradual development; unfolding

exasperated (eg zas′pə rāt′id), *adj.* extremely annoyed; very irritated

excursion (ek skėr′zhən), *n.* a going out or forth; a journey

exertion (eg zėr′shən), *n.* strenuous action; effort

exhilaration (eg zil′ə rā′shən), *n.* high spirits; lively joy

expedition (ek′spə dish′ən), *n.* journey for some special purpose, such as for military purposes

exquisite (ek′skwi zit), *adj.* very lovely; delicate

exterminate (ek stėr′mə nāt), *v.* destroy completely

exuberant (eg zü′bər ənt), *adj.* abounding in health and spirits; overflowing with good cheer

exude (eg züd′), *v.* give forth; emit

faceted (fas′it əd), *adj.* having many small, smooth, flat surfaces

fallacy (fal′ə sē), *n.* mistaken belief; error

fatuously (fach′ü əs lē), *adv.* stupidly but self-satisfied; foolishly

faux (fō), *adj.* false; fake

feign (fān), *v.* make believe; pretend

feigned (fānd), *adj.* made oneself appear; pretended (to be)

felicity (fə lis′ə tē), *n.* great happiness

feral (fir′əl), *adj.* wild, untamed

ferret (fer′it), *v.* hunt; search

ferry (fer′ē), *n.* a boat used to carry passengers, goods, and vehicles across a river or narrow stretch of water

fetter (fet′ər), *v.* bind with chains

fickle (fik′əl), *adj.* likely to change or give up loyalty, attachments, etc., without reason

flare (fler), *v.* shine; glow

flimsy (flim′zē), *adj.* light and thin

flotsam (flot′səm), *n.* wreckage of a ship or its cargo found floating on the sea

flounced (flounsd), *adj.* trimmed with a wide strip of cloth, gathered along the top edge and sewed to a dress; having a wide ruffle

flourish (flėr′ish), *n.* a showy display

flustered (flus′tərd), *adj.* nervous and excited; confused

folly (fol′ē), *n.* lack of sense; unwise conduct

foray (fôr′ā), *n.* a raid for the purpose of robbing

foremast (fôr′mast′), *n.* the long pole arising nearest the bow of a ship

foresight (fôr′sīt), *n.* power to see or know beforehand what is likely to happen

foundry (foun′drē), *n.* place where metal is melted and molded

fragility (frə jil′ə tē), *n.* condition of being delicate or frail

fragment (frag′mənt), *n.* part broken off

fraud (frôd), *n.* a person who is not what she/he seems to be; impostor

frenzy (fren′zē), *n.* state of near madness

friction (frik′shən), *n.* a rubbing of one object against another

frivolity (fri vol′ə tē), *n.* silly behavior

frivolous (friv′ə ləs), *adj.* silly

furrow (fėr′ō), *n.* a long, narrow groove or track cut in the earth by a plow; something, such as streams of tears, that resembles the tracks of a plow

furrowed (fėr′ōd), *adj.* wrinkled

gaberdine (gabardine) (gab′ər dēn′), *n.* a closely woven cloth with small, diagonal ribs on its surface; a garment of this cloth

gallant (gal′ənt), *n.* man who wears showy and stylish clothes

galleon (gal′ē ən), *n.* a large, high ship with three or four decks, used especially in the 1400s and 1500s

gaudy (gô′dē), *adj.* cheap and showy

genetic (jə net′ik), *adj.* having to do with origin and natural growth; hereditary

genial (jē′nyəl), *adj.* cheerful and friendly

genocide (jen′ə sīd), *n.* the extermination of a cultural or racial group

ghetto (get′ō), *n.* part of a city where any racial group or nationality lives; (formerly) a part of a city in Europe where Jews were required to live

ghoul (gül), *n.* a horrible demon that robs graves and feeds on corpses

glean (glēn), *v.* gather grain left on a field by reapers

gnomic (nō′mik), *adj.* full of meaning; saying much in a few words

goad (gōd), *n.* a sharp-pointed stick for driving cattle

grace (grās), *v.* adorn

greatcoat (grāt′kōt′), *n.* a heavy overcoat

grimace (grə mās′), *v.* make a facial expression by twisting the face to show disgust; frown unattractively

guileless (gīl′lis), *adj.* honest

gullet (gul′it), *n.* esophagus; throat

gullibility (gul′ə bil′ə tē), *n.* tendency to be easily deceived or cheated

habitually (hə bich′ü əl lē), *adv.* customarily; usually

haggard (hag′ərd), *adj.* looking worn from pain, fatigue, worry, etc.

haggling (hag′gling), *n.* disputing, especially about a price

hapless (hap′lis), *adj.* unlucky; unfortunate

harangue (hə rang′), *n.* a long, pompous, formal speech

haughtiness (hô′tē nəs), *n.* condition of being too proud and scornful of others

haughty (hô′tē), *adj.* too proud and scornful of others

havoc (hav′ək), *n.* devastation; ruin

heinous (hā′nəs), *adj.* extremely offensive

herbivorous (hėr′biv′ər əs), *adj.* feeding on grass or other plants

heredity (hə red′ə tē), *n.* transmission of traits from parents to offspring; qualities that have come to children from parents

heresy (her′ə sē), *n.* opinion opposed to what is generally accepted

hostage (hos′tij), *n.* person given up to another or held by an enemy as a pledge that certain promises will be carried out

hostel (hos′tl), *n.* a lodging place; inexpensive quarters

hover (huv′ər), *v.* hang suspended in air

hulking (hul′king), *adj.* big and clumsy

hymnal (him′nəl), *n.* book of songs of praise; a book of songs in praise and honor of God

ideological (i′dē ə loj′ə kəl), *adj.* having to do with a set of doctrines or beliefs of a person, class, or group

illegally (i lē′gəl lē), *adv.* not lawfully; in violation of a rule or law

illiterate (i lit′ər it), *adj.* unable to read or write

illustrious (i lus′trē əs), *adj.* very famous; outstanding

immense (i mens′), *adj.* extremely large; huge

immigration (im′ə grā′shən), *n.* a coming into a foreign country or region to live there; the persons who immigrate

imminent (im′ə nənt), *adj.* likely to happen soon

impalpable (im pal′pə bəl), *adj.* that cannot be felt by touching; intangible

impediment (im ped′ə mənt), *n.* some physical defect, especially a defect in speech

imperceptibly (im′pər sep′tə blē), *adv.* in a manner not capable of being observed through the senses

imperil (im per′əl), *v.* put in danger

imperious (im pir′ē əs), *adj.* overbearing; domineering

impertinence (im pėrt′n əns), *n.* a being shamelessly bold or greatly rude

imposing (im pō′zing), *adj.* impressive because of size, appearance, dignity, etc.

inadequacy (in ad′ə kwə sē), *n.* a condition of not being sufficient; deficiency

inalienable (in ā′lyə nə bəl), *adj.* that cannot be given or taken away

inarticulate (in′är tik′yə lit), *adj.* not uttered in distinct syllables or words

incarnation (in′kär nā′shən), *n.* a taking on of human form by a divine being; embodiment

incision (in sizh′ən), *n.* cut made in something; gash

incredulity (in′krə dü′lə tē), *n.* lack of belief; doubt

indelible (in del′ə bəl), *adj.* that cannot be erased or removed

indescribable (in′di skrī′bə bəl), *adj.* beyond description

indignation (in′dig nā′shən), *n.* anger mixed with scorn

indiscreet (in′dis krēt′), *adj.* not wise and judicious; imprudent

indispensable (in′dis pen′sə bəl), *adj.* absolutely necessary

ineffable (in ef′ə bəl), *n.* that which is too great to be described in words

ineradicable (in′i rad′ə kə bəl), *adj.* that cannot be rooted out or got rid of; **ineradicably,** *adv.*

inevitable (in ev′ə tə bəl), *adj.* not to be avoided

inexhaustible (in′ig zô′stə bəl), *adj.* that cannot be emptied completely

inexorably (in ek′sər ə blē), *adv.* relentlessly; unyieldingly

infuse (in fyüz′), *v.* instill

ingratiating (in grā′shē āt′ing), *adj.* bring (oneself) into favor

inhospitable (in′ho spit′ə bəl), *adj.* barren

innumerable (i nü′mər ə bəl), *adj.* too many to count; countless

inquisitive (in kwiz′ə tiv), *adj.* prying into other people's affairs; curious

inscrutable (in skrü′tə bəl), *adj.* that cannot be understood; incomprehensible

insidious (in sid′ē əs), *adj.* seeking to entrap or ensnare; developing without attracting attention

insolently (in′sə lənt lē), *adv.* with bold rudeness

instinct (in′stingkt), *n.* a natural tendency or ability

intelligible (in tel′ə jə bəl), *n.* capable of being understood

intercede (in′tər sēd′), *v.* plead for another; ask a favor from one person for another

interminable (in tėr′mə nə bəl), *adj.* so long as to seem endless

interval (in′tər vəl), *n.* period of time between

intransigence (in tran′sə jəns), *n.* a being unwilling to agree or compromise

intuition (in′tü ish′ən), *n.* immediate perception or understanding of truths, facts, etc., without reasoning

invoke (in vōk′), *v.* call on in prayer; appeal to for help or protection

involuntarily (in vol′ən ter′ə lē), *adv.* without one's free will; unintentionally

irreconcilable (i rek′ən sī′lə bəl), *adj.* that cannot be made to agree or make friends

irreproachable (ir′i prō′chə bəl), *adj.* faultless

irrevocable (i rev′ə kə bəl), *adj.* impossible to call or bring back

irrigate (ir′ə gāt), *v.* supply (land) with water by using ditches

isolation (ī′sə lā′shən), *n.* a setting apart or separating from others; loneliness

ivory (ī′vər ē), *n.* a hard, white substance composing the tusks of elephants, walruses, etc.

jam (jam), *v.* make (radio signals, etc.) unintelligible by sending out others of approximately the same frequency

jeopardy (jep′ər dē), *n.* risk; danger; peril

jubilant (jü′bə lənt), *adj.* expressing or showing joy

jubilation (jü′bə lā′shən), *n.* rejoicing

jurisdiction (jür′is dik′shən), *n.* power; control

just (just), *adj.* in accordance with what is right and honest; fair

kerchief (kėr′chif), *n.* piece of cloth worn over the head or around the neck

kimono (kə mō′nə), *n.* a loose outer garment held in place by a wide sash worn by Japanese men and women

knell (nel), *v.* ring slowly; toll; make a mournful sound

kowtow (kou′tou′), *v.* kneel and touch the ground with the forehead to show deep respect, submission, or worship; show slavish respect or obedience

labyrinth (lab′ə rinth′), *n.* maze

lacerated (las′ə rāt id), *adj.* deeply or irregularly indented as if torn

lance (lans), *n.* a long wooden spear with a sharp iron or steel head

landing (lan′ding), *n.* a place where persons or goods are landed from a ship or boat

languishing (lang′gwi shing), *adj.* becoming weak; losing energy

latch (lach), *n.* a movable tongue or bar of metal or wood for fastening a door or window

laurel (lôr′əl), *n.* a small evergreen tree of southern Europe, with smooth, shiny leaves; sweet bay

lecher (lech′ər), *n.* person, especially a man, who displays gross indulgence in lust

ledger (lej′ər), *n.* book of accounts in which a business keeps a final record of all transactions, showing the debits and credits of the various accounts

legitimate (lə jit′ə mit), *adj.* born of parents who are married to each other

lenient (lē′nyənt), *adj.* mild or gentle

leper (lep′ər), *n.* a person who has leprosy—an infectious disease that attacks the skin and nerves

lien (lēn), *n.* a legal claim that one has on the property of another for payment of a debt

limn (lim), *v.* paint; describe

loiter (loi′tər), *v.* linger idly or aimlessly on one's way; stand around

louse (lous), *n.* a mean, contemptible person (slang)

lucidity (lü sid′ə tē), *n.* a being easy to follow or understand

ludicrous (lü′də krəs), *adj.* ridiculous

luminous (lü′mə nəs), *adj.* full of light; shining

lunatic (lü′nə tik), *n.* an insane or crazy person

lurid (lür′id), *adj.* shockingly terrible, repulsive, etc., startling

luxuriant (lug zhùr′ē ənt), *adj.* lush; tender and juicy
lynx-eyed (lingks′īd′), *adj.* having sharp eyes; sharp-sighted
macaw (mə kô′), *n.* any of several large parrots of South and Central America
machete (mə shet′ē), *n.* a large, heavy knife, used as a tool for cutting brush, sugar cane, etc., and as a weapon
madrone (mə drō′nyə), *n.* an evergreen tree or shrub of the heath family
magnanimity (mag′nə nim′ə tē), *n.* nobility of soul or mind; generosity
mainmast (mān′mast′), *n.* the principal pole for attaching sails and rigging on a ship
maintenance (mān′tə nəns), *n.* subsistence; support
malicious (mə lish′əs), *adj.* showing active ill will; wishing to hurt or make suffer; spiteful
malign (mə līn′), *adj.* hateful; malicious
mango (mang′gō), *n.* the tropical evergreen tree on which a fruit with thick, reddish-brown rind grows
mantilla (man til′ə), *n.* veil or scarf, often made of lace, covering the hair and falling down over the shoulders
marrow (mar′ō), *n.* the inmost or essential part
materialize (mə tir′ē ə līz), *v.* appear in material or bodily form
matriarch (mā′trē ärk), *n.* mother who is the ruler of a family or tribe
meditation (med′ə tā′shən), *n.* quiet thought; reflection
mercenary (mèr′sə ner′ē), *n.* person who works merely for pay
meticulously (mə tik′yə ləs lē), *adv.* with extreme or excessive care about details
miasma (mī az′mə), *n.* a bad smelling vapor rising from decaying organic matter in swamps; anything which resembles this in its ability to spread and poison
midship (mid′ship′), *adj.* in or of the middle part of a ship
minaret (min′ə ret′), *n.* a slender, high tower of a Moslem mosque, from which a muezzin calls the people to prayer
minister (min′ə stər), *v.* to be of service or aid; be helpful

mirage (mə räzh′), *n.* an optical illusion; anything that does not exist
modicum (mod′ə kəm), *n.* a small or moderate quantity
modulated (moj′ə lāt əd), *adj.* regulated or adjusted so as to tone down; softened
momentum (mō men′təm), *n.* force with which a body moves
mongrel (mung′grəl), *adj.* of mixed breed
moribund (môr′ə bund), *adj.* at the point of death or extinction; dying
morrow (môr′ō), *n.* the following day or time; morning
mortal (môr′tl), *adj.* causing death; fatal; of human beings; very great
mother-of-pearl, *n.* the hard, smooth, glossy lining of certain mollusk shells, such as oysters, that changes color in light and is used for buttons and other decorations; a milky-white, iridescent shell layer
mourning (môr′ning), *n.* period of time during which one grieves
mouthing (mouth′ing), *v.* utter words in an affected or pompous way; to repeat without comprehension or sincerity
muse (myüz), *v.* be completely absorbed in thought
musicianship (myü zish′ən ship), *n.* musical ability
mutant (myüt′nt), *adj.* that is the result of change or alteration
myriad (mir′ē əd), *adj.* countless; innumerable
naive (nä ēv′), *adj.* simple in nature; like a child
narcissism (när′sə siz′əm), *n.* excessive love or admiration of oneself
nausea (nô′zē ə), *n.* the feeling a person has when about to vomit
nefarious (ni fer′ē əs), *adj.* very wicked; villainous
nephritis (ni frī′tis), *n.* inflammation of the kidneys
neutrality (nü tral′ə tē), *n.* quality or condition of not taking part in a quarrel or war
nil (nil), *n.* nothing
noble (nō′bəl), *adj.* high and great by birth, rank, or title
nocturnal (nok tèr′nl), *adj.* of the night
nonchalantly (non′shə lənt lē), *adv.* with cool unconcern; indifferently

nostalgia (no stal′jə), *n.* a painful or wistful yearning for one's home, country, city, or for anything far removed in space or time

novelty (nov′əl tə), *n.* new or unusual thing

nuanced (nü änsd′), *adj.* having a shade of color or tone

nucleus (nü′klē əs), *n.* a central part or thing around which other parts or things are collected; a beginning to which additions are to be made

nurture (nėr′chər), *v.* nourish

object lesson, a practical illustration of a principle

obsolete (ob′sə lēt), *adj.* no longer in use

obstinate (ob′stə nit), *adj.* not giving in; stubborn

obtrusive (əb trü′siv), *adj.* inclined to put forward unasked and unwanted

odious (ō′dē əs), *adj.* hateful; offensive

okra (ō′krə), *n.* a plant grown for its sticky pods, which are used in soups and as a vegetable

omen (ō′mən), *n.* sign of what is to happen

option (op′shən), *n.* thing that is or can be chosen

oracle (ôr′ə kəl), *n.* the priest, priestess, or other means by which the god's answer was believed to be given; a very wise person

oratory (ôr′ə tôr′ē), *n.* eloquent speaking or language

ostracize (os′trə sīz), *v.* shut out from society, favor, or privileges, etc.

overture (ō′vər chər), *n.* proposal or offer

pad (pad), *v.* walk or trot softly

pamper (pam′pər), *v.* indulge too much; spoil

parable (par′ə bəl), *n.* a brief story used to teach some truth or moral lesson

paradoxically (par′ə dok′sə kəl ē), *adv.* involving a statement that may be true but seems to say two opposite things

parch (pärch), *v.* make hot and dry or thirsty

paroxysm (par′ək siz′əm), *n.* a sudden outburst of emotion or activity

partisan (pär′tə zən), *n.* a strong supporter of a party, person, or cause

party (pär′tē), *n.* group of people organized to gain political influence and control, especially of the legislative and executive branches of government

passé (pa sā′), *adj.* out of date

pasture (pas′chər), *v.* feed on growing grass; *n.* grasslands on which cattle, sheep, or horses can feed

patronisingly (pā′trən īz′ing lē), *adv.* with a haughty, condescending way; in a manner of stooping to the level of one's inferiors

pawn (pôn), *v.* leave (something) with another person as security that borrowed money will be repaid

pedigree (ped′ə grē′), *n.* list of ancestors of a person or animal; **pedigreed,** *adj.* having a known list of ancestors

peevish (pē′vish), *adj.* cross; complaining

pension (pen′shən), *n.* a fixed sum of money paid at regular intervals by the government, a company, etc., to a person who is retired or disabled

peon (pē′on), *n.* any unskilled worker

peremptory (pə remp′tər ē), *adj.* leaving no choice; decisive

perfunctory (pər fungk′tər ē), *adj.* mechanical; indifferent

periphery (pə rif′ər ē), *n.* an outside boundary

perjure (pėr′jər), *v.* swear falsely; lie under oath

perjurer (pėr′jər ər), *n.* person who commits an act of willfully giving false testimony or swears falsely

pernicious (pər nish′əs), *adj.* that will destroy or ruin; deadly

perpetual (pər pech′ü əl), *adj.* lasting forever; eternal

perspex (pėr′speks′), *n.* a transparent acrylic resin, similar to Lucite

phantom (fan′təm), *n.* image of the mind that seems to be real

phenomenal (fə nom′ə nəl), *adj.* remarkable

physiognomy (fiz′ē og′nə mī), *n.* art of estimating character from the features of the face or form of the body

pinch (pinch), *v.* steal (slang)

plague (plāg), *n.* highly contagious, epidemic, and often fatal bacterial disease that occurs in several forms; any epidemic disease; thing that torments, annoys, troubles, or is disagreeable

plait (plāt), *n.* braid

pledge (plej), *n.* solemn promise

pliant (plī'ənt), *adj.* easily influenced; yielding

poise (poiz), *n.* composure; self-possession

pole star (pōl'stär'), *n.* a guiding principle; guide; North Star

pomp (pomp), *n.* splendor; magnificence

poppy (pop'ē), *n.* a bright red

posterity (po ster'ə tē), *n.* generations of the future

potential (pə ten'shəl), *n.* something that can develop or become; possible chances

poverty (pov'ər tē), *n.* condition of being poor; destitution

pram (pram), *n.* baby carriage

precariously (pri ker'ē əs lē), *adv.* not securely

predatory (pred'ə tôr'ē), *adj.* of or inclined to plundering or robbery

prefect (prē'fekt), *n.* a student monitor in certain schools

premises (prem'is əz), *n. pl.* house or building with its grounds

prestigious (pre stij'əs), *adj.* honored; esteemed

presumptuous (pri zump'chü əs), *adj.* acting without permission or right; too bold

principle (prin'sə pəl), *n.* an accepted or professed rule of action or conduct

privy (priv'ē), *n.* a small outhouse used as a toilet

probability (prob'ə bil'ə tē), *n.* quality or fact of being probable; good chance

proctor (prok'tər), *n.* official of a university or school designated to supervise students

prodigiously (prə dij'əs lē), *adv.* in extraordinarily large quantity

prodigy (prod'ə jē), *n.* a remarkably talented child; marvelous example

promontory (prom'ən tôr'ē), *n.* a high point of land extending from the coast into the water; headland

prosecutor (pros'ə kyü'tər), *n.* the lawyer in charge of the government's side of a case against an accused person

prospect (pros'pekt), *n.* thing expected or looked forward to

prospective (prə spek'tiv), *adj.* future

protrude (prō trüd'), *v.* thrust forth; stick out

proverbial (prə vėr'bē əl), *adj.* well-known

providence (prov'ə dəns), *n.* God's care and help

provincial (prə vin'shəl), *adj.* lacking refinement or polish; narrow

purify (pyŭr'ə fi), *v.* make pure; freeing from impurities

quandary (kwon'dər i), *n.* state of uncertainty; dilemma

quarry (kwôr'ē), *n.* anything eagerly pursued; prey

queue (kyü), *v.* line up

quintessentially (kwin'tə sen'shəl lē), *adv.* having the purest form of some quality; most fully

radical (rad'ə kəl), *adj.* going to the root; extreme

rampage (ram'paj), *n.* fit of rushing wildly about; spell of violent behavior

rancid (ran'sid), *adj.* stale

rancor (rancour) (ran'kər), *n.* bitter resentment or ill will

rationalization (rash'ə nəl ə zā'shən), *n.* finding an explanation or excuse for

raven (rā'vən), *n.* a large, black bird like a crow but larger

reap (rēp), *v.* gather

reaper (rē'pər), *n.* a person or a machine that cuts grain or gathers a crop

receipt (ri sēt'), *n.* a written statement that money has been received

recess (rē'ses), *n.* an inner place or part

redolent (red'l ənt), *adj.* having a pleasant smell; fragrant

reel (rēl), *v.* go with swaying or staggering movements; stagger

refuge (ref'yüj), *n.* shelter or protection from danger

regent (rē'jənt), *n.* member of a governing body

registry (rej'ə strē), *n.* office in which written records are kept

rejuvenate (ri jü'və nāt), *v.* give youthful qualities to

relent (ri lent'), *v.* to let up

relic (rel'ik), *n.* something belonging to a holy person, kept as a sacred memorial; souvenir; memento

repertory (rep'ər tôr'ē), *n.* store or stock of things ready for use

replica (rep'lə kə), *n.* a close reproduction

repression (ri presh'ən), *n.* act of keeping down; suppressing

reproachful (ri prōch′fəl), *adj.* expressing discredit or blame

resignation (rez′ig nā′shən), *n.* a written statement giving notice that one gives up a job or position; patient acceptance

resolute (rez′ə lüt), *adj.* determined; bold

resound (ri zound′), *v.* give back sound; echo

respite (res′pit), *n.* time of relief and rest; lull

resuscitated (ri sus′ə tāt əd), *adj.* brought back to life or consciousness; revived

retort (ri tôrt′), *n.* a sharp or witty reply

retribution (ret′rə byü′shən), *n.* a deserved punishment; return for wrongdoing

revelation (rev′ə lā′shən), *n.* act of making known; the thing made known

reverberating (ri vėr′bə rāt′ing), *adj.* being reflected a number of times, as light or heat

reverie (rev′ər ē), *n.* dreamy thoughts

reviled (ri vīld′), *adv.* called bad names; abused with words

rickety (rik′ə tē), *adj.* liable to fall or break down; shaky

rite (rit), *n.* any customary ceremony or observance

rogue (rōg), *n.* a dishonest or unprincipled person; rascal

rosary (rō′zər ē), *n.* string of beads for keeping count in saying a series of prayers; a series of items strung together

ruse (rüz), *n.* scheme or device to mislead others; trick

sabotage (sab′ə täzh), *n.* an act tending to hamper

sackcloth (sak′klôth′), *n.* coarse cloth worn as a sign of mourning or penitence; sacking

sacrilege (sak′rə lij), *n.* an intentional disregard for or injury to anything sacred

salaam (selam) (sə läm), *n.* a greeting that means "Peace," used especially in Moslem countries

salvageable (sal′və jə bəl), *adj.* that can be saved

salvation (sal vā′shən), *n.* deliverance from sin and from punishment for sin

sanctify (sangk′tə fī), *v.* make right; justify or sanction

sanction (sangk′shən), *v.* approve; allow

sarcasm (sär′kaz′əm), *n.* a sneering or cutting remark; harsh or bitter irony

sarcastic (sär kas′tik), *adj.* sneering; cutting

satin (sat′n), *n.* a silk, rayon, nylon, or cotton cloth with one very smooth, glossy side

saunter (sôn′tər), *v.* stroll

savor (sā′vər), *n.* think about with great delight; relish

scansion (skan′shən), *n.* the marking off of lines of poetry into feet; scanning

score (skôr), *n.* a written or printed piece of music arranged for different instruments or voices

scropbrush (skrop′brush′), *n.* scrub brush

scythe (sīт͟н), *n.* a long, thin, slightly curved blade on a long handle, for cutting grass, etc.

seawall (sē′wôl), *n.* a strong wall or embankment made to prevent the waves from wearing away the shore

secular (sek′yə lər), *adj.* not religious or sacred; worldly

self-effacing (self′ə fā′sing), *adj.* keeping oneself in the background

sexton (sek′stən), *n.* person who takes care of a church building

shackles (shak′əlz), *n. pl.* chains; anything that prevents freedom of action, thought, etc.

share (sher), *n.* each of the equal parts into which the ownership of a company or corporation is divided

shrewd (shrüd), *adj.* having a sharp mind

sisal (sis′əl), *n.* a strong, white fiber, used for making rope, twine, etc.

slattern (slat′ərn), *n.* woman or girl who is dirty, careless, or untidy in her dress, her ways, her housekeeping, etc.

smug (smug), *adj.* self-satisfied

snowdrop (snō′drop′), *n.* a small plant of the amaryllis family, with drooping white flowers that bloom early in the spring

snuff (snuf), *n.* powdered tobacco, often scented, taken into the nose

solace (sol′is), *n.* comfort or relief

soy (soi), *n.* a Chinese and Japanese sauce for fish, meat, etc., made from fermented soybeans

species (spē′shēz), *n.* a group of related organisms that have certain permanent characteristics in common

spectroscopic (spek′trǝ skop′ik), *adj.* of or having to do with the examination and analysis of spectra; of a continuous sequence or range

speculator (spek′yǝ lā′tǝr), *n.* person who buys or sells when there is a large risk, with the hope of making a profit from future price changes

speedometer (spē dom′ǝ tǝr), *n.* instrument to indicate the speed of an automobile or other vehicle, and often the distance traveled

spigot (spig′ǝt), *n.* faucet

spleen (splēn), *n.* bad temper; spite; anger

squadron (skwod′rǝn), *n.* any group or formation

squander (skwon′dǝr), *v.* spend foolishly; waste

staff (staf), *n.* a stick, pole, or rod used as a support

stalwart (stôl′wǝrt), *n.* loyal supporter of a political party

stanch (stänch), *v.* stop or check the flow of blood (from a wound)

statistics (stǝ tis′tiks), *n. pl.* numerical facts about people, the weather, business conditions, etc.

sterile (ster′ǝl), *adj.* not producing results; mentally or spiritually barren

sterling (stėr′ling), *adj.* thoroughly and genuinely excellent

stifled (stī′fǝld), *adj.* kept back; suppressed; stopped

stock (stok), *n.* domestic animals kept or raised on a farm for use or profit, such as cattle, pigs, or sheep; the shares or portions into which a company or corporation is divided

strategic (strǝ tē′jik), *adj.* based on skillful planning and management

strategy (strat′ǝ jē), *n.* plan based on skillful management

strident (strīd′nt), *adj.* shrill

strop (strop), *n.* a leather strap used for sharpening razors

stupefaction (stü′pǝ fak′shǝn), *n.* a dazed or senseless condition

stupefying (stü′pǝ fī′ing), *adj.* amazing; astounding

subjugation (sub′jǝ gā′shǝn), *n.* bringing under complete control

subterfuge (sub′tǝr fyüj), *n.* trick or excuse used to escape something unpleasant

subversive (sǝb vėr′siv), *adj.* tending to overthrow

suede (swād), *n.* a soft leather that has a velvety nap on one or both sides

summons (sum′ǝnz), *n.* a formal order or notice to appear before a judge or court of law

sundries (sun′drēz), *n. pl.* odds and ends

supple (sup′ǝl), *adj.* bending or folding easily

supplicant (sup′lǝ kǝnt), *n.* person who asks humbly and earnestly

surveillance (sǝr vā′lǝns), *n.* watch kept over a person; supervision

suture (sü′chǝr), *n.* a seamlike line along which two things or parts are united; *v.* unite by sewing together

swindling (swin′dling), *adj.* be guilty of cheating

sylvan (sil′vǝn), *adj.* of, in, or having woods

tactics (tak′tiks), *n. pl.* procedures to gain advantage

talisman (tal′i smǝn), *n.* stone, ring, etc., engraved with figures or characters supposed to have magic power; charm

tally (tal′ē), *n.* anything on which a score or amount is kept

tempo (tem′pō), *n.* the time or rate of movement

tenacity (ti nas′ǝ tē), *n.* firmness in holding fast; stubbornness

tenet (ten′it), *n.* doctrine, principle, belief, or opinion held as true by a school, sect, party, or person

terrace (ter′is), *n.* row of houses running along the side or top of a slope

terrorist (ter′ǝr ist), *n.* person who uses or favors the use of great fear to rule or subdue others

testament (tes′tǝ mǝnt), *n.* a tangible proof or tribute; witness

thatch (thach), *n.* straw, rushes, palm leaves, etc., used as a roof or covering

tirade (tī′rād), *n.* long, scolding speech

tissue (tish′ü), *n.* web; network

token (tō′kǝn), *n.* mark or sign

tonic (ton′ik), *n.* anything that gives strength

torturous (tôr′chər əs), *adj.* causing severe pain

tradition (trə dish′ən), *n.* the handing down of beliefs, information, and customs by word of mouth from one generation to another

tranquil (trang′kwəl), *adj.* calm; peaceful

transcend (tran send′), *v.* go beyond the limits or powers of; to extend beyond a person

transfer (tran sfėr′), *v.* change from one public vehicle, such as a bus, train, etc., to another

transgression (trans gresh′ən), *n.* breaking a law, command, etc.; sin

transparent (tran sper′ənt), *adj.* having the property of transmitting light; easily seen through

traumatized (trô′mə tīzd), *adj.* state of emotional shock that has a lasting effect on the mind

treachery (trech′ər ē), *n.* a breaking of faith; treason

treasure (trezh′ər), *v.* cherish; hoard

trifling (trī′fling), *adj.* having little value; not important

trite (trīt), *adj.* worn out by use; commonplace

tyrannous (tir′ə nəs), *adj.* cruel or unjust

tyrant (tī′rənt), *n.* a person who uses power cruelly or unjustly

ulcer (ul′sər), *n.* a moral sore spot; an open sore on the skin

ulterior (ul tir′ē ər), *adj.* hidden

ululate (yül′yə lāt), *v.* lament loudly

unanimous (yü nan′ə məs), *adj.* in complete accord or agreement

unctuous (ungk′chü əs), *adj.* too smooth and oily

undulate (un′jə lāt), *v.* move with a wavelike motion

union (yü′nyən), *n.* a group of workers joined together to protect and promote their interests

unrequited (un′re quīt′əd), *adj.* not returned; unrewarded

usurer (yü′zhər ər), *n.* person who lends money at an extremely high or unlawful interest rate

utilitarian (yü til′ə ter′ē ən), *adj.* designed for usefulness rather than beauty

vault (vôlt), *n.* an arched space or passage

vaunt (vônt), *v.* boast; brag

veld (velt), *n.* the open grass-covered plains of southern Africa

vengeance (ven′jəns), *n.* punishment in return for a wrong; revenge

venture (ven′chər), *v.* dare to say

vermilion (vər mil′yən), *adj.* bright-red

vice (vīs), *n.* a moral fault or defect

vile (vīl), *adj.* very bad; disgusting

virile (vir′əl), *adj.* masculine, forceful

virtue (vėr′chü), *n.* moral excellence

vivifying (viv′ə fi ing), *v.* life giving

void (void), *n.* that which is emptied out; urine

voracious (və rā′shəs), *adj.* greedy; very eager

wake (wāk), *n.* a watch beside a corpse before its burial; track left behind by any moving thing

wan (won), *adj.* faint; weak

weld (weld), *v.* join together by heating the parts that touch to the melting point so they become one piece; closely joined

wheeze (hwēz), *v.* breathe with difficulty and a whistling sound

whorl (hwėrl), *n.* anything that circles or turns on or around something else

wicker (wik′ər), *n.* twigs, or any slender, flexible material

wield (wēld), *v.* hold and use

wisteria (wi stir′ē ə), *n.* any of a genus of climbing shrubs of the pea family

wits (witz), *n. pl.* mind; sense

wizened (wiz′nd), *adj.* withered; shriveled

wrath (rath), *n.* very great anger; rage

wreak (rēk), *v.* give expression to; inflict

wry (rī), *adj.* turned to one side; twisted

yearling (yir′ling), *n.* an animal one year old

yeast (yēst), *n.* a tiny one-celled fungus that grows quickly in a liquid containing sugar and causes fermentation; the substance that causes dough for bread to rise and beer to ferment

yokel (yō′kəl), *n.* an awkward or unsophisticated person from the country; bumpkin

zucchini (zü kē′nē), *n.* kind of dark-green summer squash shaped like a cucumber

Acknowledgments

viii Foreword by Jamaica Kincaid Copyright © 1994 by ScottForesman, Glenview, Illinois.
2 "Rules of the Game" from *The Joy Luck Club* by Amy Tan. Copyright © 1989 by Amy Tan. Reprinted by permission of The Putnam Publishing Group.
16 "The Mao Button" from *Chrysanthemums and Other Stories* by Feng Jicai. Translated and Copyright © 1980 by Susan Wilf Chen. Reprinted by permission of Harcourt Brace & Company.
30 "The Censors" by Luisa Valenzuela. Reprinted by permission of the author.
35 *The Little Man at Chehaw Station* from *Going to the Territory* by Ralph Ellison. Copyright © 1986 by Ralph Ellison. Reprinted by permission of Random House, Inc.
40 "The Shoe Breaker," from *Les Noces Du Merle* by Daniel Boulanger. Copyright © 1963 by Daniel Boulanger, published by Editions de la Table Ronde. English translation copyright © 1989 by Penny Million Pucelik and Maryjo Despreax Schneider. Copyright © 1985 by Editions Gallimard. Reprinted with permission of Editions Gallimard.
46 "A Man" from the *Anthology of Contemporary Romanian Poetry*, edited and translated by Roy MacGregor-Hastie. Reprinted by permission of Peter Owen Publishers, London.
47 "Black Hair" from *New and Selected Poems* by Gary Soto. Copyrighted © 1995 by Gary Soto. Published by Chronicle Books. Reprinted by permission.
50 "Paper" from *Little Ironies: Stories of Singapore* by Catherine Lim. Copyright © 1978 by Catherine Lim. Reprinted by permission of Heinemann Educational Books (ASIA) Ltd.
62 "Another Evening at the Club" by Alifa Rifaat from *Arabic Short Stories*, translated by Denys Johnson-Davies. Reprinted by permission of Quartet Books, Ltd.
70 "Forbidden Fruit" by Fazil Iskander from *Soviet Life* (September, 1968).

Copyright © 1968 by Fazil Iskander. Reprinted by permission of Novosti Press.
80 "The Girl Who Would Not Assert Herself" from *The Woman Warrior* by Maxine Hong Kingston. Copyright © 1975, 1976 by Maxine Hong Kingston. Reprinted by permission of Alfred A. Knopf, Inc.
92 "Getting Nowhere" from *When I Dance* by James Berry. Copyright © 1991 by James Berry. Reprinted by permission of Harcourt Brace & Company.
93 "Clouds on the Sea" from *Collected Poems* by Ruth Dallas, University of Otago Press. Copyright © 1987 by Ruth Dallas. Reprinted by permission of John McIndoe, Printers & Publishers, Ltd.
96 "Amnesty" from *Jump and Other Stories* by Nadine Gordimer. Copyright © 1991 by Felix Licensing BV. Reprinted by permission of Farrar, Straus & Giroux, Inc. and Penguin Books Canada Limited.
106 "Fable — Detail from KZ — Oratorio: Dark Heaven" from *The Desert of Love* by János Pilinszky, translated by Janos Csokits and Ted Hughes. Copyright © 1976 by János Pilinszky, translation copyright © 1976 by Ted Hughes. Reprinted by permission of Anvil Press Poetry, Ltd.
106 "Lot's Wife" from *Walking to Sleep, New Poems and Translations* by Richard Wilbur. Reprinted by permission of Harcourt Brace & Company.
109 "Bread" from *The Little School: Tales of Disappearance and Survival in Argentina* by Alicia Partnoy. Copyright © 1986 by Alicia Partnoy. Reprinted by permission of Cleis Press.
114 "Tell Them Not to Kill Me" from *The Burning Plain and Other Stories* by Juan Rulfo, translated by George D. Schade, Copyright © 1967. Reprinted by permission of the University of Texas Press.
126 (Pages 98–104) from "The Handsomest Drowned Man in the World" from *Leaf Storm and Other Stories*

Photograph Credits

Index of Authors and Titles